BODY GENRE

Bernadette Marie Calafell, Marina Levina, and Kendall R. Phillips,
General Editors

BODY GENRE

Anatomy of the Horror Film

David Scott Diffrient

University Press of Mississippi / Jackson

The University Press of Mississippi is the scholarly publishing agency of the Mississippi Institutions of Higher Learning: Alcorn State University, Delta State University, Jackson State University, Mississippi State University, Mississippi University for Women, Mississippi Valley State University, University of Mississippi, and University of Southern Mississippi.

www.upress.state.ms.us

The University Press of Mississippi is a member of the Association of University Presses.

An earlier version of portions of chapter 6 appeared previously in *New Review of Film and Television Studies* 16, no. 2 (2018).

An earlier version of portions of chapter 9 appeared previously in Gary Bettinson and Daniel Martin (eds.), *Hong Kong Horror Cinema* (Edinburgh University Press, 2018).

Copyright © 2023 by University Press of Mississippi
All rights reserved

∞

Library of Congress Cataloging-in-Publication Data

Names: Diffrient, David Scott, 1972– author.
Title: Body genre : anatomy of the horror film / David Scott Diffrient.
Other titles: Horror and monstrosity studies series.
Description: Jackson : University Press of Mississippi, 2023. | Series: Horror and monstrosity studies series | Includes bibliographical references and index.
Identifiers: LCCN 2023030776 (print) | LCCN 2023030777 (ebook) | ISBN 9781496847966 (hardback) | ISBN 9781496847973 (trade paperback) | ISBN 9781496847980 (epub) | ISBN 9781496847997 (epub) | ISBN 9781496848000 (pdf) | ISBN 9781496848017 (pdf)
Subjects: LCSH: Horror films—History and criticism. | Human body in motion pictures. | Senses and sensation in motion pictures. | Horror films—Production and direction. | Horror films—Psychological aspects. | Motion picture audiences—Psychology. | Fear in motion pictures.
Classification: LCC PN1995.9.H6 D47 2023 (print) | LCC PN1995.9.H6 (ebook) | DDC 791.43/6164—dc23/eng/20230803
LC record available at https://lccn.loc.gov/2023030776
LC ebook record available at https://lccn.loc.gov/2023030777

British Library Cataloging-in-Publication Data available

CONTENTS

ACKNOWLEDGMENTS VII

1. Books, Bodies, Beliefs:
   Introducing a Genre That Needs No Introduction 3

Section One—Somatic Spectatorship: Believing, Bleeding, Hearing, Seeing

2. Heads Will Roll, Bodies Will Shake, Souls Will Shatter:
   Horror Film's Formative Stages and Physical Changes 27
3. Corporeality, Materiality, Mortality:
   The Horror Film as "Body Genre" 56
4. Going Deep, Sticking to the Surface:
   Bad Deaths and Wet Bodies 82
5. Sliced Eyeballs and Severed Ears:
   On (Not) Seeing and (Not) Hearing Horror Films 106

Section Two—Beyond Sight and Sound: Breathing, Smelling, Tasting, Touching

6. Dead, But Still Breathing:
   The Problem of Postmortem Movement in Horror Films 137
7. Smelling Like a Slaughterhouse:
   Cinematic Olfactics and the Stench of Horror 169
8. Shitty, Slimy, Smelly, Smiley:
   Dirty Spaces, Funny Faces, and the Textural
   Pleasures of "Laughably Bad" Texts. 198
9. Spooky Encounters of the Humorously Disgusting Kind:
   Clutching Hands and Hopping Corpses,
   from Hollywood to Hong Kong. 235

Coda. Preparing to Be Unprepared:
   Horror Film's Predictable Unpredictability 263

NOTES 271
BIBLIOGRAPHY. 279
INDEX 292

ACKNOWLEDGMENTS

I would like to begin by thanking the talented staff at the University Press of Mississippi, including Emily Bandy, Joey Brown, Shane Gong Stewart, Pete Halverson, and Corley Longmire, who—along with the outside readers—have nurtured this book from its earliest incarnation and assisted me in turning an initially shaky manuscript into something that I can be proud of. UPM's Horror and Monstrosity series editors, Bernadette Marie Calafell, Marina Levina, and Kendall R. Phillips, have each inspired me with their own publications over the years, and I feel honored to have *Body Genre: Anatomy of the Horror Film* join a growing list of books with their names attached.

A few individuals have played a vital role in helping me hone my arguments throughout the seven years it has taken me to complete this book's chapters. They include Jean-Thomas Tremblay, whose work on the topic of breath in cinema was invaluable as I sought to apply his ideas to the study of horror film, and Gary Bettinson and Daniel Martin, who were both instrumental in getting me to dig deeper in my exploration of the sociopolitical meanings of Hong Kong horror films (also, much of my knowledge of South Korean horror films, which I only briefly make reference to in this book, comes from reading Daniel's work on that subject). I am also thankful to Cüneyt Çakırlar, Rebecca Stone Gordon, Andrew Jackson, Mark Jancovich, Craig Ian Mann, Alison Peirse, Iain Robert Smith, Andrew Sydlik, Constantine Verevis, and Barbara Wall for their support of my work over the years, in many cases giving me the opportunity to present early versions of this book's chapters at conferences and symposia. My annual trips to Albuquerque, New Mexico, where I have been attending the Southwest Popular/American Culture Association conferences each February since the early 2010s, have given me the motivation to complete several of the chapters, and I would be remiss if I did not mention the kindness and generosity of Steffen Hantke (chair of the SWPACA's "Horror" SIG), who has consistently supported me even when I brought some truly disgusting topics to the table. Steffen gave me my first opportunity to publish a piece on horror cinema two decades ago (for a volume that he edited), and I will forever be in his debt. Over the years, he has gone from being a mentor to being a trusted friend whose insights I value and whose encyclopedic knowledge of the horror genre in all of its guises (film, literature, television, video games, etc.) is second-to-none.

More so than any of the books I have written prior to this one, graduate students—including summer research assistants and those who have taken my fall and spring courses on horror films and the human sensorium at Colorado State University—have been key to much of the research work that went into this volume. Indeed, many grad students at CSU—including a few who have gone on to become professors at other colleges—played a significant part in gathering documents and other materials, tracking down bibliographic references, transcribing audio commentaries from DVDs and Blu-rays, and making sure that I did not miss any information conveyed via the accessibility features of contemporary home-video formats (e.g., SDH, audio description services, etc.): Tyler Brunette, Lisabeth Bylina, Michael Foist, Nancy Frimpong, Ryan Greene, Brad Kaye, Chance Lachowitzer, Emma Lynn, Henry Miller, Amy Moore, and Riana Slyter. My fellow faculty members in the Department of Communication Studies who specialize in film and media studies—Usama Alshaibi, Carl Burgchardt, Evan Elkins, Kit Hughes, Nick Marx, and my partner in life Hye Seung Chung (who never batted an eye whenever I made some rather expensive additions to our already vast collection of horror DVDs and Blu-rays for the purposes of seemingly never-ending research)—have lifted me up and patiently listened to my nuttiest ideas. The same goes for Jeffrey Snodgrass, in the Department of Anthropology, one of my oldest friends at CSU who is perhaps unaware just how important our occasional online and tabletop gaming sessions have been to my mental and emotional well-being. Similarly, outside the university, James Schwindt and Joel Dickens have reminded me of the value of lasting friendship and—for reasons that I cannot fully fathom—they keep humoring me by playing the many horror-themed board games I bring to our weekend meetups (and which will be the focus of my next book project). Mike Paige, a fellow movie-lover whose taste for "tasteless" cult and exploitation cinema mirrors my own, watched many of the Friday-night episodes of *The Last Drive-in with Joe Bob Briggs* along with me (including a few of the ones I reference in chapter 4). I owe much of my rekindled interest in schlocky horror films and stylish *giallo* films from the 1970s and 1980s to both that Shudder program and to Mike.

Finally, I could not have written this book without the support of my family: chiefly, my mother and father—Donna and Harry Diffrient—whose willingness to overlook some of the nastier elements of horror cinema (which, unfortunately for them, I dwell on in the following pages) is matched only by their attentiveness to my needs as a fifty-something son who still feels like a film-addicted teen in their loving presence. One could not ask for better parents—or grandparents, for that matter—and my daughter Pepper is a better person thanks to them. As for Pepper (who has already begun dipping her toes into PG-rated horror films), I can only hope that, once she is old enough to read this study of the gross and ghastly, she will recognize the joy I experienced when writing it as well as the cultural significance of a genre that matters precisely because it allows us to confront our fears together, as a family and as a society. This book is dedicated to Vivian Sobchack, who, as my dissertation advisor at UCLA many years ago, laid the groundwork for much of what I investigate in the following pages and encouraged me to think about cinema—and my own affective/bodily/sensorial relationship to the medium—differently.

BODY GENRE

1

BOOKS, BODIES, BELIEFS

Introducing a Genre That Needs No Introduction

> This morbid doodling with human body parts... is *this* what it's all about? Is this what all our great work has led to?
> —DR. DAN CAIN (Bruce Abbott) to Dr. Herbert West (Jeffrey Combs)
> in *Bride of Re-Animator* (1990)

Like the bodies of slain teenagers in a slasher film, books about horror cinema—and the trees that have been felled, ground into pulp, and sliced into paper-thin sheets for the purpose of producing those books—are numerous. A veritable mountain, large enough to engender a Lovecraftian level of madness in anyone so foolish as to scale its loftiest peaks, the many tomes devoted to the genre run the gamut from high-theory meditations on the philosophical meanings of horror to lowbrow celebrations of cult stars, exploitation filmmakers, and other studio personnel (including special-effects artists) whose once-neglected contributions to the medium have now been thoroughly documented. Indeed, a voluminous amount of critical, historical, and theoretical literature, on top of countless fan-written accounts of horror's distinctive, paradoxical appeals, attests to its ongoing fascination for scholars and lay readers alike. Simply trying to read even a small percentage of the many published studies about horror film can be just as intimidating—if considerably less stomach-churning—as the prospect of watching a notoriously disgusting motion picture like *Cannibal Holocaust* (1980) or its modern-day equivalent, *The Green Inferno* (2013). With so many written texts already available, what value does yet another book concerning the subject of cinematic fright—especially one that is as committed to the disreputable strain of body horror that *Cannibal Holocaust* literally embodies as it is to the so-called elevated horror that recent releases such as *The Witch* (2015), *Hereditary* (2018), and *A Quiet Place* (2018) are said to represent—possibly have either in academia or the larger marketplace of ideas that has given us questionable terms like "elevated horror"?[1] Simply put: why write another examination of the horror film when so much has already been written about it, and when so little about the genre's inner workings—its figurative "guts"—appears to have been overlooked by earlier scholars whose own studies are scalpel-like in their incisiveness?

Brian Albright, author of the 2012 book *Regional Horror Films, 1958–1990*, begins his state-by-state assessment of cheaply shot, independently produced motion pictures by posing a similar question. In the Introduction to that volume, the author puts it bluntly when he asks, "So why did I write this book?" (3). Claiming that there have been "thousands" of manuscripts written about the genre over the years, and that they have been "organized almost every way imaginable: chronologically, by sub-genre, by studio, by director, by subject matter, by country of origin, and even by the amount of gore spilled per film," he explains that there is still room for novel, unorthodox approaches like his own (Albright 2012, 3). By teasing out the "distinct local flavor" discernible in dozens of 16mm films and shot-on-video (SOV) movies that were made outside of California over a thirty-year period, from the Louisiana-based *Night of Bloody Horror* (1969) to the Connecticut-based *Cannibal Campout* (1988), Albright shines a light on largely forgotten or critically neglected curios from the past. He also reminds us of the limitless range of options available to present-day cultural historians and film scholars who wish to breathe life into a genre that is paradoxically predicated on the inescapability of death—a genre that, far from being exhausted or depleted through formulaic repetition, is just as stimulating and as overflowing with creative possibilities as it was over 100 years ago (when the first experiments in cinematic horror were being made during the silent era).

My respiratory metaphor in the preceding paragraph is deliberate, for *breath itself* is at the heart of cinematic horror. However, few scholars have paused to consider its significance as both an audible and sometimes visible reminder of the mortal threats faced by characters over the course of emotionally and physically exhausting narratives that, not unlike zombies, either lumber or sprint toward their rarely happy endings. As I elaborate in the second half of this book, something as seemingly unremarkable as the inhalation and exhalation of air, which all of us—those of us who are not undead, at least—do every few seconds throughout our lives (if sometimes through the assistance of mechanical ventilators), becomes weighty with meaning in the context of horror films, which habitually draw attention to lifeless bodies and breathless beings played by actors who are very much alive. Besides breathing, other commonplace activities, such as the blinking of one's eyes, the opening of one's mouth, or the releasing of one's bowels likewise assume deeper connotations when performed in narratives where the bodily phenomenon of fright—the physical sensation of being terrified or horrified—moves from diegetic to extradiegetic settings, spilling over into very real, flesh-and-blood spectatorial arenas where audiences might cover their eyes, let out a scream, or figuratively "shit their pants" from sheer fear. This book not only takes seriously a diverse array of superficially silly cultural productions—from ballyhoo-driven studio releases like William Castle's typically gimmicky *The Tingler* (1959) to pitch-black horror comedies like Jack Hill's *Spider Baby* (1967), martial-arts films like Sammo Hung's kung-fu classic *Spooky Encounters* (1980), and literally shitty gross-out movies such as Lawrence Kasdan's *Dreamcatcher* (2003) and Jesse Thomas Cook's *Septic Man* (2013)—but also dwells on seemingly banal sensorial activities that are crucial to an understanding of horror as an affective "body genre." Indeed, the simple acts of seeing, hearing, smelling, tasting, and touching—taken for granted as something that most audiences do unconsciously during their everyday lives—become affectively intensified in narratives whenever the organs that are called upon to do that sensing (the eyes, the ears, the nose, the tongue, and the skin) are targeted by human and nonhuman monsters.

The title of this book is not unlike that of Gary D. Rhodes's *White Zombie: Anatomy of a Horror Film* (2001) or, more recently, Sotiris Petridis's *Anatomy of the Slasher Film: A Theoretical Analysis* (2019), insofar as it conjures the investigatory zeal with which genre enthusiasts put on their proverbial lab coats and probe a subject that is as entrancing as it is revolting. By analyzing cinematic horror in scientific or pseudoscientific detail, opening it up in the way that a coroner or medical pathologist might (with bone saws, rib shears, toothed forceps, and the like), one can adopt a forensic gaze that sees past the surface signifiers of a text into its deepest structures. However, because horror is ironically *structured around surfaces*, any attempt to go below a given film's laminate effects will generally bring the investigator back to the things that shocked or repulsed him or her in the first place: the bloody wound, the disfigured face, the severed appendage, and other semantic staples of the genre. Nevertheless, "anatomizing" a horror film, which Rhodes does in his meticulous reading of the independently produced pre-Code feature *White Zombie* (1932), means breaking it apart so as to scrutinize the thing as thoroughly as one can. For him and other film historians, including those who devote themselves to a single case study presented in painstaking detail (with attention paid to its production background, theatrical release, and cultural impact), such a methodology makes it possible to, in Rhodes's words, "flesh out" or materialize a work of art that otherwise exists primarily in the abstract, confined to the minds of spectators who imagine it as a metaphysical rather than physical thing (2001, 6). As I argue in the pages that follow, *flesh itself* deserves scrutiny as not only the surface but *substance* of cinematic horror, just as the many other physical characteristics of the genre (its "sharpness," its "smelliness," its "wetness," and so forth) are also worthy of sustained analysis.

SENSES AND SENSIBILITIES
(AND NONSENSICAL INQUIRIES)

> I build bodies. I take them apart and put them back together again.
> —SETH BRUNDLE (Jeff Goldblum) in *The Fly* (1986)

True to its title, *Body Genre: Anatomy of the Horror Film* dissects corporeal forms in much the same way that a mad scientist or masked stalker might, cleaving individual parts like hands and heads from the whole only to reconstitute them into a stitched-together form that is recognizably, uncannily human. In doing so, I am following in the footsteps of Ian Conrich and Laura Sedgwick, whose recently published volume *Gothic Dissections in Film and Literature: The Body in Parts* catalogues the various ways that anatomical features have been treated, or rather *mistreated*, in cinematic and literary texts over the years. Moving chapter by chapter from the brain to the anus, and covering just about every gooey or hairy thing in between, Conrich and Sedgwick present a comprehensive inventory of the body's constituent parts, though for the sake of brevity they limit their overview to *anatomy itself* rather than to those parts' "associated fluid(s), sense(s) or expression(s)" (meaning that they are primarily interested in "the nose before a study of mucus and smell, the ear above hearing, and the brain before the mind") (Conrich and Sedgwick 2017, 2). My study differs from theirs by going beyond the anatomical referent to address horror's reflexive foregrounding of the human sensorium more broadly. But it also narrows the focus to comparatively fewer body parts whose centrality to the genre is hard to dispute. Adopting such an approach will hopefully bring another type of anatomy—that of the horror film itself—into view with a clarity that might illuminate the genre's inner workings and further reveal how social divisions or a fragmenting of the body politic are often allegorized in this most disintegrative of cultural forms.

As with the aforementioned breathing metaphor, my vision-centric wording in that last sentence, with its emphasis on "seeing clearly" and "illuminating" otherwise invisible structures, might serve as a reminder of the centrality of a specific type of "body language" within most critical interrogations of horror, including those that do not start from the basic premise that the latter is a body genre. To an extent, such language is warranted, given the motion-picture medium's ontological privileging of visual images over other signifiers. But it is also "short-sighted" and ableist, for it presumes that seeing is commensurate with understanding and that all audiences share the same physical capacity for grasping a movie's meanings through their eyes. It thus rhetorically obscures the role that other sense modalities play in the sense-making process, and which are powerfully evoked in films that call upon audiences' ears, noses, mouths, and other body parts when presenting a multisensory "view" of a world that, while fictive and often farcically far-fetched, bears a disturbing resemblance to our own. Though critical of such rhetorical maneuvers, I readily admit that a sight-based hermeneutics—an interpretative predisposition to foreground the things viewers might *see* when watching a horror film—suffuses the present study as surely as it does other books devoted to the genre. Nevertheless, I endeavor to recast the spectatorial gaze as a means of *unseeing* horror, or rather seeing it anew, through conceptual lenses quite different than what have heretofore been favored in academic writing (e.g., aesthetics, auteurism, Marxism, psychoanalytic theory, etc.). Whether it is reading Subtitles for the Deaf and Hard-of-Hearing (SDH), searching for signs of an actor's breathing while he or she "plays dead," flinching at the splatter of fake blood on the lens, or getting snagged on the punctum-like piercing of a film's "skin" through the spotting of cigarette burns (or reel changeover cues), scratch marks, hair in the gate, and other celluloidal distractions (which have all but disappeared in this age of digital filmmaking), viewing a horror film is far more complex than what it has been made out to be. And to really *see* it entails looking not only with the eyes but through other sense organs as well.

As Julian Hanich argues in *Cinematic Emotion in Horror Films and Thrillers*, "the attraction of seeing and hearing" that audiences experience while seated in a darkened theater, their eyes drawn to the illuminated screen and their ears attuned to the sounds emanating from amplified speakers, is often so strong that they "have to become active in order to avoid it—a fact that has a considerable weight in terms of frightening movies." According to Hanich, "there is little with which we could actively distract ourselves" in such a traditional viewing arrangement, and indeed "the enforced attraction of the screen is particularly apparent in fearful scenes of horror that we try to resist watching by looking away" (2010, 54–55). However, one could also make the case that the intended dread or terror of certain scenarios, regardless of the screen's gravitational pull, is sometimes mitigated by unintentionally distracting elements that are all-too-prevalent in low-budget exploitation films, including bad prosthetics, cheap-looking special effects, glaring continuity errors, shaky camera work, flimsy sets, and excessively campy or incompetent performances.

Though not restricted to threadbare productions, such distractions, which are more likely to generate chuckles than screams, are especially pronounced in the kind of schlocky cult favorites that Albright explores in the previously mentioned *Regional Horror Films, 1958–1990*, including the squishily gross yet humorously titled *I Eat Your Skin* (1964), *Flesh Feast* (1970), *Blood Sucking Freaks* (1976), *Bloodeaters* (1980), and *Skinned Alive* (1990). Those elements furthermore highlight the convergence of comedy and horror, two seemingly

Figure 1.1. In motion pictures ranging from *The Raven* (1935) [top left] to *Lady Frankenstein* (1971) [top right], and *Tales That Witness Madness* (1973) [bottom] prosthetic effects applied to actors' faces can sometimes call attention to a story's fictiveness (owing to their obvious fakeness) and bring the latent humor of most horror films to the surface.

antithetical categories of low cultural standing that actually share much in common as body genres. Akin to a running gag, that intergeneric slippage, whereby humor bleeds into terror (and vice versa), will become an increasingly obvious motif over the course of this study.

Building upon Hanich's and other theorists' work, including the pioneering contributions of Carol Clover, Linda Williams, and Barbara Creed (who collectively paved the way for subsequent studies of the genre's affective and corporeal dimensions), *Body Genre: Anatomy of the Horror Film* seeks to expand the critical vocabulary of existing scholarship and introduces alternative ways of feeling and thinking about horror. Of course, *feeling* and *thinking*, as Xavier Aldana Reyes reminds us in his important application of Affect Studies to the genre, are not so easily disentangled, and it has become increasingly apparent that a kind of *corporeal cognition* results from our bodily engagement with films that—though frequently propelled by characters' desire to solve mysteries (inviting the audience to "play along" in this brain game through the mental piecing together of clues)—dance upon our flesh and activate our senses in a phenomenologically acute way. Referring to the recent "corporeal turn" in film studies, partly inspired by Vivian Sobchack's foundational work in the area of film phenomenology, Reyes notes how the "Cartesian models of thinking" that had "previously rendered the body a 'mere material handmaiden of an all-powerful mind'" have given way to new reckonings with filmic *feeling* (2016, 9). Indeed, "the particularities of *thinking through our flesh*" are such that a rigorous yet flexible model of somatic perception is needed in order to pinpoint those precise moments when, in the words Angela Ndalianis, "the medium and the human body collide" (2012, 3). In the same way that Reyes and Ndalianis have established such a framework in their respective attempts to account for the unique cognitive and physiological demands placed on horror audiences, I formulate an approach to the subject that is sensitive to film's affective and sensorial features, including those that have been overlooked even by the scholars who have steered the field toward that corporeal turn.

For that reason, throughout this book I pose a series of seemingly impertinent or nonsensical queries, which turn out to be the only *sensible* ways to go about further unpacking what Ndalianis refers to as the "horror sensorium." For instance, the question of what horror films might "smell" like has crossed my mind on numerous occasions, including every time I sit down to watch *Rosemary's Baby* (1968), *The Texas Chain Saw Massacre* (1974), *The Amityville Horror* (1979), *Edge of the Axe* (*Al Filo del Hacha*, 1989), *House of Wax* (2005), *Severance* (2006), *Let the Right One In* (2008), *Raw* (2016), and countless other motion pictures in which odors are directly referenced through spoken dialogue or visual images (for instance, whenever a character holds his or her nose when confronted by an offending stench). What effect does the perceptible breathing of presumably dead bodies—those of ill-fated characters played by still-living actors—have on spectators who are asked to suspend their disbelief more frequently as consumers of horror films than they are during other types of viewing? How is "disbelief mitigation," which is central to the manipulation of audiences' responses (and, according to Aaron Smuts, is what "prevents [horror] from sliding into comedy"), undermined by the material properties of the medium, the physical conditions of spectatorship, and the disruptive presence of laughably "bad" practical effects or CGI-work (Smuts 2003, 158)? How does consumption itself, foregrounded in scenes that depict individuals eating food and other, less appetizing things (including human flesh), collapse the distinction between pleasure and displeasure and implicate the viewer in another, more dubious type of nonculinary ingestion? At what point does such literal or figurative mastication become *masochistic*, a painful experience leading to a vomitous physical expulsion or, more problematically, a cultural cleansing by which "impure" elements within a society (itself a kind of bodily organ) are cast out? Do the two ostensibly unrelated definitions of "taste"—referring to the ability to distinguish between sweet, sour, bitter, or salty qualities as well as the critical discernment needed to evaluate the aesthetic value of something—correlate in any way?

With regard to taste, additional questions concerning the discursive formation of fan communities around so-called "bad objects," including films that are widely perceived as being aesthetically unsophisticated, amateurishly produced, and technically inept, will bubble up from time to time in my study. This is done to problematize the standard evaluative criteria brought to bear on cinematic texts that, I believe, are compelling precisely *because* they do not fit prescriptive categories of artistic value or cultural worth. Several of the case studies that I explore in this book, from low-budget exploitation films like Dwain Esper's *Maniac* (1934) and S. F. Brownrigg's *Don't Look in the Basement* (1973) to critically disparaged entries in long-running franchises such as *Amityville 4: The Evil Escapes* (1989) and *Amityville: It's About Time* (1992), might inspire ironically detached audiences to excuse creative missteps or textual flaws (e.g., cheap-looking special effects, crummy production design, glaring plot holes, hammy acting, incompetent directing) through "so-bad-it's-good" rhetorical moves that end up reproducing the cultural logics of mainstream appraisal. But "badness," if partly derived from an abundance of audiovisual and performative signifiers that do not appear to be motivated by purely narrative concerns, can also be understood as a dysmorphic *bodily* phenomenon insofar as the anatomical makeup and cosmetic appearance of a given movie—its misshapen appendages, flabby features, and unsightly blemishes (metaphorically speaking)—are what often get derided by even the most affectionate of viewers.

Too often, lay audiences as much as professional reviewers evince an almost pathological commitment to what critical disability theorists would call *normative embodiment*, with ostensibly well-made, handsomely mounted, symmetrically apportioned motion pictures—the cinematic equivalent of a runway fashion model or some other physical specimen prized for its conventional attractiveness—being held up as examples of what artists working within a film industry or favoring a particular genre should aim for. The anatomically unusual "badfilm," part of the larger cultural category of "paracinema" that Jeffrey Sconce elaborates in his 1995 essay "'Trashing' the Academy: Taste, Excess, and an Emerging Politics of Cinematic Style," prompts ironic reading strategies among fans whose opposition to mainstream sensibilities makes them strange bedfellows with members of the artistic-political avant-garde as well as academic elites and highbrow critics who guard the cinematic canon as devotedly as their lowbrow brethren attend midnight screenings of *The Room* (2003) or *Troll 2* (1990). The latter film, one of many comedy-horror "trainwrecks" that can be understood differently through one's sense of touch,

Figure 1.2. A group of goblins in the illogically titled cult movie *Troll 2* gobble up the soupy remains of a young woman, whose physical transformation is nearly as gross as anything that occurs in more critically lauded body-horror films.

is noteworthy for being consistently singled out by online commentators as an exemplar of the "so-bad-it's-good" school of unschooled filmmaking. It is, to be sure, a bad object. But it is also an object of cult worship and subcultural distinction with something to say about nonnormative bodies and questionable consumption practices.

As the subject of a 2009 documentary titled *Best Worst Movie*, writer-director Claudio Fragasso's *Troll 2* hardly needs any introduction in this age of internet memes, so notorious is it as a textbook illustration of what distinguishes a "bad" film from a "good" film. One of the many reasons it has a "Tomatometer" score of 5 percent on the aggregator website Rotten Tomatoes, where review blurbs like "a disaster from start to finish," "epically terrible," and "godawful" accompany nearly two dozen appropriately green splats, has to do with its title. *Troll 2*'s title is doubly inaccurate since this sequel has no connection to its "in-name-only predecessor" *Troll* (1986) and, funnily enough, *features no trolls* (Kern 2010, 72). Instead, another mythical species of forest-dwellers—hairy, large-nosed *goblins*—take center stage, occasionally assuming human form in order to gain the trust of a vacationing middle-class family in the Midwestern farming community of Nilbog ("Goblin" spelled backward). As hungry vegetarians, the diminutive creatures want to make a meal of the Waits family. To do so they need to feed them a diet of poisoned concoctions that look like green cake frosting and yogurt so that these meaty interlopers might become digestibly plant-like. One of the film's most memorable scenes depicts a young woman mutating into a literally vegetative state—a physical transformation that is as gross in its gelatinous moistness as most body horror films are (figure 1.2). However, it is garnished with unintentionally comic schlockiness that distinguishes this woodenly acted, poorly directed "monstrosity" from the arthouse shockers directed by David Cronenberg and other auteurs.

In fact, audiences who might be drawn to *Troll 2* out of sheer curiosity, if not for its defamiliarizing, paracinematic potential, *do* encounter a troll during their viewing. The "troll" that I am referring to is *the film itself*. If countless online diatribes are any indication, *Troll 2* is as "offensive" to mainstream and middlebrow tastes as that specific type of folkloric creature—distinguished by its large body, small brain, and ugly appearance—is to anyone who subscribes to traditional notions of physical beauty. And if this film is indeed troll-like in its failure to perfectly emulate the aesthetic ideals associated with "great" cinema, it is still *good* at being "bad," in part because so many of its onscreen bodies—those of the monstrous abominations passing for goblins—elicit visceral responses from spectators (laughter and revulsion in place of screams of terror). Of course, those obviously fake creatures are as fantastical yet grounded in material production practices as the film is. Nevertheless, that mutually reflected artifice and unreality paradoxically strengthen *Troll 2*'s authenticity as an object of cult worship, one that is best appreciated by audiences with a taste for tastelessness.

The question of taste also comes into play when we consider the kinds of cinematic productions that are seen as violating accepted standards of decency rather than just the protocols of "proper" filmmaking. Banned from public exhibition in several countries and famously condemned by Roger Ebert as a film "so sick, reprehensible and contemptible" that its very existence boggled the mind, the rape-revenge-themed *I Spit on Your Grave* (1978) is both exceptional and indicative of the cultural and industrial shifts occurring in the United States at the time of its theatrical release, when extra-grimy slices of cinematic horror were being served to customers growing inured to explicit scenes of sexual violence (1989, 359). Ultimately, I have chosen not to explore this controversial and divisive motion picture, which Ebert called a "vile bag of garbage" upon its original theatrical release, but which has since been defended (if not praised) by feminist theorists who recognize its value as a crude, uncompromising, and possibly cathartic critique of the very misogyny it was once believed to be perpetuating. Nevertheless, *I Spit on Your Grave*'s paradoxically vaunted status, not only as a work of trash art that is central to what Alexandra Heller-Nicholas calls the "rape-revenge film canon" but also as a potentially *good* (i.e., instructive) bad object, calls attention to the conflicting views on screen violence that have been part of the ongoing conversation about horror film spectatorship since the 1970s. Regarded by some critics as a cruelly sadistic form of pleasure-taking in another person's misfortune and by others as a masochistic positioning of spectators within a culture of misogyny that runs deep in American society (much deeper than what a single motion picture is able to suggest), the violence on view in this and other horror films remains a point of contention among scholars and lay audience alike.

With that in mind, portions of this book revolve around the gendering of onscreen bodies as well as the violation of those bodies that speaks to the horror film's long history of sexist representations. As Matt Hills has noted, the gendered representations found in horror films, past and present, are not unrelated to "the gendered reception of the genre" (2005, 202). This brings us back to the topic of fandom—specifically, to the fannish proclivities of audiences who might gravitate toward or steer away from particular types of screen violence for reasons that would appear to have nothing to do with a given film's story or characters, and whose pleasure or displeasure in viewing horror cannot be disentangled from their own lived experiences outside the movie theater or away from the TV screen. In Hills's words, the frequently graphic displays of female victimization and vengeance-seeking that flare up in specific subgenres, such as the slasher film and torture porn, can "become emotionally troubling because they are treated, imaginatively, as real-seeming rather than as predominately symbolic or metaphorical" (2005, 202). Any subversive power that we might attribute to the horror film, across and within its various junior categories, is balanced by a countervailing tendency (discernible within several online fan communities) to glom onto images of women in distress and partial or full undress, something that surely drives some people to seek out films that *play into* rather than problematize the purportedly voyeuristic aspects of the genre. If horror is, as several other theorists have argued, a *body genre*, it is also a genre of "boobs, butts, and blood," to quote one online critic (who cites this "Three Bs" attraction of horror in his review of Vinegar Syndrome's Blu-ray release of the Richard Styles–directed film *Shallow Grave* [1987]) (Filipowicz 2021).

Heavily censored grindhouse releases of the 1970s like *I Spit on Your Grave* and the better-received but similarly explicit films directed by iconoclasts such as Paul Morrissey (e.g., *Flesh for Frankenstein* [1973], *Blood for Dracula* [1974]) and David Cronenberg (*Shivers* [1975], *Rabid* [1977]) are worthy of a deeper exploration than what I can offer in this book, in part because they call attention to the broader cultural implications of showing men and women in horribly compromised states. To be sure, there is nothing titillating or arousing about the extended scenes of "atavistic brutality" depicted in *I Spit on Your Grave* or any of the other rape-revenge films that followed in its wake, such as *Mother's Day* (1980) and *Ms .45* (1981) (Crowdus 2017, 235). And, to his "credit" (although that sounds like too strong a commendation), director Meir Zarchi does not use the camera to turn Jennifer's (Camille Keaton) body into an erotic spectacle during the twenty-five-minute rape sequence that occurs in *I Spit on Your Grave*. Instead, as Peter Lehman argues, Zarchi opts for extreme long shots of the young woman's dirt-covered body (rather than close-ups that might fragment or fetishize her genitalia) and ensures that the four men's actions are "painfully difficult to watch"—so much so that viewers, thoroughly disgusted by what they have witnessed, actively root for the attackers' "just desserts" by narrative's end (Lehman 1993, 104). Culminating with scenes of Jennifer turning the table on her aggressors and cutting off one man's penis (killing the other three men in creative though more "conventional" ways: hanging one, lodging an axe into the back of another, and disemboweling the last with a motorboat's propellers), *I Spit on Your Grave* set the stage for comparatively "lighter" contemporary productions such as Mitchell Lichtenstein's *Teeth* (2007) and Karyn Kusama's *Jennifer's Body* (2009), which have sparked similarly divisive opinions since their controversial theatrical releases.

Both of these latter films will reemerge at a later point in this book, when I look at and listen to them with an eye and an ear to their horrifically humorous approaches to the rape-revenge subgenre of horror as well as to the threat of castration, which for decades has been woven into the genre's "monstrous-feminine" depictions of women breaking free from oppressive, socially circumscribed protocols of "proper" behavior and disrupting the "normal" state of things (Creed 1993). Space has also been reserved in forthcoming chapters for an assessment of horror's queering potential, or, rather, filmmakers' capacity to imagine alternatives to the genre's built-in structural binaries while creating empathy and opportunities for self-determination for people who have been marginalized because of society's limited understanding of their sexual identities. Additionally, a more thoroughgoing consideration of recent developments in assistive technologies, which might level the perceptual playing field for audiences whose accessibility to images and sounds is otherwise impacted by embodied differences (colloquially known as physical and sensory impairments), would add much to our understanding of horror as a body genre. As Travis Sutton argues, those two ostensibly unrelated areas of activist-led scholarship—Queer Theory and Disability Studies—overlap in their respective efforts to make visible the otherwise invisible forces of oppression in society and to speak truth to the unspoken standards upon which so many big-screen fictions are predicated (Sutton 2014, 75). From compulsory heterosexuality to compulsory able-bodiedness, the mutually dominant systems of "being" a body onscreen are just as conspicuous in horror as they are in other categories of cultural production. However, horror's tendency to associate monstrosity with *ab*-normality, *de*-formity, *dis*-ease, *dis*-order, and *dis*-ability distinguishes it as a genre that is sorely in need of queer, non-ableist, and intersectional interventions (Sutton 2014, 75; see also Norden 1994, 12).

The questions put forth in the preceding paragraphs propel this book's exploratory tour of the human anatomy and the human sensorium. But I also devote pages to the use (and misuse) of *nonhuman* creatures in horror films that unwittingly reveal the medium's anthropocentric view of a world in which beings are arranged hierarchically according to their capacities for language, introspection, and complex reasoning. At the anatomical and physiological levels, humans and animals are remarkably similar, and many nonhuman creatures carry within their bodies the same organs (e.g., brain, heart, lungs) and organ systems (e.g., nervous, cardiovascular, respiratory) that we do. And though horror films often remind us of that comparability by reducing human beings to "meat" (something that, in the wrong hands, can be flayed, butchered, frozen, and even eaten), animals frequently receive the brunt of abuse both diegetically and extradiegetically, during the actual production of motion pictures that do not abide by the safety protocols established by American Humane and other nonprofit organizations around the world. A living bat is tortured by children in Jorge Grau's *Blood Ceremony* (*Ceremonia sangrienta*, 1973). Real chickens and squealing pigs are slaughtered in the Paul Naschy vehicles *Vengeance of the Zombies* (*La rebelión de las muertas*, 1973) and *Blue Eyes of the Broken Doll* (*Los Ojos Azules de la Muñeca Rota*, 1974). A large turtle is decapitated and gutted in a non-simulated scene of the aforementioned *Cannibal Holocaust*. A cat is eaten by a swarm of rats in the Hong Kong historical horror film *Men Behind the Sun* (aka, *Black Sun: 731*; *Hēi tài ang 731*, 1989) and several more actual dead felines have been strung up outside a house in the opening scene of *Stephen King's Sleepwalkers* (1992). These and other physically and morally revolting images suggest that nonhuman creatures have long been part of horror's taxidermic fascination with bodily pain. More to the point, they have been put on grisly display as a practical, if ethically dubious, "solution" to the problem of achieving deathly verisimilitude onscreen. The question that begs to be asked, though, is how much the genre might contribute to an interspecies empathy conducive to a feel-based reimagining of animal-human relations or, conversely, to a further entrenchment of humans' presumed superiority over "lesser beings," whose bodies cease to matter in the same way that ours do.

The latter idea is complicated by the fact that animal flesh is often substituted for human flesh during the making of horror movies, as Rob Weiner and A. Bowdoin Van Riper remind us in their discussion of Herschell Gordon Lewis's notorious splatter classic *Blood Feast* (1963). This film's "most iconic scene" shows a psychopathic food caterer forcing his hand into the mouth of a young woman and ripping her tongue out (Weiner and Van Riper 2017, 229). Disgusting though it is, knowledge of the circumstances surrounding the filming of the scene, in which a sheep's tongue was used in place of actress Astrid Olson's tongue, alleviates some of the emotional and physical stress placed on spectators who are able to "swallow" animal deaths more easily than they can human deaths (figure 1.3). Notably, on the bonus audio commentary track

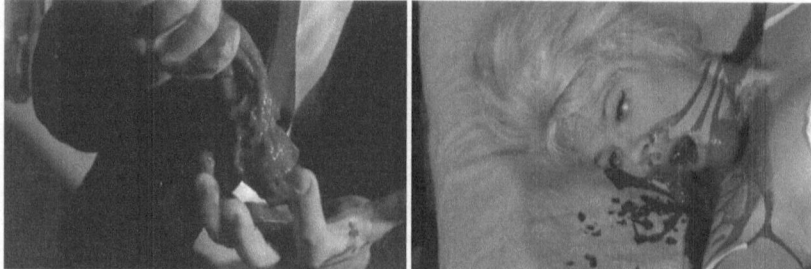

Figure 1.3. A rancid sheep's tongue was used in place of an actual human tongue during the production of *Blood Feast* (1963), one of many instances across the history of the horror when animals' body parts serve as convenient (if smelly) props.

of Arrow Video's recent Blu-ray release of *Blood Feast* (ported over from the interview included on Something Weird Video's 2017 DVD release), director Lewis and producer David F. Friedman laugh about the fact that the sheep's tongue, purchased from a local butcher's shop, had begun to spoil due to a power outage at the sleazy motel in Miami where this scene was being filmed. A small portion of this movie's $25,000 budget thus went to paying the cost of Pine-Sol, a household cleaning product in which the gloppy appendage was doused so as to cover up the stench of rotting meat.

This and other production-related tidbits, though trivial within the larger history of cinematic horror, are precisely what a "fleshed-out" comprehension or "anatomy" of the genre relies upon, and which are provided in the supplemental features of several classic and cult films' home-video releases. Indeed, the director's commentary tracks, cast interviews, making-of documentaries, and behind-the-scenes footage included on the special-edition DVDs and Blu-rays produced by Blue Underground, Mondo Macabro, Scorpion Releasing, Scream Factory, Severin, Synapse Films, Vinegar Syndrome, and other boutique companies specializing in horror make it possible to "see" the genre differently, from humorously skewed and historically informed vantages far removed from the straightforward mode of passive spectatorship that is wrongly assumed to be the standard way of watching films these days. Thanks to such artifactual/paratextual add-ons, greater attention can be directed not only toward onscreen details (related to a film's camera movement, cinematography, mise-en-scène, etc.) that tend to slip past most casual viewers, but also to the often physically demanding work required to bring stories about death to life. Moreover, the dangerous conditions of moviemaking that occasionally give rise to on-set injuries and more tragic outcomes (see, for instance, *Vampire in Brooklyn* [1995] and *Incident in a Ghostland* [2018]) are brought forth in the supplemental features of some DVDs and Blu-rays, a topic that I touch upon throughout the first half of this book (comprising its first five chapters), which is devoted partially to the dual, or rather dueling, prospect of *seeing* and *unseeing* horror films. Because the bodies of actors and stunt performers, as visible and invisible members of the genre's corporeal labor force, both reveal and mask some of the more serious, consequential aspects of making ostensibly silly cinematic fare, a sustained look at the things to which we are encouraged to "turn a blind eye" will help to bring horror's ethical dimensions to the fore.

Throughout this book, I interweave anecdotes drawn from such unconventional sources for the purpose of explaining how horror differs from other genres yet shares some of the affective qualities of comedy, its phenomenological flipside. Today it is not uncommon to hear directors, producers, and cast and crew members snickering quietly or guffawing loudly on the commentary tracks of digitally remastered horror films, whose newly cleaned-up images and clearly audible sounds reveal gaffes or goofs that were easier to miss during the era of VHS tapes (i.e., the late 1970s to the early 1990s) or even earlier, when drive-in movie theaters were the only places to watch certain low-budget releases. I was reminded of this when I rewatched the 2019 Arrow Video Blu-ray release of director Richard Friedman's *Scared Stiff* (1987) while listening to the audio commentary, which is one of several supplemental features included on the disc. During an early scene of this once-obscure, recently rediscovered motion picture, as psychotherapist David Young (Andrew Stevens) attempts to calm an agitated mental patient who has to be physically restrained by hospital orderlies lest he hurt another innocent victim, the commentary's moderator (a cultural historian and longtime fan of the film, Robert Ellinger) reminds listeners that "what we're watching here is the new restored version." "It looks *amazing*," Ellinger enthuses to his fellow commentators (director Friedman and the film's producer, Daniel Bacaner), before noting that until this screening he had "never noticed there was some blood on the right side of [the patient's] mouth." Funnily enough, he says this at the exact moment when the man angrily spits into David's face, forcing the protagonist to wipe the stuff from his eyes. His action conveys something about the manner in which this horror film—previously available only on murky VHS tapes—has been "cleaned" up by the video distributor and given new life as something that can now finally be seen in the way that its creators had intended. Upon hearing Ellinger marvel at how much more "detail" there is "in this restored version, including the makeup job" on the patient's forehead (which bears a deep gash, or rather what looks to have been a hastily applied facial prosthetic whose fakeness is pronounced thanks to this digital restoration), Friedman quips, "Yeah . . . not necessarily a *good* thing."

The filmmaker's humorous aside, aimed at the occasional schlockiness of an ambitious production that had to "make do" with a limited budget and whose cheesy effects stand out now that Arrow Video has removed over thirty years of dirt and debris from the original 35mm negative, is balanced at a later point in the commentary when Friedman enthuses that this "crystal clear" restoration "is actually the way [the film] *should* look, and it has never looked like this before." Notably, his remark, coming from "outside" the text (as part of the Blu-ray's paratextual material), corresponds to what is happening inside the house. Specifically, it coincides with shots of David, a new homeowner, discovering the entrance to a hidden attic behind a boarded-up wall and stepping cautiously into that heavily cobwebbed, pigeon-filled space, flashlight in hand. "It was *well-lit,* and *now* you can see it," Bacaner chimes in, just as the protagonist shines his light across the attic's contents and, amidst decades of accumulated dirt and debris, discovers a few old objects left behind by a previous occupant (a former slave owner whose malevolent spirit haunts this cursed mansion). Suggestive of the manner in which this and other characters' pursuit of literal and figurative clarity in horror films (as part of their efforts to shed light on inexplicable events or supernatural phenomena) parallels our own extratextual hunt for the best audiovisual presentations of those digitally restored films, these comments on the *Scared Stiff* disc are reminiscent of what occurs on the 2012 Blu-ray release of Tobe Hooper's 1981 slasher film *The Funhouse*. Interviewed by fellow filmmaker and horror enthusiast Tim Sullivan, Hooper remarks at one point that "Blu-ray has a way of seeing things that the projected film doesn't have," to which his companion on the commentary track adds that when he first saw *The Funhouse* at a drive-in theater decades ago the projected images were washed out by car headlights, making it almost as frustrating as watching the film on cropped videos in the years that followed. Concluding that "it was like [he] never really got to see the movie" until Shout! Factory released this digitally restored version, Sullivan hints at the fact that audiences' responses to onscreen stimuli are historically situated and contingent on the material conditions or contexts of their presentation. And he does so in the presence of the film's director, who is forthcoming about details of its production and thus offers audiences an insider's view that contributes to a clearer, fuller picture while pulling back the proverbial curtain to reveal how the "magic" of this movie about carnival sideshows was achieved.

Returning to Herschell Gordon Lewis and David F. Friedman's laughter-filled audio commentary chat as they watch the equally carnivalesque *Blood Feast* together, it is noteworthy that, at the midpoint of the film, they cannot help but mock actress Louise Kamp's inability to hold her breath while playing a virginal priestess who has just had her heart removed by a crazed, knife-wielding follower of the Egyptian goddess Ishtar. That simple description of the scene is risible enough to undercut the terror of witnessing the deadly instrument plunge into the woman's chest (which, as the director reveals, was actually chicken skin). But Lewis's verbalized complaint about Kamp's visible breathing amplifies the humorous effect while adding much to our understanding of the challenges involved in making something truly scary or shocking for modern-day spectators—viewers who, to borrow on old adage, have "seen it all."

SEEING IT ALL, BELIEVING IN NOTHING

> Do you want to be left as you are? Or do you want your eyes and your soul to be blasted by a sight that would stagger the devil himself?
> —MR. HYDE (Fredric March) to his disbelieving colleague Dr. Lanyon (Holmes Herbert), seconds before drinking from a potion-filled flask, in *Dr. Jekyll and Mr. Hyde* (1931)

In recent years, variations on that "seen it all" expression have become a prominent feature of both academic and journalistic accounts of horror's built-in familiarity as a genre that, for all its jump scares, shock cuts, and other startle effects, fails to surprise the most jaded of viewers. This was Joe Dante's main complaint when, during a 2011 interview led by his friend and fellow filmmaker John Landis, he opined that audiences have "seen every plot . . . seen every twist . . . seen every gore effect" (Landis 2011, 63). As the director of such perennial fan favorites as *Piranha* (1978), *The Howling* (1981), and *Gremlins* (1984), Dante played his part in helping to fortify some of the conventions of the genre through the skillful repurposing of material that would have been familiar to anyone raised on a diet of classic creature features from the 1930s and cheesy B-movies made before and during the Cold War era (from "nature-run-amok" animal horror to werewolf folklore and giant radioactive bug movies). But now, in the "twilight" of his career, and saddened by the popularity of commercially successful romantic fantasies like *Twilight* (2008) and its sequels, the septuagenarian can only sigh at how little young people know about the "old, low-budget serials" that are the basis for so much of what gets produced by studios these days (Landis 2011, 63). Therein lies the irony of his comment that "they"—mainstream audiences who have multiple media outlets at their fingertips (all competing for their increasingly divided attention) as well as twenty-first-century gore-hounds who appear to be unfazed by the spectacle of ever-more-explicit "maiming and killing"—have "seen it all," when in fact it would seem that they have seen very little.[2]

I have no interest in either disputing or supporting such claims, or in drawing a dividing line between groups of hypothetical spectators whose access to cinema's past is contingent on a host of socioeconomic factors and technological affordances, not to mention shifts in taste cultures as a result of increased (or decreased) availability of once-marginalized films in home-video and online formats. I will say, though, that the recent surge of interest in horror, both inside and outside academia, parallels the genre's renaissance over the past two decades, not just in the United States but internationally, with French productions such as *High Tension* (*Haute Tension*, 2003), *Frontière(s)* (2007), *Inside* (*À l'intérieur*, 2007), *Martyrs* (2008), *Raw* (2016), and *Climax* (2018), Japanese productions such as *Pulse* (*Kairo*, 2001), *Suicide Club* (*Jisatsu Sākuru*, 2001), *Ju-On: The Grudge* (2002), *One Missed Call* (*Chakushin ari*, 2003), *Noroi: The Curse* (2005), and *One Cut of the Dead* (*Kamera o Tomeru na!*, 2017), South Korean productions such as *Sorum* (2001), *A Tale of Two Sisters* (*Janghwa, Hongryeon*, 2003), *Thirst* (*Bakjwi*, 2009), *The Wailing* (*Gokseong*, 2016), *Train to Busan* (*Busanhaeng*, 2016), and *Gonjiam: Haunted Asylum* (*Gonjiam*, 2018), and Spanish productions such as *The Devil's Backbone* (*El espinazo del diablo*, 2001), *The Orphanage* (*El orfanato*, 2007), *[REC]* (2007), *Julia's Eyes* (*Los ojos de Julia*, 2010), *Sleep Tight* (*Mientras duermes*, 2011), and *Verónica* (2017) attracting strong fan followings through global film festivals and online platforms like Shudder, Netflix, Hulu, and Amazon Prime. These and dozens of other, equally audacious works of the twenty-first century can stand toe-to-toe with the greatest horror films of the previous century, making any such complaints about the current state of genre-based filmmaking and reception a moot point.

At the time of this writing (in the summer of 2021), several theatrical and streaming releases have appeared in mid-year lists of the "best" horror films of the past six months. The strength of such works as Amelia Moses's *Bloodthirsty* (2020), Bryan Bertino's *The Dark and the Wicked* (2020), David Prior's *The Empty Man* (2020), Natasha Kermani's *Lucky* (2020), David Bruckner's *The Night House* (2020), Rose Glass's *Saint Maud* (2020), Madeleine Sims-Fewer and Dusty Mancinelli's *Violation* (2020), Prano Bailey-Bond's *Censor* (2021), Anthony Scott Burns's *Come True* (2021), Jaco Bouwer's *Gaia* (2021), Ben Wheatley's *In the Earth* (2021), and Jane Schoenbrun's *We're All Going to the World's Fair* (2021) is a testament to the genre's enduring power to address important social issues (ranging from domestic abuse and sexual assault to racial injustice and the increased rate of suicide among vulnerable populations) while making the viewer's skin crawl with truly terrifying visions of what we have become in an age of global health crises, growing economic inequality, and deepening political divisions.[3] Even a film like Mike P. Nelson's *Wrong Turn* (2021), a "reboot of Rob Schmidt's 2003 backwoods slasher about a group of teenagers being hunted by mutated serial killers" along the Appalachian Trail, but modified by turning the physically deformed cannibals from West Virginia (the monsters in the original) into an isolated cult in Virginia led by a cruel father figure, captures something of the zeitgeist in its portrayal of an urban-rural cultural clash while also generating pleasure in its "predictability," according to Adam Nayman. Significantly, Nayman's April 28 list of "The Best

Horror Movies of 2021 (So Far)," posted on the pop culture website *The Ringer*, begins by observing that narrative coherence, logic, and plausibility are not prerequisites for greatness. Instead, he argues, what matters most is whether or not a film is "convincing" in its depiction of *belief*—an attitude that even the most skeptical characters eventually adopt, but which is harder to impress upon audiences who have "seen it all" (Nayman 2021).

Nayman uses that "seen it all" phrase when discussing *Wrong Turn*, not only because this latest in a long string of franchise reboots is directly based on another film of the same title and replays its basic premise ("city kids become lambs to the slaughter"), but also because, like Joe Dante, he understands that contemporary audiences—especially those who are roughly the same age as this film's millennial protagonists—have a larger array of viewing options at their disposal than their parents and grandparents did just three or four decades ago. As such, they are perhaps less prone to devote time to earlier generations' cinematic output when so much of what is being made today is worth watching. The "all" of that well-worn statement thus refers to the standard iconographic and narrative elements of cinematic horror, initially developed by Dante's predecessors inside and outside Hollywood during the silent and early sound eras and subsequently inherited or updated by contemporary cultural producers (and their visual effects teams), rather than to the many historical touchstones of the genre that he and other cinephiles believe are being forgotten or left behind in our pursuit of more graphically violent, physically nauseating thrills. Nevertheless, the idea of seeing "everything" is inflected with two distinct meanings that dovetail in unexpected ways. Indeed, the literal "opening up" of the body in gory detail onscreen in splatter film franchises ranging from *Final Destination* (2000–present) to *Saw* (2004–present) oddly correlates to the figurative "closing down" of the mind to earlier productions' less-gratuitous representations (i.e., images of death and physical violation in 1920s- and 1930s-era films that now seem tame by comparison).

Of course, greater knowledge of and appreciation for classic movie monsters and the larger history of horror would enable viewers to look upon a recent metafictional work like *Cabin in the Woods* (2011) with an eye to its combined indebtedness to prior productions and novelty as a postmodern "deconstruction" of the genre (Murphy 2013, 15). However, to quote numerous online commentators as well as the film's own tagline, there is "more than meets the eye" in *Cabin in the Woods*, and "if you think you know the story"—a premise that has been replicated on multiple occasions—"*think again.*" Indeed, as Bernice M. Murphy points out, director Drew Goddard's much-discussed motion picture, whose "freshness" and textual self-awareness are ironically tied to its adoption of "stale" generic formulas as well as its recognizable and obscure intertextual allusions, paradoxically undermines audience expectations through the scenario's "very predictability" (starting from its title, a reference to that most clichéd of settings in the slasher subgenre). "The audience doesn't need to have it explained to them that the isolated cabin in the midst of the deep, dark forest is a locale in which horrific events will take place: *they've seen it all before*," Murphy writes, emphasizing that the film's "reality-warping revelations" are all the more effective at "wrong-footing" us because "we *think* we 'know' the story" (2013, 15, emphasis added).

Those musings in the preceding paragraphs, derived from three very different sources (one a nonacademic chat between two horror auteurs/enthusiasts [Dante and Landis], the second an insightful blog about the year's best horror films [Nayman], and the third a scholarly study of the rural gothic in American popular culture [Murphy]), underscore a common refrain in contemporary discourse surrounding the genre. Just as horror is thought to hinge on the "repetition of certain recognizable formulas and scenarios" (Reyes 2016, 165), so too does the critical and quotidian language surrounding the genre repeatedly frame it as something begging to be *seen* in all of its entirety, whether historically (as something that hardcore fans and completists attempt to do by tracking down *every* horror film ever made) or imagistically (by refusing to turn away from the most retina-searing, stomach-churning visions of violent mayhem and human carnage found in either artfully made or tastelessly exploitative motion pictures). In both cases, horror is treated as a Sisyphean challenge to the viewer—a cruel "Squid Game" to be played but never won, since "seeing it all" (in both senses of that phrase) is ultimately unachievable, even for someone with all the time and/or nerves required to attempt such a fool's errand.[4] And yet, as I stress throughout this book, *pleasure* rather than pain can result from playing that game, an experience akin to what Isabel Cristina Pinedo refers to as "recreational terror" (1996, 17–31; 1997).

Although I will return to Pinedo's important study of the various pleasures experienced by viewers of horror films in upcoming chapters, including those that are either primarily or partially devoted to the genre's comedic leanings and to audiences' propensity to laugh (rather than scream) when seated before an ostensibly terrifying scene, it bears mentioning that she was among the first scholars to theorize such an approach a quarter of a century ago. Moreover, she posits "mastery"—or the sense of gaining control over the genre's tropes through repeated exposure—as one reason why horror entertains as much as it frightens. Audience members habituated to horror become "seasoned" or skillful at reading the warning signs of danger in a film (e.g., camera angles, musical cues, offscreen noises, performative gestures, etc.) while still appreciating those storytelling detours and textual ruptures that, like the big plot twist near the end of *Cabin in the Woods*, "violate audience expectations" (Pinedo 1996, 28). However, as Jasun Horsley warns in his book *Seen and Not Seen*:

Confessions of a Movie Autist, such increased narrative competency, exacerbated by the "ironic detachment" that protects people from being overwhelmed by existential dread and moral as well as physical revulsion, can also lead to "a 'seen-it-all' superiority and cynicism that's at the same time pathetically naïve, because it magically locates all the horror outside of our own direct experience, on the other side of a movie, TV, or smartphone screen" (2015, 210).

"Ironic detachment is made easy by certain kinds of movies and TV shows," Horsley adds, "because they allow us to feel like we're being exposed to life's brutal, bleak realities (violence, corruption, drug addiction, disease, poverty, insanity, moral collapse) without ever having to bear the brunt of those realities ourselves" (2015, 210). In a similar vein, Pinedo argues that, besides offering "a welcome release from the fiction that life is ordered and safe," horror grants us the opportunity to dance through a minefield without the fear of detonation (1996, 29). We experience, in other words, "controlled loss" rather than the "loss of control" that sometimes affects our own lives. Or, to put it in even simpler terms, cinematic horror makes it possible for people to confront death "without having to really die," as Dante notes in his discussion of why the genre still resonates with so many audiences (even if some of them actually *do* believe that they have "seen it all") (Landis 2011, 62).

Returning briefly to Dante's lament over the current state of horror film spectatorship and most moviegoers' general lack of historical knowledge about the genre's origins, it is important to consider the unspoken bias that is detectable in this and other commentaries. Here I am not referring to any animosity or prejudicial attitude directed toward particular groups of people, but rather to the perceptual favoritism bestowed upon one sense above all others—a widespread partiality toward *seeing* as the basis for knowledge claims. It is a bias that no one person is guilty of alone, and which I too have been prone to fall back on as a film scholar groomed in theoretical traditions that privilege sight as the sensing ability best suited to perceiving the motion-picture medium's distinct features. Accordingly, I spend portions of the next four chapters of this book discussing the general tendency, apparent within both academic and nonacademic writings about horror film, to not only see but *think* through the eyes, as if one organ above all (conveniently located near the tops of our bodies) were capable of enabling cognition, when a more corporeally inclusive concert of the senses could be called upon to get a better handle on the genre—that is, to more fully understand the strange hold that it has over us.

Just as many motion pictures have done, this book aims to put the literal and figurative anatomy of the genre front and center. But it also delves into some of the philosophical questions posed by cinematic horror (and by theorists writing about it) that pertain to the dialectics of belief and disbelief, of life and death, of normality and abnormality, and of self and other. Such antinomies, though discernible in other categories of cultural production, are central to the organizational logic of more than a few horror narratives. This is certainly true of *Dr. Jekyll and Mr. Hyde* (1931), a studio release produced in Hollywood during a period of industrial transformation (befitting the title character's physical change) that, as I will elaborate in the next chapter, hinges thematically on a "two-selves" thesis only to problematize such distinctions through *the embodiment of the soul* and *the ensoulment of the body*. By building upon yet moving beyond the ocularcentrism of film criticism, by synthesizing materials across a range of different taste cultures and disciplines, by moving largely marginalized sensory pathways and organs to the fore of the discussion, and by posing odd, previously unasked questions about a genre that is itself weird and provocative (and thus conducive to such left-field theorizing), I hope to demonstrate horror's underlying complexity and provide a springboard for future studies of the genre.

Ultimately, *Body Genre: Anatomy of the Horror Film* provides a "head-to-toe" approach to its subject by zooming in on the actual body parts that are so often fetishized—if fearfully so—as objects of our own embodied gaze. But I also zoom out to reveal the sociopolitical and cultural contexts in which those corporeal sites of meaning symptomatically correspond to anxieties more broadly experienced by people in different areas of the world. The widespread appeal of horror—the fact that a film made in one country or region can translate so well across cultures and in contexts far removed from its originating source, according to Dana Och and Kirsten Strayer—is due to "the prominence of the body" within the genre (2014, 6–7). In their words, "While social, historical, and cultural particulars may be lost in international reception, the core identification process with the body remains intact, even as the body mutates, transforms, becomes-animal, or fractures" (2014, 6–7). This will become especially apparent to readers toward the end of this book, the final two chapters of which explore the relationship between horror as a culturally translatable body genre and comedy as one that suffers considerable loss or undergoes significant change whenever it crosses national borders (for instance, moving from Hong Kong to the United States) and circulates in different linguistic communities. Further establishing a conceptual framework for the entire book, the next chapter directs the reader's attention toward critical, historical, and theoretical approaches that have been instrumental to my own understanding of what horror is, how it works on our bodies, and why even the silliest examples of the genre should be taken seriously as slightly (or grossly) exaggerated representations of real-world concerns.

SECTION ONE

Somatic Spectatorship
Believing, Bleeding, Hearing, Seeing

2

HEADS WILL ROLL, BODIES WILL SHAKE, SOULS WILL SHATTER

Horror Film's Formative Stages and Physical Changes

> Scream your way through the haunted house, and experience the sounds, smells, lights, and actions of the original movie right before your eyes. Feel like you are a part of the film as you become the victim of your own horror movie!
> —ad for the 2021 *Exorcist*-themed Halloween Horror Nights at Universal Studios Florida, which promises to involve "all five" of the visitors' senses

It all began, some historians have said, with a decapitated head. On August 28, 1895, employees at the Edison Manufacturing Company in West Orange, New Jersey, filmed a short, tableau-like historical scene that was intended to demonstrate the Kinetograph's technological capacities as a relatively new recording medium, but which has since been seen as the first stirrings of cinematic "body horror." In his role as newly promoted supervising director of Edison's film division, Alfred Clark arranged for a small group of actors to take part in a staged reenactment of one of Western civilization's most uncivilized acts: the beheading of Mary Stuart of Scotland, whose 1587 death had already been memorialized in several novels, plays, and poems prior to this earliest motion-picture treatment. What sets Clark's film apart from the cultural productions that preceded it was its unusual—and unusually *violent*—approach to showing the imprisoned woman's death-by-decapitation. Framed as a static long shot, at a strangely respectful distance from the dozen or so performers who, adorned in what look to be period-appropriate uniforms (albeit those "of the Vatican's Swiss Guards, at best a weak approximation of sixteenth-century English military wear") (Yue 2021, 80), form a backdrop to the title character's grisly demise, the main event depicted in *Execution of Mary, Queen of Scots* (1895) is, on the surface, simple and straightforward. The ill-fated woman calmly gets on her knees and bends forward, placing her neck on the chopping block. A masked executioner, towering above the kneeling woman with an axe raised to the heavens, brings the weapon down and lops off that most vital and irreplaceable of human appendages in a single swift motion. Finally, he grabs Mary's head, which has rolled to the ground, and holds it up high for all to see. The End.

Fewer than fifteen seconds have elapsed since the scene began, and no intertitles or contextualizing preface appeared onscreen prior to the action. From this we can postulate at least two things: first, the creative staff at Edison's company surmised that the film's audiences (who watched it on Kinetoscope machines four months before the Lumière brothers held the world's first public screening of motion pictures at Paris's Grand Cafè in December of 1895) would have been able to discern its historical subject with little-to-no handholding beyond its telltale title; and second, the act of *showing* took precedence over that of *telling* via printed text, turning the wordless (and, of course, silent) spectacle of a woman's bodily destruction into a catalyzing illustration of where the medium was "heading" near the turn of the twentieth century. As film scholar Gary D. Rhodes has argued, with *Execution of Mary, Queen of Scots* "the moving picture had embraced horror for the very first time, but certainly not the last" (2018, 2).

In *The Birth of the American Horror Film*, Rhodes discusses this progenitive moment in the history of the genre, when not just this film but a slew of other motion pictures "depicted authentic deaths." In doing so, they carved out a safe cultural space for the morbidly curious to confront images of physical suffering from the spectatorial remove afforded by the medium. Besides fictional recreations of historical events, on view in everything from legendary French magician Georges Méliès's lost film *The Spanish Inquisition* (*La cremation*, 1899) and countryman Lucien Nonguet's *Martyrs of the Inquisition* (*Les Martyrs de l'Inquisition*, 1906) to stateside productions like the Lubin Manufacturing Company's *Beheading the Chinese Prisoner* (1900) and American Mutoscope & Biograph's *Execution of a Murderess* (aka, *Execution by Hanging*, 1905), several "nonfiction images of animals dying onscreen" circulated in Kinetoscope parlors at that time (Rhodes 2018, 222–23). In addition to those showing stockyard animals being slaughtered, the latter set of turn-of-the-century horrors included Edison's seventy-four-second short *Electrocuting an Elephant* (1903), which Rhodes refers to as a "gruesome record of animal cruelty," one that involved not just a deadly amount of electrical shock being applied to the unfortunate pachyderm but also poisoning and strangulation. The notion that Topsy, the titular creature who was killed on January 4, 1903 (following a deadly run-in with a human), is presented to the audience as a source of rogue *terror* rather than cross-species *empathy* is further complicated by the fact that this public spectacle of *human* cruelty was staged at an amusement park (that of Coney Island) where other types of thrilling entertainment could be experienced in less vicarious ways. Unlike the heavily promoted killing of Topsy, whose rigid body falls to the ground in a cloud of smoke, the quicker death dealt to Mary in the aforementioned execution film is *fake*, further "protecting" spectators from the actual effects of corporeal destruction, if not the ethical consequences of beholding such a gruesome sight.

Execution of Mary, Queen of Scots is significant not only as the first of several cinematic slayings produced within a few years of the medium's "birth," but also as an early example of special effects in film (Rhodes 2018, 2). In lieu of actually removing a woman's head from her body, Clark did the only sensible thing and used a mannequin, which was substituted in for the living, breathing performer through a "barely noticeable splice that interrupts the falling motion of the executioner's blade" (Yue 2021, 73). As detailed by Genevieve Yue in *Girl Head: Feminism and Film Materiality*, this sleight-of-hand illusion on the part of the production crew (who stopped the camera temporarily in the course of shooting the scene so that "Mary," a historical personage played by male actor Robert Thomae, could be switched out with a dummy before cinematographer William Heise resumed filming) marked the first instance of stop-motion editing in cinema. Belying its outward simplicity and straightforwardness, the layers of trickery in this film function in triplicate to displace the woman, who is *there but not there* in the framed image. Indeed, her body "disappears three times over," according to Yue: "first, in the portrayal of a female character by a male actor, Robert Thomae; second, in the substitution of a dummy body; and third, in a splice that conceals the traces of the stop-motion effect, thereby omitting a substantial length of film footage." And yet, the material remains of the woman, in the form of movie props (the head that tumbles to the ground and rolls away from the mannequin's body), have a weight, solidity, and motility that register as palpable residue of the past, despite the film print's own material degradation. Such corporeal trauma, visited upon a person whose death is transformed into a "spectacular visual stunt," is not far removed from the acts of decapitation that appear in horror films from the past fifty years, including critically disparaged slashers from the 1980s (e.g., *Death Screams* [1982], *Superstition* [1982], *Sleepaway Camp* [1983], *The Mutilator* [1984], *Hide and Go Shriek* [1988]) as well as more visceral yet lauded recent releases in which heads are lopped off, such as *I Saw the Devil* (*Angmareul boatda*, 2010) and *Hereditary* (2018).

Written and directed by Ari Aster, *Hereditary*—one of several contemporary works to be labeled by critics and fans as "elevated horror"—features a famously "shocking" scene in which a thirteen-year-old girl, Charlie (Milly Shapiro), leans out a car window and has her head taken clean off by a telephone pole when her older brother, Peter (Alex Wolff), swerves to avoid hitting a deer in the road (figure 2.1). Although the title of Aster's work specifically refers to

Figure 2.1. The bloodied head of thirteen-year-old Charlie bakes under the sun in this shot from *Hereditary* (2018), a film that, despite its "elevated horror" label, is grounded in gut-wrenching images and the earthy materiality of human bodies.

a bloodline of people who, possessed by an ancient demon known as King Paimon, might serve as its earthly hosts, *Hereditary*'s own indebtedness to previous cultural productions dating back to that first attempt at cinematic decapitation (*Execution of Mary, Queen of Scots*) can be construed as a kind of intertextual inheritance or cinematic birthright in its own right, as just one of the latest in a long string of horror films reliant upon generic conventions that can be traced back to the late nineteenth century. Stated differently, as someone who inherited the Scottish throne from an early age and would later claim Queen Elizabeth's English throne as her own before being confined to prison and eventually found guilty of an assassination plot (leading up to her death-by-decapitation), the title character in the 1895 short film would cast a long headless shadow over generations of horror films for decades to come, including those like *Hereditary* that foreground their "family resemblance" to earlier works through the once-shocking, now-commonplace trope of the severed head. Laying on the pavement in medium close-up, Charlie's detached body part—covered in blood and ants and crushed nearly beyond recognition—is merely a more graphic representation of the violence that has been a latent part of American cinema since its initial flickerings over 120 years ago. Indeed, the severed head's centrality to the psychological trauma experienced by the young girl's family over the course of the narrative indicates how "grounded" and "messy" even the most "elevated" or "transcendent" of horror films are when it comes to the earthy, physical presence of bodies on screen.

"RIGHT BEFORE YOUR EYES"

> Certainly, film is not life, nor images of the world the same as the world itself, but . . . film and the physical world are in some measure analogous in the ways they proffer the primacy of the seen and heard as the repository of meaning.
> —JAMES PALMER and MICHAEL RILEY, "Seeing, Believing, and 'Knowing' in Narrative Film"

Flip through any academic book about the history of cinematic horror and you are likely to find that the genre dates back not only to "frightful exhibits" such as *Execution of Mary, Queen of Scots* (Kracauer 1997, 57), but also to some of the earliest experiments in motion-picture storytelling, including Georges Méliès's *The Devil's Castle* (*Le Manoir du diable*, 1896), Edwin S. Porter's *Uncle Josh's Nightmare* (1900), Walter R. Booth's *The Haunted Curiosity Shop* (1901), and a host of other comically macabre shorts from the turn of the century that likewise featured trick photography and rudimentary special effects (Dixon 2010, 3–4; Weismann 2021, 9). While very few of those productions were "particularly horrifying" (Morgart 2013, 377), they showcased many of the visual elements that retroactively can be seen as iconographic staples of the genre (e.g., crucifixes, demons, detached heads, ghosts, skeletons, witches, etc.). To be clear, the actual category of "horror film" did not emerge—discursively, rhetorically, and through a complex process of genrification—until three decades later, around the time of *Dracula*'s 1931 theatrical release (Rhodes 2018, 8; Leeder 2018, 6–8). However, the initial stage of the motion-picture medium's development, as it moved from a spectacle-driven and gag-based peepshow phenomenon to a story-driven form of entertainment in the nickelodeon era of the 1900s and 1910s, witnessed the production of several silent-era precursors to what would eventually be labeled as such by reviewers in the early 1930s (in lieu of other terms, such as "gothic melodramas," "startling films," and "weird tales") (Phillips 2018, 26–86).[1]

By the time Karl Freund's *The Mummy* (1932) was produced and distributed by Universal Pictures on the heels of that studio's previous hits (Tod Browning's aforementioned *Dracula* and James Whale's *Frankenstein* [1931]), the public had apparently become so familiar with the genre's tropes that Gordon Hillman, writing for the *Boston Daily Record*, could count on his readership knowing exactly what kind of effect a "really good horror picture" like this Boris Karloff vehicle *should* have on audiences: namely, "to send cold chills creeping down the spectator's spine" (1933, 14). According to the hard-to-impress Hillman, "In general, horror films never attain [that] object[ive]," hence his enthusiasm for *The Mummy*, the creators of which took a "macabre, fantastic, and highly unbelievable story" concerning Karloff's character Imhotep (a mummified priest from ancient Egypt) and "invested it with a high degree of weirdness, a great deal of suspense, and much excitement" (1933, 14). As Kendall R. Phillips emphasizes in *A Place of Darkness: The Rhetoric of Horror in Early American Cinema*, the promise of *weirdness, suspense,* and *excitement* had been plastered on theater marquees and incorporated into several films' ad campaigns well before *The Mummy*'s December 22, 1932, release (during and after the nickelodeon era), when similar words like "startling," "thrilling," and "mysterious" were mobilized so as to capture audiences' interest in subjects that flirted with the exotic, the foreign, and the taboo (2018, 19). During the 1910s, the whiff of something different, something *dangerous*, was enough to tempt many moviegoers into small storefront theaters, packed with people from all walks of life, at a time when the United States was, in Phillips's words, "steeped in dualities" and contradictions. Those dualities include the split between an "old world," suggested by increasing numbers of immigrants from European and Asian countries (but also indicative of this nation's rural past) and a "new world," signaled by technological advancements in mass communication and transportation that, ironically, shrank the distance between "here" and "there" while pointing toward an industrial future that seemed more like the stuff of science fiction.

"The split between religious and spiritual beliefs and the promise of scientific certainty," which can be superimposed atop that old world/new world dichotomy (Phillips 2018, 125), was another internal conflict apparent in American life at that time, making it all the more reasonable that there should be so many big-screen adaptations of that most dualistic of gothic narratives—Robert Louis Stevenson's *The Strange Case of Dr. Jekyll and Mr. Hyde* (1886)—in the three decades leading up to the 1931 limited release (and 1932 wide release) of the Rouben Mamoulian-directed version produced at Paramount. One of the most noteworthy adaptations from that formative period is *Dr. Jekyll and Mr. Hyde* (1913), a twenty-six-minute two-reeler produced by Carl Laemmle, directed by Herbert Brenon, starring King Baggot, and referred to by historian Charles King as "the first horror film made by Universal Studios (under their Imp label)" (1997, 15). In his contemporaneous review of the film for the influential trade journal *Moving Picture World*, George Blaisdell praises Baggot's performance in the dual role, stating that it is through his portrayal of Mr. Hyde that "the horror of it holds you" (1913, 899). Printed in 1913, Blaisdell's commentary is one of the first indications that critics writing for English-language publications during the second decade of the century were already aware of the genre's capacity to take *possession* of its spellbound audience, even in its embryonic form. The reviewer also singles out the "peculiarly effective" use of a slow lap dissolve to show the title character's chilling transformation from a "man of good" to a "man of evil" (1913, 899). The fact that this change, imbued with moral significance but rendered as a physical shift from one state of being (that of the upright Jekyll) to another (that of the hunchbacked Hyde), occurs "right before your eyes" (to borrow Blaisdell's phrase) makes the film all the more impressive as a demonstration of the medium's power to dismantle moviegoers' (dis)belief systems and to mask its own material presence, as if there were *nothing in between* viewers and the objects of their collective fascination.

Blaisdell's two figures of speech—"the horror of it holds you" and "right before your eyes"—are noteworthy for the way that they foreground phenomenological and sensorial aspects of the genre familiar to contemporary audiences, suggesting that what moviegoers at the time of *Dr. Jekyll and Mr. Hyde's* 1913 release *felt* and *saw* is not all that different from what those of us who watch horror films today experience. *Holding* and *beholding* are not unrelated in terms of "disbelief mitigation," an idea that is central to how the protagonist of the recently produced horror film *Trick* (2019)—a deeply disbelieving detective named Mike Denver (Omar Epps) on the hunt for a masked serial killer—claims to trust in only those things which he can *touch with his own fingers* and *see with his own eyes*. Not coincidentally, when the animalistic, monstrous side of Baggot's Jekyll-Hyde character confronts his skeptical colleague (played by Howard Crampton) with the truth of his hideous transformation, he proclaims, "Dr. Lanyon, man of unbelief, behold!" Those words, printed as a dialogue intertitle, are spoken by the character as he changes back into Jekyll, sending Lanyon—a diegetic surrogate or onscreen stand-in for the film's spectator—*reeling*, his arms outstretched and his hands frozen in a grasp as if he were endeavoring to get a literal hold on what he is witnessing. Of course, the title character's words cannot be heard by the audience, since this is a silent film requiring the use of *eyes* to "behold" the very thing being forced upon Lanyon's vision and which takes hold of *him* in a visceral way. In that respect, his words, like an earlier intertitle conveying Jekyll's plan to unleash his evil self "in the dead silence of the night," push the absence of sound to the foreground and make one's ears seem irrelevant to the comparatively "superior" sensing organ singled out by Blaisdell in his review of the film.

Notably, the phrase "right before your eyes" would reemerge in printed form, as text in another film's intertitle, seven years after *Dr. Jekyll and Mr. Hyde's* 1913 release. As one of the key works of German Expressionism, an artistic movement that spanned the cultural arenas of architecture, dance, painting, sculpture, and eventually cinema during the 1910s and 1920s, *The Cabinet of Dr. Caligari* (*Das Cabinet des Dr. Caligari*, 1920) is steeped in the kind of "weird" signifiers associated with silent-era horror. That weirdness is heightened through director Robert Wiene's innovative use of sharp angles, streaks of light and shadow painted directly onto the sets, and other visual accoutrements that, in the words of a *Variety* reviewer at the time of its belated US release, "squeeze and turn and adjust the eye and through the eye the mentality." Indeed, *Caligari*'s very oddness or foreignness as a cultural import, released to US theaters in the late spring and early summer of 1921, was exploited as a selling point by its distributor Goldwyn, though lingering anti-German sentiments might have impeded this early effort to bring European art to American shores. For its New York premiere, the film was prefaced by a live theatrical prologue that lent the presentation a formal yet carnivalesque atmosphere, with a man named "Crawford" stepping onto the stage next to the screen and introducing himself as the person to whom Francis (Friedrich Feher), "in the opening sequence of the film, is telling his story" (Robinson 2013, 57). That kind of introductory frame corresponds to the manner in which the mysterious sideshow operator Dr. Caligari (Werner Krauss) takes to the stage in an early scene of the film, inviting the crowd of onlookers gathered outside his fairgrounds tent to behold the miraculous Cesare the Somnambulist (Conrad Veidt), a man who has been asleep for all of his twenty-three years on earth. The intertitle that immediately follows shows the title character's words (printed in a suitably expressionistic style as English text for stateside audiences): "*Right before your eyes* Cesare will awaken from his death-like trance."

That four-word expression would continue to pop up in both the textual and paratextual discourses of motion pictures in subsequent decades, when films like Universal's sci-fi-horror production *The Invisible Ray* (1936), which shows Boris Karloff's radiation-exposed astronomer "burning up right before your eyes," and Universal's comedy-horror mashup *Abbott & Costello Meet Dr. Jekyll and Mr. Hyde* (1953), which shows Karloff's murderously love-struck Dr. Jekyll transforming "into a monster right before your eyes" (Anon. 1936, 8; Weaver 1953, 2), carried the silent era's sight-based predilections into the period of sound film production. However, the phrase was especially resonant during the years when *silent* film production was the industrial norm, prior to the introduction of synchronized sound technologies in the late 1920s. Interestingly, when Chicago's McVickers Theater placed an ad in *Exhibitors Herald and Moving Picture World* in the summer of 1928 to announce its forthcoming screenings of transitional sound films, including director Frank Borzage's dramatic feature *Street Angel* (1928), readers were informed that "FOR THE FIRST TIME, YOU WILL HEAR VOICES SPEAKING. CLEARLY—DISTINCTLY— You will hear music, beautiful, mellow, as though sung or played by real, talented humans, *right before your eyes*." Going on to proclaim that "You Will Be Amazed! You Will Be Startled!" the exhibitor's promotional copy, like other ads that appeared in trade magazines that year, adopted a rhetorical mode that, on the one hand, is unusual insofar as insinuated that audiences would not only hear but *see* the medium's newfound competence in delivering sound and, on the other hand, is in keeping with how horror films—even before that category had been discursively created—were being promoted to a public hungry for something new. The newness of synchronized sound, even that which is only partially present in music-filled motion pictures like *Street Angel* (which still used intertitles rather than recorded dialogue), was not unlike the weirdness of cinematic horror, in that it had to be *seen* to be believed.

Fittingly, Lisa Purse, when describing a more recent period in motion-picture history (that of the early 1980s), uses the same phrase that George Blaisdell did several decades earlier, when he gave a glowing review to the trick photography and theatrical performances in the 1913 film *Dr. Jekyll and Mr. Hyde*. As part of her discussion of the groundbreaking special effects pioneered by Dick Smith, Rick Baker, Stan Winston, Tom Savini, and other artists responsible for the prosthetics, makeup, puppetry, and stop-motion animation featured in relatively low-budget horror films like *The Evil Dead* (1981), *An American Werewolf in London* (1981), *Creepshow* (1982), *Videodrome* (1983), *A Nightmare on Elm Street* (1984), and *Fright Night* (1985), Purse notes how onscreen transformations from that period "provided sensational spectacles of bodily mutation and gore that still managed to look like they involved living beings" (2016, 148). Such emphasis on the tangibly real, which in recent years has been promoted in advertisements for haunted attractions and other types of animatronic-filled live entertainments (including the recent *Exorcist*-themed Halloween Horror Nights at Universal Orlando Studios), has been "described by practitioners as an attempt to generate an impression of 'live-ness' through carefully designed, realistic bodies and lifelike movements (such as breathing and blinking), unfolding in real time 'right before your eyes'" (Purse 2016, 148). Here, Purse is specifically quoting Rick Baker, a makeup effects artist whose Oscar-winning work on director John Landis's *An American Werewolf in London* drew notice for the way he pulled off a lycanthropic transformation (that of David Naughton's character David) through practical effects rather than optical trickery (such as dissolves). But by framing that phrase in quotes, she also hints at how hackneyed it has become. Going further, it suggests that the ocularcentric disposition of film critics is nearly as old as the medium itself, and has perhaps even been reinforced through the horror genre's privileging of eyes.

In his book *Horror and the Horror Film*, Bruce Kawin writes that is through the eyes that the genre's untold number of victims, from Sally Hardesty (Marilyn Burns), the bound-and-gagged prisoner of a family of homicidal outcasts in *The Texas Chain Saw Massacre* (1974), to the Chinese prisoner of war whose flesh is stripped away from her arms and hands by Japanese doctors in *Men Behind the Sun* (aka *Black Sun: 731*; *Hēi tài yáng 731*, 1989), "take it all in" (2012, 5). As he explains, these and other characters are forced to gaze upon the abject horror of their own bodily violation at the hands of aggressors, and the doubling of their terrified look in *our* look makes it possible for us to imagine their subjective pain. Though I agree that the spectacle of bodily horror comes to our eyes and brain in a mediated way, it is not only the victims' (or the attackers') vision that colors what we experience or think about during such moments. Other mediating factors—from poorly Foleyed sound effects and the distracting appearance of boom mics at the top of the frame to the speckling of (fake) blood on the camera lens, the accidental onscreen presence of insects (such as houseflies and mosquitos), and the palpable visibility of film grain or digital artifacts in Blu-ray and DVD copies of *The Texas Chain Saw Massacre*, *Men Behind the Sun*, and other motion pictures available for viewing on home video—impinge upon our ability to "see it all" (or, to borrow Kawin's phrase, "take it all in"). Ironically, these and other seemingly trivial things are often overlooked in many all-inclusive accounts of what *counts* in cinema, and this is especially true of the books that have been written about that most eye-centered of all genres: horror.

Such sensorial centering is perhaps to be expected, given the perceived tendency of film historians and theorists to fetishize the image, or to treat cinema as a strictly visual medium catering to one's sight. Not only cinema scholars but seasoned practitioners as well as younger filmmakers have painted the early history of motion pictures, which emerged from humble beginnings as an optical novelty around the turn of the twentieth century to become a dynamic means of storytelling and creative visual expression by the end of the silent era, in the rosiest of hues. In other words, as cinema "evolved" into an advanced form of image-based storytelling, it and the filmmakers who pushed the medium toward new heights (such as D. W. Griffith, Sergei Eisenstein, Abel Gance, Fritz Lang, F. W. Murnau, Victor Sjöström, and Lois Weber) gained artistic legitimacy in the process. But that evolution was abruptly stymied once synchronized sound was introduced in the late 1920s. To paraphrase a sentiment uttered on multiple occasions by the cinematographers interviewed in the 1992 documentary *Visions of Light* (including Néstor Almendros, John Bailey, Michael Chapman, Conrad Hall, and László Kovács), the art of cinema was dealt a potentially deadly blow when dialogue-heavy "talkies" became an industrial norm and the various technologies required to bring recorded sound to the screen—including cumbersome boom mics and noise suppressors known as "blimps"—made the more freewheeling camera movements pioneered by their forerunners a thing of the past. Nevertheless, director Rouben Mamoulian's pre-Code horror film *Dr. Jekyll and Mr. Hyde*, one of the many early sound-era Hollywood movies extracted as a clip in *Visions of Light*, is singled out in the documentary as evidence of the *skill* with which Hollywood filmmakers and other studio personnel were able to forestall this inherently visual medium's "death" during the transition to sound and return the eye to its presumably "rightful place" as cinema's principal organ.

Figure 2.2. Point-of-view shots from the opening scene of Rouben Mamoulian's *Dr. Jekyll and Mr. Hyde* (1931) put viewers into the body of the title character.

Ironically, another organ—literally, a piped musical instrument upon which hands move so as to produce sounds—is brought to the fore in that film's opening scene, which is presented as a series of first-person shots from the title character's point of view. Played by Fredric March, whose face can first be seen as he stands before a mirror (adjusting his cravat and donning a top hat in a reflective POV shot), the organ-playing Jekyll readies himself to deliver a public address at St. Simon's University, where a group of elder colleagues and younger medical students await what they anticipate will be a "sensational" lecture. When Jekyll finally arrives and begins to speak, the camera suddenly separates from his body (or, rather, it dislodges itself from his embodied vision), taking a place alongside the esteemed crowd and forcing us—this scene's *other* audience—to look upon him just as they do, from a third-person perspective rather than first-person perspective. He opens his talk by telling the gathered listeners that "London is so full of fog that it has penetrated our minds, set boundaries for our vision. As men of science, we should be curious, and bold enough to peer beyond it, into the many wonders it conceals." It is a bracing bit of dialogue, the first of many occasions in *Dr. Jekyll and Mr. Hyde* when a character verbally calls out the cognitive limitations of one sense organ that must be supplemented by others if the mysteries that lie beyond the scientific mind are to be glimpsed.

With our eyes now unpaired from his, we look upon this scene in a detached way, from a distance that is accentuated by a subsequent shot taken from the back of the college lecture hall, timed to coincide with Jekyll's declaration that "the human body, in sickness and in health," is no longer his chief concern. Instead, a "greater marvel, the soul of man," preoccupies his thoughts. This latter remark is delivered with actorly flourish and framed in a much closer low-angle shot that makes his speech even more grandiloquent. At this point, the orator explains to the murmuring crowd that man is "not truly one, but truly two." In other words, the human psyche is essentially caught in an eternal struggle between diametrically opposed impulses: to be *good* (striving for nobility and driven by spiritual pursuits) and to be *bad* (resorting to animalistic behavior and engaging in base bodily activities). His proposal—that people might free themselves from such internal conflict by chemically separating those two selves—is met with a mixture of astonishment and derision as the other scientists, including his stuffy colleague Dr. Lanyon (Holmes Herbert), stream out of the lecture hall. Some of the men call Jekyll's pronouncements about the amoeba-like splitting of the soul "ridiculous" and jokingly question his sanity. As an audience looking upon this diegetic audience, we are invited to judge their own rush to judgment and assume a superior position to these men of science based on the belief that *their disbelief* will almost surely be proven wrong by narrative's end.

From the moment we witness the title character's hands moving atop the pipe organ to play Bach's chorale prelude "Ich ruf' zu dir, Herr Jesu Christ in F Minor" until the end of his remarkable speech at the university (leaving the auditorium abuzz), these opening minutes of *Dr. Jekyll and Mr. Hyde* introduce several important themes that will be developed throughout the film, and which I too will expand upon in the coming chapters. With its striking use of first-person perspective, the introductory scene establishes a palpable sense of "embodied subjectivity" (Lerner 2010, 55–56), and it is thanks partly to the music, dialogue, and other sounds being produced by Jekyll that we, the audience, are made to feel his presence even when he is absent from the image (as a result of the "I-camera," to borrow Carol Clover's term, taking up his position and becoming his "eyes," not to mention the microphone's proximity to March, missing from the frame yet vocally present in aural "close-ups") (Thomas 2015, 660–66; Dancyger 2010, 43).[2] Indeed, as Neil Lerner states, the film's soundtrack works "together with the point-of-view shots" to bring us "eye to eye" with our "own mortality," enhancing the sense of "dread and revulsion" that will become a more conspicuous element of the narrative once Hyde, the terrible beast within the good doctor, is finally unleashed (2010, 55–56). The moment when the camera is emancipated from Jekyll's ocular position (inside the university lecture hall, where we can finally see things more objectively, from a seating area suffused with academic skepticism) is as important as those earlier minutes spent inside his skin. That reconfiguration of the film's visual field enacts, at the cinematographic level, his own beastly release of urges that had always been a latent yet suppressed part of his identity. The difference, of course, is that Hyde is not removed from the doctor's body in the way that we are. Rather, he represents a radical re-fleshing of man into monster, aided by a cinematic apparatus that can "do" things to bodily forms that would be difficult (or impossible) to achieve on stage. Regardless of whether one agrees with Michael Sevastakis's contention that this particular version of *Dr. Jekyll and Mr. Hyde* uses the "filmic codes associated with the subjective camera and various forms of montage (including wipes, editing for symbolic effect, dissolves, superimpositions and sound montage)" more effectively than any other motion picture of the 1930s (1984, 15), it is hard to deny the film's suggestiveness as a text that reflects—not unlike the "mirror" that first shows us what *we*, as Jekyll, look like—our spectatorial urge to "see it all."

BODY AND SOUL, DEATH AND DAMNATION

> The dissolution of the boundaries of death and life has . . . destroyed any simple concepts of soul as an "eternal" or essential self. Its loss raises disturbing questions about identity that have fostered new mythologies of the body.
> —LINDA BADLEY, *Film, Horror, and the Body Fantastic* (1995, 24)

Not long after Jekyll delivers his barnstorming talk at St. Simon's University, the film takes up the good doctor's position on the splitting of selves as well as his suggestion that scientific vision is "fogged" or hemmed in by a lack of curiosity—an unwillingness to suspend disbelief and imagine the wonders that cannot be seen—once he imbibes an experimental drug that brings out his bad side (i.e., his impulsively violent alter ego). The first of those half-dozen physical changes is what appears as a clip in the documentary *Visions of Light*, and, if reports of the 1931 film's original release are to be believed, is reputed to have been so "electrifying" that some women in the preview audience ran "screaming up the aisles . . . in horror of the awful transformation which seemed to be happening before their very eyes" (Anon. 1936, 115). The scene showcases how fluidly Mamoulian and his cinematographer Karl Struss (who, four years earlier, had picked up an Oscar for his work on F. W. Murnau's largely silent *Sunrise* [1927]) moved the camera, despite technical restrictions placed on the production, while employing a number of innovative tricks and practical effects to accentuate Hyde's "'troglodytic' countenance" (Turner 2020) (figure 2.3). Besides attaching red and green filters to the lens, they used swish pans, focal shifts, and lap dissolves, which make the character's shocking alteration in appearance look believable within the generic confines of this fantastical tale while demonstrating how expressionism and realism can coexist within horror cinema's far-fetched yet materially grounded scenarios.

Significantly, Mamoulian is said to have taken as innovative an approach to sound design as he and Struss took with regard to the visual effects of Jekyll's physical transformation. In his own words, he combined "eerie sounds of high and low frequencies, approaching subsonic and supersonic levels,

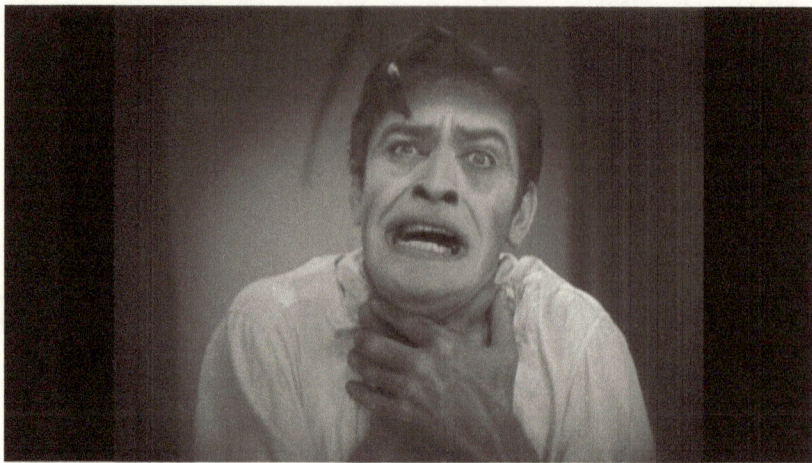

Figure 2.3. As the first of several physical changes that Fredric March's character, Dr. Henry Jekyll, undergoes, this shot allows audiences to witness his transformation into the hairy Mr. Hyde "right before their eyes."

photographed directly from light; soundtracks of gongs being struck, with the impact cut out and the resulting tracks run backward" (quoted in Turner 2020). One of his most inventive approaches involved putting a microphone on his chest, over his heart, after running "up and down a staircase for a couple of minutes," an "aural concoction" that, once recorded and mixed into a bath of other noises, "became known in the studio as 'Mamoulian's sound stew'" (Turner 2020; Lerner 2010, 70).

What at first glance (or first listen) might seem to be an interesting if incidental footnote in the history of a Hollywood production (distributed by Paramount during the final week of 1931 and given a wider release in early 1932, only a few years after the industry-wide adoption of synchronized sound) is, as Lerner emphasizes, the thing that most "deepens the audience's sense of shared interiority with onscreen characters while also bringing a dream-like quality to the film" (2010, 57). Indeed, our aforementioned "eye to eye" confrontation with life's impermanence becomes a kind of "ear to heart" encounter with the ticking clock of impending death, brought closer with each cardiac beat of a blood-pumping organ belonging to someone—a studio filmmaker—who, though no longer alive today (Mamoulian passed away in 1987), achieved a kind of immortality through his art. That sensorial shift from the "outside" appearance of the main character, whose latent capacity for evil is visually expressed by way of his hideous monstrosity, to his "insides" (including, but not limited to, that audibly palpitating heart) opens up the hermeneutic possibility of reading the film through the *ears* rather than, or in addition to, the eyes. It also draws attention to a false dichotomy that continues to impress itself upon the cultural imaginary of horror fans who, even if they *could* achieve the impossible feat of "seeing it all," are not able to perceive the presence of a soul in the absence of that soul's "container," the *body*.

Even before he ingests an experimental drug that will change his physical appearance into that of a violently impulsive monster, Jekyll has already undergone a significant transformation, and his newfound interest in that most incorporeal marker of a person's existence, the soul, has supplanted his erstwhile focus on the human body. Rooted in the ancient Greek concept of "ensoulment" and central to several religious teachings about the spiritual "essence" of humans (above and beyond their physical selves), this most metaphysical of philosophical constructs is the subject of many a horror film, including those such as *Angel Heart* (1987), *Needful Things* (1993), *The Day of the Beast* (*El día de la bestia*, 1995), and *The Devil's Advocate* (1997) that revolve around people selling their souls to Satan or some other supernatural entity. Indeed, one of the conceptual cornerstones of both the classical movie monster cycle of the 1930s (of which Mamoulian's film is one example) and more contemporary iterations (including superhero movies such as *Spawn* [1997], *Constantine* [2005], and *Ghost Rider* [2007], which combine comic-book images and horror iconography) is the idea of the soul as something to be either forcibly taken or begrudgingly handed over in exchange for certain favors (including fame, power, wealth, and youth), with the ultimate cost being eternal damnation to anyone who surrenders to temptation. In nearly all of these films, a clear delineation is made between, on the one hand, the *body* as an exterior shell of a person's essence or spirit and, on the other hand, the *soul* that somehow represents the "true" self or "real" presence of that individual (despite it being invisible to the eye). And yet, time and again this dichotomy collapses under the material and machinic weight of a representational system that depends on physically present beings and recording technologies to reveal the *absence* of life; or, rather, to show us a pale imitation of death. Simply stated, there can be no "soul" onscreen without a bodily signifier already in place and ready *to take its place*—to be its corporeal stand-in—once all such spiritualist talk about immaterial ideas is translated into the materialist language of the medium.

Throughout the history of the genre, from director Tod Browning's 1931 Universal production of *Dracula*, distributed a few months before Paramount's *Dr. Jekyll and Mr. Hyde* was released, to Terence Fisher's Hammer production of *Frankenstein Created Woman* (1967), one of several postwar British horror films to build upon the iconography and themes of their Depression-era predecessors, the *soul*, rather than the body, has consistently been sought after by both antagonists and protagonists bent on defying the laws of nature and conquering death in a most unnatural way. This is explicitly referenced in the latter film, when Baron Victor Frankenstein (Peter Cushing), experimenting with an apparatus that he believes can transfer the soul of a recently deceased person to another corpse (thereby restoring its life), informs the self-described "muddle-head" Doctor Hertz (Thorley Walters) that "death is a *physical* thing, not spiritual."

A similar sentiment is voiced in Svyatoslav Podgayevsky's *The Bride* (*Nevesta*, 2017), which revolves around a narrative conceit that is both familiar and far-fetched. This Russian film's opening sequence provides expositional orientation by way of a CGI-animated journal and a man's spoken voiceover, which combine into a visual-aural recounting of yet another scientist's efforts to convince his colleagues at Saint Petersburg's Academy of Sciences that his latest invention—a camera lens and photographic plate made of a new type of silver—can capture a person's soul. Atop drawings of an early camera device recording the anatomical chart image of a human body, whose penciled-in flesh wipes off to reveal the organs and skeleton underneath, the offscreen narrator explains that the chemistry professor's technological breakthrough, which occurred in 1832, was initially met with disbelief, but would gradually be accepted by people who sought to cheat death by keeping the spirits of their dearly departed alive (figure 2.4). One such person is a photographer from roughly that same historical period, who, in the scene that immediately follows, poses his dead wife before the camera, her closed eyelids covered by fake wooden eyes that are wide open. Taking his ever-staring, eerily "undead" bride's photo, which is hampered by the corpse's tendency to droop her head at inopportune times, is part of this man's plan to transfer her soul to the body of a peasant girl in a nearby village. Besides recalling the premise of *Frankenstein Created Woman*, this plot point of *The Bride* reminds us that the horror genre is as fixated on *life* as it is on death, though the anatomical effects of the latter often assume greater salience than the mystical drivel purporting to be science and concerning the spirit.

Once a person's animus becomes "animal," as reflected in Hyde's wild feral countenance (described by Gregory William Mank as that of a "sinister chimp" [2010, 14] and by Martin M. Winkler as that of a "simian beast" [2020, 233]), it becomes easier for audiences to sever any sentimental attachments they might have had and accept his or her death as "nature taking its course." Moreover, once the soul is made flesh through the kind of secular or religious transubstantiations on which the genre is sometimes thematically predicated, then the mortal wound—be it self-inflicted (as in the 1920 Paramount production of *Dr. Jekyll and Mr. Hyde*, starring John Barrymore as the fiendish antihero driven to suicide) or triggered by someone else (as happens at the end of this 1931 version)—becomes the point where physical destruction converges with spiritual damnation. It is telling that, in the immediate aftermath of Jekyll's death (after he has been shot by the police), Mamoulian and Struss's camera retreats

Figure 2.4. Anatomical charts showing the muscular system and internal organs of humans proliferate in horror films, as seen in this opening image from *The Bride* (*Nevesta*, 2017).

from his body back through the fireplace and "over the blazing cauldron, bubbling madly," a cinematographic gesture that could be said to symbolize the damnation that his departed soul "faces for eternity" (Mank 2010, 19). On the other hand, that concluding image could be interpreted as the "everlasting hell he perhaps *escapes* in his penance of surrendering [his fiancée] Muriel (Rose Hobart) before Hyde overtook him." Leaving the audience to decide its meaning, the film presents, in Mank's words, "Hollywood's own cauldron—the melting pot of man's battle with his soul that is the true trademark" of horror's cinematic golden age (Mank 2010, 19). However, any suggestion of hellish perdition that might be gleaned from that concluding scene comes from the director's inclusion of a material object—an actual boiling pot (or, rather, a movie prop)—located in the same space (a soundstage dressed to appear like a scientist's lab) where the main character has been gunned down (rather than in the Biblical version of Hell that many American audiences have in mind when they hear the word "damnation").

As much as the threat of spiritual damnation might exert sway over the actions of people like Jekyll, who, as Eric Austin Thomas points out, is actually more of a "creature of sexual desire" than is Hyde (an alter ego through whom that once-repressed desire is transferred into "uninhibited violence" leading to murder) (2015, 665), as a recurring motif in cinematic horror, it hardly seems more important than the representation of physical destruction, which occurs more frequently throughout the history of the genre. As Rick Worland argues, these two generally unavoidable outcomes faced by "horror's most unfortunate characters," be they monsters or their victims, may or may not be synonymous in a given story (2007, 7). But the fact that so many of the genre's most prominently featured creatures, from vampires to zombies, straddle the domains of the living and of the dead and seem to be stuck in a liminal state (as the "living dead" or "undead")—on top of the fact that the metaphysical concept of damnation (which "describes a state in which the immortal 'soul' is condemned to eternal suffering and punishment") can only be expressed via *physical* forms (including onscreen bodies and the motion-picture medium's own materiality)—makes it difficult to separate the two as effortlessly as Jekyll does during his university lecture (Worland 2007, 7).

Besides emphasizing the splitting of a single being into two selves or contrasting personalities, *Dr. Jekyll and Mr. Hyde* also gestures toward another kind of separation—a perceptual rift between what is heard by the ears and what is seen by the eyes—that the US motion-picture industry had attempted to bind together in the years leading up to this film's theatrical release. On the one hand, it is a visually audacious film, breaking ground for its special effects and thematically justified split-screen shots, while harkening back to the previous generation's cinematic output, prior to the arrival of sound. As a highly regarded director at Paramount who once proclaimed that "the visual must predominate in a motion picture," Mamoulian set about to make this—the twenty-third cinematic adaptation of Robert Louis Stevenson's 1886 novella *The Strange Case of Dr. Jekyll and Mr. Hyde* (King 1997, 14–20)—as a throwback to the kind of gothic horror films that had been produced in Germany a decade earlier (silent classics such as Robert Wiene's *The Cabinet of Dr. Caligari*, Paul Wegener's *The Golem* [*Der Golem*, 1920], and F. W. Murnau's *Nosferatu: A Symphony of Horror* [*Nosferatu, eine Symphonie des Grauens*, 1922]). But, like his contemporaries making monster movies at crosstown rival Universal (including directors Tod Browning, Edgar Ulmer, and James Whale), Mamoulian did not neglect the film's sonic elements, which he believed "had to be as unreal as the visual effects" if it was to unsettle audiences with a "beast-within" storyline familiar to anyone who had already read Stevenson's novella, and which was reminiscent of earlier Gothic morality tales about dark doppelgängers and hairy lycanthropes (e.g., Edgar Allan Poe's 1839 short story "William Wilson," G. W. M. Reynolds's 1847 novel *Wagner the Wehr-Wolf*, etc.) (Turner 2020). In uniting the ears and eyes in this way, and by combining what Mamoulian referred to as a "surrealistic mélange" of sounds with an expressionistic yet realistic use of POV and other visual effects, *Dr. Jekyll and Mr. Hyde*—a film ostensibly rooted to the past, to previous cultural productions—anticipates much of the horror cinema to come, including Alfred Hitchcock's *Psycho* (1960), which would have an even bigger impact on subsequent examples of the genre as it shifted more decisively away from philosophical talk of the soul toward shocking displays of the body.

I will return to that much-discussed Hitchcock film in chapter three, which presents a conceptual overview of horror as a body genre and elaborates what Linda Williams refers to as that genre's principal affective and material manifestations: the shudder and blood. Trembling in the presence of a monster or on the precipice of some as-yet-unknown threat is as glaring a marker of physical excess as bleeding is, and *Psycho*'s nearly unparalleled success at

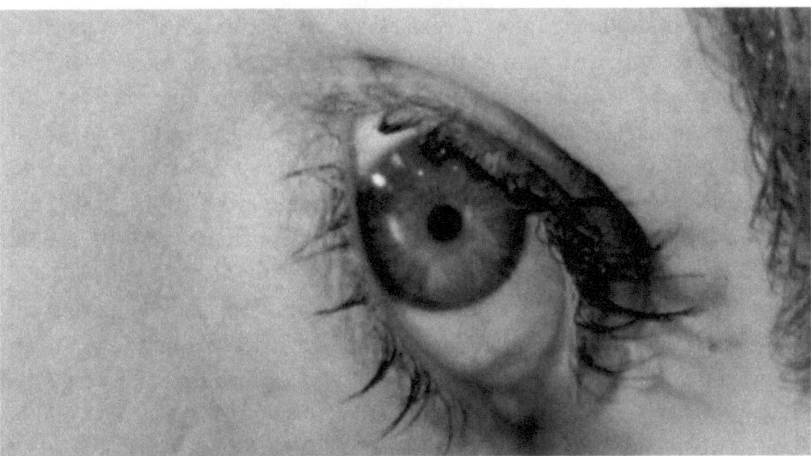

Figure 2.5. The eye of Janet Leigh's Marion Crane, who has recently been murdered in a motel shower, stares at the camera/audience in this extreme close-up shot from Alfred Hitchcock's *Psycho* (1960).

sending a shudder down the spines of audiences partially derives from the revelation—novel if not unprecedented at the time of the its theatrical release (but commonplace among horror films of the past sixty years)—that "normal-looking" humans can be just as monstrous as the most hideously deformed figments of our imagination. Near the end of this film's most famous scene, when the blood of Marion Crane (Janet Leigh) washes down the drain of a bathtub at the Bates Motel, we are given an extreme close-up view of her right eye following a lap dissolve of that drain—two orifices located where a person's foot would typically be (since the dead woman's knife-gashed body has just fallen forward onto the bathroom floor while her unseen assailant has slipped away) (figure 2.5). That shot, perhaps the most famous in horror's stockpile of staring eyes, brings first-time viewers face-to-face, or orifice-to-orifice, with their own epistemological uncertainty as to what has just taken place and how Marion's death will reverberate throughout a motion picture in which another character—the one responsible for her early departure from the narrative—steps in to take her place as the film's "true protagonist." In fact, the brutal killing of this "false protagonist" would have a ripple effect beyond the confines of *Psycho*'s detour-laden storyline, influencing countless other horror films that show men and women being suddenly blindsided, savagely attacked, or subjected to the kind of bodily abuse that often precedes a "bad death."

As Rick Worland reminds us, "the most basic fear in the horror story is the fear of death" (2007, 7). In fact, it is not just death but what Stephen King and other writers have called "bad death" that partially distinguishes the genre from other categories of cultural production, and which makes it difficult for the spectator to imagine a worse fate for those whose bodies are ruined beyond repair and recognition, regardless of whether or not their souls have been damned or spared from an ultimately unrepresentable eternal suffering (which can only be suggested through symbolic imagery, hinted at by sounds and noises, or referred to through spoken words). Indeed, "the hideous, excruciating torture of the physical body" is perhaps the *best* (worst) way to render "the soul's eternal damnation," according to Worland, who acknowledges that the unimaginable suffering of the latter is sometimes made *imaginable* through representations of the former (2007, 26).

As mentioned in the previous chapter, the first half of 2021 has already witnessed the online distribution and limited theatrical exhibition of several noteworthy motion pictures that are expanding the boundaries of horror while drawing upon genre conventions and earlier films' storylines that would be familiar to many fans. A few of those recent releases, including Bryan Bertino's *The Dark and the Wicked*, David Bruckner's *The Night House*, Rose Glass's *Saint Maud*, Kim Tae-hyoung's *The 8th Night (Je8ileui Bam)*, Banjong Pisanthanakun's *The Medium (Rang Song)*, Shari Springer Berman and Robert Pulcini's *Things Heard & Seen*, and Evan Spiliotopoulos's *The Unholy*, deal with religiously tinged efforts to either demonically claim or righteously save a person's soul. But considerably more of them grapple with matters of *physical* rather than spiritual turmoil, and if the latter is expressed at all it is only made tangible through the kinds of emotional and bodily excess (e.g., anguished screams, hysterical crying, nervous trembling, profuse sweating, the spilling of vital fluids) that make horror such a disturbingly "real" fiction in a world that seems hell-bent on denying death or insisting, through religious institutions and their teachings, on an afterlife (though many examples of the genre do this as well).

One newly produced work, director Peter Winther's *Aftermath* (2021) wastes no time in staying true to its title, showing the gory outcome of a deadly shooting during its opening title sequence. What looks to be a murder-suicide, leaving two people dead (one of whom has lost his head), has occurred inside a middle-class suburban home. Its viscera-smeared, blood-splattered walls, which will later be compared to a Jackson Pollock painting by a member of the crime-scene clean-up crew, are an early indicator that physical violence will be a recurring motif throughout this superficially "supernatural" haunted house movie (which, as we are told at the beginning, is "based on a true story"). Another recent production, Patrick Brice's *There's Someone Inside Your House* (2021), takes only slightly longer before getting to its first kill scene, a brutal attack inside another American home (this time located in rural Nebraska) where a teenaged intruder takes out his vengeful anger against a high-school jock who had bullied others in the past (as part of a hazing ritual). Here, though, we see not only the aftermath but also the moment of a "bad death" taking place, starting with the slashing of the football player's Achilles tendons, and

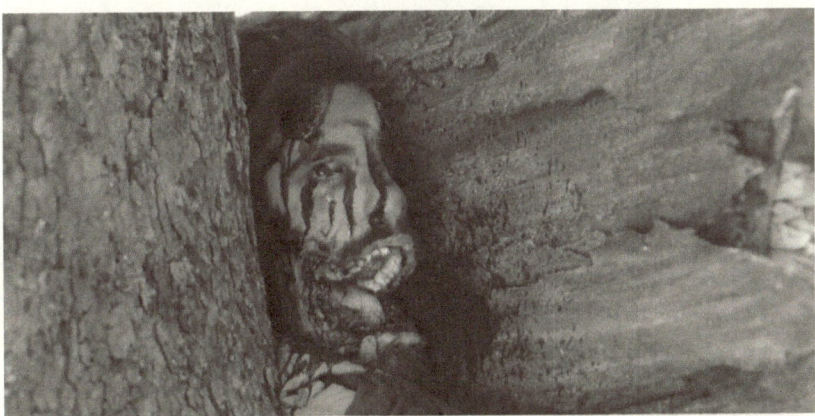

Figure 2.6. The first of several "bad deaths" in the 2021 horror film reboot *Wrong Turn* occurs when one of a half-dozen tourists hiking the Appalachian Trail is crushed against a tree by a rolling log.

culminating with the masked killer plunging his knife into the victim's varsity-jacketed chest, a merciless form of vigilante "justice" enacted at the six-minute mark of this "Generation Z" tribute to earlier slasher films (demonstrating once again how *physical* rather than spiritual pain is often frontloaded into horror narratives).

The first of several ghastly fatalities depicted in the horror film reboot *Wrong Turn* (2021) happens not long after the half-dozen young protagonists begin hiking the Appalachian Trail, failing to heed a local business owner's warning to not stray from the path. Gary (Vardaan Arora) is the first of the six tourists to die when a huge log rolls down a hill in the forest and crushes him against a tree. When Luis (Adrian Favela) sees the remains of his dead boyfriend, the audience is granted a view of the young man's pulverized head (figure 2.6). This shocking image anticipates a later moment of cranial trauma when another of the hikers, Adam (Dylan McTee), has his faced pounded into slushy pulp by the leader of the Foundation, a cult residing in the woods and led by a man named Venables (Bill Sage) who sentences Adam to death for doing much the same to a member of that backwoods community.

Notably, in the immediate aftermath of Gary's death, Adam attempts to soothe Luis's emotional anguish by telling him, "That's not *Gary* anymore. That was his *body*. His spirit has moved on." At this point, Adam pauses, and then asks, "That's what he *believed*, right?" This question, tacked on as reminder that belief systems work by convincing people that one's spiritual self can be separated from his or her bodily self, does little to dispel the physical disgust that lingers as a result of seeing the character's head crushed like a melon. In a way, the horrible fate awaiting Luis, once he is captured by members of the Foundation and blinded with a red-hot fire poker, relates back to his act of seeing his dead boyfriend, though having his own eyesight stolen from him and being thrust into a world of darkness does not erase the image that he and we were forced to look upon early on in *Wrong Turn*. Ultimately, Luis's friend Jen, the only one of the main characters to eventually escape with her life from their captors, puts an end to the blind man's suffering by shooting him with a gun that she has stolen. It is a mercy killing that terminates his life but which is understood as a less miserable way to die than what has befallen their friends.

From having one's skin scaled off by thousands of gastropod mollusks (in *Slugs* [1988]) to getting strung up and torn apart by barbed wire (in *Silent Hill* [2006]), or having one's head split into two hemispheres by an eye-gouging Nazi zombie (in *Dead Snow* [2009]), or being stabbed in the skull with a can opener before one's brains are scooped out by an ice-cream server (in *Stitches* [2012]), the "badness" of said deaths is excessive to the point of becoming as unbelievable—at least to the minds of many skeptics—as the idea of a soul that lives on after the body's destruction. In fact, the sheer outrageousness of such acts, regardless of how realistic their visual representation might be, draws attention to the inherent artifice of horror as a cultural form that becomes *harder to believe* the more grotesque it becomes, the more it leans into the very thing that distinguishes it from other genres (which showcase considerably fewer decapitations, drownings, electrocutions, immolations, impalings, stabbings, stranglings, throat-slittings, and scenes of people getting eaten alive by animals). In the words of one harried character in William Castle's *House on Haunted Hill* (1959), as he explains to a group of fellow guests who are planning to spend the night at the titular dwelling why doing so is a bad idea, "It's a funny thing, but none of the murders here were just *ordinary* . . . they've all been sort of wild, violent, *different*." Indeed, it *is* a "funny" thing. While nothing as hilariously gruesome as any of the aforementioned deaths (in *Slugs*, *Silent Hill*, *Dead Snow*, and *Stitches*) occurs in Mamoulian's *Dr. Jekyll and Mr. Hyde*, contemporaneous reports of audiences laughing at the sight of the animalistic character breaking free from the dictates of good taste and social propriety hint at the way that the stretching of credulity can take the sting out of scenarios hinging upon the supposed difference between the body and the soul (Lerner 2010, 67).

Prompted by the many POV shots and mirror images that appear in *Dr. Jekyll and Mr. Hyde*, which invites audiences to see themselves in the face of the already-doubled man-monster, I seek to show how motion pictures solicit spectatorial participation through a phenomenological engagement with the medium's material properties. In the context of horror film spectatorship, such cinematic "interfacing" might result in a mutually reflective form of physical expressivity; as embodied viewers before the screen (be it that of a cinema or that of a television monitor), we sometimes mimic the reactions—the looks of fright and terror—performed by actors and photochemically registered on strips of celluloid (or delivered electronically via video technologies). This is not a novel idea. Carl Plantinga, in his study of facial feedback, emotional contagion, and affective congruence, draws upon the work of the classical film theorist Béla Balázs, who argued that "if we look at and understand each other's faces and gestures, we not only understand . . . [but] also learn to *feel* each other's emotions" (Plantinga 1999, 243). Nor is this idea unique to horror film, as highlighted in Noël Carroll's reading of director King Vidor's studio-era Hollywood melodrama *Stella Dallas* (1937), which culminates with empathy-engendering shots of the title character (Barbara Stanwyck) watching her estranged daughter's wedding from afar (a series of close-ups that elicit a "bittersweet" emotion that is part-dysphoric, part-euphoric) (Carroll 1999, 36). However, Plantinga emphasizes that "the horror film . . . reserves *a special place* for the face, as the prevalence of close-up face shots of victims in anguish demonstrates" (2009, 126). In a way, our own perceiving faces metaphorically fuse with the faces of characters in film: people who are forced to confront nightmarish visions on the path to enlightenment, freedom, redemption, or death. Accordingly, throughout this book I highlight some of the ways horror films present spectators with a physiognomy of affective extremes, showcasing the face as a hyper-visible yet often-obscured sign of the genre's paradoxical appeals as a source of pleasure and fear, amusement and dread.

Building on Philip Brophy's theory of "horrality," or "the construction, deployment and manipulation of horror—in all its various guises—as a textual mode" (1986, 5), several sections of this book explore how these affective extremes or emotional polarities, situated at the far ends of an experiential continuum signified by Jekyll-Hyde's positively charged and negatively charged facial features, are *the* constituent features of the genre as it metaphorically moves through the body and is felt by the audience. Coined in 1983, Brophy's notion of horrality—a neologism that conflates horror and hilarity (on top of textuality and morality)—was not the first attempt to conceptualize the genre in such a way. Writing a quarter of century earlier, Derek Hill, in a piece for *Sight & Sound* titled "The Face of Horror," acknowledged that 1950s audiences frequently laughed "at the most repugnant details of the new horror films" (2000, 53). "As a release from suspense and nervous tension," this tendency produced "the same kind of laughter that accompanies a successful comedy sequence—laughter not to relieve tension, but to express amusement or satisfaction" (Hill 2000, 53). Although Hill employs the word "face" in a general way (as part of a title that essentially evokes the "state" or "appearance" of horror, and not its actual *faces*), and while considerably different from my own attempt to locate specific features of the genre within the physiognomy of onscreen performers, his writing gestures toward an idea that is central to the current study. Horror, I argue, is most *horrific* when its constituent polarities are fully operative, when the contrast yet commensurability between emotional extremes is most pronounced, and when amusement, hilarity and pleasure coexist alongside dread, terror, and pain.

WARNING SHOTS: PREPARING FOR THE HORRORS (AND HUMOR) TO COME

> ATTENTION . . . YOU HAVE 30 SECONDS TO LEAVE THE SCREENING OF THIS FILM.
> —English translation of text that appears onscreen near the climax of Gaspar Noé's *I Stand Alone (Seul contre tous*, 1998), followed by the word "DANGER" flashing in red and black

Following the theatrical release of Hitchcock's *Psycho*, several of the American and British directors churning out horror films during the 1960s seemed to have appreciated the counterintuitive reasoning that I sketched out above and not only adopted but *embraced* humor as a means to achieve their goal of frightening audiences. A few of them were practically unabashed in their willingness to be part of the carnivalesque promotional discourses that framed their work as something to be enjoyed in the same way that a circus sideshow or amusement park ride might be. Inspired by Alfred Hitchcock and William Castle, two cinematic "showmen" who appeared in their own films' theatrical trailers to inform audiences of the chills and thrills that awaited them, Warner Bros.' *Chamber of Horrors* (1966), written by Stephen Kandel and directed by Hy Averback, illustrates this tendency perhaps better than any other release from that period. Originally conceived of as a feature-length pilot episode for a proposed CBS television series to be titled *House of Wax* (a nostalgic callback to the studio's Vincent Price vehicle of the same title, made over a decade earlier), this production was deemed "too lurid for the small screen" by the network's advertisers (Davies 2015). As a result, and as a "last-ditch effort by the studio to recoup money invested in the project," it was redeployed from primetime television to movie theaters in the days leading up to that year's Halloween festivities (Higham 2020, 170). Not unlike a seasonally themed "haunted house," the film that debuted on October 28, 1966, features Grand Guignol-style sets and props left over from the earlier period piece *House of Wax*, making it more of a morbidly funny (and fun) "attraction" sure to put smiles on the faces of horror fans than a deadly serious psychological study of a one-armed homicidal maniac who, drawn to necrophilia and known to the authorities as the "Baltimore Strangler," preys on prostitutes. Though that plot synopsis hints at the dark and twisted undercurrents of this Warner Bros. release, the gimmicks that were used to hook potential ticket-buyers—including an audiovisual cue that warns audiences of any particularly scary moments seconds before they occur (and which recalls the timed "Fright Break" that accompanied the 1961 release of Castle's *Homicidal*)—work to offset such sinister implications by calling attention to the ludicrous nature of the entire outing.

In the opening seconds of *Chamber of Horrors*, as a kind of metatextual warning about those textually embedded warnings, onscreen text and an off-screen voiceover (spoken by actor William Conrad, who does not appear in this film) inform the audience of what's to come. Speaking solemnly, Conrad reads the following pre-credits script as its scrolls up the screen: "Ladies and gentlemen, the motion picture you are about to see contains scenes so terrifying the public *must be given grave warning*. Therefore, the management has instituted visual and audible warning at the beginning of each of the *Four Supreme Fright Points*." He then demonstrates what is meant by the "Fear Flasher," which he refers to as the film's "visual warning" (a strobing red light) and the "Horror Horn," which he refers to as the film's "audible warning" (a blaring alarm sound). Capping this spookily amusing preamble with his admonition that you should "turn away when you see the FEAR FLASHER [and] close your eyes when you hear the HORROR HORN," the disembodied voice ironically *draws spectators in* by instructing them on how to *distance* themselves from the frights that will follow, a means of mitigating any disturbing effects that might otherwise detract from the enjoyable aspects of the narrative. As such, even before the appearance of the Warner Bros. logo and the title of the film—a reference to the famous waxworks exhibition of notorious murderers at London's Madame Tussauds (which dates back to the early 1800s)—*Chamber of Horrors* interpellates its audience as a malleable mass subject whose responses to fearful scenes can be not only predicted but also shaped by rhetorical maneuvers that would be more than a little unusual outside the overlapping generic enclaves of horror and comedy, but which somehow make sense in these two most nonsense-driven categories of cultural production.

Similarly informing audiences about this gimmick in advance of the film's Halloween-timed theatrical release, the three-minute trailer for *Chamber of Horrors* is of additional interest for the paradoxical way that it stages bodily fear as a humorously pleasurable experience to be avoided by moviegoers, who are nevertheless encouraged to take part in the act of watching the film. Escorting viewers into the wood-paneled office of a fictionalized spokesperson for the Society for the Protection of the Easily Scared, the trailer shows this protector of the public's interests seated at his desk and initially smiling for the camera in a self-satisfied way. He is pleased with his group's efforts, after a lengthy period of "negotiations" with the film's producers, to figure out a way for "chickens" like himself to watch *Chamber of Horrors*, a film with four scenes "so horrendous, so hair-raising, so absolutely chilling" that the Society's "Seal of Approval" could not be given until some kind of warning had been devised. At this point, the trailer switches to footage from the film. Specifically, we are shown one of the "Four Supreme Fright Points," or rather the lead-up to a moment when the amputee killer—a hatchet blade attached to his hand stump—attacks an older man who, unlike the audience, is not able to escape with his life or avert his eyes from the violent mayhem about to occur (Higham 2020, 170).

At the moment that the Baltimore Strangler (a charismatic fetishist of wedding dresses whose real name is Jason Cravette [Patrick O'Neal]) is set to bring his bladed weapon down, the footage freezes into a still frame. With his arm still raised above his head, the killer is momentarily interrupted from committing his heinous crime by a flashing red light (the "Fear Flasher") as well as a high-pitched alarm (the "Horror Horn"). This is the same audiovisual system that is demonstrated in the film's aforementioned pre-precredits sequence. Once the five-second freeze frame ends, and in lieu of being shown a grisly depiction of murder, we return to the offices of the Society for the Protection of the Easily Scared. Now visibly agitated, the spokesperson warns, "This is your last chance to close your eyes!" At this point, another person's hand enters the frame and moves toward the lens to block our view of the office, blacking out the screen just as a woman's voice can be heard screaming offscreen. A few more seconds transpire before the spokesperson appears again, this time framed in a medium close-up and now physically panicked. His eyes wide open, mouth agape, and the hair on his head standing on end, the man, who looks to have been shocked by an electrical charge, is a caricatured embodiment of the fear that most audiences were presumed to be seeking when they stepped into theaters to watch *Chamber of Horrors* (figure 2.7).

Though exaggerated and campy, the man's exhortations in this movie trailer, which culminates with the printed words "FOR THE SCARE OF YOUR LIFE . . . SEE IT!," ring "true" in the sense that they reflect some of the contradictory impulses that distinguish horror film spectatorship from other modes of reception. As a genre that is partially defined by the dueling desires to look and to not-look, to behold but not literally *hold* something so terrifying as to be almost "funny" (in the way that it either exceeds the limits of propriety, frustrates categorization, or breaks the laws of physics), horror poses a fundamental challenge to the way that we order the world and understand our place in it (Creed 2015, 59). Having someone else's hand placed before our eyes, or rather in front of the camera lens that extends our vision beyond our bodies, only increases our desire to see what cannot be shown in this trailer. Undoubtedly, the William Castle-inspired "Fear Flasher" and "Horror Horn" that bring a momentary halt to *Chamber of Horror*'s unfolding narrative on four different occasions, and for which first-time viewers perhaps experienced a heightened

Figure 2.7. In this humorous trailer for the film, a spokesperson for the Society for the Protection of the Easily Scared reacts to spine-tingling scenes from Warner Bros.' *Chamber of Horrors* (1966)

sense of anticipation, were meant to rouse them to *attention*. And, indeed, the things that many viewers will most *want* to see are those deadly encounters with the killer that were deemed too gruesome or too tasteless to include in a film without the built-in opportunity to turn away.

Fascination with monstrosity and the taboo, as Brigid Cherry notes, is one reason why horror film audiences, women in particular, derive subversive pleasure from the genre. But "refusing to refuse to look," as Cherry goes on to explain, is complicated by the fact that many of horror's most horrendous acts take aim at female bodies (2002, 169–78). An early scene in *Chamber of Horrors* points toward that potential for misogynist violence, showing Cravette looming over a young woman in a brothel whom he plans to strangle with her own hair, before he is caught by the police and prevented from fulfilling his necrophiliac desire. However, the four most terrifying scenes depict violent acts directed toward men. In fact, the first of those so-called "Supreme Fright Points" occurs when the villain, handcuffed to a rail car's brake wheel on his way to prison, uses an axe to free himself, hacking at the steel and eventually—several seconds after the red-light warning has sounded—cutting off his hand after jumping from the speeding train into a river below. In a way, the detached appendage, sinking to the bottom of the river and leaving a bloody cloud in its wake, reminds us of the startling way that another unseen person's hand suddenly enters the frame during the film's trailer. Ostensibly done to shield us from a sight too horrible to behold, that oddly disembodied hand is just as invasive as Cravette's had been when he took the life of his first victim (a woman whose death occurred before the start of the narrative). Though not literally as aggressive as being hacked to death by a hatchet, having one's eyes covered by someone other than oneself is tantamount to an attack, a kind of ocular violation in which the imagined physical presence of another person intrudes upon the perceiving faculties of the viewer. Gimmicky though it is, the hand that covers the lens in the *Chamber of Horrors* trailer and which is meant as a humorously helpful rather than harmful illustration of what audiences should do whenever the "sight/site" of horror, to quote Barbara Creed, "can no longer be endured" (or the "pleasure in looking is transformed into pain"), physically enacts the kind of de-suturing process that she and other theorists have identified as a key feature of the genre (2015, 59).

In her pioneering study of horror and abjection, Creed contrasts the genre with more classically structured texts, which tend to "suture the spectator into the viewing processes" through continuity editing, eyeline matches, and other "invisible" aspects of cinematic storytelling that were developed over one hundred years ago. Because horror so often depends on scream- and giggle-inducing "gotcha" moments on top of shocking displays of bodily harm, which can be said to arrest narrative flow, as well as practical effects and visual effects (from prosthetic makeup to computer-generated imagery) that call attention to the inherent artifice of fictional scenarios (regardless of how "believable" those effects might be), narrative immersion and character identification are not as persistently felt as they sometimes are while watching other types of films. Even when a strong attachment to a character is facilitated through the filmmaker's use of point-of-view shots and other devices meant to put viewers inside his or her "skin," the force with which abject images impress themselves upon that extradiegetic gaze can prompt viewers "to look away, to not-look, to look anywhere but at the screen" (Creed 2015, 59). What is particularly interesting about the four audiovisual warnings that occur in *Chamber of Horrors*, besides how premature each one is (occurring several seconds before the anticipated moment of bloodshed does), is that they *negate* the very thing responsible for undoing narrative suture in the first place, interrupting an interruptive moment when the spectator would normally be "punished for his or her voyeuristic desires" (Creed 2015, 59). Here, somewhat perversely, "punishment" comes from being *denied* the unsettling visual representations and somatic sensations associated with scary scenes and graphic bodily harm, which the camera shies away from and leaves to the viewer's imagination.

Contemporary audiences who watch the film today might feel cheated by the lack of sexual frankness in Kandel's script and by director Averback's visual restraint with regard to content that they were promised would be *terrifying* (if not physically nauseating or morally objectionable). Anyone who has subjected themselves to the Japanese production *Guinea Pig 2: Flower of Flesh and Blood* (*Ginī Piggu 2: Chiniku no Hana*, 1985), the Spanish production *In a Glass Cage*

(*Tras el cristal*, 1986), the West German production *Nekromantik* (1987), the US production *Murder-Set-Pieces* (2004), the Serbian production *A Serbian Film* (*Srpski film*, 2010), the Dutch-UK coproduction *The Human Centipede 2 (Full Sequence)* (2011), or any of the other deeply disturbing, highly controversial motion pictures that have been banned in various parts of the world over the past four decades (owing to their depictions of incest, necrophilia, pedophilia, rape, sadomasochism, and torture) will find *Chamber of Horrors* about as offensive and cartoonish as a G-rated Disney movie. Such recent films as Gaspar Noé's early example of "New French Extremity," *I Stand Alone* (*Seul contre tous*, 1998), which notably features a thirty-second onscreen warning that gives viewers the opportunity to close their eyes, cover their ears, and exit the theater before its shocking conclusion, are often said to "leave nothing to the imagination." And yet, as vastly different as these films are from *Chamber of Horrors*, the latter's paratextual materials—from the aforementioned trailer to its one-sheet poster (which shows a severed, green-tinted hand next to the red, blood-dripping title as well as the grimacing face of the deranged killer, a hatchet where his own hand should be)—point toward the cultural shifts to come, once gorier effects began to fill in for the relative absence of abjection that characterized cinematic horror prior to the 1960s. Although at no point during a viewing of this film is a spectator likely to feel the same excessive amount of fear expressed on the face of that easily shocked spokesperson for the Society for the Protection of the Easily Scared, contemporary audiences would do well to heed his advisory warning when seated before a truly revolting example of the genre. Moreover, in whetting the public's appetite for cinematic content sufficiently disturbing to actually *earn* such warnings, it taps into a latent aspect of horror film spectatorship, one that can be traced back to *Execution of Mary, Queen of Scots* and which reveals how *we* are as contradictory as the genre is in our gravitation toward yet repulsion from the traumatized body.

3

CORPOREALITY, MATERIALITY, MORTALITY

The Horror Film as "Body Genre"

> We're human too, you know. Eyes, teeth, hands, blood. Exactly like you.
> —RED (Lupita Nyong'o), a "Tethered" version of Adelaide Wilson (Lupita Nyong'o),
> speaking to her physical/mirrored double in Jordan Peele's *Us* (2019)

From head to toe, the body has been a central component of horror films since the genre's origins as a discursively formed category of cultural production after the turn of the twentieth century. As the physical proof of a human or nonhuman existence, the body manifests one's inner being and makes it possible for the most unbelievable of stories—those involving supernatural events or far-fetched scenarios (e.g., demonic possession, paranormal phenomena, the walking dead, etc.)—to attain a degree of plausibility through material solidity, via the actual presence of corporeal forms. Although audiences might be comforted by the thought that the monstrous figures onscreen are merely "lights and shadows" (to borrow Julian Hanich's description of cinema's phantom-like projection of flickering images), and thus not a real threat to one's physical or emotional well-being, horror's affective power lies in its ability to take hold of the spectator and elicit bodily responses that sometimes mirror the actions of those monsters' ill-fated victims (Hanich 2010, 96). Indeed, as Hanich, Xavier Aldana Reyes, and other scholars have argued, somatic empathy and sensation mimicry are two forms of phenomenological engagement that partially distinguish horror film spectatorship from other modes of cinematic reception, and the transferability of feelings from one body (that of a character) to another (that of an audience member) necessarily involves a host of aesthetic configurations as well as ethical considerations around such issues as point-of-view, focalization, gender, identification, and the "negative pleasure" or "positive pain" that results from such experiences (Hanich 2010, 81–107; Reyes 2016, 150–85).

The idea that horror is a "body genre"—a category of cultural production tied to diegetic and extradiegetic forms of corporeality—is not a new one. Indeed, the expression that lends this book its title was introduced in academic literature over thirty years ago, when Linda Williams explored the effects that horror and other genres of low cultural standing (melodrama and pornography) have on spectators whose emotional and physical reactions to onscreen stimuli—screams of fear, sobs of anguish, cries of pleasure—are nearly as excessive as anything found within an especially "gross" or "sensational" motion picture (Williams 1991, 2–13). Here, the word "sensational" carries a double meaning: It refers not only to certain films' capacity to play on or prey upon a sensate being's feelings by way of powerful images and sounds (in addition to suggestions of smell, taste, and touch that might surreptitiously enter a moviegoer's body through her eyes and ears), but also to the *exceptionalism* of cultural productions that, regardless of their lowly status, are remarkable in their textual too-muchness (i.e., their larding up of signifiers that cannot be completely rationalized or contained within the classical narrative system). Here and elsewhere, Williams is building upon the pioneering work of Carol Clover, whose 1987 article "Her Body, Himself: Gender in the Slasher Film" (first published in a special issue of the journal *Representations*) heralded a new era in horror studies, when previously overlooked examples of the "cinematic underbrush," from Razzie-winning cult films like *Hell Night* (1981) to the many entries in the *Friday the 13th* franchise, were deemed worthy of scholarly investigation. And, like Clover, Williams draws attention to the structures of fantasy and perversion that prompt identificatory shifts between active victimizer and passive victim. In fact, such simplistic dichotomies are challenged by horror's presumed tendency to put viewers into a sadomasochistic subject position, one that is as fluid as the genre is "gratuitous" in its deployment of sex, terror, and violence for the sake of physical titillation.

Because of its signifying surplus—its tendency to treat sex, terror, and violence as objects of pure spectacle—the horror film harkens back to the comparatively chaste but no less sensational "cinema of attractions" that gained popularity during the first decade of the twentieth century, prior to the entrenchment of a storytelling mode that has been referred to by Tom Gunning and other historians as "narrative integration" (Gunning 1994, 290–91). As Williams herself claims in another article written nearly a decade after the 1991 publication of "Film Bodies: Gender, Genre, and Excess," a motion picture like Alfred Hitchcock's *Psycho* (1960), while certainly not devoid of story and plot, has enough of the "deviant" sensory pleasures associated with the horror genre to be both "primitive" and "modernist" all at once. In "Discipline and Fun: *Psycho* and Postmodern Cinema," she argues that this much-discussed work by the Master of Suspense is pleasurable precisely because it is sensational, a thrill ride, not unlike a roller coaster at an amusement park, that recalls a much earlier mode of bodily engagement with the cinema (2000, 356–58).[1]

Even as it transported audiences at the time of its ballyhooed theatrical release (in the summer and early fall of 1960) back to the past (i.e., the era of *pre*-classical films made before 1907 that were not yet slaves to seamless storytelling), *Psycho* signaled the arrival of a *post*-classical moment in motion-picture history. Indeed, the very things that have since come to partly define modern (and postmodern) horror—rupture, destabilization, and the ironic fun that comes from being run through the gauntlet—were thrust upon unsuspecting viewers with devilish glee by a master showman who, like a sadist, sought to discipline their behavior both inside and outside the movie theater (for instance, asking exhibitors to enforce a no-late-arrival policy and beseeching viewers not to give away the film's surprise ending). Though such disciplining presumes docility on the part of the audience, their performances of fear inside the many theaters around the world where it was shown ("screaming, hiding eyes, clutching the self as well as neighbors") indicate a highly animated state as well as a degree of agency to knowingly "play the part" of individuals whose collective response to the film's visceral thrills contributed to its counter-instinctual *appeal* (Williams 2000, 372). For Williams, this latter element of *Psycho*'s initial reception—the meta-emotional ability of audience members to perceive their own corporeal performances as being "part of the show"—was central to any pleasurable feelings that might have been engendered by a film whose violence, primarily (but not exclusively) directed toward women, has long been criticized by feminists as a painful reminder of the genre's underlying misogyny. Though she had earlier placed herself in the latter camp (and was a key figure in the development of feminist film theory), by the time Williams wrote "Discipline and Fun" she had begun to appreciate the sensory pleasures of *Psycho*, which, she argues, brought about a new "scopic regime" of visual attractions and fundamentally "altered viewing habits" forty years prior to her essay's publication (351, 367).

This black-and-white film's most "shocking display of sexualized violence," of course, is its famous shower scene (358), a technically brilliant assemblage of fifty-two cuts (from seventy-eight shots or camera setups) that lasts forty-five seconds and occurs a third of the way into the narrative: Marion Crane (Janet Leigh), a real-estate secretary from Phoenix who has stolen $40,000 from her company's client and has decided to stay overnight at a roadside motel on the way to her boyfriend's home in California, is attacked by a shadowy figure who stabs her several times with a knife. Individual frames of this scene, which online fans of the film have pored over with the kind of attention to detail that borders on the fetishistic (a somewhat icky, iffy proposition given the way that Marion's exposed torso—provided by Leigh's body double,

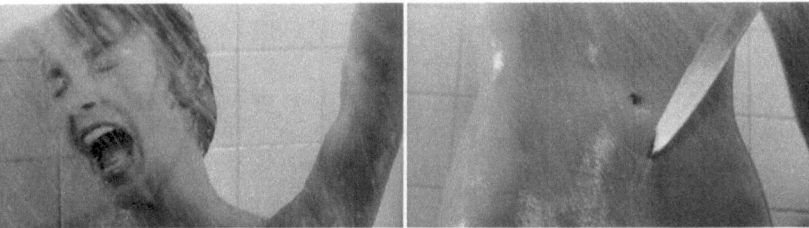

Figure 3.1. Two shots from the shower scene in Alfred Hitchcock's *Psycho* (1960), including one that clearly shows the prop knife touching the wet abdomen of Marli Renfro (Janet Leigh's body double).

Marli Renfro—receives the sustained gaze as defenselessly, and nakedly, as it does the blade), highlight aspects of cinematic horror that, ironically, are often overlooked (figure 3.10). With water and blood dripping onto the tub's floor, and with the steel weapon cleaving into Marion's flesh with the same slashing movements that are sonically conveyed by composer Bernard Herrmann's musical score, *Psycho*'s shower scene demonstrates how different textural surfaces and material sensations—wetness, softness, sharpness, and hardness—can be combined to achieve an effect that would be considerably less unsettling if only one of these were called upon to engender a feeling of disgust, nausea, or terror on its own.

After Marion drops to the floor of the motel bathroom, the killer flees the scene of the crime before the audience can make out who he or she is. That pronominal ambiguity is fitting, given the way that gender is staged as a line-blurring performance throughout the second half of *Psycho*—a literal "put-on" most clearly foregrounded during the film's big reveal near the end, when, in the climactic scene, Anthony Perkins's homicidal motel manager Norman Bates appears dressed as his dead mother (a drag show to end all drag shows) before being subdued by Marion's boyfriend Sam (John Gavin). Contrary to other theorists who maintain that viewers of Hitchcock's film are twice punished or "castrated" over the course of its lacerating narrative (first when the journey of neurotic Marion is brought to an abrupt and bloody end in the Bates Motel, and later when the male-female proprietor of that establishment is apprehended by police and charged with murder, making our "errant identification" with this psychotic character doubly criminal), Williams puts a positive spin on all this abject mayhem. Where others saw pain and "perversely thwarted desires," she sees pleasure and a "roller-coaster sensibility" (353). The fact that several elements of that sensibility, "grounded in the pleasurable anticipation of the next gut-spilling, gut-wrenching moment," are now commonplace among contemporary horror films, is a testament not only to *Psycho*'s enduring influence but also to the durability of Gunning's initial thesis that absorption into a diegetic world is hardly necessary to sustain spectatorial interest, especially when a movie's surface appeals—its amusement park-like attractions—are so endlessly fascinating.

Today, over sixty years removed from the time of *Psycho*'s original theatrical release, it is not too difficult to imagine what first-time viewers might have felt during the summer of 1960. Archival evidence, including still photographs taken at the Plaza Theatre in London not long after the film's British release (and which Williams reproduces in her essay), confirms reports of audiences—women especially—reacting in much the same way that their grandchildren would do decades later, while watching *Paranormal Activity* (2007), *The Conjuring* (2013), *The Gallows* (2015), or any of the other cinematic "thrill rides" that are marketed to the public through green-tinted, night-vision trailers showing packed theaters erupting in startled fits (Benson-Allot 2013, 188; Swanson, 2015; Reyes 2016, 100–101; Clasen 2017, 11–12) (figure 3.2). None of the publicity images reprinted by Williams in her essay depict the kind of "unprecedented" behavior that *Psycho* is reputed to have elicited, in the form of people running up and down the aisles, bolting for the exit doors, and fainting in their seats as though they had been "trapped on a roller coaster through the spook house" (in the words of J. Hoberman, who has also written about the "convulsive mixture of screams and laughter" that could be heard during many first-run screenings of Hitchcock's film) (Hoberman 2010). However, those photos show female moviegoers covering their mouths, eyes, and ears and generally cowering in fear while seated beside men whose commitment to steeliness under duress is no less a performance (Williams 2000, 362). At first glance, the women's "closing-down" response of *not looking*, in contrast to the masculine reaction of "opening up" to the image (or, adopting Carol Clover's words, "taking it in the eye"), is a reasonable defense against violent assault or the threat of penetration. However, as Williams would note in a subsequent revisitation of *Psycho*, the "gendered fun" of the film is "clearly visible on the face of one woman" seated in London's Plaza Theatre—a record of a spectator *laughing* while performing her fear (2004, 1265).

Again, one should not presume to know why this particular audience member, or any others not included in the photo, is laughing. Perhaps her neighbor—a woman to her left, head buried in lap—has just cracked a joke or let out a sound that struck her as humorous. Maybe, along the same lines that Carl Plantinga discusses in his book *Moving Viewers: American Film and the Spectator's Experience*, a feeling of embarrassment hits the woman at the moment of fright, a meta-emotion in which she self-mockingly polices her own proclivity to being scared or having her puppet-strings pulled (2009, 73, 161). Or her giggle could simply be that of giddiness at having experienced something like a roller-coaster ride, a thrilling, attraction-filled distraction or titillating break from her everyday routines. Regardless of the reason, and

Figure 3.2. A now-standard publicity stunt is the inclusion of night-vision audience reaction shots in contemporary horror films' trailers, which highlight the fun to be had while watching terrifying scenes among a group of strangers.

putting aside the possibility that the photo was staged (though that would only further substantiate claims that Hitchcock's disciplinary gaze had penetrated the actual spaces where his film was being shown), *pleasure*, not pain, is expressed on the partially shielded face of the woman. Or, rather, if pain *was* something that she experienced in that moment, it appears to have been leavened by a contrasting feeling that illustrates how horror film spectatorship, especially in the years following *Psycho*'s 1960 release, is a "much more complex and disciplined negotiation" of conflicting emotions and bodily sensations than what has previously been argued (Williams 2000, 371).

ANATOMIZING HORROR, JERKING THE AUDIENCE

> Let me speak to you about the ... *anatomy* of terror.
> —ALFREDO (Patrick Magee) to a group of revelers at a medieval costume ball in *The Masque of the Red Death* (1964)

In her 1991 essay "Film Bodies: Gender, Genre, and Excess," Linda Williams identifies "lack of proper esthetic distance" as one distinguishing feature of horror film spectatorship, although, as she notes by drawing comparisons between it and two other disreputable genres of low cultural standing, such "closeness" is akin to the emotional and physical "over-involvement" associated with watching melodrama and pornography (1991, 5). In some ways, much of the academic writing about horror—at least, that which insists upon the genre's homogeneity or unoriginality—inscribes a critical distance that is not in keeping with the way that fans might pore over details and bring an attentiveness to small, seemingly trivial moments. Perhaps that spectatorial separation from the text—a perceived need to keep it at arm's length for the sake of a more objective or honest appraisal of its evaluative "worth"—is driven less by the concern that one's judgment might be clouded by subjective "feelings" than by the fear of being "jerked" around or "victimized" by filmmakers skilled at manipulating emotions. To paraphrase Williams, as a "fear-jerking" equivalent of melodrama's "tear-jerking" tendencies, the sensational appeal of horror rests in its ability to induce not just emotional but physical responses, including screams, fainting, and in some cases heart attacks (5). In her essay, she references the ballyhooed theatrical releases and publicity stunts of producer-director William Castle, an influence on Hitchcock whose films (including *Macabre* [1958] and *The Tingler* [1959]) were marketed to the public as literally spine-tingling thrill rides in which electrical jolts or far worse fates (including death) awaited even the least cowardly of audiences.

Such big-screen ballyhoo—the cinematic equivalent of carnival barkers and circus sideshows—would continue to be integrated into the theatrical presentation and promotional exploitation of horror films in the years leading up to Castle's death. Examples include Warner Bros.' *Chamber of Horrors* (1966), which cues audiences to impending scares through a "Fear Flasher" and "Horror Horn," and the West German production *Mark of the Devil* (aka, *Witches Tortured till They Bleed* [*Hexen bis aufs Blut gequält*, 1970]), which was jokingly rated "V for Violence" by distributor Hallmark Films and promoted to stateside audiences, who (reminiscent of Herschell Gordon Lewis's *Blood Feast* [1963]) were given "vomit bags" in case of upset stomachs, as "positively the most horrifying film ever made" (Hallenbeck 2003, 125; Cooper 2011, 91) (figure 3.3). However, the kind of gimmickry that so many horror fans find endearing has abated considerably since the time of Castle's passing in 1977 (and even more so since the publication of Williams's essay thirty years ago). Nevertheless, reports of people passing out and losing consciousness or vomiting during the screenings of recent horror films (including Darren Lynn Bousman's *Saw III* [2006], the multi-director omnibus production *V/H/S* [2012], Eli Roth's *The Green Inferno* [2013], Chad Archibald's *Bite* [2015], and Julia Ducournau's *Raw* [2016]) have further substantiated Williams's claims that the various bodily excesses of the text (including the kind of gross-out moments depicted in *Saw III*, *V/H/S*, *The Green Inferno*, *Bite*, and *Raw*) spill over into the contextual sphere of reception whenever the "esthetic distance" between it and the spectator closes (Fleming Jr. 2012; Connolly and Duell 2012) (figure 3.3).

Notably, in the 1991 essay where she initially developed her ideas about horror, melodrama, and pornography as body genres, Williams included a chart labeled "Anatomy of Film Bodies" that neatly delineates the types of physical excess as well as the presumed target audiences, perversions, origins, and temporalities of the "fantasies" bound up in each of those three genres. In the

Figure 3.3. One-sheet posters for two of the many horror films that were promoted through ballyhoo-style gimmicks during the 1960s and 1970s.

column devoted to horror, she indicates that the "ecstasy" of bodily excess specific to that genre is shown by way of the shudder and blood, as distinguished from the orgasm and ejaculation of pornography (which is organized around "ecstatic sex") and the sob and tears of melodrama (which is organized around "ecstatic woe") (Williams 1991, 9). As the primary means through which the "ecstatic violence" of horror materializes onscreen, the shudder and blood are indeed the basic physical movement and material substance of this body genre, saturating it thoroughly with images of convulsive trembling and ceaseless hemorrhaging—so much so that it is hard to name more than a few examples of the genre that do *not* show people doing those two things in the lead-up to or aftermath of their run-in with human or nonhuman monsters. Although several other types of physical (re)actions and fluidic "stuff" flood the screen, and at the risk of essentializing the genre in a way that I problematized in the previous chapters, the shudder and blood are so central to horror that the first of those terms is the name of a popular video-on-demand website (Shudder .com, a streaming service owned and operated by AMC Networks) catering to fans of the genre; and the second of those terms appears in horror film titles more frequently than any other noun (e.g., *A Bucket of Blood* [1959], *Dr. Blood's Coffin* [1961], *Blood and Black Lace* [1964], *Blood Bath* [1966], *Blood Drinkers* [1966], *I Drink Your Blood* [1970], *Bay of Blood* [1971], *The House that Dripped Blood* [1971], *The Blood-Spattered Bride* [1972], *Blood Orgy* [1973], *Blood for Dracula* [1974], *Blood Diner* [1987], *Bordello of Blood* [1996], *Blood Junkie* [2010], *Blood Glacier* [2013], *Blood Moon* [2014], etc.).

For all of its usefulness in highlighting the two most rudimentary syntactic and semantic ingredients in cinematic horror, not to mention its provocative suggestion that horror synthesizes the "sadism" of pornography and the "masochism" of melodrama, Williams's "Anatomy of Film Bodies" is devoid of any actual *anatomizing* of the genre in question. Instead, she, like many of the theorists following in her footsteps, opts for a psychoanalytically informed approach to "the trauma of castration" and "the problem of sexual difference" that make horror distinct as a cultural form yet similar to pornography and melodrama in its depiction of "passive and innocent female victim[s]" (8, 10). In the chapters that follow, I build upon Williams's foundational work in an effort to flesh out a topic that, ironically, has largely been treated in such a serious and detached—dare I say "bloodless"—way that scholars seem to have forgotten what drew them to horror in the first place. Moreover, in much the same way that a camera lens does, I zoom in and focus on actual anatomical features of onscreen bodies, including those that figure almost as prominently as blood does in the promotional materials surrounding motion pictures (including movie posters, print ads, and trailers). In fact, the titles of several horror films—feature-length productions as well as shorts—point toward the corporeal underpinnings of the genre. Going from top to bottom (anatomically speaking), examples of horror cinema's paratextual framing of particular body parts include Antonio Margheriti's *The Long Hair of Death* (1965), Danny and Oxide Chun Pang's *The Eye* (2002), Joe Badon's *The God Inside My Ear* (2017), Kōji Shiraishi's *A Slit-Mouthed Woman* (2007), Jean Rollin's *Lips of Blood* (*Lèvres de Sang*, 1975), Terry Miles's *Even Lambs Have Teeth* (2015), Takeshi Shirakawa's *Neck* (*Nekku*, 2010), Alex Visani's *Stomach* (2019), Sergio Martino's *Torso* (1973), John Bradburn's *Wrists* (2010), Oliver Stone's *The Hand* (1981), Harry Basil's *Fingerprints* (2006), Naoyuki Tomomatsu's *Scissorpenis* (2018), Matthew Sean Francis's *Thigh Meat* (2009), Adam Minarovich's *Ankle Biters* (2002), and Darla Enlow's *Toe Tags* (2003). While this book does not presume to account for the ways that each and every one of these (and other prominently displayed) body parts assume places of hermeneutic significance in horror, I shed light on some of the ways that excessive displays of sadomasochistic violence might make audiences shudder with fear and possibly shake with laughter as a way of dispelling such negative emotions.

BARING *TEETH* AND SCO(O)PING OUT *JENNIFER'S BODY*: GENDER, SEXUALITY, AND SUBDERMAL MICROSCOPY

> These "gross" body genres which may seem so violent and inimical to women cannot be dismissed as evidence of a monolithic and unchanging misogyny, as either pure sadism for male viewers or masochism for females. Their very existence and popularity hinges upon rapid changes taking place in relations between the "sexes" and by rapidly changing notions of gender—of what it means to be a man or a woman.
> —LINDA WILLIAMS, "Film Bodies: Gender, Genre, and Excess" (1991, 12)

With a title that is both more specific and more general than those cited in the preceding paragraph, owing to its use of a possessive marker and proper noun as well an all-inclusive word to denote the *entirety* of the human form, *Jennifer's Body* (2009) provides another lens through which to view the horror film's anatomical features as well as the genre's compatibility with comedy. This darkly humorous, socially relevant cult film, written by Diablo Cody, directed by Karyn Kusama, and distributed by 20th Century-Fox with great fanfare (but ultimately disappointing box-office results), has already received ample coverage for the uncompromising way that it satirically intervenes in horror's presumed tendency to position women as helpless victims of monstrous men. It showcases a teenaged antihero who, like a succubus, seduces and literally devours fellow high-schoolers—the "extra salty" ones, at least—as part of a Faustian plot that leans as heavily on rape-revenge films of the 1970s (e.g., *The Last House on the Left* [1972], *I Spit on Your Grave* [1978], etc.) and slasher films of the 1980s (*Graduation Day* [1981], *Slaughter High* [1986], etc.) as it does on demon-possession films and other supernatural subgenres.

Within days of its stateside theatrical release, *Jennifer's Body* was being celebrated in small circles as a feminist subversion of the genre's most pernicious tropes even as its controversial marketing campaign drew wider criticism for its hypersexual objectifying of scantily clad star Megan Fox, whose short miniskirt in the movie poster and exposed midsection on subsequent DVD and Blu-ray covers suggest a less-progressive, semi-pornographic effort to appeal to horror's "core demographic" (i.e., straight male viewers) (Paszkiewicz 2018, 72). Directly referencing the poster that was created for the theatrical release of the slasher parody *Student Bodies* (1981), titillating publicity images such as these harken back to the way that Janet Leigh—wearing nothing more than a bra and half-slip—was depicted in the promotional materials accompanying the theatrical release of *Psycho*, which, as Carol Clover remarks, are "all about . . . those breasts" (1987, 199) (figure 3.4). Unlike the generally positive critical reception of Hitchcock's film, most professional reviewers agreed with *Washington Post*

Figure 3.4. One-sheet posters for three of the many horror films that have been marketed to the public through images of scantily clad women.

critic Ann Hornaday's dismissal of *Jennifer's Body* as "the stuff of lurid adolescent distraction, not great cinema," and several commentators complained about its triteness, crassness, and (you guessed it) *predictability* (Vrabel 2009). Even its few champions at the time of its release (such as Roger Ebert and Peter Travers) expressed only mild satisfaction with Cody's pop-culture-literate, "Hello Titty"-punning script and Kusama's lively, misdirection-filled direction.

Over the past decade, and especially after the #MeToo movement gained traction on social media sites following allegations in 2016 of sexual abuse against powerful men in the entertainment industry, the blustery winds of consensus have calmed, and opinions have shifted in the film's favor (Grady 2018). The harsh condemnation that greeted the theatrical release of *Jennifer's Body* has since given way to subtler approaches to the subject of women in horror that reveal how Cody and Kusama's artistic "failure" actually succeeds as a playfully postfeminist (if not always politically savvy) critique of genre conventions, one that has special appeal for audiences who are drawn to horror's queering potential (Wilson 2020, C1). This latter element, highlighted by but not limited to a scene showing the title character (a free-spirited cheerleader played by Fox) and her nerdy, accurately named best friend Needy (Amanda Seyfried) sharing a passionate kiss, goes beyond any such intimations of lesbian desire to hint at the more sweeping, radically deconstructive thrust of a narrative that is not content to settle into the tired binaries on which "a straight comedy, a straight horror film, [or] a straight high school movie" is structurally reliant (e.g., active vs. passive, dark vs. light, male vs. female, insider vs. outsider, etc.). (Kusama, quoted in Grady 2018). Not only does the film take aim at the kind of "toxic heterosexuality" that tends to thrive in high schools, to borrow the words of Andrew Owens (quoted in McCormack 2021), but it also maps a postmasculinist path toward present-day and future reckonings with women's fluctuating "place" in cinematic horror, a genre that is as politically reactionary in its untold number of misogynistic "tits-and-screams" scenarios and its historical privileging of the male gaze as it is progressive in its depiction of an obscenely fleshed-out fantasy of female empowerment (Clover 1987, 201). Thankfully, the latter theme has begun to counteract the more conversative aspects of a cultural form that has long treated sexual transgression in a morally circumscribed, violently punitive fashion, especially within the subgenre of slasher films where, as Clover points out, there is a strong cause-and-effect relationship between illicit desire and swift death, and where the spectacle of women's bodies—living or dead—tends to be lingered upon voyeuristically (200).

Over the past decade alone, several examples of queer, feminist, and postfeminist horror (or in some cases comedy-horror hybrids), including Jen and Sylvia Soska's *American Mary* (2012), Leigh Janiak's *Honeymoon* (2014), and Alice Lowe's *Prevenge* (2016), have contributed to diversifying not only the genre's representational politics but also its visual syntax, especially with regard to the flagrant display of body parts that were virtually verboten (if not unthinkable) in mainstream horror releases two or three generations ago. As for the latter development, a number of recently produced motion pictures ranging from the multi-director horror anthologies *The ABCs of Death* (2012) and *V/H/S: Viral* (2014) to such high-profile films as Panos Cosmatos's *Mandy* (2018), Luca Guadagnino's *Suspiria* (2018), Ari Aster's *Midsommar* (2019), Tate Taylor's *Ma* (2019), and Brandon Cronenberg's *Possessor* (2020) as well as more obscure international works like Steinþór Hróar Steinþórsson and Gaukur Úlfarsson's gay vampire splatter comedy *Thirst* (*Þorsti*, 2019) have put nearly as much visual emphasis on *male* genitalia as their predecessors placed on female anatomy decades earlier.

So widespread has this trend become that an entire program of nearly two dozen films devoted to the theme of "Penis Trauma" was included in the 2021 Fantastic Fest film festival hosted by the Alamo Drafthouse in Austin, Texas, giving audiences multiple opportunities to cross one of horror cinema's final anatomical frontiers through screenings of Katrin Gebbe's *Nothing Bad Can Happen* (*Tore tanzt*, 2013), Tamae Garateguy's *She Wolf* (*Mujer lobo*, 2013), and other globally distributed films. While many of these latest reminders of horror's predictable unpredictability were directed by women, filmmakers who self-identify with the pronouns "he/him/his" have also expanded the semantic and syntactical possibilities of the genre through the foregrounding of strong, assertive women who hit back—or, in some cases, *bite* back—against their male attackers, as evidenced in such small-scale yet ambitious productions as Jim Mickle's *We Are What We Are* (2013) and Kevin Kölsch and Dennis Widmyer's *Starry Eyes* (2014). A notable standout among this recent batch of film festival hits is Mitchell Lichtenstein's *Teeth* (2007), which has drawn considerable attention from media scholars ever since its debut at Sundance (where lead actor Jess Weixler, who plays the main character Dawn O'Keefe, won the Special Jury Prize for Dramatic Performance).

Although I will not explore the thematic underpinnings of *Teeth* as thoroughly as other critics have done, it is worth mentioning a few things about the film's handling of the subject of sexual assault and of the perennial theme of castration anxiety, which—typically framed as a metaphorical effect of what Barbara Creed calls the "monstrous-feminine"—is literalized here through Lichtenstein's unique take on the *vagina dentata* folk-myth. In the film, that anatomical anomaly belongs to Dawn, a proud high-school virgin living on the outskirts of Austin, Texas. An early scene in the film shows her preaching abstinence to younger members of her evangelical church group. Soon enough, however, she develops a budding sexual interest in boys her own age. This is offset by physical and emotional trauma once she is attacked by another, slightly hornier student with pent-up hormonal desires. When Tobey (Hale Appleman), the ostensibly God-fearing object of her attraction, removes his underwear and forces himself on Dawn, pinning her to the jagged rocks behind a waterfall in a remote forest and knocking her temporarily unconscious, her sharp-toothed vagina (which is not shown) bites off his penis (which *is* shown). Leaping to his feet and screaming in terror as his eyes dart between his bleeding groin and the severed appendage on the ground, Tobey is unable to process what has just happened. Standing motionless for a few seconds, he finally flees the cave only to disappear into the lake that had initially seemed like an idyllic make-out spot when the two teenagers first laid eyes on it, but which might as well be a primordial cesspool from some mythic story or centuries-old morality tale. Dawn, in a state of shock herself (as frightened of her own body as he was), can barely believe her eyes, but unlike her attacker she survives the ordeal. Over time, she comes to understand the nature of her newfound power and learns to harness it over abusive men, including her pervy gynecologist Dr. Godfrey (Josh Pais), who likewise screams in terror when he loses his illicitly probing fingers during a medical exam-turned-sexual assault midway through the film, and her own stepbrother Brad (John Hensley), whose amputated penis falls to the bedroom floor only to be gobbled up by his Rottweiler, named Mother, near the end.

As several scholars have noted, Dawn becomes an "independent and physically confident young woman" over the course of an otherwise "familiar" coming-of-age narrative, mirroring how her vagina has progressively mutated into an "evolutionary defense mechanism" (Craig and Fradley 2010, 90). In fact, that movement from passively reactive victim to violently proactive vengeance-seeker is one reason why so many scholars have singled out *Teeth* as an "intelligent (post-)feminist movie mobilizing dark comedy and recurrent images of penile trauma to explore serious youth-oriented social issues" (90). Not all critics agree with that assessment, however, and a more balanced take on *Teeth*'s treatment of a painful subject might question the appropriateness of using tongue-in-cheek humor and the familiar tropes of the teen movie to acclimate audiences to an otherwise oppressive world "full of predators and misogynists," or to the troubled life of a young woman whose rape takes a backseat to the graphic representation of castration (Harrington 2018, 71).[2]

Indeed, the first of the three castration scenes in *Teeth* is more than a little problematic for the way that it suddenly shifts focus away from Dawn's frightening experience of physical violation toward her assailant's own bodily trauma. As Claire Henry argues in her perceptive analysis of the film, the all-too-real horror of the female protagonist's victimization at the hands of young men who will not take "no" for an answer is "usurped by the graphic castrations that quickly follow," and any motivation that Dawn might have for exacting revenge against them is further undercut by the fact that she has no control over her vagina (whose "bite" is "reflexive/accidental," at least until the end of the film) (2014, 62). In a similar vein, Eddie Falvey comments on the film's "problem of incompatibility," whereby "viewers are required to at once celebrate her body's ability to fight back against the threats posed to it and, conversely, accept the denial of her agency to it" (2021, 209). Initially unable to keep her "masticatory contempt" for those who would harm her in check, this already-conflicted hero is held hostage to her own gynaehorrific condition before she gains partial mastery over it and thereby becomes the archetypal "castrating woman" (someone who, according to Barbara Creed, is an indelible part of horror's "monstrous-feminine," which the theorist traces back to maternal figures like "Mrs. Bates" in *Psycho* and several more classic tales predating the invention of cinema).

Erin Harrington, the author of a recent book about "gynaehorror," furthermore casts doubt on this film's success as an "empowerment narrative," given its elision of "what has historically been an important part of feminist struggle: collectivity and community" (2018, 74). To be sure, Dawn's vengeance-seeking and sexual self-actualization offer satisfaction, catharsis, and even pleasure, especially to anyone with firsthand knowledge of what she undergoes in the lead-up to her first traumatizing experience with a member of the opposite sex (Falvey 2021, 210). However, hers is a "deeply individualistic" form of vigilante justice that accords with a particularly American view of victimhood and punishment, thus downplaying the responsibility of the state and other governing bodies in holding abusers responsible for their actions or enacting laws that might protect women as much as they have historically privileged men (Harringon 2018, 74). I do not necessarily blame writer-director Lichtenstein for failing to include references to the collective political struggle that has long been part of feminist calls for social reform (and which has largely been ignored by men making movies in the United States). Nor do I think that it is wrong for his film to adopt a "victimhood-to-violence" narrative arc that has been "a staple of the rape-revenge subgenre" since the early 1970s (74). However, *Teeth* should be scrutinized for the way that it inadvertently *reinforces* different forms of "conservative identity politics" even as it leverages a smart critique against hegemonic/toxic masculinity and the prevailing ideological "norms" of a deeply patriarchal society. As Harrington emphasizes, *Teeth*, though a seemingly progressive work celebrating its main character's sexual autonomy, is ultimately compromised by its insistence that "only by embodying and deploying masculine fears of voracious female carnality can women best protect themselves and exert an active subjectivity that refuses to be co-opted or constrained" (73, 75).

Whatever one might think about *Teeth*'s literalization of the *vagina dentata* folk-myth or its "monstrous reconfiguration of the female body"—the genitals in particular—as a site of socially isolated strength and resistance (one that has become all the more relevant in the years since the film's 2007 debut at Sundance) (Falvey 2021, 209, 211), it is hard to deny that its unnerving effect largely derives from Lichtenstein's combination of comedy and horror, a potentially combustible cocktail of conflictive feelings or tonal registers that is most pronounced during the humorously overdramatic castration scenes (which juxtapose quick glimpses of the bloody man-meat and exaggerated, grossed-out reaction shots meant to mirror the audience's response). As *Den of Geek* contributor Hannah Bonner muses, "This film, not for the heterosexual male faint of heart, delights in its salacious, if silly, gore" (2016), and the more that Lichtenstein, composer Robert Miller, and the sound department crew lay on the big musical stingers and noises (audible, for instance, when a crab scuttles across Tobey's now-shriveled penis or when Brad's dog licks the young ne'er-do-well's lopped-off dick), the more it begins to seem like the sillier sibling of *Hard Candy* (2005), another, more deathly serious study of a teenaged vigilante who confronts and tortures a man suspected of being a sexual predator. Unlike the latter psychological thriller, *Teeth* is prone to generate as many laughs as screams, and my own (admittedly anecdotal) experience of seeing this film in a nearly packed theater on three occasions suggests that audiences find much humor in its gruesome scenes of bloodletting.[3]

Funnily enough, the same theater where the 2021 Fantastic Fest recently featured a "Penis Trauma" program of festival screenings (the Alamo Drafthouse in Austin, not far from where *Teeth* was shot) is mentioned by critic Melanie Haupt in an article that she wrote not long after the film played there. In her piece for the *Austin Chronicle*, Haupt notes that, in the days leading up to *Teeth*'s January 2008 rollout (one year after it had become a word-of-mouth sensation at Sundance), its theatrical trailer was shown before a sold-out screening of Jason Reitman and Diablo Cody's coming-of-age comedy *Juno* (2007). For many people seated in the theater, this was their first time to hear about *Teeth*, and the trailer's histrionic mode—reaching a fever pitch when the film's cheesy tagline "Every Rose Has Its Thorns" fades in—only slightly exaggerated the combined hilarity and horror that awaited audiences who, like Dawn, felt compelled to go back into the theater's cave-like setting thanks to a piqued curiosity (Haupt 2008). Writing about the audible groans, titters, and outright guffaws of the people seated in that auditorium on a cold Texas night (summed up by one woman's audible protest, "Eww!"), Haupt could just as well be describing any number of other horror films—or horror film trailers—in which the excessiveness of aural and visual stimuli assumes laughably large proportions (Haupt 2008).

Speaking of "large proportions," let us consider the opening title sequence of *Teeth*, which gives viewers the impression of looking through a microscope

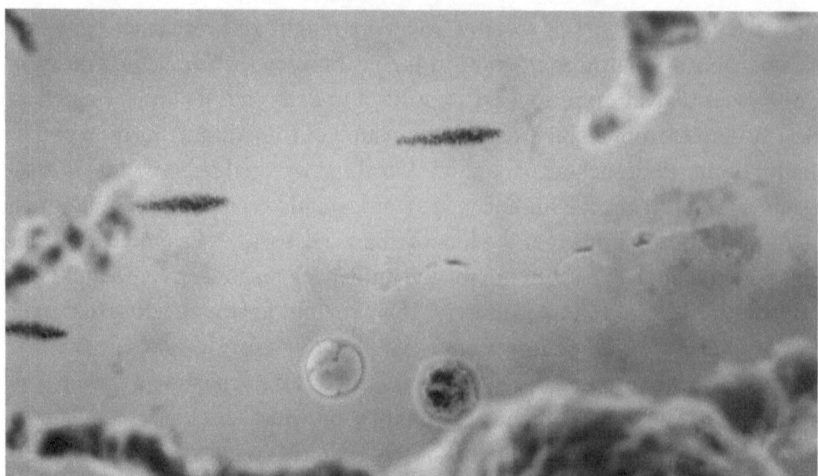

Figure 3.5. During the opening title sequence of Mitchell Lichtenstein's *Teeth* (2007), microscopic images of cellular activity depict the film's narrative in miniature while bringing to mind other horror films in which tiny organisms in the bloodstream become monstrously large on screen.

and peering at things that are too small to be seen with the naked eye. Specifically, images of cellular activity, like those found in a molecular biology lab video, flood the screen: a group of predatory bacteria swim shark-like through a blue-green bloodstream in pursuit of egg-like organisms (figure 3.5). One of the evading spherical organisms appears different from the others, with a dark pulsating energy at its center, suggesting a mutation of some kind. Suspenseful orchestral music, driven by heavy percussion and skittish violins, accompanies this "chase scene," as one-by-one the organisms are picked off by the ravenous parasites. The sequence reaches a climactic crescendo once the last remaining organism, now backed into a corner by two aggressors, finally unleashes its dark energy to fight back against them, ingesting them with a violent force that anticipates what Dawn will do to Tobey, Brad, and other characters over the course of *Teeth*'s ninety-four-minute running time (Kelly 2016, 93–94).[4] In the manner of a *mise-en-abyme*, these opening credits—obviously manipulated through computer-generated digital effects—can be said to reflect in miniature the entire narrative. But the title sequence also leads the eye and mind to sites of meaning *outside* the text, allowing spectators to draw comparisons between *Teeth* and any number of other horror films featuring microscopic views of cellular life—atoms, bacteria, genes, microbes, viruses, and other scientifically scrutinized minutiae—that have been an important facet of the genre ever since the 1922 release of F. W. Murnau's *Nosferatu: A Symphony of Horror (Nosferatu, eine Symphonie des Grauens)* (Abbott 2016, 45). Indeed, cellular imagery like this is key to understanding how the genre's various "excesses" are

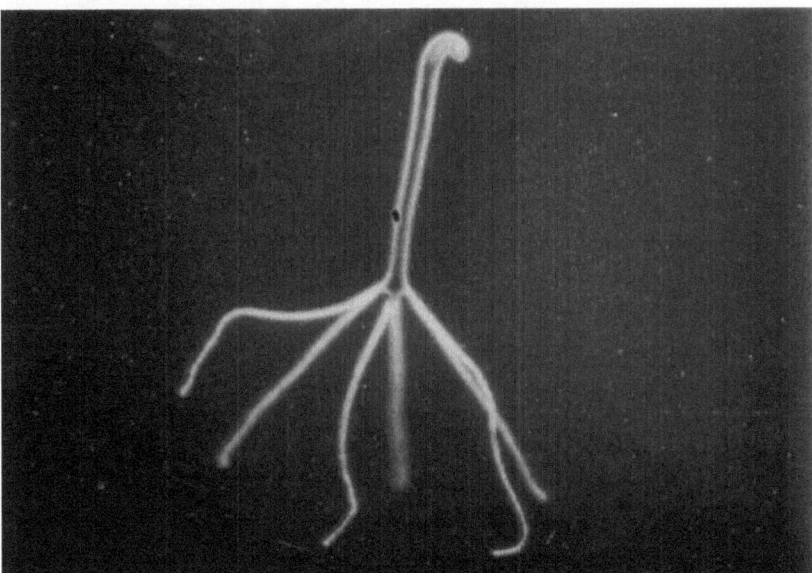

Figure 3.6. A strange cellular creature, as seen through a microscope in *Nosferatu* (1922), assumes monstrously large proportions and reminds audiences that horror is a body genre concerned not only with anatomical features and sensing organs but also histological and embryological elements not apparent to the naked eye.

merely magnified renderings of basic human conditions biologically shared across our species.

The latter film, a classic example of German Expressionism that drew liberally from Bram Stoker's 1897 novel *Dracula*, was groundbreaking on several counts, but one of Murnau's most striking innovations involved the presentation of monstrous microorganisms—made to appear unnaturally large on the big screen—that demonstrated the complementarity of two otherwise distinct optical devices (Ford 2013, 64). As Tom Gunning elucidates in an article about *Nosferatu* (published the same year as *Teeth*'s release), the microscope and the motion-picture camera each provide glimpses "into an invisible world," one that—to paraphrase Professor Bulwer (John Gottowt), a scientist showing his students a clawed, carnivorous polyp (*Hydra viridis*) inside a glass vial—is filled with ethereal, phantom-like creatures (Gunning 2007, 94–95) (figure 3.6). Like the spherical organism that lashes out against its attackers in the more recent production's title sequence, the polyp that is given pride of place in the silent film's atmospheric visual syntax (a semitransparent superimposition calling attention to the motion picture medium's own phantasmatic status) is a "microscopic monster" whose claws and tentacles "grasp another cellular creature and seem to devour it," resulting in a "death" as gruesome as any other that occurs in *Nosferatu* (94–95).

By "displaying the most primitive form of cellular life through the most modern of media," both films draw a connection between "the uncanny powers of the cinema" (CGI-enhanced cinema in the case of *Teeth*) and a medical-scientific gaze that, searching for the hidden secrets of life and the universe (whether through microscope or telescope), is not content to limit itself to what can be seen by the naked eye. That idea, Gunning stresses, carries significant weight, hinting at how cinematic imagery—itself a mutation of previous forms of visual culture founded upon "observation and display"—tests the limits of visibility while remaining grounded in the physicality of the real world. In much the same way that the microscopically magnified polyp in *Nosferatu* is "almost as translucent as the water that bears it," the motion-picture medium is phantomic, a "filter of light" and a "caster of shadows" that appears to disappear whenever spectators find themselves so immersed in its fictions that the fact of its own (machinic) materiality dissolves into thin air (Gunning 2007, 95). Horror brings this latent aspect of cinema to the surface even as its technologically mediated images serve to accentuate the immersive aspects of unbelievable scenarios and otherworldly environments that *pull us in* as forcefully as those tentacled microorganisms do to other, unsuspecting ones.

Besides recalling Professor Bulwer's scene in Murnau's film, the opening title sequence of *Teeth* resembles other instances of microcinematography in horror films, including those depicting vampiric creatures indebted to *Nosferatu* and its own literary source material, *Dracula*. As Stacey Abbott states, microscopic imagery has appeared "across a long history of visual representations of the vampire in film and television and increasingly highlights the generic hybridity" between horror and science fiction (2016, 45). Her examples include the Universal production *House of Dracula* (1945), the international coproduction *The Hunger* (1983), and *Bram Stoker's Dracula* (1992). The latter film is an apt illustration of how close-up images of blood cells, as seen from the perspective of a doctor peering into the eyepiece of a scientific yet oddly magical optical device, began to soak up additional meanings following the global outbreak of AIDS in the 1980s (46–67). Of course, vampirism had served as a metaphor for disease or contagion well before director Francis Ford Coppola and screenwriter James V. Hart adapted Stoker's turn-of-the-century Gothic tale. But the theme began to resonate differently once the bloodsucker's bite was seen as a means of spreading a sexually transmitted disease that was less a reflection of the previous century's bacterial/syphilitic threats than a thinly veiled commentary about pressing concerns of HIV infection. In his exploration of the film, Fred Botting, author of *Gothic*, writes, "The 1990s, like the 1890s, saw terrors linking sex and death," and the threat posed by sexuality was "both global and microscopic, internal and external, crossing all borders with impunity and disturbing the security of body, home and culture" (2014, 190).

Though similar microscopic images—taking viewers beneath the organs and tissues of bodies into the cellular and molecular "unknown"—can be found in everything from low-budget drive-in fare such as Al Adamson's *Horror of the Blood Monsters* (1970) to highbrow art films such as Claire Denis's *Trouble Every Day* (2001) and commercially viable franchise films including Juan Carlos Fresnadillo's *28 Weeks Later* (2007), the close-up shots of blood cells in *Bram Stoker's Dracula* stand out as salient reminders of the ever-mutating metaphors at the heart of horror, which depends as much on *context* for its meanings as it does on any given *text*.

While *Teeth* is far removed from the settings of these and other films featuring microscopic cinematography, its remediation of footage that at first glance appears to have been taken from a science documentary situates it within a broader history of cultural productions linking sexuality, illness, and infection. Moreover, readers who have watched *Ginger Snaps* (2000), a Canadian werewolf movie directed by John Fawcett (who cowrote the screenplay with Karen Walton), might detect multiple points of convergence between it and Lichtenstein's film, from their puberty-as-monster metaphor (which furthermore anticipates subsequent productions such as the Danish werewolf film *When Animals Dream* [*Når dyrene drømmer*, 2014] and the Swiss coming-of-age fantasy *Blue My Mind* [2017]) to their provocative, over-the-top staging of sexual encounters that turn deadly in the blink of an eye. Such parallels are only strengthened through the inclusion of a high-school science class scene in *Ginger Snaps* that shows the two main characters—sisters Brigitte (Emily Perkins) and Ginger Fitzgerald (Katharine Isabelle)—watching a video about meiosis. Footage from the electronic lecture is accompanied by a narrator's description of cellular activity (spoken by a man) that presages what will happen to Ginger once her body gives itself over to the infection caused by a werewolf bite: "Preying upon normal healthy cells, the intruder gradually devours the host from within. Eventually, the invader consumes its host completely, and finally destroys it" (figure 3.7).

As Xavier Aldana Reyes points out, Ginger, who has recently gotten her first period, "lets her head bang against her desk in either agony or exhaustion" during the science class screening, driving home the point that "the discomfort of ovulation becomes virtually indistinguishable from, although not equated with, her body's reaction to the infection" (2016, 39). As in *Teeth*, microscopic representations of what cannot be seen without technological intervention spell out the existential plight of the main character as a biological condition, through scientific terms that would seem to further objectify her as an object of the medical gaze, a curiosity to be studied in much the same way high school students are asked to do with organic specimens through the aid of microscopes. Such images, however, demonstrate the pervasiveness of what at

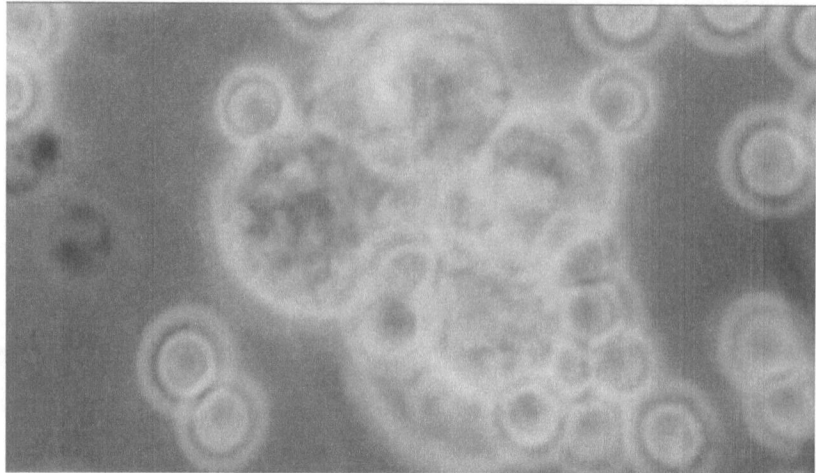

Figure 3.7. Microscopic images showing healthy cells being devoured by an "intruder" appear during a high-school science class scene in the 2000 film *Ginger Snaps*.

first glance appears to be a singular experience (unique to one teenager) yet is latent within every young woman in a patriarchal society where "intruders" and "invaders" seem to be everywhere.

It is important to note that the title character in *Jennifer's Body* only becomes "monstrous"—that is, a blood-spattered figure of terrifying abjection, vomiting up black bile and tearing into the flesh of others—after she has been tied up, held at knifepoint, and sacrificed to Satan by members of a struggling indie rock band, the anatomically named Low Shoulder, whose mistake in presuming that she was a virgin is what leads to her demonic possession. Her metamorphosis is therefore predicated on another type of victimizing monstrosity, coming at the hands of young men seeking fortune and fame on the back of a sacrificial "lamb" who ironically becomes wolf-like in her voracious appetite for fresh meat. As Katarzyna Paszkiewicz notes in her reading of the film, *Jennifer's Body* owes something of its success as a postfeminist take on female empowerment to earlier motion pictures in which similar transformations of teenage characters occur as a result of their encounters with young men whose bullying, belittling, or outright physical abuse must be countered through vengeful might. Her examples, ranging from the original *Carrie* (1976) to the abovementioned literalization of the *vagina dentata* folk-myth *Teeth*, each demonstrate a commitment to holding perpetrators of misogynistic acts accountable while unmasking the "horrors of high-school socialization" (Paszkiewicz 2018, 60–99; Craig and Fradley 2010, 89). Such an undertaking falls heavily on the shoulders of female protagonists who, lacking peer support and victimized at home by abusive family members, are isolated from others and therefore left to their own devices. By "devices," I mean their craftiness or ingenuity but also, primarily, their *bodies*, the various pathologies of which give rise to exceptional, *superhuman* abilities that exceed the limits of what people are physically capable of, as demonstrated by Carrie White's (Sissy Spacek) object-moving telekinesis and by Dawn O'Keefe's penis-severing genitalia.

Given its focus on the sisterly yet strained bond between two adolescents (Jennifer and Needy) whose already-fragile friendship is tested by increased competitiveness over the course of the narrative, Cody and Kusama's film is perhaps more reminiscent of the Canadian werewolf movie *Ginger Snaps*. This much-loved film is also cited by Paszkiewicz, who alludes to the similarly turbulent relationship between sisters Brigitte and Ginger Fitzgerald as well as to the latter's tendency to adopt a traditionally "masculine" position during her sexual trysts with schoolmates following her lycanthropic transformation, which was itself preceded by her getting her first period (2018, 80). Notably, all three of the aforementioned films—Brian De Palma's *Carrie*, John Fawcett's *Ginger Snaps*, and Mitchell Lichtenstein's *Teeth*—were directed by men, making *Jennifer's Body* all the more significant as both a carnivalesque rejection of "culturally prescribed gender roles" and a parodic reworking of the "Final Girl" archetype (embodied by Needy once she dispatches Jennifer with a box-cutter, similar to the phallic instrument used by the lead singer of Low Shoulder). Significantly, Needy inherits her dead friend's abilities following that climactic showdown, albeit without the vomitous side effects that made Jennifer—the conventionally beautiful cheerleader whose "dirty" mind is externalized in the form of an "unclean" body—such a contradictory figure in the first place.

Besides vigorously sinking its teeth into the topics of female sexuality, teenaged promiscuity, and other tropes associated with the slasher film, *Jennifer's Body* reminds us of the need to bring a more sensorially holistic sensitivity to onscreen and offscreen signifiers in order to "see" how corporeal excess, which Linda Williams cites as a distinguishing feature of body genres, is not limited to what is literally shown on the image track. In fact, a motion picture's soundtrack is where a great deal of horror's bodily activity takes place; aural events, as much as visual representations, help spectators to build up a mental picture of the diegetic world while ratcheting up dramatic tension to the point where terror becomes amusing. Here it is important to underscore the key roles played by music, sound effects, and spoken dialogue in granting the genre's storytellers a similar type of freedom, enabling them to roam unreservedly over anatomical referents in search of something that might shock, titillate, or unnerve audiences. Something as seemingly insignificant as the "sloshing" of guts, a Foleyed sound that can be heard in *Ginger Snaps* when Ginger eviscerates the high-school custodial worker (and which is described as such through the captioning service provided by Amazon Prime), is actually instrumental to the piecing together of a more fully realized, sensorially holistic storyworld inhabited by physical bodies. On a related note, when Dawn, the female protagonist in *Teeth*, severs the penis of a teenaged rapist with her unseen *vagina dentata*, the crunching noise of that violent encounter, as well as the sound of "[water running]" outside the cave where it occurs (captioned as such on Amazon Prime), are as central to the scene's affective play of sickly sharp and wet sensations as is the fleeting shot of the young man's detached member on the ground.

Through extratextual tools like Subtitles for the Deaf and Hard-of-Hearing (SDH), which are included on several online streaming platforms and as an added "bonus" feature of home-video releases, sighted viewers can even *see* some of those anatomically resonant sounds that partially distinguish horror from other genres, in the form of onscreen text that appears at the bottom of the screen. SDH is one of the supplemental features that can be activated on the 20th Century-Fox Home Entertainment DVD and Blu-ray releases of *Jennifer's Body*, giving audiences the ability to visually engage this film's fleeting verbal references to muscle groups like triceps, hip flexors, calves, and abs (all of which are spoken about during a butt-squeezing exercise equipment paid advertisement that Jennifer distractedly watches on TV after the opening titles). SDH enables audiences, including those who are not deaf or hard-of-hearing, to perceive sounds synesthetically while imagining a broader array of corporeal components comprising this and other films' titular bodies. For the sake of elaborating what this means in relation to the present discussion, let us consider the following passages of dialogue from *Jennifer's Body*, which—perhaps easier to overlook (or, rather, underhear) when they are not subtitled—hint at this film's own head-to-toe approach to anatomical horror.

- "I could expose my *stomach*, but never my *cleavage*. *Tits* were her trademark." (Needy in voiceover as she sizes herself up in the mirror)
- "I can almost see your front *butt* . . . I can see, like, your *womb*." (Needy's boyfriend, Chip [Johnny Simmons], commenting on her revealing outfit)
- "You could hear their *bones* breaking." (Needy speaking to Chip on the phone)
- "Feel my *heart*, Jonas. I think it's broken." (Jennifer fake-commiserating with soon-to-be-disemboweled football jock Jonas [Josh Emerson], as she places his hand on her breast)
- "You're *penis* cheese!" (Chip's younger sister Camille [Nicole Leduc] when he complains that she is playing a toy piano too loudly)
- "My *skin* is breaking out and my *hair* is dull and lifeless." (Jennifer to Needy after class ends, responding that she looks as tired as one the "normal girls")

- "He wears *nail* polish. My *dick* is bigger than his." (Jennifer speaking to Needy about Colin [Kyle Gallner] after he has asked her out on a date)
- "Dirk here is going to wear your *face*." (Nikolai [Adam Brody], the lead singer of Low Shoulder, explaining to Jennifer what he and his bandmates are planning to do to her)
- "They did go all 'Benihana' on my *ass*." (Jennifer to Needy, explaining what happened when she was sliced like sushi by the members of Low Shoulder)
- "Lasagna with *teeth*." (What Colin looked like when his mutilated body was found, according to Chip)
- "C'mon Chip, show me your '*breast*stroke.'" (Jennifer euphemistically flirting with Needy's boyfriend while walking along the edge of a blackened, filthy swimming pool)
- "My *tit*." "No, your *heart*." (Jennifer being corrected by Needy, who has just plunged a utility knife into her demonic best friend's chest)

Seemingly superficial, these and other lines written by Diablo Cody or devised by Karyn Kusama and her performers during the film's shooting, on top of Low Shoulder's cliché-filled, anatomically obsessed song lyrics (e.g., "I'm biting my *tongue*," "Wrapped around your *waist*," "Shake your *ass*," "You smashed a plate over my *head*"), reveal a deeper truth only hinted at by this film's title. Couched in the colloquialisms and slang terms common to young people's informal speech, the vocal stylings and linguistic shadings of contemporary horror films (as well as teenpics) are only slightly exaggerated renderings of what target audiences sometimes say in their own everyday lives. Although few viewers would see themselves mirrored in either the physical appearance or destructive actions of Megan Fox's slim, runway-ready, cannibalistic character, Jennifer's innuendo-sprinkled dialogue—in the form of snarky put-downs and quippy come-ons directed at fellow high-schoolers—approximates the diction and repartee of many people who identify with the filmmakers' *intended* demographic (young women as well as nonbinary and genderqueer audiences in their late teens, twenties, and thirties).

In this way, *Jennifer's Body* exemplifies what Katharina Lindner, author of *Film Bodies: Queer Feminist Encounters with Gender and Sexuality in Cinema*, describes as the phenomenological similarity between the bodies of characters and the bodies of spectators. Although those two sets of corporeal entities are not "ontologically analogous," audiences frequently detect something of their own physical-kinetic presence in the "movements, postures and gestures" of movie characters (in addition to the verbal tics, phrasings, and actual content of those characters' spoken lines). As such, they experience what Lindner—queerly recalibrating the theoretical writings of Vivian Sobchack—refers to as "resonant" embodiments (2017, 53). The fact that the various embodiments on view and audibly present in *Jennifer's Body* resonate so strongly with fans suggests that those physical configurations have been made "sufficiently comprehensible" through visual and verbal means, including actual anatomical references (sometimes vulgarized as "asses," "dicks," and "tits").

In much the same way that the titular victim-turned-monster is corrected by someone who, putting the teenaged girl's hidden "heart" before her visible "tit," is finally able to end her murderous ways, so too do audiences need occasional reminders of those important features of cinematic horror that lie below the surface of the text, and which cannot be accessed through eyesight or hearing alone (though SDH, akin to a microscope, does bring otherwise overlooked or underheard aspects of the soundtrack to light). In being able to imagine the beating organ below the surface of Jennifer's body-as-text, Needy displays this need to "go deeper." But the price she pays for her heroic if ultimately self-destructive act—ending up institutionalized inside a mental asylum and being blessed/cursed with her dead friend's superhuman abilities—also suggests the lingering effects of horror on viewers whose own subdermal or multisensory perception might be similarly activated.

Significantly, this idea of plunging below the surface, itself a kind of violent interrogation of the film as textual body (not unlike the way Jennifer kills Jonas, tearing into his neck and ripping out his guts only to leave his corpse behind for woodland creatures to nibble), has been taken up rhetorically by scholars who share my interest in horror's metatextual tendencies (figure 3.8). For instance, in his examination of the appropriately titled home-invasion thriller *Inside* (*À l'intérieur*, 2007), Dario Marcucci notes that the theoretical frameworks of horror as a body genre enable critics to "go deeper into the mechanisms of the subgenre" that this French production epitomizes (2020, 258). Importantly, he makes his argument after pointing out that both actual and symbolic bodies—those of *victims* who suffer at the hands of the killer and those of the *homes* being invaded by strangers—are violated over the course of a film that takes the idea of "forced penetration" as literal and figurative means to an end (258). What Marcucci refers to as "spatial rape," prevalent within but not limited to home-invasion narratives, can be stretched even further to suggest how horror film hermeneutics turns us all into textual "penetrators," looking for the meanings of things that cannot be fully fathomed by sticking to the sticky or slick surfaces of visual images.

Rather than simply *scope* out the surface appeals of a motion picture, including one as outwardly "sensational" as the belatedly appreciated film *Jennifer's Body* (marketed to audiences who were presumably hungry to see the sexy star's partially naked body, but now appreciated as a cult classic-in-the-making that is "*really about* female friendship," to quote one online critic) (Robertson

Figure 3.8. A literally gut-wrenching scene from *Jennifer's Body* (2009) showcases director Karyn Kusama and writer Diablo Cody's dark sense of humor.

2018), those of us who align ourselves with feminist politics yet are still fans of horror might follow the title character's lead in *scooping* out or externalizing the inside "stuff" of the genre. Supplemental features included on DVD and Blu-ray releases of horror films, including audio commentaries and behind-the-scenes documentaries that provide "insider" information about the making of those films, have proven to be effective tools for scholars seeking to do just that. Here we might feel compelled to follow Dawn's lead in *Teeth*, when, sitting in that now-conventional high-school setting of a science classroom, she peels back a large sticker from her human reproductive biology textbook (one that had been used to censor the anatomical illustration of female sexual organs) to confront the truth of her body. Even so, cinematic horror tells us repeatedly and with unparalleled vigor that surface *is* substance, just as *texture* or the so-called skin of the film can be thought of as a kind of *text* to be analyzed—poked and prodded—in its own right. In the next chapter, I turn to those frequently gooey and slimy surfaces as part of our gradual move into the interior of a body genre whose *figurative* guts are not always as visible to the eye as its literal ones are. In doing so, I will evoke images and ideas that are more than a little disturbing, but necessarily so if we are to address another perennial theme—namely, mortality—with the same unblinking frankness as do the most resonant horror films.

4

GOING DEEP, STICKING TO THE SURFACE

Bad Deaths and Wet Bodies

> Unlike classical horror films, which tell and imply but show very little of the destruction wrought upon the human body, the postmodern horror film is obsessed with the wet death, intent on imaging the mutilation and destruction of the body. The genre's fascination with the spectacle of the ruined body necessitates its privileging of the act of showing. But the act of showing the ruined body is only half the story; the other half is the act of concealing, of producing a partial vision.
> —ISABEL CRISTINA PINEDO, *Recreational Terror: Women and the Pleasures of Horror Film Viewing* (1997, 51)

There is an almost limitless variety of ways in which human life can be snuffed out and the body can be destroyed in horror cinema, with death coming as a result of beheading (*Trauma* [1993], *30 Days of Night* [2007], *Hereditary* [2018], etc.), disemboweling (*Dawn of the Dead* [1978], *Satan's Little Helper* [2004], *The Descent* [2005], etc.), drowning (*Creepshow* [1982], *Cabin by the Lake* [2000], *Lake Mungo* [2008], etc.), electrocution (*Shocker* [1989], *Pet Sematary Two* [1992], *Bride of Chucky* [1998], etc.), impaling (*The Omen* [1976], *The Mutilator* [1984], *Tucker and Dale vs. Evil* [2011], etc.), incineration (*Sorority Row* [2009], *The Purge* [2013], *The Babysitter: Killer Queen* [2020], etc.), melting (*The Beyond* [1981], *Street Trash* [1987], *Killer Klowns from Outer Space* [1988], etc.), shredding (*Sleepaway Camp III: Teenage Wasteland* [1989], *The Collection* [2012], *Freaky* [2020], etc.), and strangulation (*Bloody Birthday* [1981], *The Dentist* [1996], *The Greasy Strangler* [2016], etc.), to name only a few. The number of times characters have been gobbled up by alligators and crocodiles alone, in films such as *Black Magic 2* (1976), *Eaten Alive* (1976), *Dark Age* (1987), *Lake Placid* (1999), *Primeval* (2007), *Rogue* (2007), and *Crawl* (2019), among many others, is large enough to remind us of how frequently "bad death"—a particular subset of cinematic mortality largely reserved for horror—figures in narratives that exceed the boundaries of reason (and taste) while stretching believability to the point of breaking.

Even within a single film—sometimes within a single jaw-dropping sequence, set piece, or scene—viewers will occasionally encounter a full arsenal of killing tools as well as a small mountain of hacked or injured body parts. For instance, *The Collector* (2009), a pastiche of genre elements cobbled together from previous decades' home-invasion films and more recent examples of so-called torture porn, offers a grab bag of bodily shocks, showing different characters not only being blasted with shotguns, electrocuted, pushed down staircases, and stabbed multiple times but also getting their guts ripped out, fingers cut off, hands impaled, tongues removed, mouths skewered, necks snapped, and heads caught in bear traps. "Teeth are chiseled away, fingernails are scraped off, and fishhooks are plunged into eyelids," one online reviewer says, adding to a growing list of this film's stomach-churning offenses but also noting that, for all of *The Collector*'s shortcomings, "it's interesting to see primal fear put back on the screen, forcing the crowds to twist and shout their way through the agony" (Ornsdorf 2009).

In each of these examples, the graphic display of characters going to an early grave—their bodies horribly mutilated or desecrated—distinguishes them as *contemporary* examples of a genre that, decades ago, once leaned on the atmospheric evocation of dread rather than on gory images meant to disgust or shock the audience. As numerous scholars have pointed out, the bodily fear evoked by classic horror films of the 1930s, 1940s, and 1950s is partly triggered by the spectator's active imagination, put to service in the name of a narrational system that, for reasons of censorship and industrial regulations concerning screen content (which, in the US cultural context, was internally "policed" by members of the Production Code Administration), simply *could not show everything*. Instead, motion pictures from that period *told* rather than showed the details of a person's bad death.

This occurs, for instance, in the science fiction-horror film *Them!* (1954), a Cold War creature feature revolving around the national threat posed by giant irradiated ants that have sprung up in the New Mexico desert. One of the first victims of these unnaturally large insects is "Gramps" Johnson (Mathew McCue), a local storeowner whose horribly mangled body—*not* visible on the screen—is taken by state police to the county medical offices of Dr. Putnam (Joseph Forte). Having completed the autopsy report, the coroner tells the officers that Gramps's "neck and back were broken, his chest crushed, his skull fractured." Adding that what he is about to say would likely stump Sherlock Holmes, Putnam remarks, "There was enough formic acid in him to kill twenty men." As he puts into words what, in the mid-1950s, could not be visually depicted (but which can be shown today, even in PG-13-rated films or their

Figure 4.1. Before the era of more graphically excessive representations, films like *Them!* (1954) for the most part only verbally described (through spoken dialogue) the abject state of bodies violently harmed by natural or supernatural threats. Here, a medical coroner details the physical injuries that led to the death of this latest victim of giant bug attacks, though spectators are left to imagine the appearance of the mangled body below the sheet.

equivalent outside of the United States), audiences are called upon to sketch a mental picture of the dead man's body, making them accomplices in a narrational act that requires a filling-in of gaps if they are to have a more complete understanding of what actually happened. Another instance of this occurs later in *Them!*, during a scene when another victim of the giant ants, a man named Thomas Lodge, lies tastefully hidden beneath a white sheet as the coroner details the latest incident (figure 4.1). Noting that the dead man's chest has been deeply lacerated, that his face has been chopped up, and that his arm has been pulled off at the shoulder and is now missing, the coroner verbally conjures the same kind of horrendous fate that awaits characters in contemporary horror films, which are much more likely to *show* things that previous generations' audiences were only asked to *imagine*.

With Hollywood studio productions like *Them!* in their rearview mirror, low-budget films of the late 1960s—partly inspired by Hitchcock's *Psycho* (1960) and a few other releases from the first half of that decade that pushed the limits of onscreen violence—played a crucial role in putting flesh on the idea of bad death. One need only refer to George A. Romero's *Night of the Living Dead* (1968) and Michael Reeves's *Witchfinder General* (1968) in discussing the importance of this transitional period to the recalibration of a genre that would no longer be content to keep its wrecked and violated bodies tucked safely away in the shadows or left inoffensively offscreen. Released in theaters at a time when people were growing accustomed to witnessing real-world horrors flicker across their television screens (thanks to nightly news reports showing actual dead or dying bodies during the Vietnam War), American and British productions such as these—chock-full of flesh-eating zombies and literally torturous scenes of physical anguish—augured a new era in motion-picture content. Of course, less brazen attempts to horrify or repulse viewers would continue to be made during that period of greater permissiveness, well into the 1970s (when a handful of made-for-TV movies such as Don't Be Afraid of the Dark [1973], Bad Ronald [1974], and Trilogy of Terror [1975] were broadcast).[1] But, by and large, the post-Vietnam zeitgeist was when people's growing frustrations and feelings of powerlessness, shared by other audiences around the world who had witnessed violent US military incursions as well as the soft-power spread of its cultural exports, found purchase in a new breed of filmmakers' work that only became more vicious and rage-filled in its apocalyptic visions and critique of the political establishment—if not of sexism and other aspects of the social status quo—as the decade wore on. With that move toward a more direct, if still allegorical, sort of horror cinema in the 1970s came the kind of spectacularly graphic representations referred to above, part of what Beth A. Kattelman calls the first wave of "carnographic culture," which continued into the prosthetics-heavy 1980s and intensified throughout the post-9/11 second wave of gore-filled horror films noted for their thematic emphasis on literal and figurative torture (2010, 5).

Some of the filmmakers contributing to that intensification throughout the 1970s and 1980s are household names to genre enthusiasts: George A. Romero, John Carpenter, Wes Craven, Brian De Palma, Tobe Hooper, and David Lynch. However, several less well-known specialists in horror and its sister categories (science fiction and fantasy), from Bob Clark (the director-producer of Children Shouldn't Play with Dead Things [1972], Deathdream [1974], and Black Christmas [1974]) to Larry Cohen (the director-producer of It's Alive [1974], God Told Me To [1976], and The Stuff [1985]) and Don Coscarelli (the director-producer of Phantasm [1979] and three of its sequels), were also instrumental in breaking down the barriers that had been placed on previous generations' cultural productions and in bringing the visceral, intestinal subtext of their stories to the surface. Besides these US-based filmmakers, a number of international auteurs with connections to stateside distributors and producers, from Canada's David Cronenberg to Italy's Dario Argento, played a vital role in collapsing the distinctions between art and trash, or between technical sophistication and sleazy exploitation, while demonstrating the genre's power to "rupture the surfaces of the flesh and violate the organic integrity of the body" (Shaviro 1993,

202). This latter aspect of horror had been latent throughout the genre's history, but was kept in check by surveillant mandates concerning acceptable screen content until the dam began to burst with the plunging knifes of Norman Bates and his proto-slasher descendants. As Lorna Piatti-Farnell emphasizes, the gooey, slimy, and sticky features of certain cinematic texts call upon viewers' haptic sensitivities and necessitate a *textural* approach to the very "thingness" or materiality of the medium (2017, 72). Her argument, I believe, is best applied to those productions of the 1970s and 1980s that took the lessons learned from Hitchcock's *Psycho* and recalibrated them in a practically *tactile* way, grafting thrill-ride sensationalism to then-emerging sensibilities surrounding the spectacularizing of death on the big screen.

If *Psycho* is to be singled out as an exemplary case of "popular modernism" at least partly responsible for introducing "new ways of seeing, and new ways of *feeling*, films," according to Linda Williams (2000, 351), then some attention should also be given to those "postmodern" examples of cinematic horror that, in Isabel Cristina Pinedo's words, brought the genre's "fascination with the spectacle of the ruined body" to the fore, and often in a knowing, satirically humorous way (1997, 51). Obsessed with what she calls "wet death," films such as Romero's *Dawn of the Dead* (1978), Carpenter's *The Thing* (1982), and Craven's *A Nightmare on Elm Street* (1984), which show shopping-mall zombies ripping out people's glistening intestines, a defibrillating physician's arms being ripped off by another man's beartrap-like chest cavity, and a ten-foot-high geyser of blood erupting from a teenager's bed, respectively, seem "intent on imaging the mutilation and destruction of the body" to the point where laughter at the sheer excessiveness of it all is an appropriately immoderate response on the audience's part (figure 4.2). Brimming in blood, feces, pus, semen, snot, urine, vomit, and other abject markers of bodily excess, several motion pictures that have been produced since the 1970s take the thrill-ride sensations and amusement-park metaphors associated with the reception of Hitchcock's film (as discussed in the previous chapter) into more physically revolting territory. What this suggests is that there is a charnel house behind every cinematic "funhouse," to borrow the title of Tobe Hooper's 1981 slasher film (which, not coincidentally, begins with a shower scene presented from the first-person perspective of a masked "killer" that pays metatextual tribute to *Psycho* as well as to Carpenter's *Halloween* [1978] only to subvert audience expectations with a false startle effect). The carnivalesque setting of Hooper's *The Funhouse* is fitting, then, given how horror had become a means of playfully debasing established protocols of classical storytelling and raising the vulgar, earthly improprieties associated with the lower bodily stratum to a level of mainstream acceptance (if not highbrow approval) by the time of that film's theatrical release.

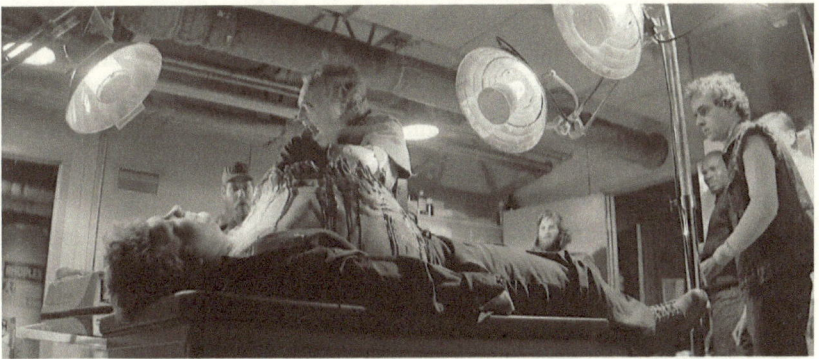

Figure 4.2. One of the biggest "jump scares" in John Carpenter's *The Thing* (1982) occurs when Dr. Copper (Richard Dysart) brings a defibrillator down on Norris's (Charles Hallahan) chest, only to have his arms cut off by the geologist's beartrap-like cavity. Stumbling backwards, double-amputee Joe Carone (wearing a mask modeled on Dysart's face) holds up the bloody stumps and lets out a scream that was surely echoed by several of this film's first audiences.

One of the major proponents of that carnivalesque profanation, albeit from a more cerebral perspective than that of his peers, was David Cronenberg, who began his career over fifty years ago, making avant-garde and experimental art-house films before gravitating toward horror in the early 1970s. In his study of Cronenberg's films, William Beard alludes to the fact that the Canadian auteur, whose earliest stabs at the genre took place in that transitional period when moral restrictions were loosened and once-taboo subjects, including sexual liberation and polymorphous perversity, were broached with unprecedented degrees of anatomical directness, played an important role in shifting onscreen portrayals of death and destruction away from a mode of "telling" to one of "showing." In Beard's words, "contemporary horror's intense devotion to showing the horrific in the most explicit detail possible" marks "the final manifestation of a drift from suggestion to shock" (2015, 228n5). That "drift" was a decades-spanning movement from the kind of atmospheric motion pictures produced by Val Lewton and directed by Jacques Tourneur and Mark Robson for RKO Pictures (e.g., *Cat People* [1942], *I Walked with a Zombie* [1943], *The Leopard Man* [1943], *The Seventh Victim* [1943], *Isle of the Dead* [1945], *Bedlam* [1946]), which are partially distinguished by what they do *not* show and thus leave to the viewer's imagination (Jancovich 2014, 238), to those such as Cronenberg's *Shivers* (1975), *Rabid* (1977), and *The Brood* (1979), which, sprinkled with images of slug-slithering, skin-grafting, and fetus-licking, do not flinch in their autopsy-like "exploration of the human body and its murky relationship to the human soul" (209). By the time he completed *Scanners* (1981), *Videodrome* (1983), and his squishiest film to that point, *The Fly* (1986), turning his attention to weightier themes related to techno-capitalism and psychogenetics, he had earned a reputation as a provocateur capable of stimulating the intellect (Kellner 1989, 89–101). But Cronenberg was just as prone to wallow in the messy afterbirth of a genre that had now been fully opened up to once-verboten material, including the actual *materiality* of the human body in various states of mutation, disintegration, and decay. From excremental parasites shaped like penises to exploding heads, externalized wombs, and vaginal slits in a man's abdomen, the very substance(s) of Cronenberg's early-to-mid-career output marked the end of one era and the beginning of another (though he would probably disapprove of such binaristic, black-and-white distinctions).

Like Beard, Laura Wilson discusses the distinction between "telling" and "showing" in her book *Spectatorship, Embodiment and Physicality in the Contemporary Mutilation Film*, though in doing so she gestures toward one of Cronenberg's contemporaries, John Carpenter. Building upon Philip Brophy's exploration of the many visible differences between *The Thing from Another World* (1951), a science-fiction horror hybrid directed by Christian Nyby,[2] and *The Thing*, a 1982 adaptation of that earlier film's source material (John W. Campbell Jr.'s 1938 novella *Who Goes There?*) directed by Carpenter, she draws attention to the textural physicality of a genre that, beginning in the 1980s, was busy adding "feeling" to the aforementioned tendency toward "showing" (Wilson 2015, 19). The practically tactile experience of watching *The Thing*, described by Julie Guihot as being "visually viscous" (2012, 198), is imparted to the audience through the haptic visuality of protoplasmic goo and wet, slimy surfaces. This facet of the genre, which was being publicized in the pages of *Fangoria*, *Cinefantastique*, and other magazines aimed at gore-hounds and body-horror enthusiasts around the time of the film's theatrical release (Nair 2021, 109), has only become more pronounced with the advent of "torture porn" franchises initiated by James Wan's *Saw* (2004), Eli Roth's *Hostel* (2005), and Tom Six's *The Human Centipede* (2009).[3] Quoting Brophy, Wilson notes that while both versions of Campbell's story "deal with the notion of an alien purely as a biological life force," Carpenter's film, bolstered by makeup artist Rob Bottin's breakthroughs in "creature effects," distinguishes itself from its mid-century predecessor in the way that it generates suspense not by withholding information but by offering up *too much* of the stuff. She goes on to suggest that "through 'showing' bodily mutilation via explicit images, rather than alluding to—or 'telling'—this violence through editing, framing and sound" (Wilson 2015, 19), *The Thing* turns the "thingness" of the eponymous life form (a parasitic creature from another planet that assumes the sundry shapes of its human and animal hosts) into a site of profound terror.

This "thingness" of the title creature, as Kartik Nair elaborates, is furthermore accompanied by a "thereness" that can be just as unsettling to the spectator, even when he or she can see through the artifice of the film's sticky prosthetic trickery and, to quote Steve Neale, "knows that the Thing is a fiction" (Nair 2021, 110; Neale 1990, 161). Indeed, the "weighty, wet, possibly odorous" objects that Bottin and his effects team created and placed "there" on the smoke-filled, K-Y Jelly–slathered set alongside the film's actors and crew "disturb us with their mysterious and artificial materiality" (Nair 2021, 112), and no amount of awareness of their status as "fabrications" (which Bottin himself described as "just so much foam latex") will completely offset their impact. In Nair's words, the "off-putting indeterminacy" of *The Thing*'s prosthetic effects, similar to the biological mystery of the title creature (whose cell-structure cannot be fathomed by the team of scientific researchers stationed in the Antarctic), provokes a combination of "confusion and revulsion" in audiences who are as dumbfounded and horrified as the characters are when assailed by the "suddenly exploding insides" of infected bodies (112).

KILL COUNTS: CALCULATING AND CATALOGUING DEATH

> As Joe Bob Briggs is fond of reminding us, fans of low horror are drawn by the body count ("We're talking two breasts, four quarts of blood, five dead bodies . . . Joe Bob says check it out").
> —JOAN HAWKINS, *Cutting Edge: Art-Horror and the Horrific Avant-Garde* (2000, 28)

The "carnographic" aspects of the genre that I have described above, even more pronounced today than they were during the 1970s and 1980s, are humorously highlighted in each episode of *The Last Drive-in with Joe Bob Briggs* (Shudder, 2018–present), a streaming American TV series starring cult film critic and comic performer John Irving Bloom (whose better-known stage name graces the show's title). Like Briggs's earlier late-night cable hit *MonsterVision* (TNT, 1991–2000), *The Last Drive-in* shines a light on a wide range of paracinematic offerings from the worlds of exploitation, grindhouse, horror, and science-fiction filmmaking, with episodes devoted to obscure, independently made oddities like *Spookies* (1986), *Blood Harvest* (1987), and *Things* (1989), as well as critically lauded international releases such as the Japanese cyberpunk body-horror film *Tetsuo: The Iron Man* (1989), the Spanish black comedy-horror film *The Day of the Beast* (*El día de la bestia*, 1995), and the South Korean action-zombie film *Train to Busan* (*Busanhaeng*, 2016), usually paired with a similarly themed movie as part of a roughly four-hour double feature. Besides showing two films in their entirety, interspersed with short trivia-filled breaks in which the Dallas-born host, ensconced in a neon-lit trailer home (actually, a TV studio soundstage), engages in banter with fellow genre enthusiast Darcy the Mail Girl

(Diana Prince) and any guests who might be attached to the featured movies (filmmakers, actors, celebrity-fans, etc.), each episode contains a preview segment called "Drive-In Totals." As an inventory of some of the many excessive elements to be found in the motion picture that follows, this list provides a numerical and typological rundown of that film's deaths, the gruesomeness of which is hinted at by the host's amusing wordplay. Spoken to the camera and printed as onscreen text, these "Drive-In Totals" segments not only establish a horizon of expectations for curious viewers but also comedically frame horror as a body genre whose "badness" extends beyond the manner of a character's death to the larger representational system that allows such flagrantly gruesome fatalities to consume so much screen time.

For example, in the lead-up to a screening of writer-director Don Coscarelli's *Phantasm III: Lord of the Dead* (1994), which was programmed as part of a four-film Christmas-themed marathon that aired on December 21, 2018 (and which featured three other entries in the long-running *Phantasm* franchise), Briggs provided his customary introduction, telling viewers that over the next two hours they would encounter:

> 23 Dead Bodies. 2 Breasts. Exploding Eyes. Multiple Fireballs. Exploding Hearse. Zombie Monks Feeding on Human Flesh. Multiple Exploding Heads. Electric Drill Attack. Needle to the Neck. Hatchet to the Forehead. Skull Drilling Daggers to the Forehead. 1 Flying Monster Hand with Teeth. 1 Motor Vehicle Chase with Crash and Burn. Face Peeling. Heads Roll. Hands Roll. Kung Fu. Baseball Bat Fu. Frisbee-with-a-Razor-Edge Fu. Cryogenic Spear Fu. (figure 4.3)

Capped with a shout-out to this film's "Drive-In Academy Award" nominees (actors Angus Scrimm, Kevin Connors, Reggie Bannister, and Gloria Lynne Henry), Joe Bob's paratextual framing of *Phantasm III: Lord of the Dead* might remind viewers of a theatrical movie trailer, which similarly spotlights that movie's onscreen talent and whets the appetite for the thrills to come while only *hinting at*, without actually showing or fully revealing, the monstrous creatures and plot developments that lie in wait.

We might pause here to consider how previews of coming attractions for horror films are distinguished by dueling impulses on the part of both marketing teams and audiences, each torn between the desire to show/see and the desire to hide/not see. That promotional/spectatorial tendency furthermore corresponds to Isabel Cristina Pinedo's notion of "recreational terror," the contradictory pleasures of which derive from looking and not looking. This latter aspect of horror film spectatorship, according to Pinedo and other scholars, is an "act of control" exercised by audience members who, obscuring "their own line of vision by

Figure 4.3. As one of the patented features of his Shudder series *The Last Drive-In*, host Joe Bob Briggs prepares his audience for the cinematic mayhem to come by doling out "Drive-In Totals," a tongue-in-cheek calculation of the many "bad deaths" that occur in contemporary horror films.

looking through their hands or by intermittently turning away from the screen," are able to "distance themselves during intense moments of anxiety to keep fear in check when it threatens to overwhelm them" (1997, 51, 53–54).[4] Movie trailers are not as forthright as the films they have been carefully designed to advertise, only *insinuating* narrative details while approximating and sometimes misrepresenting the overall tone or emotional cadence of particular scenes (because of the interest filmmakers have in keeping audiences "in the dark"). Because of this, trailers ironically heighten one's desire to see the terrifying spectacle—the exploding eyes, the hatchet to the forehead, and the zombie monks feeding on human flesh, in the case of *Phantasm III: Lord of the Dead*—from which that same hypothetical viewer might eventually recoil (while watching the actual film). As Pinedo stresses, "the degree to which *not being able to see* structures the act of looking" is something that is often ignored in discussions of horror's contradictory pleasures and recreational terrors (51, 53–54).

Joe Bob's "Drive-In Totals" for the 2015 New Zealand comedy horror *Deathgasm* (the first part of a season one episode also featuring *The Changeling* [1980]) are even more extravagant, in terms of the length of his summary and the descriptive specificity that he employs when drawing attention to the film's most memorable scenes:

> 35 Dead Bodies. 40 Undead Bodies. 4 Breasts. 2 Vicious Beatdowns. 3 Fistfights. Bra Lasering. Super Soaker Piss Spraying. Projectile Blood Vomit into the Face of a Girl Wearing a White Sweater. Multiple Throat Cutting. Latin Demon Music. Double Head Slicing. Head Splitting. Head Ripping, with Spinal Cord. Arm Ripping. Zombie Drilling. Ax to

the Brain Stem. Face Kicking. Horns to the Tummy. Automobile Engine Head Squashing. Clown-Zombie Hand through the Gizzards. Quadruple-Head Chainsaw Whirlybird Martial Arts Move. Chainsaw through the Gizzards (Again). Flying Head Slicing Buzzsaws. Stiletto through the Mouth. Simultaneous Electric-Dildo Ear-Canal Stabbing. Collateral Damage Head-Chopping. Guitar Lightning. Oral Zombie Sex. Demon Worship. Bloody Drumming. Bloody Eye Sockets. Blood Spewing. Blood Puking. Ear-Stud Ripping. Scimitar Plunging. Gratuitous KISS Makeup. Gratuitous Lesbian Warrior Sequence, with Ax. Heads Roll. Arms Roll. Torso Rolls....

One thing that stands out about this and each of the fifty-seven other films that comprise the show's first three seasons (not to mention the thirty-seven additional films that have been shown during ten marathons and specials) is the inventiveness of the methods used to bring about death or cause pain. Joe Bob's "Drive-In Totals" hint at the often-inspired levels of outside-the-box creativity that are brought to the production of works typically brushed off by critics as being unimaginative or "mindless" in their adherence to genre formulas. Indeed, just reading a horror film's inventory of kills can spark the imagination insofar as the most inconceivable of them might confound even the most seasoned of genre enthusiasts, as suggested by Joe Bob's descriptions of the deathly set pieces in *Tourist Trap* (1979: "Designer Scarf Strangling"), *Mother's Day* (1980: "Electric-Turkey-Carver Face Plunging"), *The Prowler* (1981: "Aquatic Throat Sawing"), *Silent Night, Deadly Night Part 2* (1987: "Deer-Antler Impalement"), *Jack Frost* (1997: "Runaway-Sled Head Slicing"), and *Society* (1989: "Projectile Suntan-Lotion Attack"). When woven into the outwardly asinine yet internally consistent, structurally complex entries in the *Saw* franchise, referred to by one online commentator as "far and away the most plot-heavy, convoluted horror film series ever," these kinds of bizarre deaths only compound the challenge of putting the jigsaw-like puzzle pieces together amidst an ever-growing number of flaunted narrative gaps (Belinkie 2010).

Knowing that none of the "zombie-drilling" and "ear canal-stabbing" in writer-director Jason Lei Howden's feature-length debut *Deathgasm* is really happening to any of the performers (i.e., no one was killed or maimed during the making of the film), some audiences—especially those who are fans of heavy metal music and over-the-top "splatstick"—will most certainly *enjoy* the spectacle of its many fictional, highly stylized deaths. Putting aside its higher-than-normal "kill count" (thirty-five onscreen fatalities), Howden's film, whose title hints at the spasmic and orgiastic pleasures of the text, is similar to the other examples of "low," critically devalued cultural productions featured on *The Last Drive-in with Joe Bob Briggs*, insofar as they all (to varying degrees) attempt to compensate for a particular *lack* (of financing/funding, of production values and A-list actors/stars, of distribution/exhibition outlets, etc.) through the piling up of corporeal *excess*.

Indeed, another standout element in the show's "Drive-In Totals" is the word "gratuitous," which appears in nearly every film's list of things to look out for. According to Joe Bob, director Wes Craven's *The Hills Have Eyes* (1977) has "Gratuitous Baby-Eating Jokes," Ruggero Deodato's *Cannibal Holocaust* (1980) has "Gratuitous Butterfly Collecting," Tony Williams's *Next of Kin* (1982) has "Gratuitous Skinnydipping," Larry Cohen's *The Stuff* (1985) has "Gratuitous Bikini Models," J. Michael Muro's *Street Trash* (1987) has "Gratuitous Nam Flashbacks, with Cannibalism," Lloyd Kaufman's *Troma's War* (1988) has "Gratuitous Hymn-Singing," William Lustig's *Maniac Cop* (1988) has "Gratuitous Bagpipers," Stewart Raffill's *Tammy and the T-Rex* (1994) has "Gratuitous Brain Probing," and Ana Lily Amirpour's *A Girl Walks Home Alone at Night* (2014) has "Gratuitous Vampire Skateboarding." Like extra appendages (or what in an ableist society are sometimes referred to as "birth defects"), these and other seemingly superfluous parts of a horror film's own material being—its "malformed" or "misshapen" body—are the very things that draw many contemporary genre fans to this updated version of the earlier "cinema of attractions" that was discussed briefly in chapter three.

It bears mentioning that, until the June 18, 2021, airing of the final episode of season three, when the host of *The Last Drive-in with Joe Bob Briggs* highlighted the comparatively tamer pleasures of Roger Corman's 1960 comedy-horror film *The Little Shop of Horrors* (paired with the sci-fi monster movie *Humanoids from the Deep* [1980]), the oldest motion pictures showcased in this Shudder series were two releases from 1975: the Italian-language *giallo* horror film *Deep Red* (*Profondo rosso*) and the Japanese-language adaptation of a popular manga series *Wolf Guy* (*Urufu gai: Moero ōkami-otoko*). The fact that nothing predating the mid-1970s had been featured in *The Last Drive-in with Joe Bob Briggs* prior to that Corman-themed episode (discounting the aforementioned marathons and specials) suggests that the particular type of "attractions" cited above, dripping in bodily fluids and revolting to most mainstream audiences, are a fairly recent phenomenon (relative to the entire history of horror). That is, the gruesome display of physical trauma, even if filtered through a comedic lens or rendered through practical, prosthetic, and puppeteering effects that call attention to the film's artifice, was *not* something that most filmmakers plying their trade before that decade had seriously considered. This is not surprising, given the industrial and cultural restrictions that were placed on studio and independent productions during the 1930s through the 1960s.

Kazuhiko Yamaguchi's *Wolf Guy*, a lycanthropic crime-sexploitation thriller starring legendary martial artist Sonny Chiba and set in a literal "urban jungle" where a phantom tiger is on the loose, was never officially distributed outside Japan before Arrow Video's 2017 DVD/Blu-ray release (though bootleg copies of it circulated in the stateside "grey market" for years). Conversely, a slightly abbreviated, English-dubbed version of Dario Argento's *Deep Red* did receive a wide theatrical release after its New York City premiere in the summer of 1976 (one year after it had debuted in Milan and Rome). Though the *New York Times*' Vincent Canby famously referred to *Deep Red* as being little more than a "bucket of ax-murder clichés" (1976, 58), time has been kind to Argento's film, which not only inspired his Italian contemporaries (including Lucio Fulci, Pupi Avati, and Ruggero Deodato) as well as US filmmakers who were, each in their own ways, attempting to become the "next Hitchcock," but has since been analyzed by scholars with the same obsessive attention to detail that Argento and his production team brought to the staging of murders. Perhaps more so than any other internationally distributed film from that period, *Deep Red* can be seen as a defining statement about what horror *as a body genre* could be at a time when filmmakers around the world felt similarly emboldened to "push the limits of visual and auditory experience" (Cooper 2012, 1). Of course, one could point toward a number of North American directors—for instance, George A. Romero, John Carpenter, Wes Craven, David Cronenberg, Brian De Palma, and Tobe Hooper—who likewise burst onto the scene in the late 1960s or early 1970s and are equally deserving of the "Master of Horror" accolades bestowed upon Argento. But few films were as influential in terms of raising the bar for "elaborate, inventive methods of dispatching . . . victims" as *Deep Red*, which put a new spin on familiar standbys of the genre (e.g., stabbing, hacking, etc.) while introducing altogether bizarre forms of corporeal abuse within baroque set pieces (accompanied by an equally extravagant score composed and performed by the Italian prog-rock group Goblin) that are as powerfully felt today as they must have been when the film was theatrically released nearly fifty years ago (Kannas 2017, 92).

Argento reaches those affective heights by plumbing the depths of human perception: our base sensations and bodily desires vis-à-vis objects of a suspiciously fetishistic gaze. Even more paradoxically, he does it by prompting audiences to see "profundity" in the surface of the world. In keeping with its Italian-language title, *Deep Red* is "deep" in the way that it reflexively frames death as a spectacularly trashy work of art, a seemingly superficial gloss on that most profound kind of loss—that of life itself—which nevertheless holds meaning for anyone who finds themselves transfixed by his films' beautifully gruesome images; at once lurid and sublime, repulsive and seductive, their colors so garish and deeply saturated that critics have called them "violent" (McDonagh 1994, 25). As if the chromatic properties of a motion picture could somehow be as aggressive or brutal as the behavior of a killer, the color red practically bleeds with meaning, "overwhelming" the spectator as viscerally as the soundtracks to Argento's films are also said to do (Heller-Nicholas 2021). But it does so with a special vibrancy or *hyper*-redness that makes something like movie blood (or stage blood, which is usually a mixture of corn syrup and red food coloring) look "fake" when compared to that of actual bodies in the real world. Such discourse, which pervades much of the scholarly responses to the director's body of work, underscores the significance of horror's sensational appeals.

As Alexandra Heller-Nicholas suggests in her discussion of style *as substance* in 1970s *giallo* films, those sensational appeals are not merely superficial promptings on the part of a gifted auteur (someone who, like Argento, is skilled at manipulating the audience's reactions), but rather the very lifeblood of cinema, as fundamental to our hermeneutic pursuit of "truth"—a spectatorial undertaking personified by the protagonist of *Deep Red*, jazz pianist-turned-amateur sleuth Marcus Daly (David Hemmings)—as any underlying structures or recurring themes. By making the "carefully arranged details" of his film ("from the sets' colors and shadows to the cameras' angles and movements") "so fundamentally *pretty*," according to L. Andrew Cooper, Argento makes it difficult for even the most easily shocked viewers (those who would otherwise be mortified by the spectacle of bloodletting) to turn away (2012, 1). Just as Marcus is shown doing in the final shot of *Deep Red*, once the identity of the previously hidden killer has been brought to light and the mysteries of its labyrinthian narrative have been solved (if only partially), audiences are forced to confront themselves—to gaze at their own blood-drenched reflections—vis-à-vis images that are mirror-like in their framing of horror film spectatorship as an artistic practice or performative act in its own right.

Another, more down-to-earth way that Argento achieves the above effects is by limiting his films' orgiastic displays of "pain, suffering, and mental anguish" to common, relatable experiences, "thus evoking more visceral reactions from viewers" (Smuts 2002; Cooper 2012, 1). As Aaron Smuts explains in his exploration of *Deep Red* (prompted by information provided by the Italian director himself as part of an interview included on Anchor Bay's twenty-fifth anniversary DVD release in 2000), because a majority of audience members do not know what it feels like to be injured by a loaded revolver or a shotgun blast, guns are less likely to appear in Argento's body of work than are more quotidian means of causing pain: hard-edged, everyday objects and physical structures found in most people's homes (kitchen knives and meat cleavers, of course, but also staircases, windowpanes, fireplace mantles, wooden desks, and end tables) that are transformed into "specters of gruesome death" in his hands. "We all know what it is like to bump our heads against a sharp table-edge and to hit our teeth on a drinking-glass," Smuts explains, "so Argento couples these two common experiences and shows people getting their teeth rammed against a table corner" (Smuts 2002). Minor household annoyances like broken glass underfoot or scalding hot water in a bathtub, which might trigger physical memories in audiences who have accidentally cut or burned themselves at some point in their lives, are thus raised to a level of mortal danger in scenes that are "splashy" in both the figurative and literal senses of that word.

Besides the gaudily ornate production design, throbbing electronic musical scores, flashy camerawork, and other "excessive, exhibitionist displays of style" that make his films' surfaces so beguiling (Isaacs 2020, 70), Argento's body of work is also splashy in the sense that those surfaces have a palpable *wetness*, a liquidic tactility that moistens the mise-en-scène—and not just metaphorically, as anyone who has seen *Inferno* (1980), which features a scene set inside a flooded, corpse-littered basement, can attest. From his undisputed masterpiece *Suspiria* (1977) to his mid-career standouts *Tenebrae* (1982), *Phenomena* (1985), and *Opera* (1987), his films are as wet as they are sharp—literally so whenever water, blood, or some other fluid is visibly present in the image. The scene from *Deep Red* that best highlights this involves a tub of bath water, a familiar sight/site that might tritely be spoken of as one of physical cleansing as well as a less-literal type of spiritual purification, but which, like the shower in *Psycho*, is transformed into a space of deadly reckoning where victims are at their most exposed in the presence of an unseen assailant.

The moment in question occurs midway through the film, when Amanda Righetti (Giuliana Calandra), the author of a book about "modern ghosts" (which might contain clues about the identity of a mysterious killer responsible for several deaths in Turin) is suddenly attacked by that book's subject inside her own apartment. Grabbing her from behind, the gloved hands of the assailant drag Amanda to the bathtub, where he, she, or they—at this point in the narrative, the person's gender is not known—has already drawn scalding hot water in preparation for what looks to be a most unholy sort of baptism. With steam rising from the bubbling tub, the image radiates heat. The audience's haptic perception of the water's boiling temperature is confirmed once the attacker dunks Amanda's head in it, a vicious act accompanied by splashing sounds and the muted screams of someone whose face has begun to blister and peel off until she is let go (dropping to the bathroom floor a few seconds before she finally expires). Unlike a similar head-dousing scene in *Halloween II* (1981), which shows the masked killer Michael Myers thrusting a nurse face-first into a hospital Jacuzzi (approaching 130-degrees Fahrenheit) from a side angle, this more disconcerting moment in *Deep Red* is shot from the ocular perspective of the killer (figure 4.4). The fact that the murderer's gloved hands are shown reaching up from the bottom of the screen and throttling the back of the woman's neck throughout this splashy example of bad death—one in which water literally splashes and threatens to hit the camera lens—is notable but not

Figure 4.4. In this scene from Dario Argento's *Deep Red* (1975), gloved hands—those of the director himself—reach into frame and push a woman, Amanda Righetti (Giuliana Calandra), into scalding hot bathwater, a moment that was reportedly difficult for the actress to film (owing to the shortness of her breath underwater).

that extraordinary given the preponderance of POV shots across the history of cinematic horror, dating back at least to the 1931 release of director Rouben Mamoulian's *Dr. Jekyll and Mr. Hyde*. What *is* significant, though, is the fact that those hands belong to the director himself, Dario Argento, who often subbed in for the unseen killers in his films by stepping out from behind the camera and placing his own body in close proximity to those of his abused characters.

As detailed by Thomas Rostock in his commentary track for the 2018 Arrow Video DVD and Blu-ray releases of *Deep Red*, the scalding water may have been "fake" (an easily achieved practical effect), but the extreme lengths to which the Italian filmmaker went in order to make the victim's plight believable and her pain palpable crossed over into reality during shooting when actress Giuliana Calandra struggled to breathe underwater, having not fully prepared herself for the suddenness with which the director pushed her head down. Noting that Calandra "almost choked to death for real in this scene," Rostock draws attention to an oft-ignored aspect of cinematic horror, a genre so eager to please hardcore fans that, in trying to top previous onscreen depictions of gruesomely bad deaths, its creators sometimes push performers and crewmembers to their physical limits or into dangerous situations.

FAKING MORTALITY, SUSTAINING REAL INJURIES, AND *SURVIVING THE DEAD*

The movie was not very kind to her.
—SCOTT BECK, speaking with his cowriter/codirector Bryan Woods about the many physical knocks (including blows to the head) that lead actor Katie Stevens sustained during the making of *Haunt* (as part of an audio commentary featured on the Ronin Flix DVD and Blu-ray releases of the 2019 slasher film)

Examples of the kind of on-set injuries and unforeseen occurrences referenced above are too numerous to cite in their entirety and can be found tucked away (if not completely buried) in the production histories of widely celebrated classics like William Friedkin's *The Exorcist* (1973) as well as little-seen cult curios like the tellingly titled *The Unseen* (1980) and contemporary survival horror-thrillers like *Open Water* (2003). In the case of the latter film, actors Blanchard Ryan and Daniel Travis, playing a couple on a Caribbean vacation who have been left behind in shark-infested waters by their scuba-diving instructor, were outfitted in chain mail beneath their wetsuits and asked by their director, Chris Kentis, to float alongside *real* sharks (rather than rubber models or mechanical props) so that their fear might register as an authentic emotion.[5] In the case of the former film, not only did Friedkin force voice actor Mercedes McCambridge to record the demon Pazuzu's many growls and roars "under great duress" (by his own admission), but in striving to get his onscreen performers to deliver genuine emotions he also "slapped Father William O'Malley (Father Dyer) before a take [and] fired blanks from a gun to shock Jason Miller [who played Father Damien Karras]" (Glasby 2020, 37).[6] Add to this Friedkin's insistence that cinematographer Owen Roizman keep his camera focused on the film's lead, Ellen Burstyn, after her back had been injured in a stunt that required immediate medical attention, and one is left feeling more than a little conflicted—if not necessarily about *The Exorcist*'s vaunted position in the pantheon of great horror films, then about the rationales that are given by filmmakers who will stop at nothing (including putting their actors into a hypnotic trance, as writer-director Bernard Rose did to star Virginia Madsen during the making of the 1992 film *Candyman*) in order to make essentially unbelievable stories believable.

Throughout the making of *The Unseen*, a horror film that was saved from obscurity in 2008 thanks to home video distributor Code Red and then, a decade later, by Scorpion Releasing (a Blu-ray company that ported over the earlier disc's commentary track featuring producer Anthony B. Unger and actor Stephen Furst), safety protocols were lax and performers were often required to do their own stunts whenever director Danny Steinmann could not locate a double. During their conversation on the commentary track, Unger and Furst make light of the questionable decisions that they and other creative personnel made over the course of this film's production, and which led to both minor and serious consequences. Furst, who appears to have endured the most physical abuse in his role as the film's titular monster, admits to drinking dirty, bacteria-filled water from the floor of a basement (where many of his scenes were shot) and says that he continues having cardiac problems today as a result of being "nearly shocked to death" after Steinmann asked him to hit a breaker panel with all his force—an action that created real electrical sparks and knocked him to the ground but which was not used in the final version of *The Unseen*.⁷ The title of this film serves as a useful reminder that much of what happens "behind the scenes" or occurs "offscreen" (and which is typically consigned to the trivia heap by cultural historians who are primarily invested in what can be visually accounted for in the image) should be looked at and listened to with the same perceptual energy that we bring to more traditional modes of textual analysis.

In his foreword to the edited collection *Korean Horror Cinema*, Julian Stringer notes that, from the beginning of motion-picture history and in contexts not limited to the Korean peninsula, "directors, actors and other movie personnel have taken significant risks in pursuit of art—actions that have potentially brought them one step closer to death" (2013, ix). Referencing both classic and contemporary examples of South Korean horror, from the Golden Age classic *A Public Cemetery Under the Moon* (*Wolha-eui gongdongmyoji*, 1967), which features a scene in which a baby cries real tears after being held at knifepoint and being throttled by a woman, to latter-day commercial hits like Bong Joon-ho's *The Host* (*Gwoemul*, 2006), a Godzilla-inspired monster movie on which the poorly compensated extras were purportedly "subjected to hazardous working conditions," Stringer acknowledges that "constraints of time and money," compounded by other high-level stresses perhaps unique to horror film production, "sometimes conspire to propel filmmakers across the line separating safety from peril" (ix). This leads him to ponder if filmmaking is itself a "pathological" exercise akin to the murderous mayhem and monstrous actions on view in horror cinema. "Are movie directors sick? Is horror film production a disease?" Stringer asks, before concluding that "the genre functions at times as an allegory of itself, a series of audio-visual documents chronicling the risks and rewards that mark its own production. . . . Films conjure nightmares, but making them can itself be a daymare" (ix–x). Indeed, even when it results in less-tragic outcomes (for instance, prosthetic makeup artist Rob Bottin's hospitalization following a physically exhausting workload as the special effects coordinator on *The Thing*, which led to him getting double pneumonia from the extreme temperature changes on top of a bleeding ulcer), horror-film productions affect the bodies of their *creators* as surely as their completed work impacts the bodies of spectators.

Many horror fans are well-versed in the history of production-related injuries and near-deaths (not to mention actual deaths, including that of stunt performer Sonja Davis, who was critically injured during the making of Wes Craven's *Vampire in Brooklyn* [1995]), though the topic is rarely covered in scholarly studies of the genre (Stringer's short excogitation notwithstanding). However, the subject is frequently broached in the various paratexts surrounding horror films, including those that are included as special bonus features on DVDs and Blu-rays like Arrow Video's 2018 remastering of *Deep Red* and the same company's earlier two-disc version of *Tenebrae*, which, as Simon Hobbs notes in his book *Cultivating Extreme Art Cinema*, promised (in its own rhetorically unrestrained ad copy) to restore Argento's 1982 *giallo* to its "depraved glory" and "[drench] the viewer in crimson arterial spray" (2018, 59). On more than one occasion while listening to a director's commentary track on a horror film's home-video release, I have learned about instances when actors and other members of a production's creative team were injured as a result of on-set accidents and failures to uphold safety regulations (including the use of real instruments of destruction in lieu of prop weapons/tools, as was the case during the making of Tobe Hooper's *The Texas Chain Saw Massacre* [1974] and John Carpenter's *The Thing*). Although Rob Bottin was the only member of the crew to experience serious health setbacks owing to his work on *The Thing*, Carpenter admits (in his running commentary on Universal's region 1 DVD and Blu-ray releases) that several members of the all-male cast were severely tested during the physically grueling shoot, from breathing in pungent smoke to burning their hands on flares; and Kurt Russell, the film's lead actor (who shares commentary duties with the director), jokes that if he ever gets cancer he'll know he got it from being on this film's set.

Putting a slightly grimmer spin on what Scott Beck, one of the cowriters and codirectors of the 2019 slasher film *Haunt*, said about the physical knocks suffered by lead actor Katie Stevens during the making of that movie (quoted above), *Halloween II* (2009) writer-director Rob Zombie states, "I'm surprised we didn't kill her, actually," in reference to his lead actor, Scout Taylor-Compton. Specifically, Zombie is referring to Taylor-Compton's willingness to shoot her cold, rainy night scenes while wearing nothing but a hospital gown (without a protective wetsuit underneath), shivering in between takes for a period of several hours. Besides gamely putting up with freezing temperatures and risking pneumonia, she opted to do much of her own stunt work throughout the making of this sequel to a remake of the original *Halloween* (1978), throwing herself down several flights of stairs in a scene involving her character, Laurie Strode, trying to escape the clutches of Michael Myers (Tyler Mane). According to Zombie (who shares this information on the commentary track of his film's DVD and Blu-ray releases), Taylor-Compton took it as a challenge to "outfall the stunt girl," a member of the second unit whose physically demanding work on the film was left on the cutting room floor as a result of the actor's willingness to put her own neck on the line (literally) and essentially double for her double.

Although I will explore this emergent area of horror film hermeneutics—scholars' reliance on DVD and Blu-ray supplemental features and other forms of paratextual meaning-making in the course of (re)constituting a more holistic version of the cinematic body—a bit later, it is worth returning one last time to *Deep Red*, specifically to that image of Giuliana Calandra's head being dunked into the bathtub. Boiling or not, the water inside that tub roils with the intensity of someone who might actually be fighting for her life, struggling to survive an attack that—though aimed at Calandra's character (Amanda) and not herself—carries an affective charge equaled only by the visceral impact of witnessing Janet Leigh's Marion getting stabbed at least eight times in *Psycho*. Made fifteen years after Hitchcock's ostensibly peerless thriller, Argento's *Deep Red* has since been hailed as the first (and perhaps only) film to "out-psycho *Psycho*" (Kannas 2017, 10), but its status as such comes at the price of abstracting the physical labor required of onscreen talent and offscreen crew members (whose names are not as well-known as that of the director). It might also necessitate turning a "blind eye" to larger ethical issues concerning the use (or abuse) of actors' and stunt performers' bodies for the sake of entertainment. With Argento's own gloved hands doing the deadly deed, similar to the way that a close-up shot of writer-director Mark Rosman's hand shows him holding an actual scalpel to a real pregnant woman's tummy in his 1982 horror film *The House on Sorority Row* (information that is likewise conveyed via Blu-ray commentary track), the already troubled concept of cinematic authorship gets further complicated by the corporeal demands of making movies in which bodily destruction and images of death are seen as a filmmaker's forte, part of that person's "signature style" as an artist with his or her hands on nearly every aspect of production.

Although such ethical conundrums are not unique to the world of cinematic horror, the genre raises these and other issues in a powerfully evocative way. Horror films ask spectators to engage subjects that are not always pleasant but which might, in the end, bring us face to face with our own mortality, or at least spark a heightened awareness of *other people's bodies* before our own bodies expire. Nowhere is this more clearly expressed than on the director's commentary track included on the Anchor Bay and Lionsgate DVD and Blu-ray releases of *The Dead* (2010), a zombie film written and directed by Howard J. Ford and Jon Ford. Referred to by one reviewer (writing for the website Dread Central) as "one of the single most interesting commentary tracks you're likely to listen to" (Barton 2012), this bonus feature is less a side dish than a meal unto itself, chock-full of insights into how the two filmmaking siblings managed to complete their low-budget labor of love—one in which there was much love lost—and survive a troubled, deeply *troubling* production plagued with illness and disease. Though hyperbolic as a designation of what other directors and their cast and crew might experience whenever they film on location in areas of the world far removed from comfort zones, the word "survive" is accurate in this instance, putting mildly what the British-born Ford brothers faced in the West African nation of Burkina Faso over a three-month shoot. Indeed, so

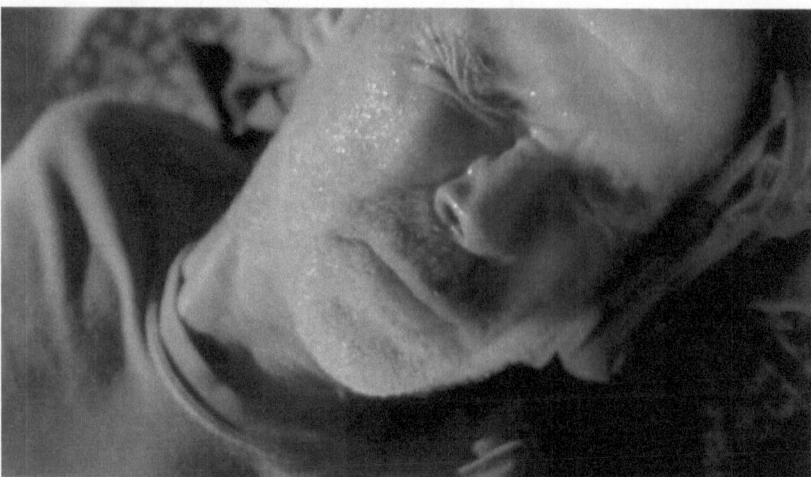

Figure 4.5. This shot from the Ford Brothers' zombie film *The Dead* (2010) shows Rob Freeman sweating profusely and writhing in pain, the result of the actor contracting malaria and almost dying during the production.

harrowing was the experience that Howard J. Ford wrote a book, *Surviving the Dead* (2012), which details the many setbacks that not only threatened to derail production and push the brothers deeper into debt but also nearly ended the life of the lead actor, Rob Freeman.

Playing a US Air Force engineer named Brian Murphy, the actor contracted malaria during the shoot, making the scenes in which he sweats profusely while writhing in pain (after his character has sustained injuries as the sole survivor of a failed evacuation effort) brim with realism. Indeed, watching Lieutenant Murphy succumb to fictional disease and dramatic weight loss is like stumbling upon a documentary of the real thing (figure 4.5). When done in the virtual company of the codirectors (via an audio commentary), as they open up about the fact that Freeman, gravely ill, began to hallucinate during the production (thinking that they were plotting to kill him), such spectatorship is compromised or at the very least *complicated* by feelings of complicity that arise from the question of whether one should be deriving pleasure from the film or even be *watching* it in the first place. Had they not driven the actor to a doctor at a hospital in time, he most certainly would have died, the Fords fess up, acknowledging that their otherwise laudable quest for authenticity led them to do things (such as filming voodoo rituals and village scenes involving the "real remains" of dead people and the "rotting flesh" of animal corpses, the smell of which "permeated everything") that would have been forbidden in their home country of England. "It had to feel *real*," one of the brothers stresses during the commentary, providing a rationale for why Freeman, who at one point actually defecated on himself in his boiler suit, was asked by them to

Figure 4.6. Many of the zombies in *The Dead* (2010) are played by local amputees with emaciated bodies from the Burkina Faso area, and the fantastical terror that they are intended to evoke is linked to their real-world physical conditions.

suck real petrol from a tube (so that his character can gas up his vehicle and escape a zombie attack).

Similar excuses have been made by other filmmakers whose desire to boost the believability of unbelievable scenarios prompted irresponsible, unethical activities on the set. But what makes the making of *The Dead* so fascinating is how the Ford brothers' commitment to verisimilitude spread like an infectious disease throughout the cast and crew, who not only put up with giant cockroaches inside the village huts where several scenes were set, freak weather conditions that caused numerous delays, violent muggings, countless roadblocks, and extreme privation, but also suffered heat stroke, food poisoning-related diarrhea, dysentery, and (in the case of one extra who appears in the background of a few shots) typhoid fever. Someone on the production (they do not specify who) lost a finger when a gun fell, and other people with disabilities—amputees and other locals who were asked to play zombies owing to their missing limbs or emaciated physiques—are depicted in ways that problematically focus on their "freakishness" (e.g., in the opening scene, one man's thin leg can be seen bending backwards) (figure 4.6). Add to this the fact that the filmmakers' prized 35mm camera (which they used throughout the first half of production) broke midway through and that a significant portion of their roughly $150,000 budget (not $2 to 5 million, which has been reported by some journalists) went toward bribing corrupt officials, and one begins to see just how remarkable it is that *The Dead* ever got completed and was released to theaters between the fall of 2010 and the fall of 2011 (mainly at horror-themed film festivals attended by fans who would appreciate the Fords' unusual if not revisionist take on postapocalyptic zombie cinema). As indicated on the DVD and Blu-ray commentary tracks, the process of making *The Dead* was not just frustrating but *embittering*, and the filmmakers' willingness to share such details makes it possible for the listener at home to both admire their dedication to getting the work done and blame them for allowing the work of making a horror film to have such a devastating effect on the crewmembers' bodies (including their own).

Not every filmmaker is as candid as this when it comes to admitting to mistakes and acknowledging that (in the words of one of the Ford brothers) "there wasn't much in the way of health and safety on this production." But when directors use their commentary tracks in this way, one is left feeling conflicted about the very act of viewing upon which most motion pictures are commercially reliant. One is also left to ponder what is *not* being said, with the recognition that, just as there were people, "right off camera, vomiting their guts out" during the making of *The Dead*, there must surely be unspoken aspects related to the many other real bodies behind this body genre—aspects that do not make their way onto a commentary track. To be sure, there is something utterly compelling about *The Dead* or any other fictional work whose production-related "daymares" (to use Julian Stringer's term) are as disturbing as any narratively contained nightmare. Similarly, there is something deliciously seductive about *Deep Red*, and Argento—christened by many fans as the "Italian Hitchcock"—was undoubtedly accomplished at drawing spectators into an "irrational world lurking just beyond the boundaries of perception" through imagery that, in another director's hands, might otherwise repel those same viewers (Newman 2011, 145). As contradictory as horror is (at once regressive and progressive, possibly even *transgressive* if also politically reactionary in some respects), it is no more paradoxical than our own spectatorial impulses to both *see* and *not see* its many hideous, frequently humorous, sometimes life-threatening things. But to limit our study of this body genre to visual images and sight alone is to ignore other experiential aspects of horror, an oversight that I hope to at least partially correct throughout the remainder of this book.

In the next chapter, I explore some of the cultural, social, and political implications of scenes in which not only eyes but ears are brutally damaged or removed from the bodies of those individuals or groups who, ironically, often go *unseen* and *unheard* by many horror film audiences. This is owing to their relative "invisibility" and "muteness" within an industrially circumscribed, racially homogenous production context that, in keeping with horror's tendency to view outsiders as monstrous threats to the status quo, can sometimes be inhospitable to anyone whose visible difference might be read as "excess." From ethnic minorities to people with disabilities and nonhuman animals whose physical presence is often abstracted as an allegorical means of emphasizing the mortal dangers or moral quandaries faced by white, straight, able-bodied humans (historically, the horror film's privileged focalizers, doubly so in terms of being narrative and social beneficiaries of others' exclusion), representations *matter* in this genre as surely as they do elsewhere. But to follow through on my earlier discussion of the hidden costs and human (as well as nonhuman) consequences of making horror films—indeed, to further underscore their relevance as a body genre—necessitates turning our attention to those scenes that are the most difficult to watch.

5

SLICED EYEBALLS AND SEVERED EARS

On (Not) Seeing and (Not) Hearing Horror Films

"Would you look at this? Something's been butchered up here."
"Let's hope it was an animal."
—two cops upon entering a blood-filled room where a boy has just decapitated his mother with an axe, in
Juan Piquer Simón's slasher film *Pieces* (aka, *The Night Has 1,000 Screams; Mil gritos tiene la noche,* 1982)

To quote Michael Stipe, lead singer of the rock group R.E.M., "everybody hurts" in horror films. More often than not, fictional characters—to say nothing about the actors who play them—find themselves on the receiving end of deadly weapons and other threats to one's life or physical well-being. In some cases, hands, arms, legs, and other appendages get severed or go missing, and no amount of preparation seems to suffice when it comes to warding off the inevitable attack that will bring bodily damage and/or emotional trauma (if not outright death) to one or more of a film's main characters as well as the "monster" (human or otherwise) responsible for all or most of the mayhem. "Blood flows freely and limbs detach easily," to borrow the words of Joe Baltake of the *Philadelphia Daily News*, whose review of Sergio Martino's 1973 *giallo* film *Torso* (*I corpi presentano tracce di violenza carnale*, literally translated as "The Bodies Bear Traces of Carnal Violence") puts plainly what I have been at pains to explain in this book. Less frequently remarked upon by reviewers who take a dismissive view of the genre is the fact that *laughter*, too, "flows freely" in theatrical venues and other settings where groups of people gather to watch horror films. Those viewers might include hardcore fans who, like so many lopped-off limbs (and regardless of their immersion in a given story), are able to "easily detach" themselves from the spectacle of fictional misery or death and take *pleasure* in the craft, ingenuity, and intrepidity required to pull off certain special effects.

In fact, horror films frequently aid in that paradoxically passionate detachment by reminding viewers that what they are about to witness, as grisly as it might be, is rooted in fantasy and not to be taken too seriously. Consider, for instance, some of the many films that have been "Rated R for Vampire Violence" by the Motion Picture Association of America (MPAA) over the past three decades, such as *Interview with a Vampire* (1994), *Blade* (1998), *Queen of the Damned* (2002), and *Dracula III: Legacy* (2005), which include scenes of neck-biting, heart-staking, flesh-burning action, as one might expect (and would presumably be pleased to see). Although other elements, including strong language, sexuality, and nudity, played a part in the MPAA's (now MPA) decision to hand the producers of these films a "Restricted" rating, the American trade association's use of the expression "Vampire Violence" acknowledges that all of the bloodshed on display in this particular subgenre of cinematic horror is a fundamentally *different* type of violence than that of action films, crime dramas, murder mysteries, thrillers, and Westerns. And part of that difference derives from the genre's very excessiveness: the idea that an extravagant number of beastly acts resulting in bodies being bloodied, bruised, and disassembled will occur over the course of a narrative that strains to hold itself together nearly as much as it stretches credulity. Not for nothing did Linda Williams title her pioneering essay about horror as a body genre, "Film Bodies: Gender, Genre, and Excess" (1991, 2–13).

"Vampire Violence" is the reason why director Wes Craven's *Vampire in Brooklyn* (1995) received an R rating, and anyone who watches this broadly farcical take on the familiar Dracula (or Nosferatu) story will understand what that phrase connotes, thanks to requisite scenes of the fanged foreigner—arriving by steamship from a Caribbean Island rather than Transylvania—prowling the streets and sewers in search of prey and leaving drained corpses (in this case, those of Italian American gangsters) in his wake. Here, the goateed bloodsucker Maximillian is played by Eddie Murphy, a former standup comedian and *SNL* star whose presence in the film ensures a certain tongue-in-cheek approach to vampiric seduction and physical transformation (figure 5.1). Besides Max's ability to shapeshift into a wolf and other animals as well as humans, his Renfield-like lackey, Julius (Kadeem Hardison), displays his own ghoulish aptitude for bodily change, gradually losing organs and limbs after drinking a few drops of his master's blood and becoming undead. Between snacks of crunchy cockroaches, he loses one of his ears, then one of his hands, and then his hair before an eyeball pops out of its socket only to get squished underfoot. His is a humorously excessive type of physical decline, reminiscent of the multiple stages of deterioration endured by the undead backpacker Jack Goodman (Griffin Dunne) in the comedy-horror film *An American Werewolf in London* (1981). Leading up to his fateful transformation and confronted by

Figure 5.1. Sex and physical attraction are central to the vampire film, as are the kinds of actions that might earn a motion picture an R rating for "Vampire Violence" (e.g., neck-biting, heart-staking, flesh-burning, etc.).

the prospect of being bitten by this newly arrived immigrant, Julius does his best to delay the inevitable, nervously telling the hungry vampire, "I won't tell nobody I saw you 'cause I can't really see. I'm blind. I got cataracts—contacts. I got astigmatism, man. I can't see, man, I'm blind. Where you at? Where you at?" Playing blindness as a defense measure (but also for a laugh), the character, performed by Hardison in a way that reminded some reviewers of a vaudeville comedian (Rosenberg 1995), ironically sets himself up for the loss of that eye—the final stage of a gruesome decomposition that began with the loss of his ear (figure 5.2).

The shot of Julius's severed organ on the grimy floor of a New York City sewer, discovered by two NYPD detectives investigating a recent rash of murders, recalls other instances in which a human ear is found somewhere far removed from its natural resting place. The first scene of David Lynch's neonoir mystery thriller *Blue Velvet* (1986) leaps to mind, as it shows college student Jeffrey Beaumont (Kyle MacLachlan) stumbling upon a severed ear on his way home from the hospital. The decomposing body part, partially hidden in the tall grass of a vacant lot, is overrun with black ants, an image that harkens back to the artwork of Spanish surrealist Salvador Dalí. Equally surrealistic is Alejandro Jodorowsky's *Santa Sangre* (1989), a feature-length blending of avant-garde experimentation and gothic horror shot in Mexico City that shows a man removing his prosthetic ear and trying to shove it down the throat of a deaf-mute girl—one of many instances in the film, according to one reviewer, when ostensibly silly ideas are broached as a way to go "straight to the subconscious" (Murray 2011). More recently, Declan O'Brien's *Wrong Turn 5: Bloodlines* (2012)

Figure 5.2. Performed with comedic flourish by Kadeem Hardison, the Renfield-like underling of the title character in *Vampire in Brooklyn* (1995) loses an ear after drinking a few drops of his master's blood and becoming undead.

features an ear-eating scene early in its narrative, a moment of unadulterated excess topped only by a head-mowing scene near the end. Several additional contemporary films could be cited as further evidence of horror's excessiveness as a genre that seems to take pleasure in going after this and other sensing organs. However, a more apt comparison to *Vampire in Brooklyn* can be found by venturing back to a much earlier motion picture that likewise hinges upon an ostensibly humorous—yet historically resonant—act of violence directed against an African American man.

That film, *Spider Baby* (1967), was written and directed by Jack Hill, who would go on to distinguish himself as a white blaxploitation auteur during the early 1970s (stepping behind the lens of the Pam Grier vehicles *Coffy* [1973] and *Foxy Brown* [1974]). Nevertheless, as an example of "psychotronic" 1960s-era cinema, *Spider Baby* seems oddly regressive next to other civil rights-era horror films featuring African American characters (such as George A. Romero's *Night of the Living Dead* [1968] and Bill Gunn's *Ganja & Hess* [1973]), and not only because it was made three years prior to its belated theatrical release. Adopting a darkly comedic mode, *Spider Baby* concerns a trio of orphaned adult siblings whose temperamental outbursts, brought about by a genetic condition unique to their inbred family (the "Merrye Syndrome," which has made them regress mentally and physically ever since they were youngsters), have begun turning violent. This makes the work of their caretaker—family chauffeur Bruno (Lon Chaney Jr.)—increasingly difficult as the narrative lurches toward its literally explosive ending, which kills off the kid-like killers through Bruno's self-sacrificing use of dynamite. The title character of this off-kilter cult film (which Hill had originally considered titling *Attack of the Liver Eaters* or *Cannibal Orgy*) is one of the three siblings, a delusional young woman named Virginia (Jill Banner) who is so obsessed with spiders that she becomes a human arachnid, eating bugs and trapping victims in her web-like net before "stinging" them to death with butcher knives.

That very thing happens in the opening scene, when an unnamed deliveryman (played by the well-known African American character actor Mantan Moreland), stops off at the Merrye house to deliver a message. Peeking into an open window of the decrepit mansion's parlor, he suddenly finds himself caught in the woman's web. In the process of brutally killing the man, whose upper torso is pinned by the window, Virginia uses her "stinger" to hack off one of his ears, which drops to the floor in a zoom shot that accentuates the unforeseen excessiveness of this initial burst of violence (figure 5.3).

As Robin R. Means Coleman, author of *Horror Noire: Blacks in American Horror Films from the 1890s to Present*, explains, *Spider Baby* is a "throwback" to 1940s narratives, including those that Moreland—a former vaudevillian-turned-film actor famous for his bug-eyed performances of fear—had appeared in, such as *King of the Zombies* (1941) and *Revenge of the Zombies* (1943). In those and other wartime productions, African American characters were often "spooked and abused for comic effect" (2011, 103). With his dangling legs flailing about outside the window "in slapstick manner," Moreland participates in this mid-Sixties reenactment of a much earlier mode of cultural representation, using his brief cameo role to resurrect his comically suffering characters from decades past. But the Black deliveryman's ear, lopped off in a fit of near-orgasmic excitement by a white character who will keep it as a souvenir, also brings to light a dark chapter in US history, when African Americans faced open hostility in the South (including in Virginia's namesake state) and sometimes bore the brunt of that hostility on their bodies.

As victims of lynch mob violence, Black men and women confronted horrors that put the relatively minor concerns of film analysis in proper perspective. Nevertheless, the significance of cinema lies partly in how it helps audiences to see and hear real-world terrors of the past that continue to resonate in the present day. Although the practice of "cropping"—removing a person's ears as a form of criminal punishment (even for minor offenses)—dates back several hundred years in other parts of the world, its adoption in rural areas of Alabama, Mississippi, Virginia, and other Southern states around the turn of the twentieth century was specifically tied to a post-Reconstruction surge in white supremacy and anti-Black vigilante violence. As documented by several historians of chattel slavery's enduring legacies in the Jim Crow South, African Americans would sometimes be shown the severed ears of lynching victims (including those of their own kin) as an intimidation tactic—a reminder of

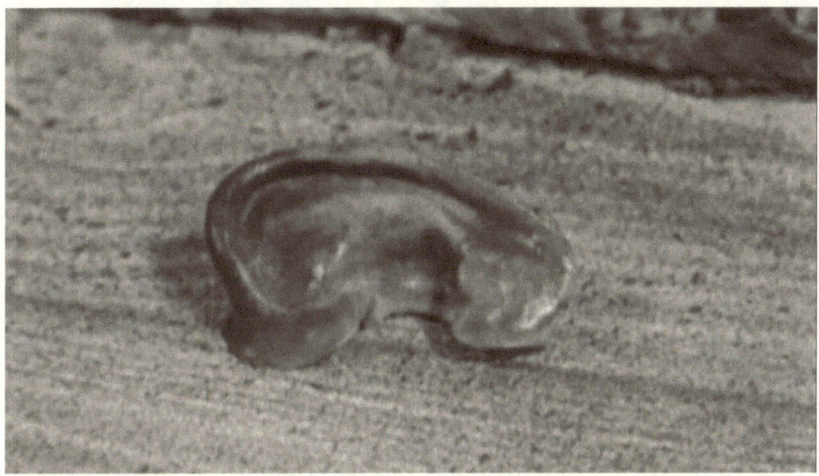

Figure 5.3. In *Spider Baby* (1967), comic legend Mantan Moreland's unnamed deliveryman character loses an ear when a member of the Merrye family lashes out at him with a knife. This shot of the detached body part (a prosthetic) conjures the very real pain associated with anti-Black vigilante violence in the Deep South (where victims' ears would sometimes be collected as "keepsakes" by members of the KKK and other hate groups after the turn of the twentieth century).

what they would face if they ever forgot their "place" in a racially stratified society (McCloud 2010, 638; Young 2005, 639–57). In many cases, the detached organs, scavenged from the bodies of individuals who were burned alive or hanged to death, were treasured as souvenirs by those who benefited from the continued exploitation of ethnic minorities, making Virginia's act of cutting off and then keeping the deliveryman's ear in the first scene of *Spider Baby* all the more disturbing.

Based on what Jack Hill states in the director's audio commentary featured on the DVD and Blu-ray releases of *Spider Baby*, none of those historical contexts or troubling implications crossed his mind during the making of the film. Instead, he simply sought to pay tribute to the comic stylings of a studio-era character actor who was fortunate enough to land lead roles in a few race movies during the 1940s (such as the comedy-horror film *Lucky Ghost* [1942]) and whose catchphrase, "Feets, don't fail me now" (which Hill quotes during the commentary) had actually been a fixture of Black burlesque stage performances since before the time of those turn-of-the-century acts of mob violence. In fact, Hill makes a point of noting that the detached ear that appears in close-up belonged to an unnamed member of the film's white crew, one of several prosthetics that the Korean War veteran had lent to the director as a prop to be "darkened" so to match the color of Moreland's skin. Even if one were to put aside the sociopolitical suggestiveness of this fleshy remnant-turned-keepsake, as a "comic prop" belonging to a war vet it still bears consideration for the way that it materializes the past (in this case, a midcentury "police action" that cost combatants their lives and limbs) and registers the physical presence of a real person offscreen (despite it being "fake"). As such, the prosthetic ear that appears in *Spider Baby* is in keeping with what historian-phenomenologist Harvey Young refers to as a racial souvenir. The latter is a fetish object collected by white onlookers or participants at public lynchings (who took not only the ears but also the fingers, toes, teeth, and other parts of Black people) that is not reducible to a single meaning, and which ensures that the damaged and/or violated body "never entirely disappears" (Young 2005, 648).

Such contextualizing also seems remote from what Wes Craven and the other creative talent responsible for *Vampire in Brooklyn* (including star Eddie Murphy, who also produced the film and cowrote the story with his brother Charlie Murphy) had in mind. Nevertheless, as the first mainstream vampire movie to feature an African American male lead since the 1972 release of *Blacula*,[1] *Vampire in Brooklyn* is perhaps unfairly burdened with expectations about its representational politics. The film's script, in fact, leans into the allegorical potential of vampire narratives to convey real-world horrors by including a comically infused yet deadly encounter between Max and two gun-toting Italian American mobsters in a dark alleyway. It is there, on the mean streets of New York, where the main character—after being shot five times in the torso—explains that this is his first time to be knocked down by bullets. "I've been stabbed, I've been hanged, and I've been burned, even broken on the rack once," Max says, dusting himself off by this minor inconvenience, "but I've never been shot before." His words, delivered a few seconds before he rips the heart out from one of the men's chests, conjures the kind of bodily trauma associated with racist violence in the United States. This interpretation is lent corporeal support once Julius (the street-savvy sidekick whom Max saved from the two gangsters) begins seeing his body parts drop off, one by one, beginning with his ear. Importantly, *Vampire in Brooklyn* treats Julius's physical pathologies—his incrementally decomposing state as an undead body taking on one form of disability after another (from partial losses of hearing and sight to amputation)—as a running gag. As such, it parallels another problematic tendency apparent in this and other horror films, which see comic potential in the endlessly exploited presence of animals—be they creatures of the wild or domesticated pets whose physical pain or outright destruction is sometimes intended as a joke.

For example, Max at one point is approached by a policeman's guard dog named Killer, who stops and stares at the vampire-in-hiding as if sensing his true nature. Without a word, Max makes Killer fly up several hundred feet in the air, leaving only the dog's collar and leash behind. It is a moment of cruel violence for which audiences are unprepared, and because of the sheer suddenness and absurdity of the act, they are expected to laugh. A similar, knee-jerk-like instance of comically absurd animal cruelty occurs when a cat named Sugar, agitated by Max's presence, leaps off a table toward him, only to be shot mid-jump by the vampire. The fact that both of these animals had been given names by their human companions suggests that their deaths will result in emotional pain, although any outward sign of that pain (in the form of tears, for instance) would not only be inconsistent with this horror film's generally comedic tone, but also a stumbling block that might slow down its fast-paced narrative (in which there is no time to linger on the consequences of death). The same cannot be said about the cockroach that is consumed by Julius at one point in *Vampire in Brooklyn*, since that order of insects—the lowest of the low—is commonly looked upon as a pest to be eradicated for the sake of human comfort. Though a real cockroach is shown scuttling away from the famished character, the American Humane Association (AHA), which had a representative on set to monitor this and other animal-related scenes during the film's production, confirms that a fake one was used "when Julius is seen eating [it]." As I will explain later in this chapter, other contemporary films—including an equally humorous vampire movie rooted in fantasy but bold enough to show *actual cockroaches* being eaten—have received "unacceptable" ratings not from the MPAA but from the AHA, indicating how much work remains to be done to ensure the safety and welfare of *all* creatures on sets that are sometimes as dangerous as their fictional locations.

Even though we know that "no animals were harmed" during the making of *Vampire in Brooklyn* (as we are informed via an onscreen disclaimer that will be familiar to anyone who sits through the closing credits of movies), there is still something unnerving about witnessing fictional acts of violence directed against nonhumans. This is partly due to the fact that the makeup and special effects teams tasked with making fake animals and flying fur seem so believable (in this case, the team included Robert Kurtzman, Gregory Nicotero, and a host of other respected artists) succeed at prompting the audience to question what they are seeing. Today's makeup artists have come a long way from the Hollywood studio system era, when something as simple as cheesecloth coated with green greasepaint and spirit gum could be glued to an actor's face to transform him or her into a monster as iconic as Frankenstein's hideous progeny (as legendary craftsman Jack Pierce did with Boris Karloff at Universal Studios during the 1930s). Special effects teams now have an array of tools at their disposal to help bring any creature to life and to recreate the look of real body parts—including the ear (something easily crafted from foam latex or silicone rubber)—deemed essential to our sensorial, spectatorial pleasure.

In an earlier chapter, I suggested that, in the United States the motion-picture industry's gravitation toward computer-generated imagery (CGI) beginning in the late 1980s and early 1990s, not unlike a similar shift toward sound film production in the late 1920s and early 1930s, brought with it a backlash among those creative personnel who felt then—and continue to feel today (if their commentaries on recently released DVD and Blu-ray releases are to be believed)—that the artistry of a previous mode of cinematic storytelling was being left behind in the rush to accommodate change or incorporate new technologies into that most ancient of human activities: storytelling. Just as there was a widespread feeling that the art of motion pictures was set back, rather than advanced, by moving away from silent film production, so too has a kind of consensus built up against CGI as a technically superior but artistically inferior way to bring horror's monstrous creatures and bloody "bad deaths" to life. Both of those shifts had enormous impacts on the horror genre during its classical and postclassical phases, respectively, entailing sensorial recalibrations on the part of audiences who would thereafter need to attend to cinematic images and sounds differently. If the industry-wide introduction of sound in motion pictures nearly 100 years ago was an affront to the eye, then that organ was soon returned to its presumably "rightful" place as the chief means of discerning the *believability* of scenarios, especially once the clean, comparatively weightless, computer-generated visual effects of the 1990s and more recent productions began to encroach upon the messy, smelly "thingness" of mechanical effects and sticky prosthetics.

ANIMALS' EYES, TRAUMATIZED

> Close your eyes. And whatever happens, *don't look.*
> —JOHN CONSTANTINE (Keanu Reeves), speaking to a group of men who are helping him
> to exorcise a demon from a young woman, in *Constantine* (2005)

Cinema's greatest affront to eye—one that has inspired countless imitators ever since it first appeared onscreen at the Studio des Ursulines in Paris nearly one hundred years ago—occurs at the beginning of a film that marked the end of the silent era in a decidedly grisly way. Conceived by Spanish filmmaker Luis Buñuel and surrealist painter Salvador Dalí as a non-rational thought experiment aimed not only at the pacifying, convention-laden storytelling that had taken root in film industries around the world but also at other purveyors of an increasingly toothless cinematic avant-garde who had fallen victim to pseudo-intellectualism and bourgeois tastes, *Un Chien Andalou* (*An Andalusian Dog*, 1929) is a landmark work of underground horror whose reputation has only grown since its auspicious debut. Some historians might take issue with my generic classification, raising their pitchforks in protest to remind me that "*Un Chien Andalou* is not a horror film" (Grant 2007, 5). Throughout much of the second half of the twentieth century, that latter statement, made by Barry Keith Grant in one of the finest, most perceptive essays ever written about Buñuel and Dalí's collaborative masterpiece, would not have been widely disputed, in part because horror was for so long written off as a lowly, cliché-ridden category of cultural production whereas the literally cutting-edge quality of that European art film—its radically unconventional use of dream imagery, which slices into the viewer's perception as swiftly as an actual razor blade does an eyeball—seemed to elevate it above the very notion of "genre." And yet, as Grant himself notes, *Un Chien Andalou* features "one of the most horrifically abject moments in film history" (5), a physical attack that was, by design, meant to upset audiences, and which was aimed at what Stephen King once called "the most vulnerable of our sensory organs" (2010, 203).

I am referring, of course, to the infamous eye-slice scene that serves as *Un Chien Andalou*'s prologue, a series of twelve shots (which together comprise only a small portion of the film's twenty-one-minute running time) that culminates with gooey gelatinous fluid—the vitreous humor behind the lens of the eye—spilling out of the corneal cut in extreme close-up. So well-known and intertextually cited is this scene that it hardly seems necessary to describe it. In fact, mere description alone is enough to disturb even the least squeamish of readers. However, it helps to recall how little screen time the audience has to prepare for what they are about to see, even when they *know* the "cut" is coming (literally in the form of the razor's movement and figuratively in the form of the film's swift editing).

Following an opening-credits sequence that lasts forty-five seconds, the film's first French intertitle, "Il était une fois" ("Once upon a time"), flashes on screen, suggesting that what is about to unfold is a children's fairy tale. Yet what follows, while fantastical and even whimsically absurd at times, is worlds away from the wonderment that one might associate with that literary genre. Instead, a man smoking a cigarette is shown sharpening a long razor on a strop attached to a door handle. This banal activity serves to contrast the horrific display of bodily trauma to come, once he opens the door to the balcony outside. Stepping out to take in the view, he casts his gaze to the moon above, smoke billowing from his cigarette in a way that emulates the vaporous clouds beginning to crowd out that nighttime beacon. Suddenly, a close-up frontal shot of a woman's passive face appears onscreen, with an undisclosed figure positioned behind her. He holds a razor blade in his right hand, dangerously close to her face, while he uses his other hand to lift the woman's left eyelid. As the weapon begins to slide to the woman's right, another rapid cut, back to the moon (this time with a sliver of cloud moving across it), interrupts the diegesis, only to be quickly followed by the aforementioned extreme close-up of the jelly-like substance spilling out from the sliced eyeball as the hand completes its horizontal movement (Williams 1976, 26–27).

Echoing Barry Keith Grant's earlier comment, William V. Costanzo refers to this precise moment, which is part of a scene that runs a mere sixty seconds, as "one of the most horrifying images ever caught on celluloid" (2014, 218). And like Grant, who compares *Un Chien Andalou* to Hitchcock's *Psycho* (1960)—another masterpiece whose images are as much an "assault on the spectator's sensibility, taking us completely by surprise," as the slashing attacks directed against women's bodies in the two films—Costanzo links Buñuel and Dalí's "scary" surrealist short to subsequent feature-length productions that sit more comfortably within the horror film canon. Those include movies that it directly inspired, such as Georges Franju's *Eyes Without a Face* (*Les yeux sans visage*, 1960) and Guillermo del Toro's *Pan's Labyrinth* (*El laberinto del fauno*, 2006), the latter an actual celluloid fairy tale deserving of that "Il était une fois" intertitle. Besides Costanzo, several scholars have drawn comparisons between *Un Chien Andalou* and other motion pictures that most people would typically classify as "horror," including international works of high artistic standing that were made before and after its 1929 release (everything from *The Cabinet of Dr. Caligari* [*Das Cabinet des Dr. Caligari*, 1920] and *Häxan* [*The Witches*, 1922] to *Ring* [*Ringu*, 1998]) (Mathijs and Mendik 2008, 165; Lowenstein 2014, 97) as well as Hollywood studio productions that came out around the same time that it was first distributed to US theaters (such as Universal's *Frankenstein*, the "surreal credit sequence" of which depicts several rotating eyes circling the face of a "weirdly exotic figure") (Perry 2017, 145–46).

Notably, John Dee, an American film critic writing for the trade magazine *The Bioscope* in May of 1931, referred to *Un Chien Andalou* as a "surrealist horror film," but he seemed less than enthused by the fact that the genre had become "the next big thing" in Hollywood (1931, 37). In Dee's words, "Screen stories grow more and more sophisticated every month, depending for their 'shock tactics' on calloused attitudes towards sex, crime and death." Using a phrase that typifies much of the writing about motion pictures at that time, he labels titillating yet objectionable movies about sex, crime, and death as "strong meat," a description that foregrounds how horror, even at this early point in the genre's "evolution," revolved around negative bodily experiences, including "revulsion" (which he singles out as a specialty of Buñuel, only a couple of years into his filmmaking career) (37). As a *New York Times* correspondent based in Paris at that time, Morris Gilbert likewise described *Un Chien Andalou* as a "horror film" dealing with "varying degrees of putrefaction and carnality" (1930, X6). His "Parisian Cinema Chatter" piece, published in the national newspaper of record on February 9, 1930, reveals how deeply the film's prologue had seared

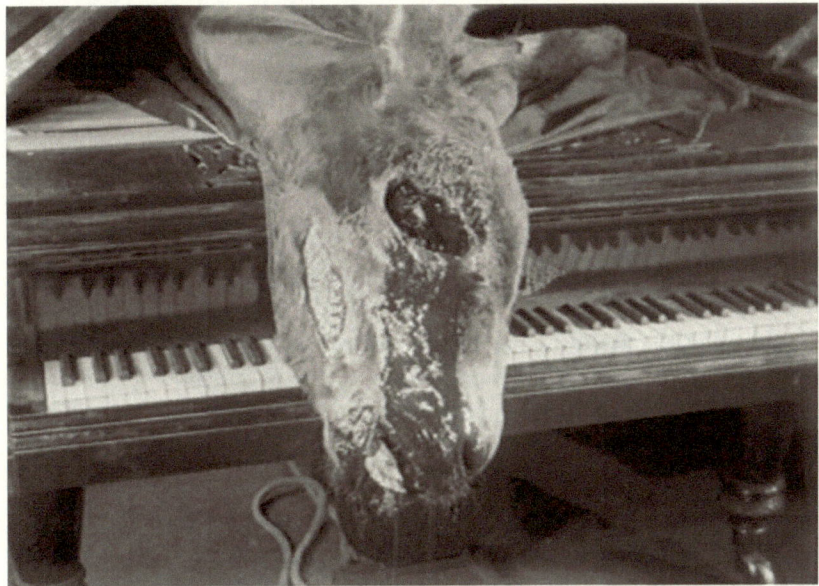

Figure 5.4. The bodies of dead animals have been used as props and generative sources of meaning in horror films since the earliest days of the genre, dating back to European art films of the 1920s, such as *Un Chien Andalou* (1929).

itself onto the retinas of its first scandalized viewers, and that the "horror" of *Un Chien Andalou* "does not depend on plot in any sense, since there is none; or on suspense, since there is none—except the fear in the audience that it may see again, before the picture is over, the same, or a *worse*, incident which passed across the film within the first two minutes of its unrolling" (Gilbert 1930, X6; Stanfield 2011, 81).

The mere mention of something "worse" than what is depicted in the film's prologue sets the mind reeling, as does Costanzo's aforementioned comment that the eye slice was not just staged before the camera but "*caught* on celluloid," as if Buñuel (who plays the man sharpening the blade, if not necessarily the partially hidden figure doing the devilish deed) had managed to *document* a naturally occurring yet wholly unnatural event by simply being in the right place at the right time. What *was* documented, however, was the slicing of an *animal's* eye, specifically that of a calf, as dead as the rotting donkey that appears later in the film—its own eye socket bloodied and its head splayed atop a grand piano's keys in what could be construed as an attack against not only cultural elitism but also that most threatening of movie "monsters": the coming of sound (figure 5.4). In both instances, these animals in *Un Chien Andalou*—to say nothing of the crawling ants that also appear in it (a precursor to the bugs that appear inside the ear of Lynch's *Blue Velvet*)—are instrumental as no-longer-living props that either fill in for the missing human (the woman whose eye, in reality, was left safely intact) or subsume their corporeal presence to the very human pastime of "making meaning" and seeing metaphors where none were intended. Stated differently, the calf and the donkey serve the meaty *practical* needs of the filmmakers and the *hermeneutic* needs of the audience. In this way, they are like many of the other nonhuman creatures that populate horror, including those that were injured or killed during or just prior to production, as if unwitting participants in a snuff film.

Although such occurrences are relatively rare, real-life animal deaths have been recorded for posterity and incorporated into the narratives of motion pictures predicated on the illicit thrill of witnessing extreme acts, from the burning of live rats in *Hunchback of the Morgue* (*El jorobado de la Morgue*, 1973) to the slaughtering of a spider monkey, a pig, and a yellow-spotted river turtle in *Cannibal Holocaust* (1980), the beheading of a clucking chicken in *The Unseen* (1980), the slicing of writhing snakes in the shot-on-video (SOV) movie *Copperhead* (1984) and the Hong Kong production *Mr. Vampire* (*Geung see sin sang*, 1985), and the ingestion of a scuttling water bug by Nicolas Cage in *Vampire's Kiss* (1989). That last film is a comedy-horror hybrid that, harkening back to German Expressionism, trades on its fearless lead actor's extravagantly antinaturalistic performance style (figure 5.5). Much more common are the fictional instances of either bodily harm or death that occur in horror films that use nonhuman beings as a convenient way to establish the threats awaiting human characters. Such "establishing shots," which tend to be close-ups of creatures rather than distant views of a film's main setting, can be found in the opening (pre-credits or post-credits) scenes of everything from Tobe Hooper's *The Texas Chain Saw Massacre* (1974) to John Fawcett's *Ginger Snaps* (2000). In the former film, a dead armadillo bakes on a desert highway as a speeding van carries the main cast of characters to their own premature deaths. In the latter film, a suburban mom living in the seemingly peaceful community of Bailey Downs is shocked by the sight of her eviscerated dog, Baxter, a "token of middlebrow normality" whose entrails are spread out on her otherwise perfect manicured lawn (Mathijs 2013, 46). Unlike the "roadkill" of Hooper's film (which, laying belly up on its leathery armored back, was actually dead), this first canine casualty of the lycanthropic "Beast of Bailey Downs" is a fake creature crafted by *Ginger Snaps*' special effects team. Nevertheless, the dog's "function," reduced to being a joke's punchline when one of the two main characters tells her older sister that "Baxter's fertilizer," is much the same as the armadillo's insofar as it sets the stage for subsequent killings yet does not appear to "count" as an onscreen embodiment of death in its own right. Indeed, numerous websites and YouTube videos devoted to "kill counts" fail to include the first animal death depicted in *The Texas Chain Saw Massacre* among its list of fatalities, suggesting that viewers do not always *see* this important facet

Figure 5.5. As a film that earned an "unacceptable" rating from the American Humane Association upon its theatrical release in 1989, *Vampire's Kiss* gained notoriety for showing star Nicolas Cage eating a live water bug on camera.

of horror cinema with the same attentiveness given to human deaths despite its visual prominence or pride of place in a narrative (not to mention the use of dead animals in the marketing and promotion of certain films) (figure 5.6).

One reason audiences do not really *see* the calf whose eye is used (or abused) to horrifying effect in *Un Chien Andalou* relates to an engrained feature of most mainstream films, one that Buñuel is ironically said to have abandoned. Namely, the continuity system of chaining individual shots together in such a way as to make narrative events legible and causal relations stronger was harnessed by the Spanish filmmaker so that the associational logic of otherwise distinct, illogical actions would be apparent to audiences. This runs counter to much of the scholarly commentary that surrounds the film, which has emphasized its randomness, its lack of suture, and its flagrant violations of spatial and temporal

Figure 5.6. Looming as large as the van spiriting a group of friends to certain doom, the armadillo that appears in the foreground of this poster for *The Texas Chain Saw Massacre* (1974) serves as a harbinger of death. However, the animal's own death is conveniently forgotten whenever fans of this proto-slasher film tally its total number of dead bodies (on websites devoted to "kill counts").

order or general disregard for narrative causality. But our tendency to read the slicing of the eye as something that happens to the unnamed *woman* and not to the faceless *animal* has everything to do with the swift suturing of the spectator into shot-to-shot relations that are made to seem "natural" (though they are anything but). Here I agree with Barry Keith Grant, who states that "our horrified response" to the film's prologue "is amplified by our willingness to accept the conventions of continuity editing, a way of seeing that is culturally produced, and to imagine an act of violence being perpetrated upon the woman." As he states,

Even if we were willing to endure this ghastly sight, we had no time or dramatic cue for us to marshal our psychic defenses; we are given no choice about whether to look or to turn away. Suddenly this abject horror is there, before our eyes, magnified on the movie screen.... To use an appropriate metaphor, given the imagery, we have been "blind-sided" by the film. The moment slices not just through an eye, but through the barrier of the film screen itself, renting our comfort zone as spectators just as Norman Bates slides through Marion's shower curtain, reaching not only into the stall but also into the private space of our viewing experience. (2007, 5–6)

Though Grant states that the viewer, if able and willing to look carefully at the extreme close-up of the eyeball, would "see clearly that [it] is not human," he mistakes it for a pig's eye. He is not alone, as different animals (sheep, goat, donkey, etc.) have been referenced by scholars in the years prior to and since Buñuel's death (which occurred not long after he clarified, in interviews, that the organ had indeed belonged to a calf). It's easy to make such a mix-up—hardly worth fussing about—and it might simply be due to the fact that the filmmaker, in preparation for shooting the scene, had bleached the area around the calf's eye, which is shown in extreme close-up (leaving other facial signifiers out of frame). But this interchangeability of creatures *does* matter in the broader sense that it speaks to their second-class status vis-à-vis more clearly delineated human characters in film, not to mention the ultimate *unknowability* of nonhuman beings in cinematic horror, which is practically unmatched (relative to other genres with an equally anthropocentric bent) in finding narrative excuses for their mistreatment.

Sometimes, the bodies of animals are dispensed with or discoursed about in a joking manner, as in the found-footage supernatural horror film *Paranormal Activity 2* (2010), which shows an ill-fated homeowner, Daniel Rey (Brian Boland), asking his daughter Ali (Molly Ephraim) if she likes her meat "medium rare" when he finds a dead bird on the ground and uses barbeque tongs to put it onto a poolside grill. At other times, animals are metaphorically "harvested" during postproduction for their distinctive sounds, something that director William Friedkin did when he added a recording of squealing pigs being led to the slaughter into the audio mix of *The Exorcist* (1973), a facet of the soundtrack that is only barely discernible whenever the possessed preteen Regan MacNeil (Linda Blair) grunts demonically (Glasby 2020, 36). The inverse of Friedkin's approach, much more common throughout the history of the genre, is to have the lifeless, voiceless bodies of animals that have been preserved through taxidermy appear onscreen, usually as props arranged within a setting that gives us some insight into the inner life of a hero or a villain. The most famous example of this comes from *Psycho*, during a parlor scene inside the Bates Motel where Norman (Anthony Perkins) is framed against a wall adorned with stuffed birds. Less widely known but just as symbolically charged are the shots of animal heads (bear, bobcat, deer) mounted as "trophies" along the walls of a truck stop in Greydon Clark's *Without Warning* (1980), a sci-fi-horror film about teenaged hikers fending off a horde of jellyfish-like aliens as well as a humanoid invader (who is later revealed to be keeping the half-eaten corpses of its human victims inside a woodland shack). Notably, the latter film's title anticipates Grant's "blind-siding" remark about *Un Chien Andalou* quoted above. However, its suggestiveness extends beyond the act of watching a fictional act of violence or witnessing a spectacularly gruesome special effect "without warning" to connote the way that audiences are frequently forced to look upon the actual physical remains of previously living creatures (e.g., a dead dog in *The Hills Have Eyes* [1977], a dead deer in *Jug Face* [2013], etc.) with little to no preparation.

Un Chien Andalou's influence on these and many other horror films goes beyond the manner in which it exploits the functional and aesthetic value of animals. Thrusting "sequences as shocking as those in any contemporary splatter film" upon the viewer, it broke new ground in putting the "primary power" of the physical jolt ahead of any metaphorical meanings or secondary interpretations that audiences might derive from any of its images (Hawkins 2000, 23; O'Pray 2003, 23). Additionally, it laid a foundation for later productions combining "European art-film cachet" with "enough sex and violence to thrill all but the most jaded horror fan" (Hawkins 2000, 23; O'Pray 2003, 23). More pertinent to the present chapter, *Un Chien Andalou*'s status as a silent-era progenitor of modern-day body horror, slasher movies, torture porn, and other disreputable subcategories is borne out by the large number of eye-related deaths and injuries depicted onscreen since its 1929 release. In a few cases, two or more of these "ripple effects" converge like a grisly Venn diagram, as in Herschell Gordon Lewis's *Gruesome Twosome* (1967), a splatter comedy from the "Godfather of Gore" that shows a woman stabbing a mentally disabled man in the eye, leaving the bloodied organ—actually a fish's eye that was subbed in for the human one—dangling from its socket. Along with a severed hand that appears on a sidewalk later in Buñuel's film (an appendage that the auteur-as-provocateur would resurrect in his 1962 supernatural surrealist film *The Exterminating Angel* [*El ángel exterminador*], and which I too will return to in this book's final chapter), the violated eye of *Un Chien Andalou* is one of two anatomical signs that the 1929 art film deserves a place at the horror table.

BLINDING PAIN AND PROSTHETIC VISIONS

> If you try to close your eyes, you'll tear them apart,
> so you'll just have to *watch everything*.
> —the unseen killer to the bound and gagged heroine, whose eyes he has forced open
> with needles taped to their bottom lids, in Dario Argento's *Opera* (1987)

A complete overview of the many motion pictures that depict ocular attacks similar to the one described above is beyond the scope of this chapter. However, for the sake of setting up my forthcoming look at how looking itself not only can be achieved through sensorial means other than sight but can also make it possible for audiences to "hear" things in a horror film that might otherwise go unseen, let us briefly consider the genre's tendency to turn the eye into a site of abject fear. One of the recurring images in cinematic horror is that of an eyeball being irreversibly damaged in scenes that test the audience's capacity to withstand ocular pain—our ability and willingness to keep our own eyes open and focused on blinding visions. This most vulnerable of sensing organs has been attacked countless times by characters wielding knives and machetes (*Phantom of the Opera* [1962], *The Sentinel* [1977], *Evil Dead Trap* [*Shiryō no wana*, 1988], etc.), arrows (*Friday the 13th Part III* [1982], *Wrong Turn* [2003], *Fear, Inc.* [2016], etc.), pickaxes (*The Hills Have Eyes* [2006], *My Bloody Valentine* [2009], *Hazmat* [2013], etc.), power drills (*D-Tox* [2002], *The Car: Road to Revenge* [2019], etc.), scythes (*Happy Hell Night* [1992], *Silent Night* [2012], etc.), and syringes (*Dead & Buried* [1981], *The Hazing* [2004], etc.). Besides those standard tools and weapons, hatpins and sewing needles (*Hands of the Ripper* [1971], *Next of Kin* [1982], *The Unborn* [2009], etc.), kitchen cutlery and eating utensils (*The Funhouse Massacre* [2015], *V/H/S/2* [2013], etc.), and even more unusual instruments, such as a boar tusk (in *Pig Hunt* [2008]), a corkscrew (in *Midnight Movie* [2008]), a crucifix (in *Fright Night 2: New Blood* [2013]), a drug vial (in *The Faculty* [1998]), a fireplace poker (in *Dawn of the Dead* [2004]), an icicle (in *Black Christmas* [2006]), a nailfile (in *Satan's Slave* [1976]), a pencil (in *Psycho Cop 2* [1993]), a stiletto heel (in *The Red Shoes* [*Bunhongshin*; 2005]), a tent stake (in *In the Earth* [2021]), and a twig (in *Romasanta: The Werewolf Hunt* [2004]), have been used to stab, cut, and bludgeon people's eyes in horror films.

At times, even the most battle-scarred of horror fans—those who have inured themselves to nearly every ghastly thing that a filmmaker can concoct in his or her quest to top previous gross-out effects—might begin to feel like Betty (Cristina Marsillach), the young heroine of Dario Argento's *Opera* (1987). Bound and gagged by a mysterious, black-gloved killer, she is forced to watch another person's death (her boyfriend's) in order to preserve her own life. With needles taped to her bottom eyelids, Betty is the embodiment of the genre's compulsory demands and contradictory appeals, someone who dares not blink lest her own eyes be punctured yet who is violated nonetheless by visions beyond her control. There is, as several scholars contend, something decidedly masochistic about a viewer submitting to such demands, since he or she "chooses to watch" and, unlike Betty, can turn away from the spectacle of violence even if he or she has been *compelled to look* by extratextual or parasocial factors. Those factors include the often-unspoken protocols related to horror fandom, which can sometimes frame viewing as a test of one's physical and emotional limits or as a prerequisite to determine whether one is worthy of being included among other "seen-it-all" fans (Cooper 2012, 10). Referred to by Peter Hutchings as "one of Argento's most unsettling images," the extreme close-ups of Betty's eyes, which lend themselves to theorizations about "the paradoxes of horror spectatorship" (2018, 27) and which provide a cross-species echo of *Opera*'s first shot (an extreme close-up of a raven's eye), are further proof of the staying power of Buñuel and Dalí's *Un Chien Andalou*. It is as if that earlier underground classic had left so traumatizing a mark on the history of cinema that it had to be compulsively repeated over the years, leading up to and following *Opera*'s theatrical release (figure 5.7).

In the estimation of many critics, the only film to approach the ocular shock of *Un Chien Andalou* is one that was made by one of Argento's countrymen, Lucio Fulci: *Zombi 2* (1979). In what James Marriott and Kim Newman call the "signature moment" in the prolific Italian director's nearly fifty-year career, a young woman named Paula (Olga Karlatos) is cornered by a decaying zombie inside her home on the cursed Caribbean island of Matul (where she has been forced to live by her domineering husband, a doctor researching local voodoo rites) (2018). Struggling mightily, she initially succeeds in keeping the reanimated corpse on the other side of a door, against which she props a heavy chest of drawers. But the creature's arm crashes through the wooden barrier, grabs her hair, and slowly pulls her head toward a long splinter jutting out from the shattered door frame while she fights to break free. As the zombie growls, she howls in desperation, edging closer and closer to the sharp piece of wood pointed at her right eye. Fulci cuts between side angles on the action and point-of-view shots from her perspective, which show the large splinter approaching the camera lens in painfully elongated intervals. Finally, this unbearable moment of tension comes to a bloody end when her eye is brought fully into the splinter, making a soggy, squishing noise that is nearly drowned out by her guttural scream. The camera now dwells on the sight of the ripped and mangled organ of the dying woman, an image that (for this viewer) is more gruesome than seeing the empty eye sockets of characters in films as diverse as *The Birds* (1963), *And Now the Screaming Starts* (1973), *Friday the 13th: A New Beginning* (1985), and *Jeepers Creepers* (2001).

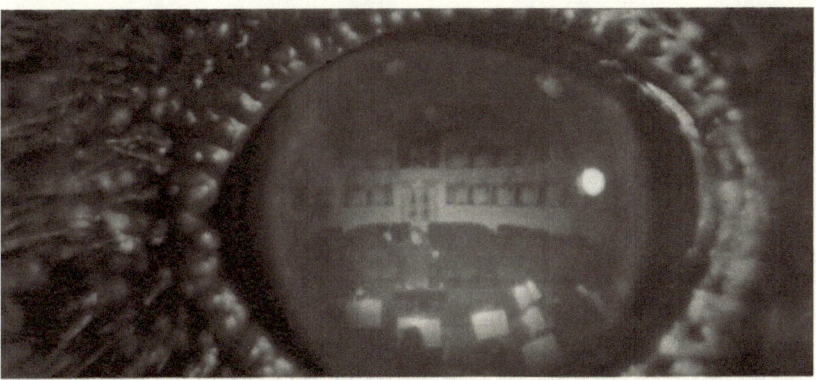

Figure 5.7. The first shot of Dario Argento's *Opera* (1987) shows an extreme close-up of a raven's eye, a reflective surface that anticipates the ocular traumas to follow.

In some ways, this scene in *Zombi 2* is the antithesis of the prologue in *Un Chien Andalou*: arriving precisely at the midpoint of the feature-length film, it is torturously drawn-out and suspenseful, whereas the opening eye-slice in Buñuel and Dalí's short film is shocking in its abruptness and brevity. It puts the viewer inside the shower-dampened, perspiration-beaded skin of the woman, whose vision of the sharp, pointy thing that will soon rob her of sight is shared with the film's viewer through POV shots not found in the earlier film. And yet, this scene in Fulci's film, like similar ones in his 1980 zombie-themed follow-up *City of the Living Dead* (*Paura nella città dei morti viventi*), his 1982 giallo film *The New York Ripper* (*Lo squartatore di New York*), and his 1989 made-for-TV movie *The Sweet House of Horrors* (*La dolce casa degli orrori*), shares something in common with *Un Chien Andalou*, which "plays on a key premise of horror: the tug of war that occurs between *wanting to look* and *not wanting to look*" (Ndalianis 2012, 32).

In her book *The Horror Sensorium: Media and the Senses*, Angela Ndalianis waxes phenomenological on this particular scene's affective power, painting a fascinating picture of how her own body—tensing up just as the victimized character's does—translated the action to her brain while watching it:

> Unable to halt the movement forward, I looked on as Paola's right eye was pushed slowly, teasingly toward a shard of wood; the anticipation of what was about to happen played itself out forcefully in the pit of my stomach. Unable to turn away, I looked on in awe at Paola as she looked on—eyes filled with terror—at the initial, almost delicate touch of wood as it pressed against the cornea, a delicate touch that was almost immediately replaced by a vicious plunge into the eyeball that proceeded to ooze and squeeze its way out of the eye socket that contained it. (32)

For Ndalianis and anyone else who watches this scene, the middle ground between Paula's eye and the viewer's eye—each "violated" in their own way—is greased with physical sensations that play upon other perceiving organs, making it possible to *feel* the "tremors that vibrated across her body and the tiny trickles of sweat that exited the pores of her skin," in addition to imagining the *smell* and *taste* of that jelly-like goo spilling from the gash (34).

What Ndalianis conjures so evocatively in her discussion of this powerfully effective and *affective* moment from *Zombi 2* is the physical relationship between three bodies: [1] her *own*; [2] that of *the character* (not to be confused with the body of actor Olga Karlatos, who survived the production unscathed); and [3] that of *the film*, whose own materiality and perceiving ability help to bring "unreal" actions to life and make it possible for spectators to imagine the screen as a mirror that "looks back." But she does not discuss *other bodies*—those belonging to fellow audience members (a justifiable omission in cases involving solo spectatorship)—whose copresence might further enrich (and complicate) a phenomenological unpacking of a motion picture's tactile, olfactory, gustatory, and auditory experiences. Drawing upon Melinda Szaloky's work on synaesthesia (the perceptual phenomenon in which the senses merge), Ndalianis suggests that an "inner hearing," reliant on individual audience members' personal memories, links those experiences (2012, 34). Importantly, for those spectators who are not deaf or hard-of-hearing, ears play a significant role in shaping their understanding of a shared viewing experience, perhaps more than one's skin, nose, or mouth does. I invite anyone who doubts this claim to seek out and experience *Zombi 2* as a midnight movie screening in a theater full of raucous Fulci fans, many of whom will be heard laughing, screaming, and flinching in collective disgust/pleasure and thus thrusting themselves into the eerily ear-centered perceptual field of individual viewers as sharply as that large wooden splinter does to Paula's right eye.

Listening to horror films, including those like *Un Chien Andalou* and other productions made before the 1930s that are "silent," is just as important to the project of embodied textual analysis as attending to their images. And, in fact, it does not always require the use of one's ears to do that "hearing." Indeed, SDH captioning options on home-video releases and online platforms such as Netflix and Amazon Prime make it possible to *see* sounds (those that have been transcribed by professional subtitlers, at least) while watching motion pictures that play upon our bodies in a more sensorially holistic fashion than what is typically described in many accounts of cinematic horror (Ndalianis's deeply felt work being an obvious exception). To use a metaphor inspired by a device in *Exorcist II: The Heretic* (1977), cinema is a "synchronizing machine," not just in terms of uniting the aural and visual operations of the medium within a temporal flow that corresponds to our own subjectively lived encounters with films as spectators, but also insofar as it engineers a uniquely communal form of space- and time-sharing involving other people. Our individual experiences, tethered to personal memories, are obviously distinct from those of other people. But they frequently line up with the feelings of fellow audience members whenever we are positioned alongside them within a single shared space at the same time—during a movie theater screening, for instance, when a "mass response" to audiovisual stimuli (in the form of collective laughter or screams) demonstrates how spectatorship is often a socially entangled, intersensorial experience.

Physical copresence with other audience members, Julian Hanich reminds us, is an important if taken-for-granted aspect of traditional moviegoing, one that affects a person's ability to derive pleasure or other, less positively valenced emotions from images and sounds that will necessarily strike that person differently in different venues, based in part on [1] who those fellow moviegoers are (i.e., strangers, friends, family, etc.), [2] how close their bodies are to one's own, and [3] how audibly present they are when caught up in the emotional or intellectual appeals of a given film (for instance, laughing at a joke in a comedy, crying during a scene in a melodrama, or commenting rudely to express their dissatisfaction with that film) (2018). Horror in particular derives much of its affective power from the situational contexts, social dynamics, and spatial contingencies of a film's viewing, and no phenomenological accounting of that experience would be complete without considering how far away the spectator is from the screen and from the loudspeakers; whether or not those other audience members are fans of the genre; and if active participation in the form of "running commentaries" or the quoting of dialogue is encouraged or frowned upon and perhaps even shushed in that setting. These and other basic questions, if not unique to the genre, are foundational to understanding how it works on our bodies.

In his book *Audience Effect: On the Collective Cinema Experience*, Hanich cites the work of Linda Williams, a key figure in genre studies who famously argued that motion pictures grant invisibility to the viewer, who is able "to see and hear everything without being seen or heard themselves" (Williams 1989, 32; Hanich 2018, 8–9). Noting that Williams's argument is "both right and wrong," the author explains that, from an "ontological perspective," a viewer remains secure in his or her invisibility, since the characters in a film (even when breaking the fourth wall while looking into the camera lens) cannot actually reach through that wall and enter into the space of the theater, though the actor playing that character could be said to perceive his or her intended audience in the abstract during the profilmic moment of performing a role and recording a scene. However, from a "phenomenological perspective," the viewer "never feels completely unnoticed," especially within viewing situations where his or her spectatorship is performed "within the immediate perceptual range of other spectators" (2018, 9).

One reason that audio commentary tracks on DVDs and Blu-rays are worthy of study, beyond what has already been covered in this book, is that they add another dimension to the intricately layered forms of shared engagement that distinguish the collective viewing of motion pictures. If not physically co-present, the viewer who accesses this now-commonly found supplemental feature (included on thousands of home-video releases) might feel like he or she is in the virtual company of the speakers, including those who represent the "inner sanctum" of production-related knowledge concerning the making of a given film. When a film director speaks via this means of knowledge-sharing, that person is also sharing an imaginary space with the spectator, who listens in on frequently funny anecdotes and eye-opening admissions that might further impact how one responds to what is occurring in a particular scene. To be sure, the "shared space of the physically close audience in the movie-theater is unlike the unshared space of the solitary and dispersed audience in front of the TV or computer screen at home" (Hanich 2018, 7–8). But a director's audio commentary partially undoes that sense of isolation and dispersal by making the viewer feel connected in ways that were not possible prior to the introduction of this supplemental feature (first as an option on laserdiscs in the 1980s before making its way onto DVD releases during the 1990s and then Blu-ray releases beginning a decade later).

It is not surprising that several directors' audio commentaries touch upon eye-related incidents, given how many scenes in horror films pivot on the threat posed to this particular body part. An example occurs on one of the two commentary tracks included on Dark Sky Films' DVD and Blu-ray releases of writer-director Adam Green's *Victor Crowley* (2017), the fourth installment in the filmmaker's *Hatchet* film series (launched over a decade earlier). While reminiscing with cinematographer Jan-Michael Losada, editor Matt Latham, and makeup-effects artist Robert Pendergraft about the making of this gore-filled slasher film, Green draws attention to a scene involving the title character—a supernaturally strong swamp monster intent on killing all encroachers on his unhallowed land—bursting through a shack door, knocking one of his many victims down to the ground, and then slamming the claw of a hammer into the young man's eye. Although a stunt double took the bone-rattling tackle of the rampaging monster, the actor who played the victim in question (Chase Williamson) sustained an injury when the actor who played Crowley (Kane Hodder) brought his hand, which was covered in small pieces of breakaway glass, down on the now-bleeding face of his scene partner. Because Hodder, a former burn victim from the neck down (whose skin, according to the director, is "all kinds of messed up"), could not feel the broken candy glass on his hand, he had no idea that he was causing Williamson real pain, despite the latter screaming so powerfully that "he blew out a blood vessel in the eye." While this might seem to be a relatively minor injury compared to what *could* have happened during the filming of the scene, it speaks to the volatile nature of a genre in which that most sought-after bodily response—an ear-piercing scream—not only conveys a person's terror and pain but also can contribute to it (at least in some extreme instances).

Human and nonhuman eyes, often singled out to the exclusion of other facial features (which are not shown or are partially obscured), loom large in dozens of movie posters and DVD/Blu-ray covers that have been produced over the past few decades, from obviously ocular-centric examples like *My Little Eye* (2002), *The Eye* (2008), and *The Child's Eye* (2010) to those for films that at first glance seem less optically fixated, such as *Frankenstein Unbound* (1990), *Candyman* (1992), and *The Grudge* (2004). Several posters foreground the iris of the eye as a kind of movie screen upon which images are projected, or a window-like surface through which spectators might access another world outside their own, as demonstrated by the paratextual materials supporting the theatrical releases of *House of 9* (2004), *The Skeleton Key* (2005), *Dark Circles* (2013), and other horror films. In some cases, the eye appears to frame another body part (for instance, a hand appears trapped inside the milky white cornea gracing the poster of *The Return* [2006]) or, conversely, is itself contained within a different orifice (such as the open mouth that appears on the poster for *The Theatre Bizarre* [2011]). A few posters illustrate the ocular threats that presumably await viewers, with sharp instruments of pain perched dangerously close to the cornea (a razor blade in the case of *Would You Rather* [2012], a wasp's barbed stinger in the case of *Stung* [2015], etc.) (figure 5.8).

Marketed as the "first gay slasher film" upon its release, screening primarily at LGBTQ film festivals in the United States (Elliott-Smith and Browning 2020, 5), writer-director Paul Etheredge-Ouzts's *Hellbent* (2004) notably has two poster designs: the first one featuring the main character, Eddie (played by Dylan Fergus), seen in profile, a scythe blade two or three inches from his eye; the second one is the same except for the fact that the pointy end of the weapon is now touching his cornea (figure 5.9). Each of those two images recalls a particular shot from writer-director Guillem Morales's *Julia's Eyes* (*Los ojos de Julia*, 2010) as well as the scene from *Zombi 2* discussed earlier, albeit at different stages of the ocular assault and with a more traditional weapon in place of a jutting piece of a broken door frame aimed at the eye. Significantly, after the midpoint of *Hellbent*, Eddie, a young man who wanted to follow in his policeman father's footsteps but was not able to pass the required physical, reveals that he has a glass eye (or what is more likely an acrylic prosthetic), the result of a childhood accident. This information, which Eddie delivers to

Figure 5.8. Perhaps even more than the films themselves, paratextual materials (like these movie posters) foreground the eye as a central anatomical feature of the horror genre.

his lover, Jake (Bryan Kirkwood), in a manner that suggests a kind of "coming out" subplot revolving around physical difference, happens after he has been cornered by a devil-masked killer on the prowl and held at scythe-point—the attack depicted in the poster. When the mysteriously silhouetted figure moves in for the kill, the metal weapon "clinks" on Eddie's glass eye, an audible reminder that another clear hard surface—the camera lens—often serves a prosthetic function in cinematic horror, whenever viewers are provided access to a victim's perspective. Importantly, this excruciating moment in *Hellbent*, echoed by an even ghastlier restaging of the same shot toward the end of the film when the so-called Devil Daddy once again corners the protagonist only to succeed in plucking his artificial eye out, was achieved by visual effects artists using CGI rather than practical means such as prosthetics.

In his exploration of *Hellbent*, Darren Elliott-Smith problematizes the film's "depiction of gay machismo," which is ostensibly deployed to subvert

Figure 5.9. Anticipating a shot from director Guillem Morales's *Julia's Eyes* (2010), the poster for Paul Etheredge-Ouzts's *Hellbent* (2004) highlights the ocular terrors awaiting audiences of this gay-themed horror film.

stereotypes related to the performance of hypermasculinity. *Hellbent*'s representational schema could be accused of reasserting the same oppressive structures of gender that Etheredge-Ouzts set out to satirize, in which "real men"—those who are powerful enough to eventually take down the monster—are "armored" with muscles and outfitted in costumes befitting hard bikers and peacekeeping cops (not to mention a pirate, whom Eddie is compared to when he is later forced to wear an eyepatch) (2016, 20, 160). The critic also notes that Eddie's "impaired gaze," a trait often associated with female protagonists of classic melodramas, is rendered vulnerable" in the face of his romantic partner's "more 'authentic' masculinity, expressed by way of an "assaultive gaze" that prefigures the moment when the male protagonist is cornered by the killer (whose own gaze, in the form of subjective POV shots, is conspicuously absent) (160–61).

Elliott-Smith also emphasizes the many feminizing "failures" of the main character, whose literal impairment parallels his figurative blindness (not noticing when others find him attractive or when his friends have been killed, for instance) leading up to the moment when the leather-clad Devil Daddy finally removes "Eddie's appearance of normality (his glass eye) with his tongue"—an act of "symbolic castration" (160–61) that links the phallus to the mouth. For all of its apparent progressiveness in foregrounding gay men as main rather than supporting characters in a slasher film that culminates with a "Final Boy" (in place of a "Final Girl") emerging victorious over the monster (albeit by once again "failing" at the task, since the one-eyed Eddie, lacking depth of field, is not able to shoot "straight" and has to aim his father's gun at *Jake*, who is being held by the killer, in order to hit his real target), *Hellbent* perpetuates ableist assumptions about people who have experienced vision loss. In fact, "loss" is translated into a more fundamental "lack" not only within the text but also by theorists who might themselves be unintentionally reproducing cultural norms and stereotypes.

The term "blind" is freighted with legal, social, and political implications, and is often used in contexts where an "impairment" beyond the visual register—say, one of the imagination or with regard to a person lacking insight or foresight—is being referenced by way of a convenient metaphor rather than an accurate descriptor. Legal definitions of blindness vary from country to country, but in the United States it refers to the condition of an individual whose "better eye is 20/200 or poorer even with the best corrective eyeglasses or contact lenses" and who, even if not totally blind (having some residual vision), would be eligible for financial benefits and rehabilitative services (Bailey and Hall 1989, 1). There are numerous examples of horror film characters whose conditions fit that definition, from those occupying small roles (the older movie theater attendee in Lamberto Bava's *Demons* [*Dèmoni*, 1985]) to those who serve as protagonists (the Vietnam War veteran Ambrose [Nick Damici] in Adrián García Bogliano's *Late Phases* [2014]) as well as antagonists (the Gulf War veteran Norman [Stephen Lang] in Fede Álvarez's *Don't Breathe* [2016]). The adjacent categories of the home-invasion film and the psychological suspense thriller also have their fair share in films such as *Wait Until Dark* (1967), *See No Evil* (1971), and *Manhunter* (1986). In a majority of the latter examples, the blind character is a young woman—a conventional means by which storytellers (many of whom are older men) can play up the "vulnerability" angle that Brigitte Peucker mentions in her discussion of *The Silence of the Lambs* (1991). In that Oscar-winning film, the main character, Clarice (Jodie Foster), is "temporarily blinded" in the basement of Buffalo Bill (Ted Levine), who has turned out the lights and who puts on infrared goggles through which to see her stumbling in the dark (2007: 191).

In many cases, characters who do not possess the visual sense of sight are still capable of "visions," insofar as they are psychics whose access to "the world behind the world" (to quote a line from the 2005 film *Constantine*) is reliant upon an "inner eye" or a "sixth sense." Such figures, able to "see" things that are beyond most people's comprehension or abilities, might be men of the cloth, as in *The Unholy* (1988), which features a priest (Trevor Howard's demonologist Father Silva) who holds the key to fighting the devil, or women seers such as Tamara Stafford's Cass in *The Hills Have Eyes Part II* (1985], whose blindness not only provides much-needed insights into the nature of the threats looming before sighted characters but also foretells their ultimate doom at the hands of malevolent forces partly defined by their superior strength or supernatural abilities. Ironically, clairvoyants and mystics whose "lack" of visual sight is compensated for by their ability to commune with the dead, to see into the future, or (in the case of Henriette [Margaret Mazzantini], a blind girl in Joe D'Amato's *Antropophagus* [1980]), to smell the presence of evil, have more than a touch of the supernatural about them, making them liminal beings positioned between two worlds. This is true of the mystical, milky-eyed seer Emily (Cinzia Monreale) in Lucio Fulci's *The Beyond* (. . . *E tu vivrai nel terrore! L'aldilà*, 1981), who issues a dire warning to the film's protagonist, Liza (Catriona MacColl), about reopening the old hotel in New Orleans that she has inherited (and which sits atop a gateway to Hell), but who might as well be "mute" given that her words go unheeded. Here and elsewhere ("beyond" this tellingly titled film, which eventually kills off Emily by having her throat be bitten by her own guide dog), blindness is exploited as a means of intensifying the audience's anxiety of *not knowing* what might be lurking in the dark while paradoxically exerting their own *agency* as literal seers whose eyes dart frantically across the image in search of what those ill-fated characters cannot see. Another reason why such figures exist is to problematize the link between seeing and believing, thus underscoring the need to look beyond traditional ways of conceptualizing the epistemological conundrums faced by characters in search of a more holistic understanding of knowledge as an imperfectly embodied relationship to the world.

SECTION TWO

Beyond Sight and Sound: Breathing, Smelling, Tasting, Touching

6

DEAD, BUT STILL BREATHING

The Problem of Postmortem Movement in Horror Films

> We're born, we breathe, and we die.
> —evil neurosurgeon Dean Armitage (Bradley Whitford) in *Get Out* (2017)

Breathing is an implicit, rarely remarked-upon bodily phenomenon in cinema. Indeed, one of the most undertheorized yet taken-for-granted aspects of the motion-picture medium, which makes an ontological break from still photography by presenting viewers with the illusion of movement, is its capacity to forge an intersubjective bond between the living, breathing bodies of characters (as well as the actors who play them) and the embodied spectator whose own respiratory activity is as key to phenomenological engagement or sensual perception as seeing and hearing are. As Davina Quinlivan argues in her book *The Place of Breath in Cinema*, a diegetic body's inhalation and exhalation of air—the biological process through which oxygen is brought into the lungs and carbon dioxide is flushed out through the nose and mouth—is fundamental to the "ethics of sharing" that the author ascribes to the medium (2012, 13). Inspired by the philosophical writings of Luce Irigaray, Quinlivan not only maintains that physically empathetic relations emerge from such "communal breathing" but also suggests that nondiegetic bodies (i.e., those belonging to audience members) experience a metaphysical connection to the motion-picture medium by way of a cinematic apparatus that is rhythmically "in tune" with the often-invisible respirations of characters (13). Here I am reminded of Carol Clover's comment about John Carpenter's *Halloween* (1978), a slasher film that invites us "to look not only through a murderous camera, but with our own murderous eyes, listening to the beat of our heart and the breathing of our lungs" in such a way that the heavy respiration of the masked killer Michael Myers becomes our own "as we wonder what he/we will do next" (1992, 185–86). However, as I explain in this chapter, breath can also sever a viewer's link to that apparatus and draw her or his attention to the fictionality/artificiality of a narrative. This is particularly true in horror films, where the themes of mortality and physical trauma figure prominently and are lent visual texture through graphic representations of the body's destruction and the taking of one's "last breath."

Death, whether by asphyxiation, dismemberment, torture, or the many other gruesome ways in which a person's heart ceases to beat and breathing is brought to an end, can only be hinted at—never actually achieved—in the context of fictional representations, which require actors to hold their breath in front of cinematographic equipment (e.g., camera lenses, lights, etc.) capable of recording and revealing subtle movements, such as the expansion and contraction of the chest or stomach. Commonly referred to as "film flubs" or "movie mistakes" (Givens 1989), shots of dead characters breathing—on view in everything from the Hammer-produced *Frankenstein Must Be Destroyed* (1969) and *Twins of Evil* (1971), slasher films such as *Graduation Day* (1981) and *The Forest* (1982), *Gremlins*-ripoffs like *Ghoulies* (1985) and *Hobgoblins* (1988), shot-on-video cheapies like *Night Feeder* (1988), and the Alejandro Jodorowsky-directed cult classic *Santa Sangre* (1989) to contemporary examples of the genre such as *The Cell* (2000) and *You're Next* (2011)—work against the "willing suspension of disbelief" that Bruce Kawin (2012, 205), John Kenneth Muir (2004, 256), Thomas M. Sipos (2010, 14, 39, 66), and other critics say is an already-fraught activity when it comes to the audience's immersion in a horror narrative. Moreover, such postmortem movements on the part of a character who is supposed to be lifeless, visible in shots that linger on his or her body after the performer is unable to hold his or her breath any longer, function metatextually (if unintentionally) as an embedded reference to the horror genre's preoccupation with undead/living-dead scenarios where such gaffes can be rationalized or naturalized, paradoxically, through recourse to irrational means or supernatural explanations.

A case in point is the first entry in James Wan and Leigh Whannell's long-running *Saw* franchise (2004–present), an intricately structured film filled with gruesome examples of bodily destruction (disembowelment, gunshot wounds, immolation, severe head trauma, etc.), but whose most shocking moment comes near the narrative's end, when *life* is presented as a specter more terrifying than any bad death. During the penultimate scene, the suicide victim lying on the floor of the film's main setting—a grimy bathroom where two other men, photographer Adam Stanheight (Leigh Whannell) and oncologist Dr. Lawrence Gordon (Cary Elwes), have been drugged and trapped by an unseen assailant—suddenly rises to his feet and removes his makeup to reveal himself as the criminal mastermind Jigsaw (Tobin Bell). Leading up to this big reveal are several moments when, between bouts of terrified confusion, moral handwringing, and the surveillance monitoring of their increasingly frantic behavior as unwilling participants in a cruel game of survival, the two men chained to the bathroom fixtures on either side of the killer engage in heated conversations on the topics of deception and truth while ruminating on the reasons why someone might "act" a certain way (for instance, "playing dead"). At one point, Adam says to his fellow prisoner that the corpse lying face down in a pool of blood is the "first dead body [he has] ever seen." "They don't move," is Dr. Gordon's response, stating a simple fact that the horror genre persists in complicating and undermining, both intentionally and unintentionally. Ironically, he is a medical doctor whose training should have enabled him to bring greater anatomical scrutiny to the presumably dead man in question, but who overlooks the latter's subtle up-and-down movements (corresponding with Jigsaw's relaxed breathing pattern, partly "hidden" thanks to a sedative that has slowed his heart rate—a plot point later explained in the film's second sequel, *Saw III* [2006]).

Not unlike the posthumous breathing of a hospital orderly who enters the bathroom near the end of *Saw* only to be bludgeoned to death by Adam out of self-defense (and whose chest and stomach can be seen moving after his head has been bashed in by a toilet tank lid), those slight physical fluctuations of a killer who has been "playing possum" and "lying" in wait (in both senses of that word) throughout the whole ordeal would be noticeable to the most attentive viewers, especially those who are rewatching the film with the benefit of narrative hindsight. To quote Adam, who has been taking pictures of Lawrence without his knowledge, the camera "doesn't know how to lie. It shows you what's put right in front of it." That sentiment gains metatextual suggestiveness in light of the fact that *Saw* cinematographer David A. Armstrong's camera reveals, early in the film, the truth of the monster's method (if not motives) to anyone who might be on the lookout for retroactively rationalized "mistakes." As Mark Bernard notes, "There is no strategic reason for Jigsaw to lie on the floor in the same room with his intended victims, other than to emphasize his invisibility and that people never notice him until it is too late" (2013, 92). Judging from the online commentary surrounding this and numerous other horror films, though, audiences *do* notice when the actors playing presumably dead characters blink, breathe, or flinch in scenes where questions of visibility and invisibility are thematically relevant to the genre's reliance on disbelief mitigation as a means of dispelling doubts about what one is seeing or hearing.

Another example of this can be found in the low-budget horror film *Psychic Killer* (1975). An early scene of this schlocky production, which was written by Greydon Clark and shot by director Ray Danton under the working title *The Kirlian Effect* (in reference to the then-fashionable interest in New Age theories about the body's natural vibrations or "aura"), shows a mortician in a

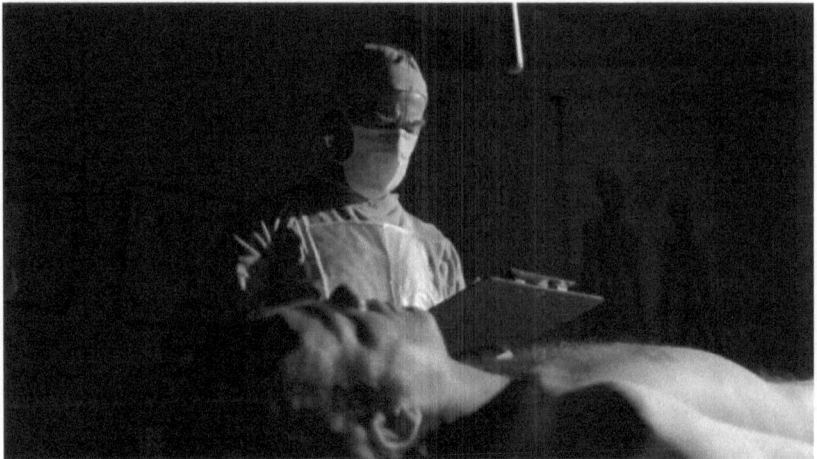

Figure 6.1. During an early scene of *Psychic Killer* (1975), a doctor performs an autopsy on the main character, whose chest and stomach can be seen expanding and contracting in the seconds before the scalpel plunges into his flesh.

mental institution performing an autopsy on a presumably dead man, Arnold Masters (Jim Hutton), whose chest can be seen moving ever-so-slightly up and down (figure 6.1). The patient's breathing, which we might initially attribute to Hutton's bad acting or Danton's careless directing, is retroactively explained once it is revealed that he was never *really* dead to begin with. Masters was simply "in a deep state of shock over the death of another patient," according to a medical specialist, who is unaware of the fact that the other inmate, before dying, had promised to protect our hero (who wakes from his deathly slumber at the touch of the doctor's scalpel) with the supernatural ability of "astral projection." From this point forward in the increasingly far-fetched narrative, the protagonist, who has been wrongfully locked up for a murder that he did not commit, harnesses his newfound telekinesis to take revenge against those who have wronged him, leading to the deaths of other characters whose lifeless but still breathing bodies cannot be so easily explained away (as unintentional mistakes perhaps unnoticed by director Danton). Notably, even after being released from the asylum, each time Masters remotely kills someone he appears to go into a vegetative state, his spirit departing as part of a paranormal, out-of-body experience. He thus seems to exist in a liminal zone of being and non-being, breathing and non-breathing.

As Quinlivan argues, breath too occupies a liminal space—that between exterior and interior—and is an (im)material presence that is rarely ever seen, beyond the white poof of vapor that blooms from lips in cold climates (2012, 67–73).[1] However, the softly heaving chests of ostensibly deceased people, be they corpses left to rot in freshly dug graves or fleshy specimens laid out on mortuary slabs, are an all-too-visible reminder of the horror film's failure to fully "live up" to its potential as a vehicle for materializing death in a truly unsettling way. Ironically, the genre's affective appeals and "perverse" sensorial pleasures, including its ability to increase the heart rate and respiratory rate of audiences through shocking images or suspenseful scenes, can be said to make viewers feel "more alive" than other categories of cultural production that are less invested in death as a thematic motif (e.g., comedy, drama, romance, etc.). Taking the title and premise of the recent US theatrical release *Don't Breathe* (2016) as a leaping-off point, but expanding the scope of this chapter to include a representative cross-section of international productions and trashy exploitation cinema, I weave together two seemingly antithetical threads, looking first at the horror film's pronounced reliance on breath as a sonic signifier of fear or terror, and then exploring those moments when actors inadvertently reveal, through visible breathing, the life still left in dead characters. Ultimately, I hope to contribute to a better understanding of the genre's unique respiratory tendencies as well as the risible yet significant textual ruptures that occur when bodies continue breathing *after* they have stopped living.

FROM *DON'T BREATHE* TO *DON'T LOOK IN THE BASEMENT*: HORROR'S NEGATIVE IMPERATIVES AND PARADOXICAL APPEALS

> Don't look, he'll see you. Don't breathe, he'll hear you. Don't move, you're dead!
> —tagline for *The Burning* (1981), spoken by a camp counselor at the
> end of the film as he issues a warning about the masked killer, "Cropsy"

Perhaps more than any other genre, the horror film habitually relies upon the act and sound of breathing as a means of forging an intersubjective relationship between material and immaterial bodies. Indeed, if the genre as a whole can be said to have a signature sound, an aural signifier that most clearly announces its aesthetic complexities and ethical conundrums as well as the limits of bodily control that are so frequently tested in representative films, it is the muffled, hypnotic respiration of the killer on the prowl. From the opening scene in Bob Clark's *Black Christmas* (1974), which introduces us to a heavy-breathing stalker (Nick Mancuso) peering into the windows of his potential victims, to the closing scene in John Carpenter's *Halloween*, which audibly reveals that Michael Myers (Nick Castle), the masked bogeyman who has been shot seven times before falling from a second-story window to his presumed death, is in fact still alive, examples of respiratory activity are so conspicuous as to perhaps be

Figure 6.2. As demonstrated in this scene from *Prom Night* (1980), Subtitles for the Deaf and Hard-of-Hearing (SDH) often parenthetically bracket the sound (and image) of "heavy breathing," one of the most identifiable markers of the horror genre.

invisible if not inaudible to audiences accustomed to this now-conventionalized part of the genre's representational system. Indeed, so conventional is the trope of the heavy-breathing serial killer, which dates back at least to Dario Argento's *Four Flies on Grey Velvet* (*4 mosche di velluto grigio*, 1971), that it has been spoofed in numerous horror parodies, including the 1981 film *The Funhouse*, which begins with a false-startle reference to both *Psycho* (1960) and *Halloween*, and that same year's *Student Bodies*, which features a comically asthmatic stalker called "The Breather" (a riff on *Black Christmas*' "The Moaner") who preys on oversexed, underdressed teenagers, frequently shown from his own identity-masking point-of-view.[2] With more horror films than ever currently available for viewing on DVD and Blu-ray as well as through online streaming services offering Subtitles for the Deaf and Hard-of-Hearing (SDH), the actual words "Heavy Breathing" appear regularly as parenthetically transcribed text onscreen, visible to anyone who utilizes that feature while watching everything from the slasher films *Prom Night* (1980) (figure 6.2) and *Pieces* (1982) to the zombie film *Mortuary* (2005) and the found-footage film *Hell House LLC* (2015).

Despite the regularity with which heavy or labored breathing—be it that of a killer on the loose or that of a dying victim gasping for air—is exploited in horror, the genre has received relatively little attention from scholars with an interest in either the physical act or philosophical meanings of respiration. Quinlivan herself, as the cultural critic most central to the emergent study of breath's "place" in cinema, has little to say about horror beyond noting that certain subgenres, such as the haunted house movie, foreground "figures whose physical absence" requires a compensating acoustic matrix (2012,

23). The audio-visual tension that partly constitutes the genre's paradoxical appeals, she suggests, contributes to an "unsettling filmic experience invested in absences and the unseen" (23). But as evocative as this final remark might be, Quinlivan stops short of unpacking the affective and corporeal aspects of the genre and concludes with the overly generalized statement that "the horror film does not refer explicitly to breathing" (24). One wonders, then, how such obvious signifiers of "breathtaking" physical terror and bodily victimization as those mentioned above can escape the grasp of theorists, especially as the horror genre has increasingly demonstrated an affinity for metatextual or self-reflexive structures that lay bare its reliance on certain narrative devices. The latter include mobile framing and subjective POV shots that put spectators inside the "skin" of a human or nonhuman monster and which are designed to alter their heart rate and breathing rate in the process.

One of the most critically acclaimed American horror films in recent years, writer-director Fede Álvarez's *Don't Breathe* is one such example: a knowing, intertextually ripe tribute to earlier motion pictures that is premised on the idea that respiratory control is necessary in warding off the mortal threats that are so endemic to the genre. Indeed, as the film's title suggests, the main characters' ability to momentarily halt, or simply silence, the intake and outtake of air (through mouth or nose) plays a pivotal role in determining their fates. Specifically, its narrative centers on a trio of teenagers—Alex (Dylan Minnette), Money (Daniel Zovatto), and Rocky (Jane Levy)—who conspire to break into strangers' houses in their home city of Detroit, selling the various goods that they have stolen as a means of earning money that will presumably bring about their individual dreams. Rocky, for instance, wants nothing more than to escape her abusive mother as well as her economically blighted urban surroundings, and plans to move to California with her little sister in tow once she has accumulated the funds to do so. Out of desperation she agrees to act on a tip received by Money, who informs her and Alex (whose father runs an easy-to-hack home security company) that their proverbial pot of gold is just a few blocks away. Learning that $300,000 in settlement money, paid to a retired US Army Special Forces veteran (Stephen Lang) whose daughter had been killed in a car crash, is hidden somewhere inside his house, the three burglars stake out the area, a conveniently deserted neighborhood street lined with boarded-up houses and overgrown lawns.

Scoping out their target, the team discover that the physically intimidating man (listed in the credits as "Norman") is accompanied at all times by a guard dog. He is also visually impaired, a sign of his time spent as a soldier in the Gulf War. Because of the blind man's disability, the thieving protagonists see him as an easy target, and are able to quickly circumvent his front line of protection by putting the growling Rottweiler to sleep with drugs. Once inside, they need only to remain calm and relatively silent in order to override the security system, sneak past the sleeping owner of the house, locate his stash of cash, and then abscond from the premises unheard and unseen. Doing so, however, necessitates not just procedural stealth but also control over the rate and depth of their breathing once the hearing-attuned army veteran wakes from his slumber. This is where much of the film's titular frisson is located: in thrilling, literally breathless cat-and-mouse sequences pitting our ethically dubious "heroes" against the ostensible "victim" of a home invasion who is soon revealed to be a victimizer himself (as someone who has trapped a young woman—the driver responsible for his daughter's death—in his basement). After gunning down Money, the blind man begins hunting the other two would-be thieves inside that prison-like place, using his heightened senses of smelling and hearing in much the same way that subterranean predators do against their prey. Tellingly, the secret truth of the blind man's monstrosity—his perverse attempt to forcibly impregnate the imprisoned woman so that she might birth a child as replacement for his dead daughter—is discovered by Alex and Rocky once they descend into that basement, a subterranean space which horror film aficionados will recognize as one of the genre's most frequently visualized, thematically resonant settings.

On view in such cult classics as *The Gruesome Twosome* (1967), *Night of the Living Dead* (1968), *The Beyond* (1981), *The Boogens* (1981), *The Evil Dead* (1981), and *Basket Case* (1982), as well as contemporary productions including *Dread* (2009), *The House at the End of the Street* (2012), *The Conjuring* (2013), *Intruders* (2015), *We Are Still Here* (2015), *Lights Out* (2016), *May the Devil Take You* (2018), and *A Quiet Place* (2018), basements and cellars have long been imagined as zones of menace and malevolence in horror cinema. There, dead or dying bodies can be stored and torture can be exacted covertly. Scott Martin calls the basement "the sinister underbelly of the house" (2016, 45), a place inside yet beneath the home that "has frequently been exploited and exaggerated for horrific effect" in films such as *The Silence of the Lambs* (1991), *The People Under the Stairs* (1991), and *Frailty* (2001), as Eleanor Andrews, Stella Hockenhull, and Fran Pheasant-Kelly likewise point out (2016, 14). Indeed, one only has to recall the dramatic climax of Alfred Hitchcock's 1960 classic *Psycho*—in which Lila Crane (Vera Miles), searching for the whereabouts of her missing sister Marion (Janet Leigh), tiptoes into the dark fruit cellar below Norman Bates's (Anthony Perkins) house—to fathom the thematic implications of such primordial spaces. For instance, in his reading of the Bates's three-tiered dwelling (cellar, ground floor, top floor), Slavoj Žižek likens the bottommost area, where Norman's mummified mother sits lifeless in a swivel chair, to the id, a "reservoir of illicit drives" and libidinal deviance that had been hidden—kept offscreen—prior to this penultimate moment in *Psycho* when the unsuspecting woman stumbles upon the corpse (Pheasant-Kelly 2013, 191). The basement, therefore, not only engenders "Gothic sensibilities of entombment, abjection, or uncanniness," but also *reveals* what would otherwise be *concealed* in many horror films (Andrews et al., 2016, 8). As such, its centrality within *Don't Breathe*, a film partially set inside the bowels of *another* Norman's house, assumes allegorical significance both as an actual place to be avoided and as the figurative expression of what Scott Martin refers to as the "hidden self" (2016, 47). This latter notion is similar to Chris Vander Kaay and Kathleen Fernandez-Vander Kaay's conception of the basement as "the destination for unnecessary but emotionally resonate things which we don't want others to see but from which we can't fully separate" (2016, 27–28). In that sense, the paradoxical logic that compels the main characters in *Don't Breathe* to hide their otherwise audible respiratory activity (in order to escape detection inside the blind man's house and thus stay alive, i.e., *keep breathing*) can be likened to the negative imperative that both encourages and discourages the female protagonist in an earlier horror film—the independently produced *Don't Look in the Basement* (1973)—to explore that titular location during its penultimate moments.

As one of a spate of "Don't" films produced during the 1970s and early 1980s (the heyday of home-invasion and slasher films, among them *Don't Torture a Duckling* [1972], *Don't Be Afraid of the Dark* [1973], *Don't Open the Window* [1974], *Don't Open the Door* [1975], *Don't Go in the House* [1979], *Don't Answer the Phone* [1980], *Don't Go in the Woods* [1981], etc., before those two subgenres began "gasping for breath" in the mid-1980s [Everman 1993, 87; Grunzke 2015, 168]),[3] the critically lambasted *Don't Look in the Basement* is, on the surface, a very different enterprise than the similarly titled *Don't Breathe*. Shot on a miniscule budget in rural Texas, this threadbare production is set inside a rural home for the criminally insane and features many of the stylistic hallmarks for which the Arkansas-born exploitation auteur S. F. Brownrigg is famous, at least among a small group of genre enthusiasts drawn to "so-bad-it's-good" cinema. This includes copious helpings of regional stereotypes, performative camp, carnal desire, and graphic bloodshed in which the bodies of dead or dying characters are lingered on—*fetishized*—by an otherwise directionless camera (Drain 2016; Thrower 2014). Textual "irregularities," including continuity errors, flubbed lines, unmotivated close-ups of leering or maniacally laughing faces, and a muddled, meandering plot filled with narrative potholes, mark this as a distinctly paracinematic work, following Jeffrey Sconce's theorization of an oppositional cultural praxis and taste politics valorizing filmic "failures" or "distortions [of] conventional cinematic style" (1995, 385). In Sconce's words, paracinema "deviates from Hollywood classicism not necessarily by artistic intentionality, but by the effects of *material poverty* and *technical ineptitude*," an apt description of the paradoxical appeals of *Don't Look in the Basement*, which was made by a director forced to work "within the impoverished and clandestine production conditions typical of exploitation cinema" (385). Those conditions, I argue, make it more likely that mistakes—specifically, the visible breathing of bodies belonging to actors "playing dead" (whose neck, chest, and abdomen movements were apparently overlooked during the shooting and editing phases)—will occur in low-budget productions characterized by shoddy visual aesthetics. More importantly, those mistakes will be noticed and even embraced by select viewers for whom such distractions are, ironically, part of the "attraction." Nevertheless, like the more technically polished crowd-pleaser *Don't Breathe*, Brownrigg's cult horror film misdirects its audience through the negative imperative of its title, in this case commanding them to *not* do the very thing—looking in the basement—that the genre keeps impishly nudging them to do.

Significantly, the underground space that is part of the title's warning, located inside a small backwoods sanitarium run by a man named Dr. Stephens (Michael Harvey), the first of many ill-fated characters to be dumped into its dark basement, appears only near the end of the film, after a lengthy build-up involving multiple acts of murder and mayhem. Leading to that penultimate moment, in which the doctor's body is discovered by a newly hired nurse fearing that she might also be losing her mind, Charlotte Beale (Rosie Holotik), are several scenes in which the patients are shown taking over the asylum. The film's roster of "crazies" includes Harriett (Camilla Carr), the murderously protective "mother" of a plastic baby doll; Sam (Bill McGhee), a recently lobotomized, popsicle-licking hulk of a man-child; Allyson (Betty Chandler), a sexually voracious woman suffering from schizophrenia; Judge Oliver Cameron (Gene Ross), a former magistrate who tries to atone for his past deeds by remaining chaste in the face of temptation; Sarge (Hugh Feagin), a shell-shocked veteran of the Vietnam War on constant lookout for invisible enemies; and Mrs. Callingham (Rhea MacAdams), a poetry-reciting octogenarian who, before getting her tongue cut out by an unseen assailant, repeatedly tells Nurse Beale to leave this godforsaken place. Lording over the rundown facilities is Dr. Geraldine Masters (Annabelle Weenick), who assumes control of Stephens Sanitarium following the death of the physician whose name graces the sign outside. Dr. Stephens's demise occurs early on, during a precredits scene showing Oliver chopping wood as part of his experimental therapy. This unconventional means of disciplining the judge's mind comes to a sudden end when the wildly swung axe lands in the asylum owner's back. The doctor's bloodied body, framed in long shot, lies on the grass as Oliver slowly lowers his chopping tool at Masters's coaxing. Even at a distance, attentive audiences will notice the slight rising and lowering of Dr. Stephens's white lab coat, which could be attributed to the gentle breeze seen blowing through the branches of a nearby tree. More likely,

Figure 6.3. The low-budget horror film *Don't Look in the Basement* (1973) is partially premised on the idea that the supervising psychiatrist at a backwoods sanitarium has been killed by an axe-wielding patient. However, even at a distance, the viewer should be able to detect actor Michael Harvey's subtle movements even as he is supposed to be "playing dead."

though, that movement is a result of actor Michael Harvey not being able to mask his real-life breathing for the duration of the shot (figure 6.3).

The doctor's body, which therefore proves to be a "problem" at both the diegetic and extradiegetic levels, is quickly disposed of in this early scene, only to reappear near the end (at the film's one hour-and-twenty-minute mark) when Nurse Beale stumbles upon it in the basement. Descending the staircase of that pitch-black place, she bristles when a hand reaches up near her ankle, then screams in terror while lashing out at it with a wooden post, which she uses in self-defense. Ironically, the shock of discovering that Dr. Stephens is not dead, but has been barely surviving in the basement after Sam deposited his body there, results in her instinctively beating him into an even bloodier pulp. As bad fortune would have it, this brings about his *actual* demise. However, once more the dead man's body is shown in long shot, and yet again we are attuned to the subtle up-and-down movement of the actor's chest, indicating the presence of life (extradiegetically) where there is none (diegetically).

Such spectatorial awareness of a textual "defect," a laughable mistake that neutralizes the dread spreading throughout this climactic scene, might seem of little consequence given the many other poorly executed moments of fear-inducement leading up to it. But its significance rests in the manner in which the horror genre's most fundamental "lie"—i.e., its reliance on still-living, still-breathing beings to stand in for the recently deceased—is revealed in a space typically reserved for characters' and audiences' transformative encounter with the Real. It is as if the illusion-shattering too-muchness of the body's lived reality bleeds through the mystifying skin of fictional representation, becoming an excess(ive) signifier of what the horror film most wishes it could hide inside its *own* dark cellar. Tellingly, *Don't Look in the Basement* shows the doctor's living-dead body one last time, during a final roll call that includes brief medium close-ups of the sanitarium's other deranged occupants. Like Dr. Stephens, they too are still breathing, despite having been slain by simple-minded Sam (as retribution for their vulture-like murder of Dr. Masters and for their unwillingness to believe his earlier claims that the asylum director was, in fact, still alive). Capping this closing scene is a close-up of Mrs. Callingham, apparently brought back from the dead for this comical coda. Her frenzied eyes fix on the camera/spectator as she beseeches anyone still watching this hilariously histrionic film to "Get out! Get out! And never, *never* come back!"

The old woman's words not only echo the ominous sentiment that she had shared with Nurse Beale during their first encounter, but also recapitulate a command uttered by several of the other asylum dwellers at different points throughout the narrative. Indeed, no phrase is spoken more often in the film than "Get out!" The words are used by Sarge against an intrusive troublemaker named Danny; by Allyson against the wet-blanket judge who rebuffs her flirtatious advances; and by Nurse Beale when she wakes to find the homicidal judge hovering over her bed, hatchet poised above her head. Like the negative imperative "Don't Look," this repeated expression directs the listener/viewer to paradoxically resist the questionable temptations of the horror genre, which gains its frisson from the audience's desire to "stay in" and confront the unthinkable, to dredge up the thing that might otherwise be consigned to their own metaphorical "basements" (the Freudian unconscious or Žižekian id referred to earlier). Not coincidentally, the space where "bad things" happen to good people in director Jordan Peele's tellingly titled *Get Out* (2017) is an underground laboratory at the bottom of the Armitage family's house, a literally "sunken place" that remains offscreen for much of the narrative. And why is the basement sealed off until *Get Out*'s final act? If we are to believe the excuse that Dr. Armitage (Bradley Whitford) concocts for Chris (Daniel Kaluuya), the film's African American protagonist, it is because he and his lilywhite family are having a problem with "black mold" (a serious health hazard with tell-tale signs of respiratory exposure).

In *Don't Look in the Basement*, upon first meeting Dr. Masters, Charlotte states, "I just *can't believe* Dr. Stephens is dead." The older woman, who is eventually revealed to be an inmate at the sanitarium simply pretending to be a psychiatrist, replies, "We *have* to accept that, Ms. Beale." Together, these two statements articulate an essential conundrum faced by viewers of this and other horror films in which the breathing bodies of actors "playing dead," if noticed, can break the diegetic spell or puncture the illusion of an already-tenuous "reality." Punctum-like, these textual ruptures disrupt the flow of narrative and mark an unwanted intrusion into the mise-en-scène, calling into question the plausibility of a scenario that demands that its characters be mortally wounded or traumatized to the point of breathing their last breath. Stated simply, in the words of Bill Milling (a Hollywood writer/director/producer who has published an online set of "acting tips" for performers drawn to this genre), "Nothing ruins the magic of a horror film [more] than being able to see the dead guy breathing." And yet, like Charlotte, we (the audience)—"we" being the word used by Dr. Masters, as if gesturing toward the film's own incredulous spectators—are asked to turn a blind eye and simply accept the inherent (un)believability of an onscreen death.

In his brief discussion of *Don't Look in the Basement*, cultural critic John Kenneth Muir begins his commentary by musing on the "willing suspension of disbelief" that is often required of horror film audiences (a facet of the genre that I touched upon in the first two chapters of this book):

> We've all heard that term, and we all know what it means. To buy into a movie (and subsequently enjoy it), a viewer must set aside some reservations and just let events happen. However, suspension of disbelief becomes harder the less probable and less realistic a movie seems. Suspension of disbelief becomes downright impossible when a movie blatantly breaks the rules of reality, yet purports to be realistic. *Don't Look in the Basement* is just such a movie. It is 89 minutes of overacting, implausible plotting, and crazy, irrational tics. (Muir 2002, 256)

For Muir, the film fails not one but several tests of "believability." First, filmmaker S. F. Brownrigg, whose directing style might charitably be described as "blunt" or "unpretentious," appears unable to establish a realistic sense of location, both inside the three-story asylum (whose room-to-room spatial layout is admittedly confusing) and outside, where the building's proximity to other locations is unclear. There is also a conspicuous lack of medical supplies within the main setting, which is "the kind of asylum that can only exist in a horror film because it is patently unbelievable" (256). Unable to appreciate the film's sweaty, over-the-top performances by a "game no-name cast," Muir finds it distracting that the actors playing the lunatics "all ham it up beyond belief," becoming grotesques in the process. "They are the insane," he grumbles, "as imagined by a writer who knows nothing about psychology, nothing about human behavior, and nothing about filmmaking" (257). Finally, Charlotte, the film's main character, does not behave in ways that a professionally trained psychiatric nurse presumably would, opting to sleep in an unlocked bedroom on the same floor with murderers and displaying no interest in learning about the shadowy circumstances of Dr. Stephens's death. Also, even when she finally heeds the warning of Mrs. Callingham and endeavors to "get out," the young nurse cannot find a way to escape her claustrophobic environment, despite the many breakable windows that would serve as possible exits for any rationally minded person.

Based on the critical consensus surrounding *Don't Look in the Basement*, Muir is not alone in thinking that it is "a terrible movie filled with dumb characters and a hard-to-swallow 'isolated' setting" (257). But those very demerits, those imperfections and absurdities of the text, also contribute to some audiences' cult-like attraction to it. Of course, this and other examples of what Jeffrey Sconce calls "paracinema" are known to "compel even the most complacent viewer into adopting a reading position marked by that rare combination of incredulous amazement and critical detachment" (2003, 21). Notably, Sconce makes this remark in an essay devoted to an earlier exploitation/horror film about the criminally insane: *Maniac* (1934), director Dwain Esper's equally campy, mistake-prone meditation on the tenuous line between madness and sanity. And, perhaps not surprisingly, that glitch-ridden text likewise features shots in which dead characters appear to breathe, lending an air of sloppiness to the already-sleazy proceedings. Moreover, *Maniac*'s frankly preposterous narrative, which appears to have influenced the plot and themes of Brownrigg's 1973 film, culminates inside a dank basement, where the body of a long-deceased mad scientist is discovered by the snooping authorities.

Significantly, the person in question, Dr. Meirschultz (Horace B. Carpenter), had been breaking into local morgues and attempting to revive the dead before being killed by his lab assistant, a struggling vaudevillian named Don Maxwell (Bill Woods) who thereafter dons the clothing of the deceased man and begins impersonating him. As a sign that he too is going mad, the lackey actor-turned-fake scientist entombs the corpse of the real scientist behind a newly built wall of bricks in the latter's basement. When the police finally arrive on the scene, the meowing of a cat that had been mistakenly buried alive alongside the scientist prompts them to knock down the wall, leading to the discovery of his body. This concluding moment, like an earlier scene showing Don popping that same feline's eyeball out of its socket before ingesting it (and even savoring its taste), is a nod to Edgar Allan Poe's 1843 short story "The Black Cat,"

Figure 6.4. In one of the most outlandish scenes of Dwain Esper's 1934 cult film *Maniac*, the presumably lifeless but still breathing body of Dr. Meirschultz (along with a meowing cat) is revealed behind a recently built brick wall inside a basement, one of the most thematically resonant settings in the horror genre.

suggesting that Esper is aiming to leverage his own cinematic outrageousness against the literary sophistication for which the nineteenth-century writer is known. But the unearthing of Dr. Meirschultz, an event that should be fraught with dramatic tension and terror, is undermined by actor Horace Carpenter's visible exhalation of breath just as his dead character topples over, face forward, from a standing position (figure 6.4). Then, in much the same way that Mrs. Callingham appears to "break the fourth wall" in the final shot of *Don't Look in the Basement* (a stylistic device more commonly associated with experimental films or self-reflexive parodies), Don, now behind bars, directs his address to the camera, telling the audience that he "only wanted to amuse, to entertain." "But here I am," he concludes with theatrical flourish, taking verbal satisfaction in his "supreme impersonation" of Dr. Meirschultz, whom no one had suspected of being dead until this literally revealing dénouement in the basement.

While this parting shot and larger-than-life performance can be chalked up as just one more example of campy excess in a film already suffused with paracinematic elements (including arbitrarily inserted intertitles spelling out the symptoms of dementia, manic depression, and other debilitating mental conditions), the character's emphasis on perfect mimicry as a goal for someone in his line of work (acting) puts the "imperfection" of Carpenter's performance—his inability to hold his breath long enough to sustain the illusion of his character's death—in a new light. Indeed, horror films are filled with *impersonations*, in the form of living actors pretending to be dead people, sometimes adopting tried-and-tested methods (e.g., low diaphragmatic breathing, meditation, etc.) and even muscle relaxers to achieve a semblance of lifelessness. Oddly, these textual aberrations at the end of *Maniac* have gone largely unnoticed by the film's online community of supporters, who, like Sconce, have focused on other moments that are just as deserving of our loving derision (e.g., the aforementioned eye-gouging scene, censor-baiting shots of topless women wrestling one another, and so forth). For Sconce, such moments, in breaking down the "representational logic" that audiences have come to expect in most fictional narratives, demonstrate exploitation cinema's potential in foregrounding "usually invisible codes organizing [those] narratives," even when the goals of filmmakers such as Brownrigg and Esper might be anything but this (as directors likely seeking, but failing, "to replicate dominant codes of Hollywood realism") (2003, 21). For all of its roadshow gimmickry as a motion picture thematizing blackmail, animal torture, heart transplants, and sex-crazed zombies (ideas dreamt up, at least partially, by screenwriter Hildegarde Stadie, Esper's wife), *Maniac* ironically ends by gesturing toward the "thing" (the Real) that is otherwise un-representable, beyond the Symbolic order. And it does so by bringing postmortem movement and breath itself to bear on a narrative premised on the seemingly impossible notion of reanimation.

LET BREATHING CORPSES LIE: HORROR'S (UN)TRUTHS AND THE (UN)REPRESENTABLE REAL

> It's *really* him. Notice how he didn't breathe, and he kept his eyes open like that. That's very hard when you have a snake coming out of your mouth, you know. That's *acting*!
> —ROBERT HILTZIK, the writer-director of *Sleepaway Camp* (1983), speaking facetiously about actor John Dunn to moderator Jeff Hayes, during the audio commentary on the Shout! Factory DVD and Blu-ray releases of the slasher film

Until this point, I have relied on a few examples of both mainstream and non-mainstream films to suggest that breathing is an indelible, thematically resonant part of the horror genre. Now, in extending Sconce's claims about the instructional value of illusion-shattering paracinematic texts, I wish to expand the scope of this study and acknowledge other instances when the respiratory activity of actors is either strategically hidden or mistakenly displayed. Doing so, I hope, will indicate the spread of certain stylistic devices—across the history of the genre and beyond American shores—that either succeed or fail in maintaining the "lie" upon which horror relies in order to achieve its effects. In lieu of using actual human corpses—as Javier Aguirre, the director of *Hunchback of the Morgue* (*El jorobado de la Morgue*, 1973), is said to have done when he asked star Paul Naschy to sever the head from a real (if no-longer-living) body during an eerily authentic autopsy scene—the makers of horror films must rely on certain "tricks" if death scenes are to seem believable. Whether it is by keeping the length of shots short and their lighting dark (as happens when Freddy Krueger's [Robert Englund] first blood-drenched victim, Tina [Amanda Wyss], appears onscreen in *A Nightmare on Elm Street* [1984]) or by utilizing handheld cameras so that the operator's physical movements mask those of the dead characters (as happens throughout the recent horror film *The Transfiguration* [2016]), several different approaches have proven to be successful at dealing with the "problem" suggested by this chapter's title. And it is a "problem for filmmaker and actor alike," according to C. Scott Combs: "[H]ow to eliminate the breathing corpse while playing still onscreen" (2014, 80).

One approach to concealing what Combs calls the "vagrant movement" of actors playing dead characters is to not use actors at all, but rather partial or full-sized body casts of the performers sculpted from various materials. Those materials—Gelatine, plaster, silicone, etc.—are familiar to anyone with a background in prosthetics and practical movie effects. This is the approach that writer-director Robert Hiltzik and makeup effects artist Edward French took when shooting one of the most notorious moments in *Sleepaway Camp* (1983), a slasher film distinguished by its passionate fan base and its twist ending (revealing that the teenaged protagonist Angela [Felissa Rose] not only is the killer responsible for most of the murderous mayhem at Camp Arawak but also has the anatomical features of a boy). Although French and his effects team decided to use a plaster mask molded from Felissa Rose's face in that famously shocking final shot of the film, placing it on the head of an uncredited male stand-in (who was paid a six-pack of beer and a small sum of money for agreeing to full-frontal nudity), they opted for a slightly different lifecasting approach when showing one of Angela's victims, Kenny (John Dunn), whose decomposing body washes to the lakeshore after being killed offscreen. When the drowned camper is shown inside a canoe that became his coffin the previous night, a snake slithers out of his mouth, cueing the audience to the fact of this body's fakeness (something that apparently irked French, who is on record expressing his regret that such a tactic was taken) (figure 6.5). Because a dummy prop was used in place of the actor's body, the problem of visible breathing in this shot was skirted, but the illusion of fictional death is undermined by the haptically perceived sense that the boy's rotting corpse is tangibly *different* from what an actual dead body might *look* and *feel* like. Playfully mocking this

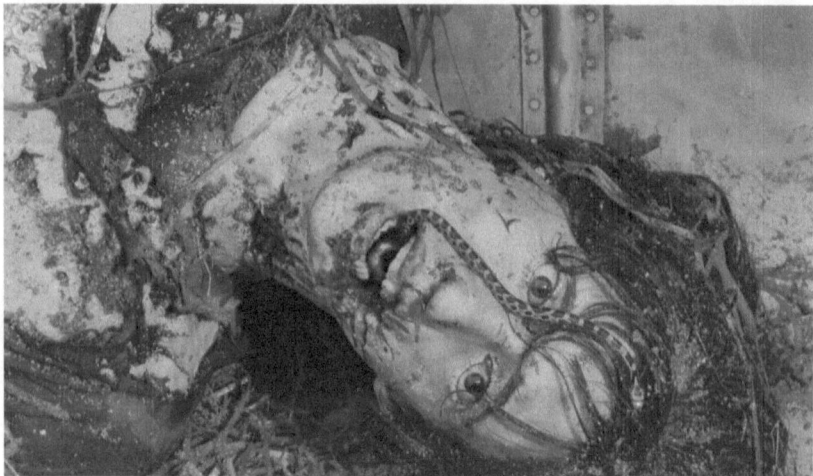

Figure 6.5. Rather than ask actor John Dunn to hold his breath for a sustained period of time, Robert Hiltzik, the director of *Sleepaway Camp* (1983), tasked Edward French and his team of makeup artists with creating a life-sized cast of Dunn's character, Kenny.

laughably "bad" effect in his director's commentary track that accompanies the Shout! Factory DVD and Blu-ray releases of *Sleepaway Camp*, Hiltzik (quoted above) doubles down on the lie that this and other horror films try to foist on disbelieving audiences, facetiously emphasizing that it really *was* Dunn in that shot, holding his breath and keeping his eyes open for a period of time in excess of the normal capabilities of most actors.

Besides the incorporation of body casts in horror films, one device in particular—the insertion of a static still frame, holding momentarily on the frozen image of a lifeless or dying character—has been used frequently enough to merit at least passing attention. As early as 1929, when the Russian formalist Lev Kuloshov wrote his *Art of the Cinema*, film theorists were speculating on the relative instrumentality of this device, which could be used whenever a filmmaker needed the audience "to imagine a dead man, who is not breathing" (1974, 61). Employing a static frame to make it seem as though someone has died in a fictional story might, on the surface, suggest "an actual realistic event," though, as Kuleshov emphasizes, "the moment you begin to imagine or suppose something, you immediately produce in film a theatrical fake" (61). That tendency toward fakery is particularly apparent in the horror genre. For instance, in the slasher film *The Burning* (1981), when nominal hero Todd (Brian Matthews) confronts the disfigured figure of Cropsy (Lou David), who has temporarily traded in his garden shears for a makeshift flamethrower, he discovers the body of a young woman named Karen (Carolyn Houlihan), who has the unenviable distinction of being the monster's first throat-slit victim. Her lifeless body is shown hanging from the ceiling, but the lack of movement in the image calls attention to the fact that this is a freeze-frame shot—an effect that director Tony Maylam and editor Jack Sholder achieved by means of an optical printer rather than more practical on-set trickery. Appearing more than once in this scene, that still image, which is itself a series of repeated images affecting the look of a stationary body, can be seen as a mise-en-abyme of the entire film, which was widely criticized for replicating the familiar tropes of the slasher subgenre. In the words of John Kenneth Muir, viewers are likely to "experience a strange sense of déjà vu" when watching *The Burning*, since its material (e.g., isolated summer camp setting, masked killer, teenaged victim base, subjective camerawork) has "been vetted before, and often more effectively" in other slasher films (2007, 229). In other words, that "seen-it-all" sense of having already experienced *The Burning* is conveyed in microcosm through the recurring yet static still frame of the dead woman's strangely immobilized, unbreathing body.

One of the best-known examples of this optical printing effect occurs at the end of George Romero's *Night of the Living Dead*, during grainy closing credits that play out like a tragic photomontage or documentary exposé of the very *real* social and political nightmares happening outside movie theaters in 1968 (the year of the film's release). Inspired by the freeze-frame climax of director Sidney Lumet's doomsday thriller *Fail-Safe* (1964) (Kane 2010, 70), this sobering conclusion to an otherwise far-fetched story about the zombie apocalypse, which shows "dispassionate posse members hook, drag, and burn" the lifeless body of the film's African-American protagonist Ben (Duane Jones) as if he were an "anonymous piece of meat," might hit as close to home as any horror film in recent memory (70). But the formal means by which Romero is able to achieve this unsettling effect—the freeze-frame—can also be seen in the final shot of the 1983 Stephen King adaptation *Cujo*, which leaves in question the fate of a family exposed to rabid dog bites (Williams 2014), as well as in several Italian zombie films of the 1970s and 1980s, which, as Donato Totaro argues, culminate with "often ambiguous or open-ending conclusion[s]" (2003, 164).

One of the most revealing uses of a freeze-frame to mask the breathing of a character occurs in an early scene of director Bob Clark's *Deathdream* (1974), when the camera zeroes in on the savagely gashed neck of a dead truck driver named Howie (David Gawlikowski) whose body is laid out on an autopsy table. The man, never to be seen again after this scene, is the first victim of the main character, a US war veteran named Andy Brooks (Richard Backus) who is likewise supposed to be dead (having been mortally wounded by sniper-fire while fighting in Vietnam) but who returns home as a pale-faced vampire. Framed in medium long shot, the actor playing Howie initially can be seen breathing, thanks to the subtle movement of his chest. Ted, a police detective investigating his murder, lifts the dead man's right arm with a jerk, asking the doctor performing the autopsy if the conspicuous needle mark means that he

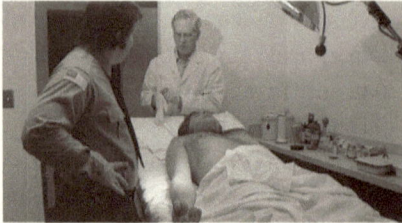 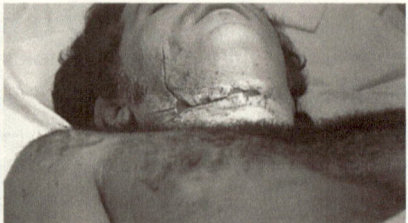

Figure 6.6. A doctor performs an autopsy on a dead truck driver, who can be seen breathing in one shot from director Bob Clark's *Deathdream* (1975), only to be captured motionless in freeze-frame after the camera has moved to a close-up image of the man.

was "on dope." This jerky movement-on-top-of-movement suddenly makes the actor's breathing less visible, as does the static insert shot that immediately follows (figure 6.6). And yet, in thrusting a close-up of Howie's slashed throat onto the unsuspecting viewer, this freeze-frame image is as distracting as the actor's inhalation and exhalation of air, as it keeps not only the physical remains of the corpse in suspended animation, but also the "breathable space" of air molecules around it suspended as well. Time, too, is momentarily arrested until the director cuts back to our earlier view of the body, once again breathing in plain sight. Tellingly, this moment when the ontological distinctiveness of the motion-picture medium is called into question through an optical-printing technique more reminiscent of still photography than of cinematography had been anticipated during the opening credits of *Deathdream*, when Andy's face is frozen in place, in mid-fall, at the time of his demise. Killed in battle but miraculously resurrected by the offscreen incantation of his mother whose muffled words ("You *can't* die. You *promised*, Andy. You promised you'd come back. You *promised*") accompany this out-of-focus shot, he becomes the living, breathing sign of what awaits his own victims, whose blood he will consume through needles, as if a drug addict.

In the words of Stacey Abbott, *Deathdream* "uses the vampire as a metaphor for the returning soldier, traumatized and changed by the events he has experienced, and unable to live up to family and social expectations. No longer the innocent teenage boy who left home to defend his country, he literally returns as a monster, dispassionate and detached from the living, revealed to be a killer capable of horrific atrocities" (2007, 83). But Andy, whose last breath before dying was held in suspension by way of a freeze frame, is also a metaphor for the delicate balance between "death" and "dream"—between *eternal* sleep and *everyday* sleep—that is brought into close contingency by the film's title. Significantly, when the blood-drinking protagonist—now decomposing and physically misshapen beyond all recognition (thanks to the prosthetics work of makeup artist Tom Savini)—finally gains his eternal rest during *Deathdream*'s closing scene, he does so by crawling, on his own volition (but viewed by his wailing, helpless mother), into an empty grave. Once inside that gaping hole, he appears to be *sleeping* rather than dead. Continuing to breathe after taking its "final" breath, the body, half-buried in dirt and half-exposed to the night, makes visible the *truth* of the lie of the horror film, lending proof to the woman's insistence that her son "cannot die."

And yet, die people *must* if the horror genre is to maintain its chokehold on the audience. Not surprisingly, death-by-strangulation or asphyxiation, when represented in horror film, requires special attention to characters' resulting loss of breath, and indeed a repertoire of visual tricks has been brought to bear on such scenes. Consider, for instance, the titular gill-man's attack of a startled deckhand in *Creature from the Black Lagoon* (1954): the amphibious monster (Ben Chapman) wraps his webbed fingers around his victim's neck and, two seconds later, Zee (Bernie Gozier), the unfortunate target of the creature's throttling, drops precipitously out of frame. The swiftness of this physical altercation, combined with the manner in which Zee disappears from view (falling onto the beach, which conveniently hides the actor's breathing), contributes to its effectiveness as a sign of the mortal threats faced by his shipmates, who for the time being gather around Zee's body and pronounce him to be "dead." Even when framed (in an ensuing shot) at a medium distance by a camera that shows nearly the entire length of his body (from his knees to his head), the actor's intake and outtake of air cannot be seen. This is owing to the low lighting and heavy shadows typical of day-for-night shooting, as well as the arrangement of other bodies (those of his fellow crew members) whose fretful movements ironically "distract" us from the distraction of a potential mistake. According to one source, this minor character's death "was originally meant to include him being thrown toward the camera," in accordance with the 3-D effects of the film as a whole, but was ultimately depicted in a far simpler way because the wires for such an elaborate stunt "kept breaking" (Anon. 2012; Weaver 2017, 191). Director Jack Arnold's practical, on-set solution, while devoid of the visceral impact that stereoscopic cinematography might deliver, nevertheless enables the audience to suspend its disbelief in the face of mounting absurdities. And that solution, it would seem, was simply a matter of composing and editing shots in such a way that spectators do not have a chance to see the thing—i.e., the breath of the actor—that *must* be hidden, kept out of frame.[4]

A considerably longer choking scene than what takes place in *Creature from the Black Lagoon* occurs during the second half of *The Living Skeleton* (*Kyūketsu Dokurosen*, 1968), director Hiroshi Matsuno's dark, expressionistic horror film in which the vengeful spirit of a dead woman named Yoriko (Kikko Matsuoka) inhabits the body of her twin sister after being gunned down by a group of modern-day pirates who seized control of her ship. The life of the possessed sibling, Saeko (also Kikko Matsuoka), also comes to a premature end when the

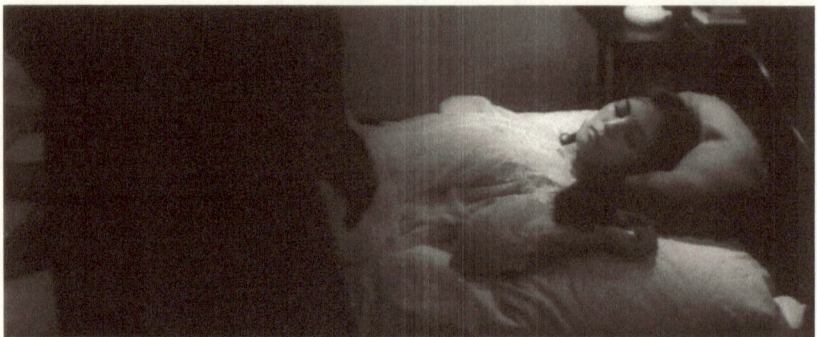

Figure 6.7. Saeko, one of the main characters in director Hiroshi Matsuno's *The Living Skeleton* (1968), has just been strangled to death, but the actor playing her (Kikko Matsuoka) continues breathing and moving slightly throughout this scene.

ringleader of the pirates, posing as a Catholic priest (Masumi Okada), sneaks up on the sleeping woman and puts his hands around her neck. Running for nearly one minute and punctuated by orchestral stabs as well as the frantic cries of the woman as she gasps for air, this scene, comprised of claustrophobic medium shots and close-ups in which her body is splayed across the length of the widescreen frame, is certainly "gripping," fraught with tension. But its unnerving effect is completely undone once the camera pauses long enough to pick up actress Kikko Matsuoka's still-heaving chest as well as the closing of her parted lips after the life has purportedly been squeezed from her character (or, to put it in more clinical terms, after the character's airways have been constricted, her larynx has been compressed, and the flow of oxygen into her brain has been severely hindered) (figure 6.7).

Saeko's attacker viciously tears away her nightgown to expose her left breast and then runs his gloved hand across the contours of her face, giving the audience yet another glimpse of postmortem movement on the part of the performer. Eventually, the black-gloved killer gets his comeuppance at the hands of both "dead" sisters, one of whom (Yoriko) has retained her beauty thanks to daily blood transfusions supplied by her flesh-eating husband, a mad scientist (Nishimura Kō) who has kept his wife's partially mummified corpse tucked away, out of sight, in the bowels of the ship where she had been killed (the nautical equivalent of a house's basement). Notably, the zombie-like doctor, nearly drained of blood himself, has managed to stay alive and keep the spirit of Yoriko alive as well by listening to an audiotape of her moaning voice, a "breathy" sound of inhalation and exhalation that had been recorded when she was still alive.

Another black-gloved killer is unveiled in the concluding scenes of Dario Argento's *Deep Red* (*Profondo rosso*, 1975), although this time the culprit is a woman (Helga Ulmann) who is herself strangled when her necklace gets caught

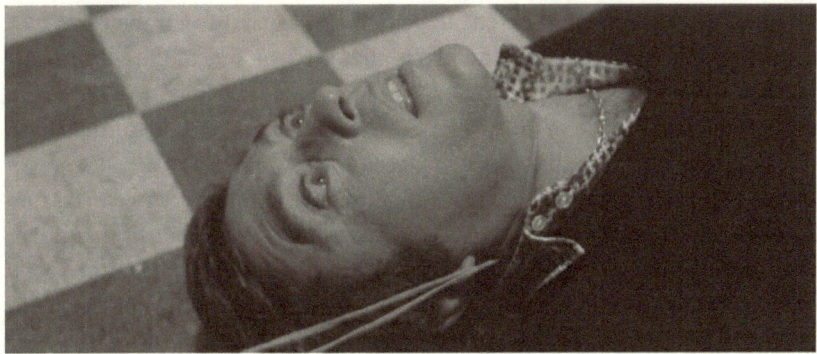

Figure 6.8. Director Dario Argento employs a left-to-right track in this brief shot from *Cat O' Nine Tails* (1971), making it difficult to spot the movement of actor Vittorio Congia's neck.

inside the gate of an elevator cage making its downward descent. Rather than dwell on the body of the dead woman, as Hiroshi Matsuno does in *The Living Skeleton*, the Italian director turns this quickly edited set piece into a Grand Guignol-like spectacle of sudden bloodletting once the chain, tightening its grip, finally slices through her neck. But Argento does not cut to the decapitated head and body, opting instead to end his *giallo* film with a shot of the dangling necklace followed by a freeze-frame of the male protagonist, Marcus Daly (David Hemmings), whose face is reflected in a pool of either his own or the dead woman's blood (it is not clear, given that, seconds earlier, he had been attacked by the meat-cleaver-wielding killer). As devilishly skillful as Argento is in conveying the brutality of this beheading and leaving intact the gravity of such a deadly encounter (which might otherwise have been undermined by the image of a breathing body), *Deep Red*'s denouement offers just one of many potential "solutions" to the problem of postmortem movement in horror film. Indeed, the filmmaker found other ways to hide human breath while playing into our collective desire to see what *cannot*, in truth, be visualized in the context of a fictional representation. For instance, in Argento's *Cat O' Nine Tails* (*Il gatto a nove code*, 1971), after a paparazzi photographer named Righetto (Vittorio Congia) is strangled to death in his developing lab, the camera, which captures his upper torso and head in medium close-up, tracks laterally from left to right, untethering our gaze from any fixed position and thus making it difficult to see any breathing that might undermine the scene's terrorizing effect (figure 6.8). If, however, the audience *does* notice any movement on the part of the actor, whose throat muscles appear to flex slightly (shifting the necklace just below the cord wrapped tautly around his neck), it is only because they have watched and rewatched this fleeting moment with the *intention* of spotting the mistake, an experience not likely to occur on first viewing (given the brevity of the shot and the mobility of the camera).

Ironically, movement—that of the cinematic apparatus (in the form of a dolly/tracking shot, zoom shot, handheld shot, etc.)—is one of the chief means by which the body's respiratory gestures are made "invisible." We see it (or, rather, *don't see it*), for example, in an early scene of another Italian *giallo* film, director Emilio P. Miraglia's *The Red Queen Kills Seven Times* (*La dama rossa uccide sette volte*, 1972). Taking place in a funeral home where two bickering sisters, Kitty (Barbara Bouchet) and Franziska (Marina Malfatti), stand over their recently deceased grandfather (Rudolf Schundlur), the scene immediately draws our attention to his body atop a coffin, a spectatorial prompting supplied by the mourning women, who direct their own gaze at him. However, as soon as this medium long shot begins, Miraglia's camera dollies forward, making the dead man's body a moving target and redirecting our gaze toward Kitty and Franziska, who are the only figures left in the frame by the time the shot ends (figure 6.9). Seemingly a textbook illustration of "unmotivated" camera movement, as defined by Ed Sikov and other theorists (2010, 28), this moment of mobile framing is in fact *motivated* by the filmmaker's desire to shift subject-object relations and to conceal the fundamental (un)truth of the horror genre, which encourages such visual flourishes (e.g., dolly shots, whip-pans, crash zooms, etc.) in much the same way that magicians practice the art of misdirection in order to fool or deceive audiences during a sleight-of-hand trick. As Sikov notes, motivated camera movements are typically "those that are prompted by the characters and events in the film" (on view, for instance, when an individual or group of people is kept in frame while walking), but even motionless characters (for instance, the dead grandfather in *The Red Queen Kills Seven Times*) can exert a kind of gravitational pull, especially when the actors playing them are unable to suppress their body's natural biological functions for a sustained period of time.

In one of the few theoretical considerations of the rift that sometimes opens between a dead character and the living, breathing actor asked to play that character, André Loiselle distinguishes between the centripetal focus typical of stage plays and the centrifugal diffusion that partially characterizes cinema. Notably, Loiselle opts for neuroanatomical terms—*afferent* and *efferent*, respectively—when describing the distinct ways that theatrical dramas and motion pictures hold their audiences' attention (2003, 159). Whereas the former denotes an inward, axonal projection of the gaze toward a point within a static, confined theatrical setting, the latter suggests an outward explosion of signifiers, including potentially distracting environmental details, aimed at (and often bombarding) the film viewer, similar to the manner in which nerve fibers carry multiple impulses away from the central nervous system toward peripheral organs. The dichotomy between afferent drama and efferent cinema is crystallized, he argues, "when the cadaver is performed on stage or in a film—that is,

Figure 6.9. An early shot from director Emilio P. Miraglia's *The Red Queen Kills Seven Times* (1972) begins by showing two sisters mourning the death of their grandfather (visible in the middle-ground) and ends after the camera has dollied forward, strategically displacing the dead man (or, rather, the living/breathing actor) out of frame and refocusing our attention on the women.

when an actor plays dead" (159). During such occurrences, "the self-controlled live body of the actor" counteracts "the boundary-breaking potential of the corpse," a notion that Loiselle inherits from Julia Kristeva, who first conceived of the radical potential of the abject cadaver to transgress social norms. In his words, "the appearance of the cadaver in a film or play implies cinematic exosmosis—the dead body's disintegration, dispersion, and merger with the environment—at the same time as the actor's very regulation of the live body to recreate the signs of death performs the centripetal concentration typical of drama" (159). It should be noted that, when watching a stage play, the audience is caught up in the liveness of the performance and is thus more attuned to the "natural motility" of the breathing "dead" body; on the other hand, the film spectator has presumably fewer opportunities to fix their gaze or even find the breath of an actor or character who is part of a constantly fluctuating and "stuffed" semiotic field (186). And yet, despite its many sleight-of-hand tricks and visual flourishes designed to distract the viewer from what might be called the respiratory Real, the horror film is still so drawn to the sight of death that, in lingering over lifeless bodies, it frequently and unwittingly reveals its own lies or artificiality in the process.

Of course, genre practitioners have also been known to gravitate toward other forms of sordid and salacious material, as alluded to in my previous references to *The Living Skeleton*, one of the countless horror films to momentarily dawdle on the sight of a partially naked woman whose heaving breasts might ironically distract audiences from seeing the breathing that produces such movement in the first place. Although a discussion of this body genre's predilection for genitalic display is beyond the scope of the present chapter, it is worth briefly considering how the often-titillating or eroticized depictions of female victims of male violence—women whose exposed breasts are framed in such a way as to make the viewer complicit in a frequently misogynistic system of visual representation—might expand our understanding of respiratory activity in horror film. At the very least, we might better appreciate how respiration and representation are linked together, each one setting corporeal limitations on particular individuals—namely, women—whose bodily movements and physical traits are subjected to a level of immobilizing scrutiny before the camera lens not typically extended to male characters.

HEAVING BREASTS, SEXUALIZING BREATH

> Doesn't seem proper, all those girls showing off their . . . "talents."
> —SUE ALLEN (Phyllis Kirk) to her friend Scott Andrews (Paul Picerni),
> after he has taken her to a sexually suggestive burlesque show, in *House of Wax* (1953)

It should not be surprising that images of heaving breasts in horror films—including those of women pretending to be dead—began proliferating at an unprecedented rate during the 1960s. Characterized by historians as a period of significant social and political changes around the world, that decade is also remembered as a time when censorship standards in various cultural industries were relaxed before being partially dismantled or replaced entirely by more liberal regulatory schemes in the years that followed (Petley 2017, 130). Notably, the decade kicked off with two black-and-white horror films—Alfred Hitchcock's *Psycho* and Mario Bava's *Black Sunday* (*La maschera del demonio*, 1960)—that foreground scantily clad women in a few scenes and thus point toward the new permissiveness of the era even as they harken back to the past through monochromatic imagery at odds with the industrial trend toward color cinematography in their respective nations. The latter film, long revered as the first real indication of Bava's directorial finesse and preeminence in his native Italy (a country that, as Roberto Curti points out, was still attached to "discriminatory and sexophobic" attitudes in the early 1960s), is also famous for introducing horror fans to the British actress Barbara Steele (2015, 42). An eventual icon of the genre—one of its most prominent "scream queens"— who would appear in such subsequent Italian-dubbed productions as Antonio Margheriti's *The Long Hair of Death* (*I lunghi capelli della morte*, 1964), Mario Caiano's *Nightmare Castle* (*Amanti d'Oltretomba*, 1965), and Camillo Mastrocinque's *An Angel for Satan* (*Un angelo per Satana*, 1966), Steele inhabits the dual roles of Asa and Katia Vajda in *Black Sunday*. When she is introduced in the first scene (set in seventeenth-century Moldavia), the former character has already been condemned to death for practicing witchcraft. Seconds before having a spiked bronze mask hammered onto her face and being left to die, Asa, bound to a rack and branded with the mark of Satan, puts a curse on her torch-bearing male accusers and their descendants. Because the man who levels the stiffest charges against this so-called she-devil is her brother, Asa effectively condemns her own successors, including Katia, to that posthumous retribution. The latter is an elegant woman several generations removed from her vengeful ancestor whose life is imperiled once the skeletal remains of Asa are magically re-fleshed thanks to an unexpected blood infusion, supplied by a stranger who happened upon her tomb and cut his hand on some broken glass above her body.

"Re-fleshing," or the refreshing of flesh, is in fact central to this gothic horror film, which at times lingers lasciviously on the body of a female actor who, in the words of Martyn Conterio, "would launch a thousand wet dreams and equally a thousand nightmares" over the course of a career that saw her repeating several of the provocative onscreen gestures which would become even more sexually charged once clothes were shed as freely as were inhibitions (2015, 31). Before Asa tries to take the place of her physically identical descendant Katia, she is shown inside the crypt opposite the man, Dr. Choma Kruvajan (Andrea Checchi), who had earlier spilled his life-restoring blood atop her body. Lying in a prone position and fixing a hypnotic gaze on him, she lures the doctor toward her now-heaving chest, the first of several instances when breathing is lent an erotic charge in *Black Sunday*. This sexualizing of breath is also apparent in later scenes showing Katia in bed, her chest expanding and contracting in a way that hints at this and other horror films' affective registers: the pull-push tension between attraction and repulsion that is itself "fleshed out" in the form of female bodies. Tellingly, when Kruvajan's assistant, a handsome young man named Andrej (John Richardson) who has already fallen in love with Katia, returns to the crypt where Asa lies in wait, he leaps back in horror, shocked and repelled by the sight of her exaggerated breathing—ironically, the very action that (if Conterio and other critics are to be

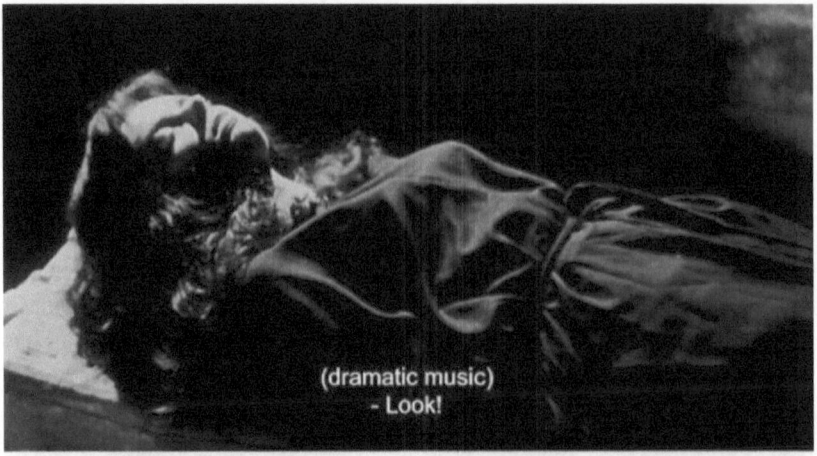

Figure 6.10. A scene from Mario Bava's *Black Sunday* (1960) that draws attention to emerging horror film star Barbara Steele's heaving chest.

believed) draws legions of straight male viewers to a genre that, in the words of John Kenneth Muir (who is specifically referring to the British Hammer production of *Lust for a Vampire* [1971]), is "all about breasts" (figure 6.10). As implied by Muir, "big breasts, little breasts, breasts under nightgowns, exposed breasts in water, [and] heaving breasts" pop up in several horror films from the 1970s onward (2012, 64), though with increasingly misogynistic undercurrents as censorship codes became more relaxed.

Whereas the Hammer Horror films "made in England from the mid-1950s through the 1970s" could be construed as "artistic classics and feminist expressions," even as they embraced new levels of violence ("complete with graphic gore") and sex ("often featuring shots of bare female breasts"), according

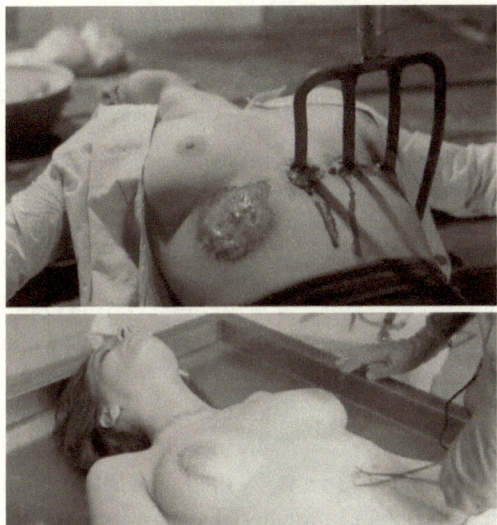

Figure 6.11. In horror films ranging from Jean Rollin's *The Grapes of Death* (1978) to Lucio Fulci's *The New York Ripper* (1982), the exposed breasts of recently killed female characters ironically distract from their otherwise visible postmortem breathing.

to Tom Pollard (2016, 34), many examples of cinematic horror coming from other parts of the world took the "idea of excess (immoral, sensual, carnal) and transgression" that Barbara Steele, Hazel Court, Ingrid Pitt, and other actors had embodied throughout their heyday as screen sirens into decidedly darker, filthier waters (Curti 2015, 42). From softcore horror director Jean Rollin's *The Grapes of Death* (*Les raisins de la mort*, 1978), which momentarily dwells on the torso of a young woman pitchforked to death by her father, to *giallo* director Lucio Fulci's *The New York Ripper* (*Lo squartatore di New York*, 1982), which shows the unseen killer's first female victim unclothed on a coroner's table, nakedness is not simply exploited for the sake of titillation, but used to "distract" from the otherwise visible respiration of actors whose *breasts* rather than *chests* flesh out or externalize what their airways, lungs, and blood vessels are primarily responsible for enabling (figure 6.11). However, like the buxom college student Sophie (Louise Cliffe), who—as the first person to die in *Wrong Turn 3: Left for Dead* (2009)—is shown playfully taking off her bikini top to let her breasts "breathe" (to the satisfaction of her fellow rafters) only to immediately be shot through one of those breasts by the arrow of a backwoods cannibal, women are frequently punished for doing the very things that the genre's most misogynistic men ask them to. This metatextually underscores why a male director's demand that his female actors mask their breathing is more than a little hypocritical or dubious when a film's visual economy rests so heavily on those breasts.

CONCLUSION: BACK TO THE BASEMENT

> It's getting hard to breathe, isn't it? I'm going to seal the last openings. You won't be able to breathe but you won't suffocate. Your heart will burst from fright before you lose consciousness.
> —the masked killer in *Tourist Trap* (1979), as he prepares to apply a suffocating amount of white plaster to the face of his victim, Tina (Dawn Jeffory-Nelson)

In this chapter, I have endeavored to build upon Davina Quinlivan's pioneering work on cinematic breathing by focusing on the conspicuously present but often-overlooked place of breath in horror films. Tellingly, Quinlivan begins her 2012 book by asking, "How can we start to think about something we cannot see?"—a nod to the challenge of visually locating something so elusive within cultural productions that are themselves ontologically difficult to pin down, shifting between material and immaterial states (2012, 1). But, as I point out above, we *can* and often *do* see people draw in and release air on screen, even when they are supposed to be absolutely motionless (something that only a still photograph or digital trickery can help them to achieve). As Siegfried Kracauer notes in his 1960 study *Theory of Film*, "What the actor tries to impart—the physical existence of a character—is overwhelmingly present on the screen," the result of the camera isolating and amplifying "a fleeting glance, an inadvertent shrug of the shoulder" (2004, 20). Indeed, the motion-picture medium is predisposed to capturing and magnifying performative fluctuations, unintentional though they might be, and therefore brings bodily consciousness to the viewer in a way that few other expressive forms are capable of doing, as Quinlivan herself observes. Horror films, as the most corporeally intense of all cinematic genres (with the possible exception of melodrama and pornography, which likewise are designed to elicit strong physical reactions from viewers) (Williams 1991), therefore lend themselves to such an analysis, with the understanding that any conclusions that we might arrive at are provisional at best, merely the first steps toward a deeper, breath-oriented understanding of the genre.

To fully fathom the affective dimensions of the genre, it might be useful for scholars to consider what is actually entailed when a person breathes, as well as what happens to a person's body when he or she passes away—the two activities most frequently depicted in horror films. The latter can result from any number of conditions and is biologically marked not only by the cessation of breathing but also by a lack of evidence of brain function, circulation, and heart activity, although, as the surgeon and writer Sherwin B. Nuland reminds us, "cardiopulmonary resuscitation (CPR) or rapid transfusion may succeed in resuscitating a person whose life has seemingly ended," at least for a few minutes after clinical death has been pronounced (1993, 121). Kevin Glynn, MD, a specialist in pulmonary medicine and the author of the recently published book *Gasping for Air*, explains the breathing process in the following way:

> Nerves in the base of the brain send rhythmic impulses down the spinal cord to the diaphragm and other breathing muscles to activate inhalation. Under normal circumstances, breathing becomes shallow during sleep, but nature controls the system tightly, and even a tiny rise in carbon dioxide or drop in oxygen causes the brain to stimulate the respiratory system to breathe more deeply and rapidly. It is like a finely tuned thermostat that turns up the furnace should the temperature fall and turns it down promptly when the proper degree of warmth is reached. (2017, 178)

It is telling that Glynn's description of breathing as an automated function of the self-regulating body rests upon an image—that of a high-temperature heating unit/oven—that many horror film fans will recognize as an entrenched part of the genre's visual repertoire. Dating back to Rex Ingram's *The Magician* (1926) and other silent-era productions, roaring furnaces became, in the words of William Everson, "an apt suggestion of Hell" (1975, 16), something recently evoked in Darren Aronofsky's *Mother!* (2017). During the ninety-year interval between the theatrical releases of those two motion pictures, a slew of other horror films—from the mainstream hit *A Nightmare on Elm Street* to the schlocky exploitation film *Nightmare Beach* (1989)—made a point of associating the furnace, the combustible heart of the basement, not with *breath* but with *death*.

In their brief overview of the "basement" subgenre of horror cinema, Chris Vander Kaay and Kathleen Fernandez-Vander Kaay refer to this cinematically privileged space as "premature burial [grounds] for things not yet dead," things that "hold onto us as much as we hold onto them." This is a fitting description of the way in which still-breathing bodies—i.e., those of actors pretending to be deceased on screen—prick our senses and draw our attention to one of the genre's most unavoidable paradoxes. Stated simply, what all but the most metatextual or parodic horror films wish to *hide*—to keep concealed inside their own metaphorical "basements"—is the inherent artifice of fictional death, which has traditionally been represented by way of living actors who must mask their breathing in order to sustain the feeling of dread on which the genre is affectively reliant. Terror thus evaporates when performers and/or filmmakers fail to disguise their breathing and/or distract the spectator from this physiological attribute of *living*, rather than dead, people. Indeed, one reason why *Don't Breathe* is able to ratchet up its tension, scene-to-scene, while maintaining its vice-like grip on the viewer is the fact that director Fede

Álvarez (working with cinematographer Pedro Luque) successfully diverts our attention from the potentially illusion-shattering presence of breathing dead bodies (those of Money and Alex), which are shown only briefly, either from a distance or in slow-motion. And yet, there is something to be said for the filmic "failures" alluded to earlier: the mistake-ridden, excess-filled examples of paracinema that inadvertently reveal what more polished productions like *Don't Breathe* conceal. Ultimately, the "problem" of postmortem movement in horror films is not that it breaks the illusion of fictional representation but that it seems to necessitate a range of stylistic and technological "fixes" that only put us—the paradoxically attracted and distracted audience—at a further remove from the always-elusive "Real."

7

SMELLING LIKE A SLAUGHTERHOUSE

Cinematic Olfactics and the Stench of Horror

> No one wants to have to smell the stuff of horror fiction.... [I]f we piped the smell of a rotting corpse into a theater showing *Jeepers Creepers* (2001), everyone would leave.
> —AARON SMUTS, "Cognitive and Philosophical Approaches to Horror" (2017, 10)

An early scene in director Tobe Hooper's *The Texas Chain Saw Massacre* (1974), following an opening-credits sequence in which the sight and sound of a hostile universe edging ever-closer toward apocalypse are signified by a boiling red sun and the discordant crashing of cymbals, hinges on a largely overlooked part of the human sensorium—one that, unlike vision and hearing, remains understudied in critical accounts of horror as a cinematic "body genre." As the film's young protagonists, Sally Hardesty (Marilyn Burns) and her brother Franklin (Paul A. Partain), along with their ill-fated friends Jerry (Allen Danziger), Kirk (William Vail), and Pam (Teri McMinn), drive toward the siblings' family homestead in the heart of the Lone Star state, their van passes by a slaughterhouse. At this point, Hooper and film editors Larry Carroll and Sallye Richardson intercut footage of fenced-in cattle with shots of the vehicle's sardine-packed occupants, struggling to keep cool in the sweltering heat. Tellingly, Franklin, a plus-sized, heavily perspiring paraplegic squeezed into his wheelchair like a hot dog sausage inside a moist bun, perceives the presence of the abattoir through his sense of *smell*, sniffing out the stinky creatures awaiting their death and explaining that such animals used to be killed by sledgehammer blows (but which are now executed through the more "humane" method of bolt-action air guns). He also briefly reminisces about his deceased grandfather who sold cattle to slaughterhouses long ago. This suggests that a particular odor—the stench of a stockyard, where living creatures become dead meat—has the power to dredge up painful memories and thus serves as a conduit between past and present (figure 7.1).

Figure 7.1. The occupants of a van detect an odor in the air—the stench of a nearby slaughterhouse—in this early moment from *The Texas Chain Saw Massacre* (1974).

Soon, and despite the fact that the group has just visited the grandfather's gravesite at a nearby cemetery (which has been vandalized), four of the five friends decide to pull the van over and pick up a hitchhiker (Nubbins Sawyer, played by Edwin Neal), ignoring Franklin's objections that the suspicious-looking stranger will most certainly "smell like a slaughterhouse." The man, whose face bears a red inkblot-like birthmark that recalls the fiery sunspots of the opening credits, indeed brings with him the malodorous associations of the killing floor. Flashing a snaggletooth grin and passing around his Polaroid photos of animal carcasses, he explains how head cheese is made from nearly every one of a cow's organs: from its muscles, ligaments, and jowls to its eyes, gums, and nose. Then, in a show of sudden aggression, he slices Franklin's arm with a razor blade before being kicked out of the speeding vehicle. His toxic intrusion into this space, like the foul stench emanating from the slaughterhouse outside, marks the first of several deadly encounters. One by one, those encounters will claim the main characters' lives over the course of this film's dread-inducing narrative, leaving only Sally—the proverbial "final girl"—to fend for herself at the end as a traumatized, frantically screaming hitchhiker herself whose face, smeared with blood, harkens back to the stranger's eerily ruddy visage.[1]

The above scene from *The Texas Chain Saw Massacre* serves as an entryway into this chapter's exploration of horror film's olfactory elements, looking specifically at how the genre's unique—and *uniquely unsettling*—smells are evoked through a combination of symbolic (audiovisual) cues and material (embodied) memories on the spectator's part. It is unlikely that many audiences will have stepped foot inside a slaughterhouse prior to viewing Hooper's film, and they probably have not had the distinct sensation of breathing in that putrescent perfume—the physically and perhaps morally revolting odor of abattoir flesh—since their initial encounter with this early prototype of the slasher subgenre. Nevertheless, mise-en-scène as well as sound design, including the palpably icky interior of the claustrophobic van and the metallic clanging of percussive instruments, contribute to an olfactory experience that can be just as real or perceptible as any other form of sensorial pleasure (or displeasure) that one might derive from the film. Drawing upon the work of Vivian Sobchack (1992; 2004), Laura U. Marks (2001), Paul Elliot (2011), Lorna Piatti-Farnell (2017), and other theorists who have investigated the mimetic function and cultural significance of smell in cinema, I strive to rectify the long-held misperception of the medium as a strictly *audiovisual* form of expressive communication—i.e., one that ostensibly lacks the means to stimulate our senses of *taste* (gustation), *touch* (somatosensation), and *smell* (olfaction) in any but the most superficial of ways.

That last sense—smell—has been especially neglected by film scholars who privilege the embodied experiences of seeing and hearing in cinema. For instance, in their otherwise thorough and inclusive book *Film Theory: An Introduction through the Senses*, Thomas Elsaesser and Malte Hagener treat the cinematic object as an anatomized *subject* in its own right, a Sobchackian maneuver in which the authors group motion pictures together under the broad categories of "cinema as eye," "cinema as ear," and "cinema as skin and touch" (2010, 82, 108, 129). However, no space in their study is given to the concept of "cinema as nose," and indeed the sense of smell is only gestured toward in a passing, perfunctory way.[2] The conspicuous absence in most critical writing of one of the five major sensory experiences—as both a biological and physiological phenomenon as well as a cultural, social, and historical construct (as we are reminded by scholars outside the film studies discipline, such as Diane Ackerman, Constance Classen, David Howes, and Anthony Synnott)—points toward a broader tendency to "deodorize" history, to present material and rhetorical renderings of past events as strangely scentless, without the least whiff of the people, places, and things that comprise that history (Classen et al., 1994). But it also speaks to the counterintuitive nature of such an undertaking, which flies in the face of several decades of received wisdom about cinema among ontological purists and technological determinists as first and foremost a *visual* medium. However, as I hope to reveal in this and the chapter that follows, the haptic quality of visual images can make one's access to certain sense-memories, including those related to smell, possible.

Beyond contributing to the larger effort to "re-odorize" film history (in much the same way that Mark Jenner has done with the social and cultural "smellscape" of early modern England [2000]), I wish to open up new hermeneutic avenues into the horror genre by way of an olfactory approach that foregrounds deeply embedded cultural fears found in representative texts, from mainstream US productions such as *The Amityville Horror* (1979) and *Dreamcatcher* (2003)—both major case studies in chapter eight—to relatively overlooked examples of international art-exploitation cinema such as *The Cannibal Man* (*La Semana del asesino*, 1972). Attention will also be paid to low-budget American and British films such as *Reeker* (2005) and *Dread* (2009) as well as more recent critical darlings such as *Raw* (2016), which are works that directly engage, in primal terms, the various stenches of horror (e.g., putrefying flesh, rancid meat, stagnant water, etc.). If cultural historians and film theorists can be said to suffer from a kind of "odophobia" that has blocked access to a corporeal engagement with the objects of their analysis, then a renegotiation of the terms by which horror cinema exploits physically felt or perceived fears might result in a more full-bodied set of interpretative tools, giving us the means to better understand that which is literally and figuratively right beneath our noses.

WHAT'S THAT SMELL (LIKE)? MAKING SENSE OF HORROR'S SCENTS, FROM *RAW* TO *SAW*

> It is the smell of the grave, he thought in revulsion. It smells like the rotting shit of a million horses. It smells like a mountain of decomposed corpses. It smells like an ocean of hot bloody pus. It smells like every desiccated and moldy piece of garbage in the world baked into a pie. It smelled.
> —a weirdly "thick" description of the reek of dried-up body wastes attached to Erick Linstrom, the paralyzed protagonist in Richard Matheson's previously unpublished first novel, *Hunger and Thirst* (2000)

What does a horror film smell like? To ask such a question—patently absurd and perhaps even laughable on the surface—is akin to inquiring what a rainbow sounds like or what a scream of terror tastes like. At the same time, this bit of rhetorical provocation, this invitation to the reader to imagine the synesthetic interconnectedness of the senses, is perhaps not so preposterous if one bears in mind the common linguistic feature linking these inquiries. Rather than posing the very different question of what *actually* comprises a motion picture's aromas (or, for that matter, the question of how the mouth and tongue's taste receptors might interact with a particular pigment), I wish to initiate this investigation into cinematic olfactics by drawing attention to the *simile*, a figure of speech that makes such comparative leaps linguistically, if not literally, possible. As I have argued elsewhere, the figurative likening of one thing to another is a form of poetic signification and sense-making that has practical uses in the real world (Diffrient 2006, 81–95). In that light, the word "like," found in the main question that animates this chapter's "sniffing out" of sensorial meaning, gestures toward broader epistemological concerns with social and cultural comparativism (something that will be more fully explored in the final chapter of this book, devoted partially to Hong Kong horror films and their relationship to English-language horror films). For the purposes of the present discussion, a brief consideration of horror film's comparative poetics should suffice in laying the groundwork for my ensuing comments about cinematic synesthesia.

As an intrinsic element in simile construction, "like" (or "as") provides the connective tissue between two essentially (or seemingly) dissimilar things. However, unlike straight metaphor, which "attempts to conceal the gap" between individual elements, simile reveals the gap and, according to Jacqueline Vaught Brogan, "provides a point of intimacy that is contingent upon . . . separation" (1986, 125). Separation folds in on itself in mediated representations of olfactory horror, which can engage one's sense of smell—if not literally (through the receptor neurons of the nose) then mentally (through cognitive cues and memories of the spectator)—across the line dividing the diegetic world of fiction and the nondiegetic world of the audience. As might be expected, such figures of speech suffuse horror literature, where the audiovisual signifiers of cinematic discourse (which relies on sounds and images to convey smells) are replaced by linguistic attempts to arouse in the mind—the "mental nostrils" or "nasal brain"—of the reader a sense of aromatic awareness. From John Skipp and Craig Spector's splatterpunk classic *The Light at the End* (1986) to Mark Z. Danielewski's darkly romantic *House of Leaves* (2000), Brian Keene's zombie-themed *The Rising* (2003), Victor LaValle's urban fairy tale *The Changeling* (2018), and Michael Rowe's vampire-themed *Enter, Night* (2020), dozens of English-language novels rooted in the semantic terrain of horror spill over with smelly similes, which gain penetrative power through excessively outrageous wordplay and comically grotesque associative leaps, forcing readers to imagine frequently disgusting odors while invasively "opening up" those readers to the less savory thematic underpinnings of their stories. As historians and theorists of the senses have pointed out, smells cannot be so easily prevented from insinuating themselves into the recipient's body as sights and sounds can be (by simply closing one's eyes or covering one's ears) (Le Guérer 1992; Le Guérer 2002). In the words of Diane Ackerman, author of *A Natural History of the Senses*, "Cover your eyes and you will stop seeing, cover your ears and you will stop hearing, but if you cover your nose and try to stop smelling, you will die" (1990, 6). That invasiveness makes cinematic and literary olfaction especially important within the field of horror studies, given the genre's gravitation toward scenes of incursion, penetration, and violation. It will be useful, then, to first think about how authors of fiction have incorporated the word "like" within written passages that hinge on olfactory horror before exploring how such prose might be ported into, and transformed by, the diegetic worlds of narrative films.

An illustration of this can be found in Stephen King's 1987 H. P. Lovecraft-inspired novel *The Tommyknockers*. James Gardener, a poet with a steel plate inside his head (which makes him immune to an invisible, odorless gas that has been transforming the residents of a small town in Maine into drone-like beings), begins to "sense" the presence of the titular aliens in his sleep. Near the midpoint of the narrative, "Gard" dreams of the Tommyknockers, who, hidden inside another writer's shed, emit "a rich, electric smell *like ozone and blood*" (emphasis added; King 2018b, 247). For the reader to share this character's perception of the telepathic threat posed by the extraterrestrials—that is, to smell them the way that he does—it is first necessary to have a grasp of what ozone and blood might do to the nose's receptor neurons. The latter substance, thanks to its high iron content, releases a pungent yet flowery metallic smell, at once sharp and mushroom-like in the way that its acridness explodes up and into the nasal canal. The olfactory characteristics of ozone, however, are harder to pin down, although anyone who has experienced the sensation of coming rain—the atmospheric aroma of imminent precipitation, similar to that of chlorine and suggestive, some have said, of both pepper and pineapple—has come into contact with it. King's choice of that word is significant, in that "ozone" is derived from the Greek verb *ozein*, meaning "to smell." Thus, this analogy in *The Tommyknockers* is at once clarifying and confusing, suggesting that the creatures smell *like smell itself*.

In this way, the quoted passage reminds us that, because we "cannot literally touch, smell, or taste" particular sensations or substances on the page (and, by extension, on the screen), the reader/spectator is forced to reverse the body's "intentional trajectory"—away from the text and toward his/her own sense memories—in pursuit of something more accessible. In the words of film phenomenologist Vivian Sobchack, one reflexively turns toward one's "own carnal, sensual, and sensitive being" to, essentially, *smell oneself smelling* (2005, 76–77). In addition to sniffing out the book's hideously deformed creatures, Gard imagines hearing them as well. Their "weird liquid sloshing" sounds to him "like an old-fashioned washing machine" (King 2018b, 248). Except, to paraphrase the narrator, *sound isn't water*—a reminder that similes and other sense-blending figures of speech are occasionally stretched thin in horror stories that strive to put readers/audiences into the bodies and minds of fear-stricken characters.

Besides *The Tommyknockers*, the word "like" pops up repeatedly in other books by Stephen King, especially during passages or scenes in which the author or narrator wishes to convey the attributes of a particular odor to the reader. For example, his 1982 novella *The Body*, the basis for Columbia Pictures' coming-of-age film *Stand By Me* (1986), is told from the perspective of an adult character, Gordon "Gordie" Lachance, who recalls the traumatic time in his early teen years when he and his three friends stumbled across the body of a dead boy. One of the most memorable aspects of that life-altering encounter with premature death was the stench of the boy's bruised and bloated body. As Gordie muses, "You remembered that gassy smell, sickish but dry, like farts in a closed room" (King 2018a, 158). Film scholar Linda Badley has noted that Gordie, clearly repulsed by what he witnessed and smelled that day, thereafter "pronounces the scene unnatural, detaches himself from the body, and enters the symbolic order of culture and language" as a writer of fiction (1996, 46). Thus, the titular corpse in this story—a human form in a degenerative state— becomes the basis for the protagonist's own generative act of storytelling. Any "loss of bodily control" that Gordie might have suffered during that horrifying moment is offset by the authorial agency that he will retrospectively exert over it—a mature yet still-boyish command of language based in part on his deployment of similes to make something that is abstract (i.e., "death") textually translatable as an olfactory sensation ("like farts") (46).

Similarly, "Gray Matter," another of King's tales (this one part of his 1978 short story collection *Night Shift*), uses the simile to translate an unholy, otherworldly odor into something graspable to anyone who has spent a significant amount of time in the kitchen. In this case, the stench emanates from the vicinity of a housebound man in small-town Maine, a heavy beer-drinker named Richard whose still-living body is decomposing into an oozing slime (perhaps because of some tainted alcohol, although no explanation is given). When three townspeople heed the call for help from the man's son, who was the first to see and smell his father's physical transformation, they trundle through the snow and make their way toward the Victorian-era building that has begun to reek as a result of its occupant's putrefaction. We learn that Richard's flat stinks "the way fruit gets when it goes to ferment with yeast," a statement that is later echoed by the narrator's description of the place as "a cider house in summer," one that smells like "rotted apples, all fermented, and under that an even uglier stink" (King 2012, 120, 122). Another food-based comparison is offered up when Richard, by now a "gray wave of jelly," is described: "a kind of rotten smell, like an old cheese someone left standing on the counter over the weekend." The stench is so awful that the narrator, who is one of the three men investigating this strange occurrence on behalf of Richard's son, starts "to feel like someone [is] stirring [his] guts with a stick"—a sensation that some readers might likewise experience if thrown back into their own past encounters with rank or rotting food (123).

Most people likely are familiar with the smell of fermented apples, stinky cheese, and many of the other culinary odors that are evoked in the pages of these and other examples of literary horror. To be sure, smell—the perception of airborne chemicals and volatile compounds—depends on a different receptor organ from that of taste. However, these two senses are "deeply interconnected," according to Lorna Piatti-Farnell, to such a degree that "the transgression of one usually entails the manipulation of the other" (2017, 49). So "intimately entwined" are they that both the *aromas* and *flavors* of food can be simultaneously detected through the stimulation of cells in different parts of the body, the activation of neural responses down different pathways, and higher-order cognitive processing in different areas of the brain (with taste being processed "at the top of the brain stem in the thalamus" before being "relayed to the frontal cortex," and smell involving the olfactory bulb and olfactory cortex before integrating emotion and cognition in the limbic system) (Marks 2002, 120; Barry 2015, 343). Moreover, the nose and throat share the same airway, allowing aromas to enter the nasal passage from the back of the mouth "even when the nostrils are closed." As explained in greater detail by Barry C. Smith, this "cross-modal interaction and multisensory integration" (whereby smell influences taste, not unlike the way that sight has an effect on smell) (2015, 348) lends any attempt to symbolically link gustatory and olfactory phenomena an anatomical, sensorial grounding. It furthermore means that the proliferation of food-based similes and metaphors in fiction and film speaks not only to the importance of smell in the evocation of dread, revulsion, and other affective dimensions of horror, but also to the significance of *taste* as a similarly intimate—and perhaps more deeply insinuating—means for audiences to imagine what the terrified or grossed-out protagonists of those stories are experiencing. Characters might employ mixed gustatory and olfactory metaphors in their speech, as Margaret (Meg Foster), the leader of a Satanic coven in Rob Zombie's *The Lords of Salem* (2012), does when she cackles, "Welcome, whores of Salem. I can *taste* the foul *stench* of your ancestors rotting in the folds of the filth between your legs." But a more pressing urge to purge people of their own pent-up emotions, through a very different sort of "oral outflux" than verbal speech, has risen to the surface of recent films in which audiovisual depictions of vomitous acts encapsulate a literally distasteful mixing of the "lower" senses.

The metaphorical resonances of film as a potentially flavor-based medium, one capable of provoking different taste sensations and "mouthfeels" depending on the genre, mode, or format of a given narrative, is worth considering. Indeed, horror's tendency to forge intersubjective bonds between characters and spectators through intersensorial means (linking the physically proximate senses of smell and taste) invites a deeper consideration of the often-stinky stuff that goes into—or comes out of—peoples' mouths. Tellingly, one of the grossest things depicted in many horror films is also the most commonplace, an activity that most audiences have firsthand knowledge of if they have ever gotten a stomach flu, suffered from food poisoning, indulged in heavy alcoholic consumption, or experienced morning sickness, motion sickness, vertigo, or any the other medical conditions that might lead to vomiting. Scenes of characters upchucking are too numerous to cite exhaustively, though it is worth mentioning that horror filmmakers frequently rely on the practical effect of actual food on sets where such nauseating acts are staged. From the green pea soup that spews out the mouth of Regan MacNeil (Linda Blair) in William Friedkin's *The Exorcist* (1973) to the rancid mix of clam chowder and bean soup that was used during the making of *Wes Craven's New Nightmare* (1994) and writer-director Mark Bessenger's decision to stir personal lubricant into a bucket full of cooked brown rice at a certain point during the production of *Bite Marks* (2011), the various concoctions that serve as "prop vomit" (and which, in some cases, have actually made cast and crewmembers physically sick, owing to their putrid smell) materialize, odorize, and flavorize the metaphors and similes referenced above—those figures of speech that do not actually "splatter" on the printed page or in the figuratively "stinky" linguistic moves of prose fiction. The splashy results of onscreen vomiting (which, from a medical standpoint, is simply the body's way of protecting itself from threats) haptically manifest, through the sound and image of that puke hitting a solid surface, both the gustatory and olfactory dimensions of cinematic horror that are otherwise left to the reader's imagination whenever writers resort to culinary wordplay.

Not surprisingly, writers have harnessed the abject power of puke to put readers in place as olfactic witnesses to what their novels' main characters encounter over the course of supernatural tales that, however far-fetched, are rooted in the immediately recognizable matter of human emesis (in addition to more basic daily activities, such as urination and defecation, which, reader-be-warned, I will leave until the next chapter). In Scottish novelist Graham Masterton's *The Manitou* (1976), a crudely effective piece of pulp fiction that was adapted into a 1978 body-horror film of the same title, the narrator, a bogus psychic named Harry Erskine, describes the experience of gazing upon a truly unusual occurrence: a Native American medicine man emerges from a tumor-sized fetus moving along the back of a young woman. But Harry does so in a way that puts the nose on equal footing with the eyes. He informs the reader that the "watery yellow fluid" that gushed from the birth sac gave off a "rich, fetid smell, like decaying fish." This comes a few pages before he encounters something "wet and messy" behind a door, the remains of a man who has become the latest victim of a Lovecraftian monster that emits a nauseating smell reminiscent of "vomit and feces." By adding that last olfactic touch, Masterton endows his book's already disturbing images (the "raw red bubbly heap" of rubbery intestines and spattered blood that make Harry feel "as if [he] was going to puke") with a verisimilar quality that not only makes it possible for readers to swallow an over-the-top, preposterous story but also might trigger smell-based memories of literally retching or shitty moments from their own pasts.

Rather than ask the reader to imagine "a scent like vomit [quotidian/familiar] mixed with infant's brains [bizarre/unfamiliar]," as comic-book writer Garth Ennis does in *The Demon: Hell's Hitman* (a DC Comics series from the mid-1990s), many authors settle on fairly straightforward food-based metaphors and similes because they spark personal recollections while collapsing nasal and oral orifices into a single "opening" where smelling can be likened to tasting. This goes for the writers of not only novels and short stories but also screenplays, including those for films in which stomach-churning shots of characters throwing up precede or follow passages of dialogue reliant upon the word "like" to enable the kind of comparative leaps that I have been discussing. For instance, in an early scene of *Jennifer's Body* (2009), written by Diablo Cody and directed by Karyn Kusama, the title character—a high-school cheerleader named Jennifer (Megan Fox) who will soon be offered up as a (non)virgin sacrifice to Satan before going on a violent rampage in her small-town community of Devil's Kettle—walks into the foyer of the house belonging to the parents of her best friend Needy (Amanda Seyfried) prior to a night of revelry at the local dive bar, sniffs the air, and remarks, "It smells like Thai food in here." Casting a sly glance at Needy's nerdy boyfriend Chip (Johnny Simmons), Jennifer asks, "Have you guys been fucking?" Her modest friend's response, "You're gross!" sets up a later scene in which Jennifer is shown spewing black tar-like vomit onto Needy's kitchen floor in the aftermath of her offscreen run-in with the devil. That scene, anticipating an analogous moment in writer-director Jennifer Kent's *The Babadook* (2014) when the trauma-stricken protagonist Amelia (Essie Davis) expels a gushing stream of inky-black liquid onto the floor, brings the earlier reference to Thai food—a literally digestible menu item that Jennifer had distinguished by its *smell* rather than taste—full circle as she prepares to feast on "extra salty" teenagers and townspeople throughout the second half of the film.

Similarly, Justine (Garance Marillier), the young female protagonist in Julia Ducournau's *Raw*, after smelling and then eating her older sister's lopped-off finger as part of her cannibalistic coming-of-age journey, jokingly informs her that it tasted "like curry" (figure 7.2). While curry can showcase a broad range of flavor profiles depending on the origin, type, and unique combination of sweet and savory spices that are used in the dish, not to mention its consistency (on a continuum between milky and pasty) atop the other ingredients with which it interacts, in general it exhibits an earthiness that accords with

Figure 7.2. Nibbling the detached finger of her older sister, Justine (Garance Marillier), the protagonist of Julia Ducournau's *Raw* (2016), describes the smell and flavor as being "like curry."

its color. More importantly, most people—even those who have tasted a wide assortment of curry styles from far-flung areas of the world (e.g., India, Jamaica, Japan, Malaysia, etc.)—will have a distinct flavor and smell in mind when they hear or read that word, and would find it difficult to unravel the gustatory and olfactory senses of that dish, which is likely to bring a "blast of emotion" to many of us based on our personal memories of eating and smelling it (Marks 2002, 120). Whether we like it or not, that emotion bubbles up (like so much heartburn or indigestion) when the curry-flavored finger-nibbling scene in *Raw* plays out—a moment that is notorious for making movie patrons vomit when it was shown at film festivals and in other public settings during its initial 2016 theatrical release.

Speaking of food, the problematic association of "fatness" and foul, sometimes indefinable odors is also a recurring feature of horror, and equally deserving of consideration if we are to fully unpack its sensorial entanglements as a body genre. This is a much-discussed facet of *Alice, Sweet Alice* (1976), a *Psycho*-inspired, *giallo*-style proto-slasher in which a troubled adolescent protagonist is wrongly suspected of multiple murders, including that of the corpulent Mr. Alphonso (Alphonso DeNoble). Before being stabbed to death in the staircase landing outside his apartment, the latter character—a "disgusting, perverted slob" who exhibits pedophilic behavior toward twelve-year-old Alice (Paula Sheppard)—is someone who, in the words of John Kenneth Muir (speaking on behalf of several viewers), "deserves to die" (2002, 445). Viewers are encouraged to root for this morbidly obese landlord's death through audiovisual prompting, with shots of his urine-coated clothing, snug against his butterball body, lending literal weight to the idea that moral turpitude has a physical component. Alice, too, turns up her nose at the abject squalor of his cramped apartment, which not only is littered with decades-old bric-a-brac but also "smells like cat's piss" (in her own words). That odor seems to emanate from the screen, and not only because several felines can be seen cavorting around the place. The ill-fated man, gravelly voiced and yellow-toothed from heavy smoking, appears to luxuriate in filth, fanning the sweat off his hirsute body like a prima donna (accompanied by the sound of a scratchy opera recording) and flashing a shit-eating grin at the girl as he paws her hair and pins her up against a brown door. These and other elements, like audiovisual similes, translate what Alice detects in the air (and verbally chastises Mr. Alphonso for) into a language befitting the medium, so much so that, as Troy Howarth states in his interview with this film's director (Alfred Sole), "you can almost smell the stench of his apartment" (2021).[3]

Since the time of *Alice, Sweet Alice*'s theatrical release, other cultural productions ranging from the Capcom-produced survivor-horror video game *Dead Rising 3* (2013) to writer-director Tom Six's notorious film *The Human Centipede 2 (Full Sequence)* (2011) have contributed to the cultural vilification of bodies deemed excessively transgressive and even toxic by dent of their size. In both examples, female and male antagonists appear dirty, greasy, and (yes) stinky to the discriminating eye, highlighting what Thomas Fahy refers to as the "negative social implications of weight-based stigma and discrimination" observable not just in the United States but around the world (2019). In *Dead Rising 3*, a game initially designed for the Xbox One platform that situates players in an open-world environment where they are forced to fend off hundreds of zombies, a monstrously dehumanized character named Darlene Fleischermacher motors around on her mobility scooter while noisily gorging herself on buffet items. As Rebecca Wenson notes in her study of the demonization of fat bodies in horror, Darlene is made to appear "grotesque" in her excessive appetite and filth, not only repeatedly burping and passing gas but also choking to death on her own vomit when her scooter finally overturns and pins her to the slimy floor. Like the death of the lecherous landlord in *Alice, Sweet Alice*, this moment of heroic victory on the part of the player's avatar (a physically fit, muscular character named Nick Ramos who helps to bring about her death) is meant to inspire cheers, since the vanquishing of this stereotypically detestable "glutton for punishment" suggests a kind of detoxifying and deodorizing of the text (Wenson 2020).

This representational tendency, as Wenson goes on to note, extends beyond horror proper into adjacent categories of cultural production, including fantasy and science fiction films. For example, in the superhero movie *Blade* (1998), the first of Marvel's many adaptations of its comic book properties, a flatulent, fleshy abomination named Pearl (Eric Edwards) emits a stench that registers on the faces of the vampire-slaying title character (played by Wesley Snipes) and his female companion, Dr. Karen Jenson (N'Bushe Wright), when they enter

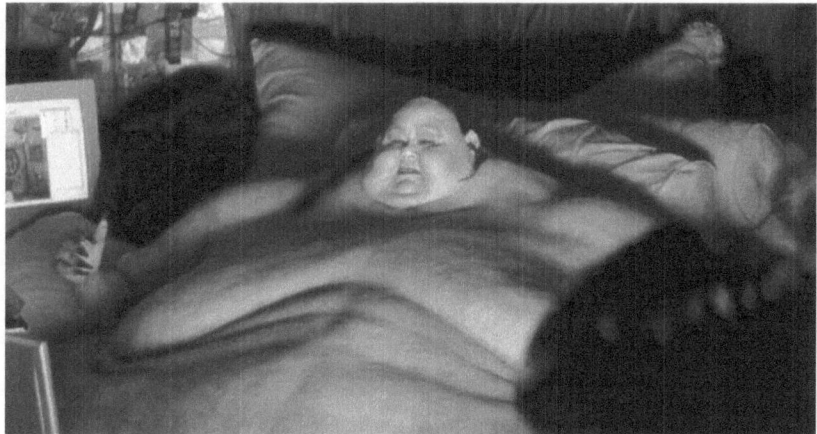

Figure 7.3. Surely one of the most corpulent beings to ever appear on screen, Pearl (Eric Edwards), a minor character in the Marvel superhero movie *Blade* (1998), emits an odor that stops the titular vampire killer in his tracks.

his tiny yet vast virtual archive of electronic files. As a "librarian," a keeper of archival documents and ancient knowledge about bloodsuckers, Pearl carries the heavy accumulated weight of vampire lore, literalized in his own physical blobbiness. Before they even step foot into his underground lair, Karen makes a face and asks, "What's that smell?" This is a sign that something disgusting or, at the very least, disturbing awaits them in that dark, musty place. Seconds later, she and we discover the source of that stench, and the Jabba the Hut-like corpulence of the naked librarian (who is so large that he is unable to move, even when they begin figuratively and literally "grilling" him with UV flashlights) suggests a toxic mixture of diaphoresis and diarrhea, strong enough to make Blade himself hold his nose (figure 7.3). In *The Weight of Images: Affect, Body Image and Fat in the Media*, Katariina Kyrölä discusses this scene, arguing that "the utter fatness of Pearl's body"—the roly-poly fold-upon-fold of that bluish flesh, which she compares to the skin of the gluttony victim in David Fincher's *Se7en* (1995)—"is anticipated and represented as abject through the bad smell of excrement that his body produces" (2016, 138).

Before moving on to explore the "excremental" stench of death (in this chapter) and the "deathly" odor of excrement (in the next chapter), let us return to Karen's line, "What's that smell?" It is a question that has been posed, verbatim, throughout the history of cinematic horror, in films ranging from little-known cult curios like *Death Bed: The Bed That Eats* (1977) to high-profile releases including Joel Schumacher's *The Lost Boys* (1987), Clive Barker's *Nightbreed* (1990), and Ari Aster's *Hereditary* (2018), and sometimes with exclamatory relish (as happens near the beginning of *V/H/S 94* [2021], when a police officer about to stumble upon an eyeless dead man inside a jail cell shouts, "What the *fuck* is that smell!?!?"). It is one of the first things that Adam (Leigh Whannell) asks his fellow prisoner Lawrence (Cary Elwes) in the nearly pitch-black opening seconds of director James Wan's *Saw* (2004), as it dawns on them that they are chained to opposite sides of a filthy restroom with a dead man's body in the middle, lying face-down in a pool of blood. The fact that Adam "went to bed in [his] shit-hole apartment and woke up in an actual shit hole," as he says only a few seconds after he makes a retching sound over a toilet bowl, brings the literalist underpinnings of cinematic olfactics to the fore. More importantly, his instinctual exclamation "What is that smell?"—uttered in the dark before a more profound, figurative sense of "illumination" comes with the flickering of sickly blue overhead fluorescent lights—hints at the fundamental role that this particular sense modality plays in cognition and detection, with odors often preceding the images of death or decay with which they are associated in the mental construction/comprehension of fearful scenarios. As Annie (Toni Collette), the traumatized protagonist of *Hereditary*, tells a fellow support group member, "*First* there's the *smell* of something wrong. And *then* the body."

The experiential primacy of olfaction over other sensations is alluded to in several examples of both cinematic and literary horror, including productions and publications that, like *Saw*, foreground smell from the opening scene going forward. Writer-director Sion Sono does this, for instance, in the Japanese-language film *Exte: Hair Extensions* (*Ekusute*, 2007), which begins with a group of customs agents covering their noses and exclaiming "Something smells bad!" when they step toward a shipping container that reeks. They soon discover that inside the container is the corpse of a young girl whose organ-harvested body has been festering for weeks, along with an ungodly amount of human hair. The movement of the guards into the previously locked space where the offending odor originates, prompted by their desire for knowledge and their duty as "detection agents," parallels the invasive way that the smell has *entered them*. It furthermore reminds us that smells seep into *our* bodies with each inhalation of air and, in the worst cases, can be said to "engulf" us until the experience becomes "unbearable" (Elliot 2011, 129). As described by Diane Ackerman, "odor molecules float back into the nasal cavity behind the bridge of the nose, where they are absorbed by the mucosa containing receptor cells bearing microscopic hairs called cilia. Five million of these cells fire impulses to the brain's olfactory bulb or smell center" (1990, 10). In addition to being indicative of a very direct and pervasive sensation, not only swirling around us and coating us but also *emanating* from us, smells exhibit a tendency toward a deceptively benign kind of violence in the way that that they "detonate softly in our memory like poignant land mines" (5). Using language that would not be out of place in a review of a horror film or a war movie, Ackerman muses, "Hit a tripwire of smell, and memories explode all at once. A complex vision leaps out of the undergrowth" (5). As we are forever being reminded in the pages of horror novels and short stories, odors "hit" the nose and brain with a sudden force, frequently without the recipient's consent. Given the fact that smell, perhaps more than hearing, "is a channel of vulnerability, whereby one often experiences something involuntarily" (Reinarz 2014, 91), it is not too much of a stretch to think of this sensation as being amenable to horrifying tales. Indeed, the frequency with which authors of fictional texts deploy the word "hit" indicates familiarity with smell's deeply penetrative, "highly emotive character" (Smith 2015, 342).

Stephen King employs such language in his 1992 novel *Needful Things*, highlighting how malodorous phenomena frequently precede terrifying visions and foretell bad deaths or situations that will haunt characters for years to come. When Alan Pangborn, the sheriff of Castle Rock, Maine, hesitantly steps into the "deep and dusty" curiosity shop that lends that book its title, readers are informed that "the smell hit him first" (2018, 749). It was not the smell of a new place of business, the narrator clarifies, but of a location "which had been untenanted for months or even years." Two things are at work here, with King bringing the rank oldness of the space to the fore while similarly pushing olfactory experiences ahead of visual and auditory elements that are less likely to accost or "hit" a person—physically and emotionally—quite so powerfully as smells can. Like Robert Bloch's description of the "faint, musty scent" detectable within the bedroom that was once inhabited by Norman Bates's mother (in his 1959 novel *Psycho*), and which seems to register the dead woman's spiritual presence in her physical absence, the reference in *Needful Things* to a place at least partially characterized by its staleness or "dampness" (a "creepy" smell that Norman from *Psycho* professes to hate) suggests the merging of past and present is potentially as terrifying as the threat of bad death. Like smells—indeed, partly *because of smells*—memories of the past are sometimes hard to shake off.

The idea that the perceptual and conscious experience of smell "is always with us," which Barry C. Smith attributes to humans breathing and living in "a world full of odours that subtly shapes our moods, influences our eating habits, our choice of sexual partner, our recognition of kin, and our response to one another's fear or aggression" (2015, 342), is broached in the 2009 horror film *Dread*. Despite its generic title, this provocative motion picture (which writer-director Anthony DiBlasi adapted from a short story of the same title by Clive Barker) delves into the unique ways that the titular emotion is experienced by different people. Specifically, several college-aged interviewees are featured as talking-head subjects in the film-within-the-film, and one of them—the embedded film's editor, Cheryl (Hanne Steen), who steps in front of the lens to deliver a painful monologue about her experience with parental abuse—dwells on an unshakeable odor that she has carried with her from childhood

Figure 7.4. In this scene from *Dread* (2009), a vegetarian whose distaste for meat is linked to a traumatic history of child-abuse is forced to eat a maggot-covered steak as part of her captor's twisted study of fear.

into young adulthood. Opening up about her violent father, a worker at a meat-packing plant in upstate New York who molested her when she was a girl, Cheryl can barely look at the film's codirectors seated behind the camera, Stephen (Jackson Rathbone) and Quaid (Shaun Evans). She lowers her head in shame as she describes the smell of his flesh "when he'd come home from work" each day. "This heavy, metallic smell that would follow him home from the plant," she says, was "like warm blood on the grass . . . cold fat in the freezers." Concluding that she "can hardly stand to look at a piece of meat now, let alone think about eating it," Cheryl unwittingly sets herself up for a third-act plot twist, which reveals that Quaid, a secretly psychopathic man looking to take their "study of fear" school project to the next level, has locked her inside a boarded-up room, empty save for a plate of beef, a bottle of water, a bucket, and a video camera that records her actions. Taking a page from Jigsaw's twisted playbook (from the *Saw* franchise), Quaid watches Cheryl squirm in desperation on a video monitor, delaying the inevitable over several days as flies lay eggs on the maggot-ridden meat and the stench from it (and her own vomit) becomes palpable. Weakened by starvation and festering in her own filth, the vegetarian finally relents and sinks her teeth into the rancid steak, eating it all the way down to the bone (figure 7.4).

Although she appears to be at her lowest point here, Cheryl sinks even deeper into (re)traumatizing depravity at the hands of this sadistic man during the film's nightmarish final scene. Having killed Stephen (the one person who, aware of what has happened, might have saved Cheryl), Quaid deposits his codirector's corpse into a basement where she is imprisoned. He tosses a knife onto the floor next to Stephen's dead body and tells her, "Let's see how hungry you have to be to get through *that*." Then, bringing this gruesome narrative about the lingering memories of bad smells to a sudden end, he slams the door shut on her (and us), trapping the woman inside a truly terrible place where the stench of rotting flesh will surely send her spiraling into madness. With earlier spoken references to her father's killing of cattle (an intertextual nod to all the slaughterhouse talk at the beginning of *The Texas Chain Saw Massacre*) establishing an olfactory basis for its visually nauseating depictions of gustatory terror during these final scenes, *Dread* provides ample evidence of the horror genre's ability to provoke that titular emotion through intersensorial means.

HELL'S SMELLS, CANNIBALISTIC CREEPS, AND AIR FRESHENERS IN FILM

> You know, speaking of noses, ever since this family has moved to this block, I've been noticing a weird kind of odor. Kind of like death.
> —RICKY (Corey Feldman), a suburban teenager who begins to suspect that his new neighbors, the Klopeks, are murderers, in *The 'Burbs* (1989)

Beyond the work of Stephen King, several other specialists in genre fiction, going back to the earliest examples of Gothic romance in the late 1700s (Horace Walpole's *The Castle of Otranto* [1764], Ann Radcliffe's *The Mysteries of Udolpho* [1794], Matthew Lewis's *The Monk* [1796], etc.), have tapped into the horrifying suggestiveness of certain odorants. In doing so, novelists and short story writers have developed innovative ways of rendering smells on the page, even as they have fallen back on a few hackneyed expressions whose repetition suggests a collective fixation on horror's most persistent tropes, including those concerning death and decay. For instance, the unnamed narrator in Edgar Allan Poe's 1842 short story "The Pit and the Pendulum"—a man condemned to death during the Spanish Inquisition and forced to await his fate inside a dark prison cell—describes the "clammy vapor" that arises from a seemingly bottomless hole in which he nearly fell as smelling like "decayed fungus" (2015, 246). This miasma, or odorous vapor, according to David Halliburton, is "the olfactory complement of slime" (1973, 326), a substance that will reemerge as a topic relevant to the study of comedy-horror films in the next chapter. But it is also a ghostly gas from some distant past, not unlike the "vaporous and nearly overpowering" smell of rot and mold that hits Charles Boone and his manservant Calvin McCann in "Jerusalem's Lot," another of King's Lovecraftian tales (also part of his 1978 short story collection *Night Shift*). Presented in epistolary form, as a letter written by Boone in 1850 to his friend Bones, that description of the Boar's Head Inn and Tavern (the first of the many old establishments comprising the deserted village of Jerusalem's Lot that he steps into) is lent further detail once the narrator explains that "an even deeper smell, a slimy and pestiferous smell, a smell of ages and the decay of ages" (such as "might issue from corrupt coffins or violated tombs") seemed to lie beneath the first. It is as if an onion-like layering of sniffable offenses—each slightly worse than the preceding one—were capable of transporting a person further back into the recesses of history, in this case, to the time of Boone's distant ancestor, who was the settlement's founder as well as the leader of a local witchcraft cult in the 1700s.

In conveying olfactory dread through a set of familiar phrases, King and other contemporary authors are effectively exhuming or revivifying the linguistic and rhetorical moves of their literary forebearers, not unlike the way that the protagonists of their tales intentionally or unintentionally uncover the physical remains of souls long departed. The fact that our olfactory lexicon is rather limited, despite the vast array of chemical compounds in the air that are humanly detectable across a hedonic spectrum (which tends to be simplified to the level of whether a smell is pleasant or unpleasant) (Yeshurun and Sobel 2010, 219), is consistent with Diane Ackerman's notion that "smell is the mute sense, the one without words." "Lacking a vocabulary," she writes, "we are left tongue-tied, groping for words in a sea of inarticulate pleasure and exaltation" (1990, 6). Although our olfactory detection abilities can be "extraordinarily precise," as she elaborates, it is "almost impossible to describe how something smells to someone who hasn't smelled it," and too often "words fail us" whenever we try to verbalize what our nose "knows" (7). Yaara Yeshurun and Noam Sobel echo that sentiment, arguing that "the boundaries of an odor object" tend to be "determined by its pleasantness, which—unlike something material and more like an emotion—remains poorly delineated with words" (2010, 219), hence the reason why a relatively limited number of stock phrases pop up in so many otherwise original stories.

Consider the common expression "smells like death," which rises up time and again (like so many animated corpses) within cinematic and literary examples of the horror genre. That phrase, or slight variations thereof (such as "the smell of death"), has been uttered by characters across the history of the genre for decades, in films such as *Madman* (1981), *The Lost Boys* (1987), *House of the Dead* (2003), and *The Amityville Asylum* (2013). In *Burial Ground* (aka, *Nights of Terror* [*Le Notti del terrore*, 1981), an Italian zombie film written by Piero Regnoli and directed by Andrea Bianchi, a traumatized boy named Michael (Peter Bark) is one of many guests inside a mansion overrun with reanimated corpses, and before he is turned into a zombie himself he holds a frayed cloth up to his nose and tells his mother (to whom he is sexually attracted) that it "smells of death." It is not likely that many audiences, even those who have spent time in the company of poorly preserved dead bodies, have a firm grasp on what the chemically complex odor of death is like (though the process of putrefaction can unleash potent odors, particularly in the bowels). However, the smell of a commonplace object like a dirty old rag, which is precisely what Michael holds up to his nose (as his own mother reminds him), should be sufficiently familiar to "click" inside the minds of audiences who might then make the associational leap that his analogy has prompted. The analogy is not unlike what the narrator of Joe Hill's debut novel *Heart-Shaped Box* (2007) employs when conveying the funky odor radiating off the body of a dead man named Craddock, whose ghost—initially attached to a hexed funeral suit—haunts the story's protagonist Judas "Jude" Coyne with dogged persistence. Though the first smell of the man's spirit, coming from inside one of the suit's pockets, is that of "something going bad," like "old food," it transforms into something that "smelled of death [and] of car exhaust," according to Jude. For many readers, the toxic pungency of automobile exhaust is more immediately recognizable than the smell of death, though the latter (by virtue of preceding the former in that passage from Hill's novel) is made more fathomable as an experiential state that might, in fact, smell like noxious fumes. Just as the associational logic of that sentence is further grounded in the setting where Jude locks eyes on the yellow-toothed Craddock (a vintage Mustang, which might actually be the source of that pungent if not deathly toxic exhaust), so too is the musty odor to which the boy's mother alludes in *Burial Ground* further suggested by director Bianchi's unusual (but, in retrospect, necessary) decision to cast a twenty-five-year-old actor in the role of Michael, someone who looks considerably older than a person his age normally would.

Given its status as a cinematic adaptation of H. P. Lovecraft's 1927 novella *The Case of Charles Dexter Ward*, as well as the fact that the words "smells like death" and other odorific similes and metaphors are sprinkled throughout its script, the 1991 horror film *The Resurrected* is appropriately titled. Written by Brent V. Friedman under the working title *Shatterbrain* (an antiquated term denoting someone with mental illness) and directed by Dan O'Bannon (who insisted that the narrator from Lovecraft's original tale, Dr. Martin Willet, be replaced with a private investigator hero named John March [played by John Terry]) (Smith 2006, 95), this film is noteworthy for the many references that its characters make to foul smells. Those odors mostly emanate from the isolated New England farmhouse where chemical engineer Charles Dexter Ward (Chris Sarandon) has been conducting tests on animal cadavers acquired from a slaughterhouse, prompting an older gas station attendant to tell John (who has been hired by Charles's wife to investigate his odd behavior) that the property "smells like death." Interestingly, the old man prefaces his remark by saying that the farmhouse smells "like that dog," pointing toward his canine companion near the pumps and putting a decidedly familiar odor front and center as a means for John (and the audience) to nasally grasp the otherwise amorphous smell of death. But, beyond this early scene, there are other moments when the film's title seems particularly apt as a reminder of how the olfactory lexicon established by the authors of gothic literature has been "resurrected" in subsequent works of cinematic fiction. Another example of this occurs immediately after the film's opening credits, when John, like a neonoir detective, speaks in voiceover and provides expositional details about the narrative's main setting of Providence, Rhode Island. Accompanied by flyover shots of the city, his narration informs us that the inhabitants of Providence "enjoy the eastern sea breeze, except in the summer when the river starts to smell." Elaborating this point, he utters words that might just as easily have been spoken by Charles Boone in King's "Jerusalem's Lot," adding, "But that smell is historic, having stunk since the time of the witch hunts. The whole place reeks of history. And history, I've learned, can jump up and bite you."

Speaking of "biting," the phrase "the smell of death" also appears in the 1897 publication of Bram Stoker's *Dracula*. In the sixth chapter of that novel, an old fisherman named Mr. Swales, before dying under mysterious circumstances, somehow senses the arrival of evil incarnate in England and, by extension, is able to envision his own imminent demise. "There's something in that wind," Swales remarks, "that sounds, and looks, and tastes, and smells like death." As foreshadowing, the old man's statement effectively whets the reader's appetite for the arrival of the book's titular figure, a Transylvanian count who, traveling by boat, brings to Western Europe a host of foreign smells redolent of his ancestral home in the Carpathian Mountains, including that of the soil itself (the source of the vampire's strength, which he has scooped up from the earth and put into fifty boxes). Significantly, this minor character's comment correlates with Jonathan Harker's acknowledgment of the "horrible feeling of nausea" that came over him upon smelling Dracula, an abject figure distinguished not only by the rank odor that emanates from his body but also by his unusual anatomical features, with Stoker lingering on the "aquiline" shapes of the vampire's sensing organs (including that of his nose, the "peculiarly arched" nostrils of which are like the "peculiarly sharp" teeth that will later taste blood) in addition to his hairiness (specifically his massive eyebrows and heavy mustache) (Mulvey-Roberts 2016, 141).[4] But what makes Swales's comment so significant is his linguistic chaining together of four, possibly five, senses: that of hearing, sight, taste, and smell. Touch, too, is hinted at in his reference to the wind, the vehicle through which the combined sound, image, flavor, and stench of death reaches British shores. This is something that the nearly one-hundred-year-old Swales "feels" in a corporeal way, "touched" as he is by the wind (literally so in *Dracula*'s seventh chapter, when he is found dead in a cemetery, his neck inexplicably broken).

A similar kind of soulful sense-blending occurs in Shirley Jackson's 1959 novel *The Haunting of Hill House*, albeit with more hedonically pleasant smells at the center of a character's embodied consciousness: "Eleanor closed her eyes and sighed, feeling and hearing and smelling the house; a flowering bush beyond the kitchen was heavy with scent, and the water in the brook moved sparkling over the stones." As will be detailed further in the remaining pages of this chapter, *feeling, hearing,* and *smelling* often work in tandem to provoke a sort of closed-eye subterranean sensing of what is *really* going on beneath the surface of a given horror film, including those whose deceptively *fragrant* odors (such as that provided by air fresheners) mask threats to life and limb that leave characters figuratively and sometimes literally "shattered" by narrative's end. Besides literary texts, that soulful sense-blending can also be found in cinematic renderings of palpably felt terror as well as more positively valenced emotional states. For instance, in director Tobe Hooper's 1982 supernatural horror film *Poltergeist* (1982), a desperate mother whose young daughter has been sucked into a televisual portal by angry spirits inside her home (built atop an ancient burial site) is suddenly hit by a blast of wind from the other side, and proclaims, "She just moved through me. My God! I *felt* her. I can *smell* her. It's *her* . . . it's my baby—she went through my soul!"

As should now be clear, odors abound in horror films—not just *any* smells, but the kind that most people would prefer to avoid in real life: that of burning fuel, leaking gasses, decomposing bodies, rotting food, and other sulfuric or toxic befoulers of one's breathable, barely inhabitable, environment. To be sure, cinematic olfactics span a broad range of hedonic tones, or pleasurable and unpleasurable smells, though the latter—a layperson's way of describing a certain molecular volatility in the air—predominates in horror, perhaps as an extension of the more recognizable physical and emotional volatility that characterizes the genre's many fear-inducing scenes. In real life, if not always in fiction and film, human beings tend to succeed at keeping those and other noxious aromas at bay, either by steering clear of places where they might be found (from garbage dumps and landfills to sewers and slaughterhouses) or by masking such smells with other, more congenial chemical obscurants (from perfumes and body sprays to candles and disinfectants) that sometimes sit as heavily on the air as do the original offending odors. The mere presence of tree-shaped air fresheners dangling from automobiles' rearview mirrors, visible in horror films ranging from *Jeepers Creepers* (2001) to *Final* Destination 2 (2003), *High Tension* (2003), *From Within* (2008), *The Human Centipede 2* (2011), *Amityville: No Escape* (2016), *Ma* (2019), and *The Arbors* (2020), indicates just how pervasive smells are within and across the genre (figure 7.5).

Funnily enough, in 2017, Severin Films (a US distributor of motion pictures catering to "the horror/exploitation/sleaze connoisseur," according to the company's website) released a limited-edition Blu-ray of Joe D'Amato's cult classic *Beyond the Darkness* (*Buio Omega*, aka, *Buried Alive*, 1979) with several

Figure 7.5. As seen in the stench-themed *Reeker* (2005), but visible in several other horror films as well, air fresheners dangling from rearview mirrors are a deceptively familiar sign that malodorous content is on the horizon.

special features, including an actual air freshener bearing a grisly image from the film: that of a single-eyed skull sinking into an acid-filled bathtub. This unusual form of twenty-first century ballyhoo, while clearly a marketing ploy designed to capitalize on the film's collectible-hungry fan base, humorously hints at the need to defend oneself from the invasive threats posed by the horror genre's various stenches. In the case of D'Amato's stomach-churning study of a psychopathic taxidermist named Frank (Kieran Canter), those smells include a recently deceased, disemboweled woman's guts. The main character not only extracts those internal organs from her body, which is thereafter preserved and put on necrophilic display like a stuffed animal, but also proceeds to lick and eat them, linking olfactory offensiveness with the gustatory distastefulness—the unappetizing sight and sound—of cannibalism (figure 7.6).

One of the most telling uses of an air freshener, albeit in the form of an aerosol spray can rather than a kitschy car accessory, occurs in director Eloy de la Iglesia's 1972 film *The Cannibal Man (La Semana del asesino)*. Despite its English-language title (which differs considerably from its more literal translation, *The Week of the Killer*), this Spanish production features none of the anthropophagous activity—the potentially nauseating ingestion of human flesh—that distinguishes D'Amato's film. Like the aforementioned American production *The Texas Chain Saw Massacre*, this cinematic Grand Guignol begins with shots of a slaughterhouse, although here the cattle inside are shown being sliced apart with all the graphic matter-of-factness of a gut-wrenching animal-abuse documentary. It is there, in the blood-filled abattoir, where Marcos (Vicente Parra), the inarticulate main character, works during the day as a meatpacker before retiring each night to the only slightly more agreeable

Figure 7.6. Severin Films' limited-edition Blu-ray of *Beyond the Darkness* (1979) was packaged with an air freshener, a gimmicky yet thematically relevant tie-in (given the cannibalism-themed film's foregrounding of offensive odors).

creature comforts of his small house. The walls of his squalid hovel, located on the outskirts of Madrid and dwarfed in the shadow of a newly constructed high-rise apartment, "are decorated with pictures of bikini-clad, semi-naked women taken from magazines," suggesting that Marcos lives with the constant social pressure of having to conform to cultural norms of gender and sexuality. As Andy Willis states, "Even his own environment," ostensibly a sanctuary far removed from the slaughterhouse and from the alienating effects of blue-collar labor, "no longer allows for peace of mind (2005, 172). In this way, "societal forces impact on his life" as a possibly closeted gay or bisexual man isolated from others and figuratively caged inside his own machismo-laden personal space (172). Tellingly, those sexualized images of women on his walls, which thrust the pressures of heteronormativity "in his face" (to use Willis's words), will become "deodorized" once the main character's work-life balance is thrown out of whack and the flimsy supports of sanity begin to collapse, bringing the stink of the abattoir floor to his own home and its already-filthy walls.

Before discussing *The Cannibal Man*'s air-freshener scene, in which those salacious magazine photos and other material objects inside the title character's apartment are sprayed down to mask the smell of rotting human flesh, it will be helpful to synopsize the film's narrative trajectory. Over the course of a single week, this socially marginalized fringe-dweller descends into homicidal madness, killing first a taxi driver (who had been offended by the sight of Marcos kissing a young woman of slightly nobler birth in the backseat), and then, when she threatens to inform the police of the cabbie's death, his girlfriend, Paula (Emma Cohen), the same middle-class woman with whom he had been necking. Soon thereafter, he bludgeons his brother Esteban (Charly Bravo) with a wrench before directing his murderous gaze toward his brother's fiancée, Carmen (Lola Herrera), who casually notes the "funny" odor inside Marcos's fly-infested home before she too is killed. Another sadistic takedown, that of Carmen's concerned father, Mr. Ambrosio (Fernando Sanchez Polak), who comes looking for his missing daughter, follows—once again inside a domestic space that is beginning to look more and more like the slaughterhouse. Chopping up his victims' bodies, Marcos stores their limbs inside that increasingly cramped dwelling. In order to conceal the smell of the decomposing bodies, he purchases ten bottles of air freshener, spraying the aerosol over everything that has been infected by death: his television set, family photos, cheap Catholic statuary, and the aforementioned "girlie" photos or pinup images.

It is certainly possible to take this air-freshening scene at face value and not read too much into its symptomatic or implicit meanings as a biting sociopolitical allegory of class warfare. More broadly, as Danny Shipka states, contemporary audiences might view the film as a whole "as simply a story of a murderous man who takes his victims to the slaughterhouse where he works and makes meat pies of them" (2011, 310). However, the historical context in which *The Cannibal Man* was produced makes any such neutral or agnostic position suspect. Indeed, just as the "surface beauty of the Fascist and neo-catholic aesthetics" of cultural productions made during the dictatorship of Francisco Franco (1939–75) could be said to barely mask the "brutality and torture" that would become his regime's legacy after "El Caudillo" finally surrendered the function of prime minister and was succeeded as Spain's head of state (Kinder 1993, 138), so too is the spray merely a cosmetic coverup, a way to temporarily vaporize something that offends the sensibilities but which is nearly as offensive as an obscurant—a distraction from the grim reality. Nevertheless, Iglesia's work, by assaulting critics' senses and sensibilities with the same "tasteless" appetite for destruction as another, more traditionally coded horror film produced in Spain that year, writer-director Vicente Aranda's *The Blood-Spattered*

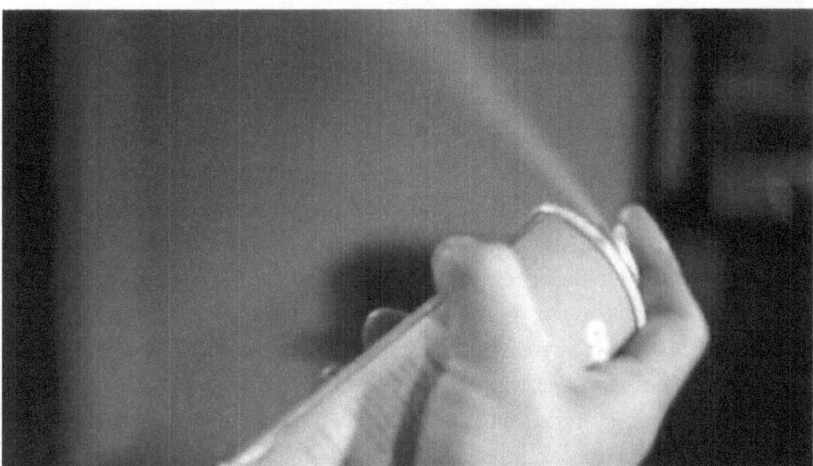

Figure 7.7. Armed with several aerosol cans, slaughterhouse employee-turned-serial killer Marcos (Vicente Parra) attempts to mask the smell of putrefying bodies (those of his victims, whom he has chopped up and hidden inside his dwelling) in this scene from *The Cannibal Man* (1972).

Bride (*La Novia Ensangrentada*, 1972), ironically helped not only to raise the cultural respectability of horror but also to highlight the genre's "radical and subversive potential" in the land of Francisco Goya, a visual artist of the late eighteenth and early nineteenth centuries who laid the groundwork for such anti-state commentary through paintings of witches, mental asylums, and fantastical creatures undergoing all manner of physical and spiritual torment (Willis 2005, 167).

In his reading of *The Cannibal Man*, Antonio Lázaro-Reboll notes Iglesia's use of Francoist icons in the air-freshening scene, singling out these and other visual elements as signs of the controversial film's critique of the status quo (2012, 148). Deemed "vile" and "dangerous" by the Spanish censorship board, which was particularly offended by the screenplay's inclusion of a sexually ambiguous character named Néstor (Eusebio Poncela), whose relationship with the butcher-turned-serial killer flirts with homosexuality, the film became a topic of debate at the time of its production in the early 1970s. As Lázaro-Reboll explains, when the script was submitted to the board under a different title (*Auténtico caldo de cultivo*, or "Genuine Meat Broth"), certain scenes—including ones in which the disposed appendages that Marcos has taken to the slaughterhouse "make their way into the production line for the broth, ready for consumption")—drew the ire of those who felt that the film would be "too gruesome" if approved for theatrical release (138). Even after he had made several recommended cuts, Iglesia's picture caused critics to metaphorically hold their noses, for it had (in the words of one contemporaneous reviewer for *Nuevo Fotogramas*) not only generated "fear" and "disgust" but also evoked "the stench of body decomposition" (quoted in Lázaro-Reboll 2012, 148). In retrospect, it is ironically possible to see *The Cannibal Man* and other socially conscious horror films that took aim at the crumbling regime as "breaths of fresh air," i.e., as counter-aesthetic alternatives to "the bourgeois values characteristic of official film culture" (141). That is, they comprised "a vulgar cinema for a vulgar world" (to borrow the words of one critic), and their diegetic smells—especially those emanating from rotting corpses—were merely onscreen whiffs of what Franco's government had been doing to Spain's politically oppressed citizens for decades.

However, at the time of these films' original distribution, few people were able to see past their "aggressive and primitive" cinematic language. Indeed, the director's "crude, visceral style," which contributes to the "moral and sexual sordidness" of this story, is said to have "exasperated critics in equal measure" at the time of *The Cannibal Man*'s domestic and international release (Lázaro-Reboll 2012, 140–41), not just in Spain but also in Germany, where it played at the 1972 Berlin Film Festival accompanied by barf bags handed out to audience members—a promotional gimmick (reminiscent of the ballyhoo surrounding the theatrical releases of William Castle's films during the 1950s and 1960s and anticipating the aforementioned grab bag of items included in Severin's Blu-ray and DVD releases of *Beyond the Darkness*) that set up certain spectatorial assumptions about the film's content (Paul Julian Smith as noted in Willis 2005, 168). Eventually, Iglesia's film made its way to Great Britain, where its cult status grew in the early 1980s when the uncut release was added to a growing list of horror titles known as "video nasties"; this was years before it was granted a British rerelease thanks to the aptly named distributor Redemption, which packaged it with a VHS tape cover showing a meat hook so as to forge a link between it and *The Texas Chain Saw Massacre* as well as exploitation auteur William Girdler's *Three on a Meat Hook* (1973) (Willis 2005, 169).

Notably, in his book *The Pleasures of Horror*, Matt Hills quotes a British devotee of the "video nasties" phenomenon—someone who describes his own embodied recollections of collecting banned tapes during the 1980s (at antiques shops, through foreign importation and trades, etc.)—in olfactory terms. In addition to explaining how the underground acquisition of "hard-to-find rarities" on that list, such as Michael Findlay and Horacio Fredriksson's *Snuff* (1976) and Umberto Lenzi's *Cannibal Ferox* (1981)—both of which ran afoul of the UK's Director of Public Prosecutions before the 1984 passing of the Video Recordings Act—could be seen as a way of "circumventing 'state-imposed' censorship," Hills draws attention to the distinctive smell of the videos, which contributed to their paradoxically alluring noxiousness as prized artifacts (2005, 104). "Kevin," the man whom Hill mentions, describes his experiences as a cult film fan drawn to the "musty," but not unpleasant, odor of those grubby yet highly sought-after objects. Stating that "a yellow film coated the protective plastic sleeve" of the videos (something that he attributes to the owner of the antiques shop where he purchased them being "a heavy smoker"), Kevin momentarily dwells on that deeply associative "video nasty aroma" (104). It is a scent that, even years after those releases obtained certification from the British Board of Film Classification, resides in the sense-memories of this and presumably other horror film aficionados for whom it conjures both the illicit and pleasurable aspects of underground collecting. Perhaps these comments about the weirdly intoxicating odor associated with the videotape releases of *The Cannibal Man* and other international horror films of that period help to explain why Blu-ray distributors today might package a title like *Beyond the Darkness* with an actual air freshener, even if that cheap piece of movie memorabilia—as material paratext—is just a jesting reference to the olfactory "nastiness" found *within* the text.

Besides the aforementioned moments when Marcos brutally kills his victims, the nastiest scene in *The Cannibal Man* is also its most quotidian, a brief interlude in the otherwise unrelenting mayhem that depicts him dining alone on a meager meal of meat broth at a nearby bar. In extreme close-up, a view of the soup's ingredients fills the screen, and just as Marcos puts the spoon to his lips a waitress, Rosa (Vicky Lagos), informs him that the beef in the dish comes from the meatpacking company where he works (and where, unbeknownst to the company's management, he has disposed of his victims' bodies) (figure 7.8). Hearing this, he puts the spoon down in disgust, as if the thought of ingesting the processed remains of human rather than nonhuman creatures is something that he—the person responsible for their deaths—simply cannot stomach.

In a sense, Marcos for the first time appears to come into consciousness as a member of the industrial working class, something that he had not done earlier in the film (when he was shown sitting alone and eating a meat sandwich at the slaughterhouse, "oblivious to the brutality going on behind him") (Willis 2005, 170). Witnessing a customer turning his nose up at the soup, the cook rushes out and inspects the dish, putting it up to his own nose and telling Marcos, who is visibly sickened, that what he really needs is "red meat" (later, Rosa, the flirtatious, ill-fated barmaid who inveigles her way into his home, says that he needs "fresh air to feel better"). Notably, a high-angle long shot, which shows Marcos getting up to leave, draws attention to an oscillating fan in the foreground. Making a complete 360-degree rotation, the fan not only blows the smell of the soup into every crevice of this working-class milieu but also metaphorically sends it wafting into the space of the audience (not unlike the same object does in the previously mentioned film *Alice, Sweet Alice*, blowing the odor of "cat's piss" from the diegetic world of the pedophilic Mr. Alphonso into the extradiegetic world of the spectator). Though visually and morally distanced from Marcos's actions, the audience is thus brought into alignment

Figure 7.8. This scene from *The Cannibal Man* indicates why the film was given such an odd English-language title (when a more accurate translation of the original Spanish-language title would have been *Week of the Killer*). Here, Marcos is served a meat broth whose ingredients have come from the slaughterhouse where he works (and where he has stashed his victims' dead bodies).

with him during this sickening culinary experience, a moment of performed mastication that stands in for their own spectatorial consumption of "unsavory" or "disgusting" films like *The Cannibal Man*.

Brigid Cherry has argued that cannibalism-themed horror films such as Ruggero Deodato's *Cannibal Holocaust* (1980), a notorious Mondo-style mockumentary that likewise earned a place on Britain's "video nasties" list, are not just "exercises in orality" but also taboo-shattering challenges to the culture's privileging of "the clean and proper body" (2009, 118). Although that theme is also discernible in more respected, less-filthy motion pictures like George Romero's *Night of the Living Dead* (1968) and Jonathan Demme's *The Silence of the Lambs* (1991), the "dirty," explicit manner in which the aforementioned exploitation films broke from cinematic decorum or "good taste" and crossed almost-sacred social boundaries at the time of their release makes them noteworthy as examples of body horror. For Cherry, these potentially transgressive works' "yuck factor"—the feeling of bodily disgust that they engender—can be thought of as another type of border-crossing, one that reveals how our own comfortable distance from diegetic representations of bloodshed, cannibalism, and mutilation (among other horrific acts) can be dissolved through aromatic and other forms of abjection (118). Turning our attention to *The Amityville Horror* and its many abject offshoots in the next chapter, I wish to explore the "yuckiest" of all substances produced by the human body—namely, feces—before segueing from a *smell*-based to a *touch*-based assessment of horror films that are more likely to generate "yuks" (laughs) than screams. By crossing that most taboo of borders and bringing the culturally marginalized topic of excrement to the forefront of our exploration of horror as a body genre, we gain a vantage point on the latter that is as fresh as it is foul. In other words, *provocation*—something that horror is reputed to excel at—can be taken up by audiences as a critical maneuver and directed at film criticism itself, especially that which persists in labeling those motion pictures that "fail" in various ways (aesthetically, artistically, financially, etc.), or which simply do not conform to the perceived standards of a "good" movie, as being "shitty."

8

SHITTY, SLIMY, SMELLY, SMILEY

Dirty Spaces, Funny Faces, and the Textural Pleasures of "Laughably Bad" Texts

> Something smells rotten in this cabin, and that's bad B-grade shit horror.
> —an assessment of Eli Roth's 2002 film *Cabin Fever*, posted on the review website Rotten Tomatoes by a user with the pseudonym "Ben H" (June 27, 2010)

In the introduction of their edited collection *B Is for Bad Cinema: Aesthetics, Politics, and Cultural Value*, Claire Perkins and Constantine Verevis ask, "If 'good' or 'bad' derives from 'shit,' how do 'badness' and 'goodness' collide, converge, supplement each other, complement each other, or perhaps annihilate each other in particular films or groups of films?" (2014, 2–3). What prompts their reference to excrement is the critical discourse surrounding *Holy Motors* (2012), writer-director Leos Carax's widely praised yet deeply confounding and "ferociously eccentric" dramatic fantasy described by one reviewer—the *Guardian*'s Peter Bradshaw (quoted in Perkins and Verevis's study)—as "a batsqueak of genius, dishevelment and derangement" (1). At the heart of *Holy Motors* is a wealthy French actor named Mr. Oscar (Denis Levant) who, for unexplained reasons, leaves his family for the day to perform nearly a dozen different roles on the streets of Paris, abetted by a limousine chauffeur (Edith Scob, wearing a mask not unlike what she wore in Georges Franju's *Eyes Without a Face* [*Les yeux sans visage*, 1960]) who spirits her employer from one neighborhood to another. Those roles, implemented through several costume and wig changes, range from a murderous gangster to an old beggar woman on the Pont Alexandre III to a man who is married to a chimpanzee. Most memorable among this menagerie of misfits and miscreants is "Monsieur Merde," a frenetic, wild-eyed persona that Mr. Oscar steps into by literally stepping into the sewers that serve as both his home and a prison where he keeps watch over a beautiful woman whom he has kidnapped (Eva Mendes's mysteriously named supermodel "Kay M."). Having first played this mute, gremlin-like character in the 2008 omnibus triptych *Tokyo!*—specifically in "Merde," a short segment directed by Carax and sandwiched between Michel Gondry's "Interior Design" and Bong Joon-ho's "Shaking Tokyo"—Levant (the actor behind the actor) embodies the anarchic energy of *Holy Motors* as a whole, a film that lurches wildly from one self-contained episode or performance-art "appointment" to the next, and which was referred to by an online commentator (writing about its rapturous reception at the 2012 Cannes Film Festival for the pop-culture website *Vulture*) as "completely bat-shit" in its craziness (Yuan 2012).

The fact that scattered boos could be heard underneath the applause, both there at the world's most glamourous film festival and throughout the general reception of *Holy Motors* once it made its way to other, less prestigious international venues, reminds us that "badness" and "goodness" are evaluative terms tied to the subjective experiences of audiences who might be predisposed to hating or loving a French neosurrealist work that is either "boorish" in its eccentricities or "balls-to-the-wall crazy," depending on that predisposition (Yuan 2012). More than that, though, "badness" and "goodness" are mutually informing conditions that, borrowing Perkins and Verevis's terms, not only "collide" and "converge" but also "supplement" and "complement" each other. If we extend their thoughts to the subject of cinematic horror, it is possible to see how a so-called "bad" film—for instance, a notoriously cheesy, kitschy, or trashy production like *The Creeping Terror* (1964), *Blood Diner* (1987), or *Zombie Nation* (2004), currently ranked as three of the worst-reviewed movies on Rotten Tomatoes—might actually be "good" when seen from vantages far removed from the conceptual frameworks of traditional critical evaluation, or through perceptual lenses not limited to the sense of sight. Historically, mainstream and academic film criticism has tended to privilege aesthetic sophistication, formal inventiveness, structural integrity, and thematic profundity (or the deeper truths about the human condition that lay dormant within most great works of art) over cinematic banality, emptiness, or misspent intensity as well as the kind of ineptness, lunacy, or raggedness that sometimes characterizes onscreen and offscreen motion-picture performances (those of the actors as well as the creative personnel working behind the camera). That propensity to separate the cinematic wheat from the chaff, and to celebrate the former while steering potentially unsuspecting audiences away from the latter, is not unique to professional (accredited or salaried) film critics. Indeed, the ascendency of nonprofessional reviewers over the past thirty years, attendant with the rise of digital media and the demise of print media (Frey 2015, 3), has only magnified the extent to which binaristic thinking and reductive terminology informs the reception of motion pictures that are either "good" or "bad" based on the number of "fresh" red tomatoes or "rotten" green splats featured on the popular review-aggregator website.

If I may borrow the language so often brought to bear on motion pictures deemed "awful," "terrible," or "worthless" by a vocal majority of reviewers, I am tempted to say that Rotten Tomatoes *stinks* as an ostensibly democratized space where the nuances of a more deeply considered meditation on a given film's strengths or weaknesses are dispensed with in favor of a simplistic summing up of its positive or negative reception. My purpose in calling out this particular website—merely one of the many for-profit "consumer guides" catering to a public hungry for quick, bite-sized summaries of reviews rather than in-depth critical interrogations or philosophical treatises—is not to debate the algorithmic effectiveness of its "Tomatometer" tabulation system or the role that it has played in "dumbing down" lay audiences whose own reductive commentary provides evidence of that effect (a claim that Mattias Frey has already refuted in his meticulous study of Rotten Tomatoes) (2015, 81–98). Rather, I would like to begin this chapter by reflecting on the way that casual users who wish to weigh in with their own opinions are given space to do so, in the form of starred capsule reviews with clickable links located near the bottom of a given film's landing page. It is there, in the users' comments, where one is likely to find the kind of dismissive rhetoric—an almost passionate love for *hating* movies—that is suggested less frequently (if no less flamboyantly) in the critical broadsides launched by professional reviewers (located higher up on the page). Moreover, the very "rottenness" of a given film, quantified by the prominence of those green tomato splats on its associated landing page, is furthermore captured in many users' predilection for "shit-talk"—a rhetorical move that is in keeping with the themes and iconography of many horror films.

Even the site's "Super Reviewers"—so named because, according to the editors of Rotten Tomatoes, they have "demonstrated consistent insight" in postings that "feature prominently on movie pages"—revert to reductive comments that say more about *them* than about the films they are reviewing. For instance, in his June 20, 2011, posting about the horror film *Zombie Nation* (written and directed by the prolific German filmmaker Ulli Lommel), "Super Reviewer" Jacob P. states, "This is the worst zombie movie . . . ever. It's so bad. Everything about it is bad. The acting, the effects, the script, the makeup, even the story is horrible! A complete waste of time, DO NOT BOTHER WATCHING THIS MOVIE." This sort of impressionistic takedown of a film, only slightly less snarky than the damning reviews of *Zombie Nation* posted by accredited reviewers,[1] is mild compared to the derogatory remarks that are aimed at films whose only success seems to lay in their ability to inspire vitriol and bring out the worst in the site's users.

Consider the following one-star and half-star reviews of the 2003 film *Dreamcatcher*, adapted by William Goldman from Stephen King's novel of the same title (published two years earlier) and directed by the generally respected Hollywood filmmaker Lawrence Kasdan:

Amy T: The shittiest movie I've seen in a long time and I'm ashamed for Morgan Freeman and the rest of the well-known and talented cast. (April 18, 2011)
Bradley N: I've seen some bad films but this tops the bill. A film of a toilet flushing would of been better then this garbage. (August 27, 2011)
Darwin K: the monster comes out of the butt & so does this movie. horrid. (October 14, 2011)
Will D: SSSSSSSSUUUUUUUUCCCCCCCCKKKKKKK (February 4, 2012)
Brett H: This movie is shittier than shit. It starts off well enough for the first 45 minutes and keeps the suspense high, then after the bathroom scene NOTHING interesting happens until the ludicrously over the top ending. The acting was bad all across the board. (May 12, 2012)
Matthew M: Probably the worst movie to hit theaters in the last 30 years. So bad it hurts. (May 19, 2012)
Oliver D: Rarely in cinema do we see a movie slowly fall apart in every respect as we do in Dreamcatcher. Though it starts out as slightly promising, it becomes so outlandish and convoluted that it's almost worth finishing the movie to see the ending, which is so comically bad that it's hard to believe that any sane person would actually end a movie in this manner. For Kasdan's sake, I hope that he was high on drugs during the entire process of making this movie. This is one of those movies that is so bad that it just might be worth seeing if only to have a ceiling (or should I say floor) for what constitutes a ridiculously horrible film. (May 22, 2013)
Claudia G: crap movie, crap book. (June 17, 2015)
evan m: one of the worst films I've ever seen. barf!! (August 20, 2017)

These and other Rotten Tomatoes reviewers' gravitation toward scatological words and slang terms ("barf," "butt," "crap," "shit," "suck," etc.) suggests horror's own predilection for base bodily activity and taboo subjects. One possible reason for the recurrence of such language in posts complaining about *Dreamcatcher*'s "badness" is the film's foregrounding of excretory activity and bathroom imagery, with the toilet becoming an entryway into the narrative's underlying themes of alien invasion, bioterrorism, fungal infection, and telepathic male bonding. It is as if the film, like its expletive-filled source material (which King wrote so that he might "do for the toilet what *Psycho* [1960] did for the shower") (Conrich and Sedgwick 2017, 256), were so mired in the muck of bodily wastes that the excretory flow of online harangues which *Dreamcatcher* seems to have inspired is strangely fitting: a coarse type of discourse about a curiously purgative cultural production in which parasitic, serpent-like aliens (dubbed "shit weasels" by the main characters) explode from the anuses of their human hosts. To put it bluntly, if this or any other film can be said to "stink," it is perhaps because the evaluative discourse surrounding them is as gauche, juvenile, or unrefined as those cinematic "failures" are purported to be, and just as prone to turn reviewers into the kind of gas-producing "asses" that *Dreamcatcher* latches onto in a shockingly explicit yet humorously corny way.

This chapter follows through on an argument introduced in the preceding one: namely, that horror films are predisposed to eliciting frisson, revulsion, and a host of other excitations of the flesh through appeals to our nasal brain—our ability to cognitively piece together the various smells of a storyworld as surely as we do its narrative details (concerning character, plot, and setting). As a genre that has long been perceived as being "beneath" more critically esteemed categories of cultural production, horror provides a good point of entry into the study of cinematic olfactics by virtue of its "badness," its baseness as a vehicle for delivering us into dangerously close proximity to aspects of the human condition that we generally close our eyes to or shut our ears to. Paul Elliott emphasizes that "smell's place as a proximal sense," its dependence on closeness or physical intimacy between the perceiver's body and the odoring object, is a major reason why it is "considered one of the lowliest" senses, situated far below sight on the sensory hierarchy (2011, 128; Marks 2013, 144). Indeed, its lowly status makes it a natural bedfellow of the horror genre. And this is despite cinematic horror's tendency to privilege eyes and seeing as well as ears and hearing as the principal means of engaging the threats to life and limb that await characters in scenarios that either pivot on battles between "good" and "evil" or revolve around the tension between purity and pollution. Such dichotomies, similar to the good/bad evaluative rhetoric that figures so prominently in the critical discourse surrounding horror films, are indicative of broader cultural logics and social imaginaries whereby the "Self" can be kept at a safe distance from the "Other." But the embodied perception of smell, especially that which is prompted by the malodorous funk of horror films (sulfuric sewer lines, rotting corpses, flatulent asses, etc.), works to close that gap or collapse such distinctions, even as it reduces an otherwise complex range of hedonics to a simple set of positive and negative values (i.e., pleasant vs. unpleasant aromas).

Even more proximal than smell are the senses of taste and touch, and portions of this chapter as well as the following one find me ruminating on their suggestiveness as haptically perceived qualities of horror films whose various textures—mainly their *sliminess*—play a part in those films' critical reception (as aesthetically devalued texts that are not just "wet to the touch" but ostensibly bereft of the more edifying, life-affirming attributes associated with "dryer," more artistic works). Just as horror persists in situating characters (and us) within "terrible places" and "dirty spaces," including private bathrooms, public restrooms, outhouses, drainage systems, and sewers, so too do we consistently return to the genre to purge ourselves of nasty feelings or dreadful ideas, as if perched above a toilet. As borne out by our own olfactory experiences in everyday life, smells are not so easily flushed away, however, and the fact that our memories are shaped and triggered by specific odors underlines the need to attend to this largely overlooked aspect of horror films. In the words of Paul Elliott, "Smell, then, does have a place within film and film appreciation—not in the synthetic creation of substitute aromas with gimmicky technologies ... but in the synaesthetic and haptic appreciation of lived sensual experience that provides the embodied ground for the brain and the mind" (2011, 128).

As Elliott and other film theorists have noted, there had been attempts to incorporate actual odors into the theatrical experience of motion pictures since well before the 1959 "AromaRama" release of *Behind the Great Wall* and the 1960 "Smell-O-Vision" release of *Scent of Mystery*, though none of those earlier efforts helped to bring about André Bazin's "myth of total cinema" (Sobchack 2013, 126–27). Jack Cardiff, the director of *Scent of Mystery*, famously came to regret participating in the project, calling the film and its "cheap" perfumes (contained in tubes timed to release certain smells, such as coffee, gunpowder, fresh salt air, peaches, and wood shavings) a "complete disaster." Nor have any of the subsequent endeavors along these lines fared much better or been viewed as anything more than a one-off gimmick. For instance, John Waters's parodic satire of the melodrama genre, *Polyester* (1981), which he coproduced through his own company Dreamland in partnership with New Line Cinema (the film's distributor), was theatrically released in "Odorama," which essentially consisted of audience scratch-and-sniff cards with numbers corresponding to certain moments in the film when mostly unpleasant smells (e.g., flatulence, gasoline, model airplane glue, skunk spray) drift through scenes. As Vivian Sobchack notes in her essay "The Dream Olfactory: On Making Scents of Cinema," the idea that "we might in some way 'smell' a film" seems, at first glance (or initial sniff), "completely counterintuitive," though, as she goes on to mention, "in vernacular English we often say one 'stinks.'" "Indeed," Sobchack states, "it seems absurd to propose a film as possessing or evoking an 'aroma' at all—aside, that is, from the various (and often hilarious) attempts to 'add' discrete scents to the cinematic scene from an external off-screen theatrical source" (126).

The play of words in her essay's title suggests that a certain *sense-making* becomes available to audiences immersed not only in a film's narrative but also in their own *smell memories*, which might be activated by visual and even aural cues, such as steam rising from a boiling pot of soup, or from a frozen lake in the dead of winter, or from dog poop left unscooped on a sidewalk (not unlike what appears at the end of Waters's gross-out cult comedy *Pink Flamingos* [1972]). Smell, sound, and vision frequently interpenetrate in motion pictures, though any such moments of synesthesia, Sobchack is quick to point out, are "not literal or direct." Rather, they occur "through the affective mediation of tonal elements that subjectively modulate and 'qualify' the objects and people we see onscreen" (2013, 237). Applying her theory to several "laughably bad" horror films, such as *Dreamcatcher* and other notorious stinkers (including the official and unofficial sequels in the *Amityville Horror* franchise that began in the late 1970s), this chapter seeks to illustrate how even the most far-fetched scenarios and fantastic creatures across the genre's history are brought down to earth and made recognizably lifelike—*human*, even—through the persistent depiction of our basic bodily functions, including those that take place on the toilet.

SHOOTING THE SHIT, POPPING THE CORN: FROM *DREAMCATCHER* TO DREAMLAND

> Yeah, it stinks, doesn't it? Ooh, I hate this movie! Yeah, thumbs down on this movie ... Ugh! Get this movie off the screen!
> —TOBY D'AMATO (Tom Villard), the monstrously scarred murderer in *Popcorn* (1991), referring to a fictional horror film within the film titled *The Stench*

Writing about the trend toward bathroom horror in contemporary examples of the "urban environmental Gothic," cultural theorist Marisol Cortez discusses King's *Dreamcatcher*, which, like its 1986 predecessor *It* (a novel also set in and around the fictional town of Derry, Maine), is "intensely corporeal ... full of flatulence, shit, blood, and vomit; gluttonous urges and bodies pushed beyond exhaustion" (2021, 165). As she states, "In both novels, the bathroom is a space for making spectacularly visible what ordinarily remains hidden: the body but also the banal secret of the body's insertion into the technological systems (utilities provision, waste disposal, communications, transportation) that make up ... 'the networked city'" (156). More so than the novel, though, the film (which Kasdan, a fan of 1970s horror, directed so that he might do to the ass what *Alien* [1979] did to the chest) renders the abject state of the parasitically ravaged body as spectacle, a thing so horrifyingly grotesque that it becomes humorous in its excessiveness. Before being taken over by a turd-shaped rectal creature (which had been growing inside the man's intestinal

Figure 8.1. The first of many "bad deaths" in *Dreamcatcher* (2003) happens to a man who has been infected by a "shit weasel," one that explodes from his anus as he attempts to relieve his pain on a toilet bowl.

tract), the body in question belonged to Rick McCarthy (Eric Keenleyside), a nearly frozen stranger whom the four main characters—lifelong friends on an annual hunting trip, Beaver (Jason Lee), Henry (Thomas Jane), Jonesy (Damian Lewis), and Pete (Timothy Olyphant)—have brought to their snowbound cabin retreat after rescuing him from the woods. Complaining of a stomachache and letting loose with "several volcanic belches and farts," Rick rushes to the cabin's bathroom, locking the door behind him and producing a smell that, in King's novel, transforms from that of "ether and overripe bananas" into "something contaminated and dying badly." It is "like mine-gas trapped a million years and finally let free," the book's narrator states (2001, 86, 138), using an analogy that recalls countless other passages in King's larger body of work (a topic discussed in the previous chapter). "I have to shit. . . . If I can shit I'll be all right!" Rick yells, stating outright the fecal imperative of a narrative that seems intent on producing similar levels of discomfort and release in its audience. All of this is but a prelude to the puke-inducing payoff of witnessing the gory aftermath of Rick's anal explosion, a "bad death" if ever there was one, leading to yet another fatality (that of Beaver, who bursts into the bathroom and is wrestled to the blood-smeared floor by one of the sharp-toothed "shit weasels") (figure 8.1).

Reassessing this poorly received film fifteen years after its 2003 theatrical release, online critic Sean Keeley dwells at length on this extended sequence (which runs over 100 pages in King's novel) (Conrich and Sedgwick 2017, 256), though he notes that everything that follows it is equally "insane" (Keeley 2018). Leading to Henry and Jonesy's defeat of the alien invader through the help of their psychically connected childhood friend Duddits (Donnie Wahlberg), a man with Down syndrome who is dying from leukemia but who is revealed to be a friendly extraterrestrial, *Dreamcatcher* is just as "batshit crazy" (to borrow Keeley's words) as *Holy Motors* is (though the latter's textual extravagance is cottoned to by critics who would otherwise turn their nose up at this stinky adaptation of King's novel). Defiantly calling *Dreamcatcher* a "good-bad movie" and "baffling in the best way," Keeley marvels at how its plot "appears to be making itself up as it goes," something that might also be said about Carax's episodic art film. Left nearly speechless by the sheer outrageousness of this big-budget production, which somehow attracted A-list actors and some of Hollywood's most respected creative personnel (including Morgan Freeman, who plays an unhinged military officer leading the effort to neutralize the alien threat), the critic can only sum up his thoughts by stating, "Holy shit, you guys" (Keeley 2018). His remark is a decidedly informal yet accurate summation of how *Dreamcatcher* makes explicit what the more highly respected *Holy Motors* and its armpit-licking, sewer-dwelling leprechaun Monsieur Merde merely gesture toward. Similar to the ill-mannered manner in which Rotten Tomatoes user "Corey E" defends the film against its harshest, most "ridiculous" critics (or, in his words, "little kids" who "have no taste") by writing, "This movie is nowhere near terrible, bad, or shit" (August 19, 2021), Keeley's rhetorical slide into conversational slang and scatological humor takes its cue from his object of analysis, "a fart- and shit-obsessed movie" that actually follows through on horror's promise of offering a bottom-up view of society's ills.

If King is correct in thinking that "what goes on behind the toilet doors is one of the last great taboos of society" (Brown 2018, 116), then the horror genre's eagerness in granting audiences access to that "dirty space"—be it a public restroom or a private bathroom—not only sets it apart from every nearly other category of cultural production (with the notable exception of comedy), but also highlights its significance as a truth-telling machine, a means of pulling back the curtain to show us what so many other works of art insist on hiding. Indeed, horror brings us face to face—or face to feces—with that part of ourselves which we would prefer to keep hidden, including base or illicit desires that can be plumbed by going through the actual plumbing systems and sewers beneath our feet. Doing so allows us to confront those things that have been flushed away, put out of sight and out of mind by representational systems that are sanitized to the point of being devoid of life (which is messy, and not just metaphorically). By design, the toilet along with other cleansing fixtures like the sink and the tub are meant to divest bodies of their dirt and odors, if only temporarily. Hence the reason why the introduction of the private bathroom over two centuries ago heralded a new era in public health, when "the practice of making excrement (and the excretory body) disappear became a hallmark of scientific progress, civilization, cleanliness, rationality, and control over nature" (Cortez 2021, 157). Consigning the practice of open defecation to the distant past, modern indoor plumbing and underground sewers also contributed to the stigmatizing of bodily functions "as contaminating, impure, primitive, and improper—something to be relegated to the realm of the 'private' bathroom," according to Cortez (157).

In her ecocritical reading of *Dreamcatcher*, Cortez makes the case that the novel's (and by extension, the film's) "intense focus on embodiment—the permeable and porous body, the body open to invasion and transformation by other agencies"—serves to foreground "the networks and infrastructures that laterally structure urban industrial subjectivity." "Like telepathy," which the four main characters all have in common (psychically linking them and Duddits, as if they can together "catch" each other's dreams), "water delivery and disposal systems suture bodies to one another, just as visual culture and information technology link minds" (2021, 169). This latter point is especially useful in thinking of the infrastructural, technological, and socially connective "tubes" of Rotten Tomatoes and other user-review websites as being similar to the local ecological and hydrological systems—the pipes behind bathroom walls and the sewers down below—in which we are "actually physically embedded" (158). In that sense, any unusually large accumulation of online "effluent," such as the piling-on of putdowns meant to bury or destroy "bad" films, can be likened to a backed-up toilet or a clogged sewer line. With greater numbers of nonprofessional reviewers publicly "poo-pooing" a wide variety of motion pictures (horror films in particular), chances increase that the purported "badness" of a production like *Dreamcatcher* will be obscured by the "rottenness" of those furiously thrown tomatoes.

Insofar as it is "gorier than virtually all the previous mainstream King adaptations" (Brown 2018, 116), *Dreamcatcher* might be unique in its commitment to bringing the figuratively shitty comments of anti-fans to life, through spoken and visual references to "woodchuck turds," rat droppings, dog doo-doo, and cat scat in addition to all the human discharge on display. But it is hardly the first or last word in fecal horror. One could go back to the 1960 release of Alfred Hitchcock's *Psycho* to see how the toilet bowl and other bathroom fixtures (including the shower and tub) might be used to heighten feelings of anxiety or menace. However, it would not be until the mid-1980s—around the time of *Psycho III*'s 1986 release, one that gave audiences a glimpse at a much-older Norman Bates (Anthony Perkins) killing a motel guest while she sits on the commode—when cinematic horror shifted into decidedly darker waters, with everything from Charles B. Pierce's famously inept sequel *Boggy Creek II: And the Legend Continues* (1985) to J. Michael Muro's intentionally schlocky "melt movie" *Street Trash* (1987) attesting to an increase in the volume of poo inside the loo. Not just poo but goo, slugs, and other slimy things slither about in horror-sci-fi hybrids such as Fred Dekker's *Night of the Creeps* (1986), comedy-horror mashups such as *Brain Damage* (1988), and slasher films such as *Sleepaway Camp II: Unhappy Campers* (1988) (figure 8.2). The leech-filled,

Figure 8.2. Thanks to films such as *Brain Damage* (1988), a space that is traditionally reserved for the removal of bodily impurities is now associated with murderous actions and deadly infections (as happens to this victim of a slug-like parasite who is killed inside a bathroom stall).

fly-infested outhouse that appears in the latter film harkens back to slightly earlier examples of the slasher subgenre—most famously, *Friday the 13th Part V: A New Beginning* (1985)—in which rickety outdoor "shitters" become the "terrible places" where bad death awaits. In this film, the first of four sequels to writer-director Robert Hiltzik's *Sleepaway Camp* (1983), a teenaged summer camper named Ally (Valerie Hartman) is stabbed in the back and then forced into the hole of an outhouse by the murderous camp counselor Angela (Pamela Springsteen), reminding viewers of other horror films in which characters are either flushed down toilets (e.g., *976-Evil* [1988]) or dragged into dark pits (e.g., *Reeker* [2005]) by monsters whose abjection is rivaled by what their ill-fated victims produce only seconds before taking the spill.

For decades, the horror genre has depicted toilets as sites of abjection where individuals are at their most vulnerable, exposed to threats lurking below the surface of the water or in seemingly cordoned-off spaces (i.e., restroom stalls) whose permeability attests to the ease with which bodies can be penetrated or violated. To the above list of titles, we can add other motion pictures depicting men and women being attacked and often killed inside private and public lavatories, from mainstream hits like Wes Craven's *Scream 2* (1997) to small independent productions like Kate Glover's *Slaughtered* (2010). Some films, such as John Hough's *The Incubus* (1981), with its demonic rapist chasing down women indiscriminately, depict sexual violence inside public restrooms. Others, among them Frank Henenlotter's *Basket Case* (1982) and Bernard Rose's *Candyman* (1992), conjure the abject nature of revulsion as an olfactory phenomenon, with the putrid stench of fecal matter and other substances creating a physically nauseating environment where characters—with their fingers to their noses or their hands over their mouths—gag on their own vomit or dry heave amid all the horrifying wetness. This is perhaps most powerfully evoked in the first forty-five seconds of Jesse Thomas Cook's 2013 film *Septic Man*, which begins with a scene of jaw-dropping frankness with respect to abject bodily states: an unnamed woman (Nicole G. Leier), covered from head to toe in her own filth and squirming atop a toilet, spews vomit onto an already dreadfully soiled bathroom floor. Not a single inch of this compact space is clean, and her feet slide greasily over the tiles as she shifts her weight on the seat. Digging her nails into her bloodied thigh and frantically looking for a pill or some other means of easing her affliction, she suddenly lurches forward and regurgitates white liquid into the blackened bathtub, her exposed derriere now aimed at a wall that receives another excremental splash. At this point, Cook cuts to an overhead shot of the toilet, filled to the brim with brown soupy poo, only to quickly zoom into the bowl, bringing this pre-credits prologue to an abrupt, but sorely needed, end.

In the words of cultural critic Charles Bramesco (writing for *The Dissolve*), this astoundingly dirty opening to *Septic Man*—unprecedented in the annals of cinematic horror and seemingly unrelated to the story that ensues—serves as "a warning shot . . . to herald what will be a long, taxing volley of scatological warfare on the viewer" (2014). More than that, though, it lays the groundwork for a narrative that tracks the downward trajectory of a self-described "civic-minded shitsucker" named Jack (Jason David Brown). Spurred on by a slimy government agent bearing a large stack of cash, Jack ventures into his hometown's subterranean sewers so that he can investigate a mysterious water contamination problem, which has led to an emergency evacuation of the area and begun turning residents into blood-vomiting zombies. After getting trapped inside a septic tank by a rat-like man named Lord Auch (Tim Burd)—a reference to Georges Bataille's transgressive novella *Story of the Eye* (*L'histoire de l'œil*, published under that pseudonym in 1928])—Jack, gagging from beginning to end, undergoes a physical and psychological transformation that more than one critic has compared to the title character in *The Toxic Avenger* (1984). Like that film's superhero protagonist, "Toxie," who changes from a flyweight janitor into a hideously deformed, mop-toting mutant after falling into a drum of toxic waste, Jack sprouts facial pustules while trying to find a way out of his cesspit prison. Unlike that intentionally campy Troma production, which has curried favor with a majority of the film critics and users posting reviews on Rotten Tomatoes, audiences have found little to appreciate about *Septic Man*'s commitment to gross-out effects, which are actually put into service as a tool for social commentary (about worker exploitation and shoddy "infrastructure," a word uttered numerous times throughout the narrative). The critical disdain for the movie, which has a Tomatometer score of 16 percent (far below *The Toxic Avenger*'s 68 percent rating), is tersely summed up by Bramesco, who ends his review by stating, "It's a loose turd of a film that's best flushed back down the toilet it crawled out of."

In a far more agreeable but no less provocative way, director Mark Herrier's *Popcorn* (1991), a self-reflexive celebration of "B-movie" spectatorship, not only foregrounds the malodorous associations of bathroom horror but also features a scene in which the rottenness of a film within the film is snarkily commented on by the killer, a man who masks his identity behind prosthetic face coverings modeled after the visages of his victims. Not long after the midpoint of the film, it is revealed that Toby (Tom Villard), a college-aged film student who has devised an all-night movie marathon along with his classmates, concocted the mini-festival being held at a soon-to-be-closed picture palace as a way to take revenge against the daughter of the person responsible for his mother's death, an experimental filmmaker named Lanyard Gates (Matt Falls). Because Toby's mother had been an audience member at a theater to which Gates set fire years ago (as part of a performance art snuff-screening of his film *Possessor*), the young man plans to return the favor by killing Gates's daughter Maggie (Jill Schoelen) on the main stage of the Dreamland Theater, following a triple bill showing of vintage B-movies accompanied by William Castle-style promotional gimmicks. Following screenings of *Mosquito* (a 3-D "big bug" movie modeled after *Them!* [1954]) and *Attack of the Amazing Electrified Man* (a "Shock-o-Scope" release modeled after Castle's *The Tingler* [1959], complete with electrical buzzers under the auditorium seats), the final film of the horrorthon—a literally stinky motion picture titled *The Stench*—is projected on the Dreamland's screen, prompting the costumed audience seated before that screen to put on the "Aroma-Rama" nose guards that they had been given upon entering the theater (figure 8.3).

It is during that screening when Toby strides toward the stage, revealing his true face (horribly burned as a result of having survived that fire as a baby) and repeatedly yelling at the screen, "Yeah, it stinks doesn't it? Ooh, I hate this movie! Yeah, thumbs down on this movie. . . . Ugh! Get this movie off the screen!" Funnily enough, his meta-commentary, delivered in jest and mocking the kind of midnight-movie spectatorship that derives pleasure from mocking laughably bad genre films, anticipates the snide or snarky postings thrown up by nonprofessional reviewers on Rotten Tomatoes, a website that notably uses the image of a full popcorn bucket whenever at least 60 percent of all users give positive reviews, and a tipped-over popcorn bucket whenever a film has been deemed to be "rotten."

The monstrous figure's jeering ("it stinks!"), itself a performance meant to agitate the audience, achieves its intended effect once the crowd of costumed spectators—many of whom are dressed as monsters—turn on him and advance toward the stage. The hostile mob is further egged on by Toby's replacement of *The Stench* with *Possessor*. Extreme close-up shots of a person's eye and then mouth—stream-of-consciousness flickerings from Lanyard's avant-garde film—suddenly flash onscreen during this penultimate scene, suggesting the erasure of the previous movie's smells through the insertion of sight- and taste-based interfaces designed for organs not protected by the "Aroma-Rama" nose

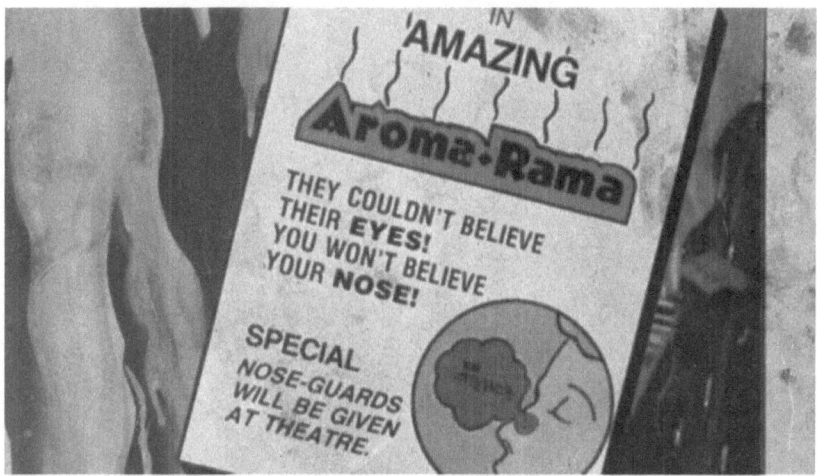

Figure 8.3. As a throwback to the kind of ballyhoo-style gimmickry popularized by William Castle during the 1950s and 1960s, *Popcorn* (1991) features a film-within-the-film titled *The Stench*, the theatrical release of which is accompanied by "Aroma-Rama" nose guards (which are handed out to audiences prior to the screening).

guards. Significantly, in the lead-up to the screening of *The Stench*, Toby attacks one of his classmates, Leon (Elliott Hurst), in the men's restroom. Dressed in the same asylum patient getup that Leon wears and masking his identity behind a prosthetic mask that looks exactly like his friend's, the doppelganger first pees on Leon's leg at the urinal and then pushes him into a bathroom stall before dumping an explosive device into the toilet and walking away. The smoky, gassy BOOM that brings this scene (and Leon's life) to an end paves the way for a similarly noxious encounter with odor pellets, which another of the main characters, Joanie (Ivette Soler), activates and sends wafting through the auditorium's air vents during the audience's viewing (and smelling) of *The Stench*. Having already learned which specific pellets she and her friends were planning to use during the movie marathon ("fish smell, locker room, road kill, fart plain, fart stale, dead dog"), we are primed to imagine those odors and can metaphorically stick our own noses into the tellingly named Dreamland once their visible vapors drift out of the vents. Importantly, the main vent is positioned where the mouth of a large wall-hanging mask is located, part of the theater's interior decor that links the olfactory and the oral.

As the gaseous exhaust pours from the architectural orifice, viewers might recall an earlier instance when something suggestive of a bad taste spills from a character's mouth. Specifically, a scene showing members of the diegetic audience milling about outside the theater, dressed in costumes and engaging in the kind of party atmosphere that distinguishes a horror-themed movie marathon from run-of-the-mill film screenings, depicts a young man vomiting

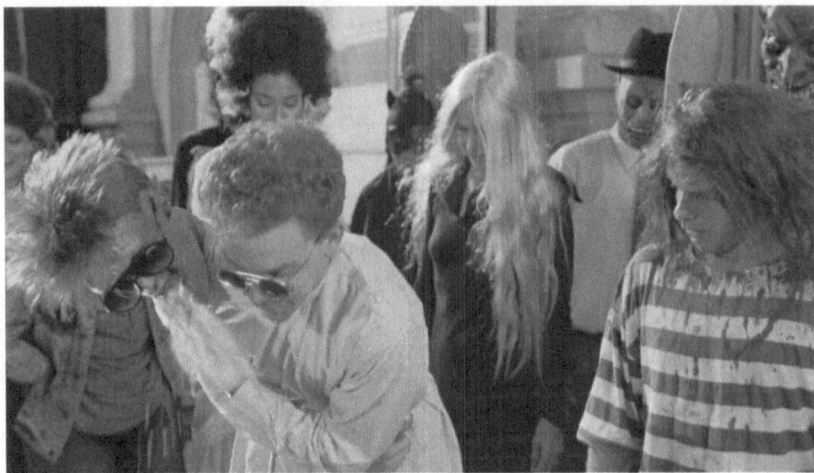

Figure 8.4. Vomiting occurs frequently in horror films, but rarely is it presented in such a humorously metatextual way as what occurs in this scene from *Popcorn* (1991), when an audience member upchucks green slime as part of his elaborate cosplay.

green slime onto the sidewalk. Or, rather, the prop head attached to his costume upchucks the stuff, an image that points to the fact that other "fake movie" fluids besides urine flow through this and similarly comedic forays into body horror (figure 8.4). As will become apparent in the coming pages, horror is as slimy as it is shitty, just as it is can be funny (or humorous) while also being terrifying (or revolting). To borrow the title of a notoriously cheesy sci-fi blaxploitation comedy from 1972, the genre with which this book is concerned might be thought of as *The Thing with Two Heads*. One of those heads either grimaces in pain or screams in terror while the other laughs uproariously or snickers devilishly at all the mess that it has made. Before proceeding to the intentionally comedic sort of horror films that practically swim in slime, let us turn to a well-known if understudied franchise that has returned more than a few times to the proverbial well of bad smells since its launch in the late 1970s.

THE ANALITY OF EVIL AND THE BOWELS OF THE EARTH: FROM RECTORY TO RECTUM IN *THE AMITYVILLE HORROR* AND OTHER EXCREMENTAL TEXTS

> [W]hen she entered her bathroom, she was struck by a completely different odor, an overpowering stench. Kathy gagged and started to cough, but before she ran, caught a glimpse of her toilet bowl. It was totally black inside!
> —a passage from Jay Anson's novel *The Amityville Horror* (1977)

Published in 1977 and adapted into an independently produced American film of the same title two years later, Jay Anson's supernatural ghost story *The Amityville Horror* has attracted surprisingly little critical attention outside of a few books questioning its accuracy as a novelistic rendering of an ostensibly fact-based haunting: that of a suburban Long Island house purchased and quickly vacated (after a twenty-eight-day stay) by George and Kathleen Lutz in 1975. The relative dearth of academic investigations into *The Amityville Horror*'s formal and thematic elements inversely reflects the extreme degree to which both the controversial novel and the paranormal phenomena that inspired it (e.g., "human levitation, the regular appearance of a large, black, talking, spectral pig with red glowing eyes, ghostly marching bands parading through the home in the middle of the night," etc.) have been scrutinized by those who remain dubious of the author's and married couple's claims (Broderick 2012, 14). Rather than contribute to the voluminous discourse surrounding the text's status as "hoax," I want to use this second half of the chapter focusing on the manner in which Anson's novel and its first cinematic adaptation each generate fear and revulsion while engaging the reader/audience's sense of *smell*—a largely overlooked bodily experience in literary criticism, horror film, and genre studies. One odor in particular—that of excrement—wafts through the story in each telling, assuming greater salience as George and Kathy (played by James Brolin and Margot Kidder in the 1979 film) begin to unearth the source of their waking nightmares: a previous homeowner's recent slaughter of his entire family, whose vengeful spirits linger as a result of the Dutch Colonial house having been built atop a Shinnecock Indian burial site (one of the many aspects of the Lutzes' account that have been disputed by researchers). Tellingly, the couple's figurative exhuming of the truth, their gradual encounter with the reprehensible Real that otherwise exists beyond—or, rather, *below*—the symbolic order, is accompanied by a literal turn toward the "bowels of the earth."

That latter expression, common within horror-filled tales (dating back at least to Edgar Allan Poe's 1833 short story "MS Found in a Bottle") and spoken by a psychic demonologist or "ghost hunter" in *The Amityville Horror*, reminds us of the genre's intestinal spread of dread—that is, its alimentary descent into the most unpleasant smells of the anus as well as the freshly fertilized earth. On several occasions, the foul stench of fecal matter—an invisible odor whose source initially appears to be the house's blackened toilet bowls—flares up and intensifies the reader/audience's revulsion (figure 8.5). That perception of something gone wrong, something outside the bounds of normal existence, is grounded in the ordinary (i.e., the everyday, familiar smell of our own bodies' discharge) yet elevated to the level of the extraordinary once another character, a local priest named Father Mancuso (renamed Father Delaney, and played by Rod Steiger, in the film), senses the presence of a malevolent force inside and

Figure 8.5. A blackened toilet bowl appears to be the source of a nauseating stench in *The Amityville Horror* (1979).

outside his own domicile. Noting that the church's rectory sits atop a cesspool (one that, according to plumbers, is in "good working order"), this man of God initially cannot fathom why such noxious fumes should befoul the air of this holy site. Like the Lutzes, whom he visited not long after their arrival in Amityville, Mancuso/Delaney senses the unholy presence of spectral others through his nostrils, as part of that most banal of biological processes (i.e., one in which oxygen is breathed into the lungs and carbon dioxide is flushed out through the nose and mouth). Thus, the banality of evil—its multi-associative location in the nostrils and lungs as well as in the bathrooms and basements of this and other horror film families—is linked, analogically and anatomically, to its anality.

As Ian Conrich and Laura Sedgwick argue in *Gothic Dissections in Film and Literature*, the intestines and the anus are the "most taboo parts of the body," owing to the fact that, along with the stomach, they are responsible for "processing food intake and passing waste out through the rectum" (2017, 259). Building upon these and other scholars' work, I seek to reveal how a mixture of "purity and pollution, privacy and expulsion," so central to horror in its cinematic and literary guises, results from the imaginative linking together of bodily orifices, the "sensitive 'end' parts of the anatomy," to borrow the words of Conrich and Sedgwick (259). Notably, the strange odors that permeate George and Kathy's newly purchased five-bedroom home (but which seem to issue from some unseen, subterranean space below it) are alternately described as that of sweet perfume or gut-churning excrement, a disgustingly musty yet oddly agreeable confluence that hints at the genre's contradictory appeals and spectatorial (dis)pleasures. After addressing these elements within *The Amityville Horror* (both the 1979 film directed by Stuart Rosenberg and the novel upon which it is based), I gesture briefly toward other excremental cinematic and literary texts in which characters' sometimes nauseating olfactory experiences are conveyed audiovisually (through aural cues or images on the screen, including that of buzzing flies) and linguistically (through similes, metaphors, and other figures of speech on the page). Moreover, the faint whiff of additional *Amityville*-related works, including critically lambasted sequels, remakes, spin-offs, and spoofs that followed the original film's release, will drift in and out of the present discussion, bringing with them their own metaphorical odors as entries in an ever-expanding franchise that, in the words of one unimpressed Reddit poster (speaking for several other non-fans), "stinks."[2]

To accept the notion that the nearly two dozen theatrically released or straight-to-video motion pictures with "Amityville" in their titles, on top of the countless published books, graphic novels, and other cultural productions inspired by the Lutzes' experience, comprise a single yet multifarious *text*—an "Amitytext" made up of both canonical and derivative works that are directly or indirectly concerned with the paranormal goings-on at 112 Ocean Avenue—is to first acknowledge the historical *context* for such transmedia franchise-building. Doing so also presumes at least passing familiarity with the tragic circumstances that led one of the house's previous occupants—a mentally deranged twenty-three-year-old man named Ronald DeFeo Jr.—to murder his family members in their beds on November 13, 1974. Told and retold through its myriad iterations (albeit with inaccuracies and pseudonyms obscuring the truth of what actually transpired), the story of what happened to the real killer's father (Ronald DeFeo Sr.), mother (Louise), sisters (Dawn and Allison), and brothers (Marc and John Matthew), like the story of what happened to George, Kathy, and their three children one year later, hardly needs summarizing, so deeply has it seeped into the popular consciousness of movie audiences over the years. Nevertheless, it behooves us to use historical context as a *pretext* for a more thorough evaluation of the story's fixation on the causes or origins of seemingly supernatural events and malodorous emanations. Doing so necessitates a brief consideration of how the DeFeo family murders—and the Lutz family hauntings that presumably resulted from that grisly episode—have informed the Amitytext as a whole.

Let us start, somewhat counterintuitively, with *Amityville 3-D* (1983). Midway through this second official sequel, directed by the seasoned Hollywood veteran Richard Fleischer, two teenage girls, including the daughter of the new homeowner, John Baxter (Tony Roberts), discuss the history of the house as they traipse through it, room by room. Conveniently delivering exposition for the benefit of any uninitiated viewers not already familiar with the legend, Lisa (Meg Ryan), the best friend of Susan Baxter (Lori Loughlin), informs

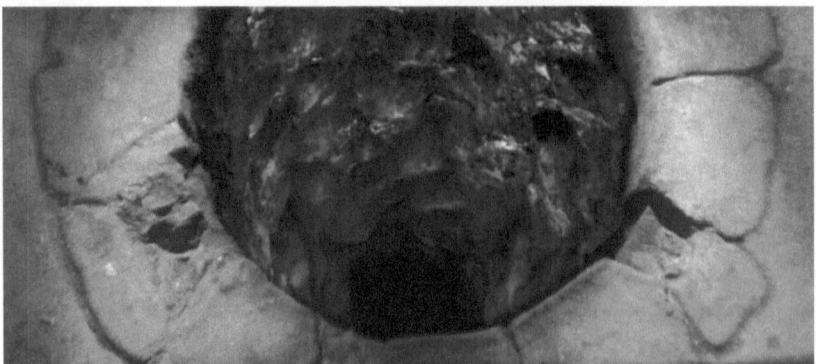

Figure 8.6. A deep hole is discovered inside the basement of the haunted house in *Amityville 3-D* (1983), a sequel whose reputation for being figuratively "shitty" (according to some online critics) finds literal expression in this confrontation with the bowels of the earth.

her companion that she has read all the newspaper articles about the DeFeo murders (including those written by John Baxter himself) and therefore knows "the whole story." The master bedroom, Lisa glibly notes, is where Ronald began his killing spree, dispatching his father and mother before moving on to the upstairs bedrooms where his siblings were sound asleep. The sound of rifle fire, she claims, was "muffled by the crash of thunder outside," a detail that seems wholly concocted to put Susan (and the audience) into a state of fearful apprehension. This bit of poetic license on the part of the teenaged storyteller, plus her insistence that DeFeo had been "possessed by the spirit of the devil," cannot be verified by any factual evidence, of course. But these and other fabulations have exerted sway on the cultural imagining of the Amityville residence as an unholy place where wave after wave of foolhardy homeowners face mortal danger.

At Lisa's urging, Susan unwisely descends into the house's basement, because that is where, according to legend, "the entrance to hell" is to be found. "It was burst open by some colossal supernatural power from the depths of the earth," the girl states as they both gaze into a cavernous brown hole that is indeed bowel-like in its baseness (figure 8.6). Notably, Lisa's curious use of the word "colossal" to describe the force required to explode the earthly surface beneath the basement's floorboards is later echoed when Susan's mother, Nancy (Tess Harper), furious that her ex-husband has taken their daughter to this "infamous" place, laments John's "colossal ego" as a risk-taking investigative journalist who will do anything (including jeopardizing the lives of loved ones) to get to the bottom of a story. As such, a rhetorical connection is forged between the demonic and patriarchal evils that lurk inside family structures in which men (overcome by either supernatural spirits or their own hubris) threaten women and children with violence. This idea was introduced in *The Amityville Horror* four years earlier, whenever George Lutz, "the haunted middle-class Dad" inside a "haunted middle-class home," directs his mounting rage against his wife and kids (Sobchack 2015, 180).

Writing over thirty years ago about an increasingly discernible trend in horror films of the 1970s and early 1980s, Vivian Sobchack notes that the anxiety and dread associated with the genre, once the province of distinctly "other" places and times (abstractly evoked in the "there" and "then" of narratives set in distant lands and historical or fantastical pasts), had entered the "hereness" and "nowness" of the contemporary American home. "It is within the home and family," she states, "that the institutionalization and perpetuation of the bourgeois social world is now seen to begin—and end" (Sobchack 2015, 174). From *The Exorcist* (1973) to *Poltergeist* (1982), the "sanctity" of the domestic sphere is threatened from without and from within, and the once-solid edifice of the nuclear family—a "structure" inside the architecturally encasing structure of house and home, and even more delimiting—begins to show cracks that hint at the physical and psychical destruction to come. As the most privileged icon of bourgeois mythology, the child, whether stuck in infancy or transitioning into adolescence, personifies the positive virtues of the familial structure that further contains it, evoking innocence and purity but also the vulnerability that will surely be exploited by external threats. Notably, Sobchack describes the baby or small child that so often appears in horror as a "figure of poignant sweetness," and that latter word is made all the more relevant as a defining characteristic of culturally constructed infancy when the "sour" smell of a rotting middle-class family threatens to overpower or befoul it *from within* (176).

Before exploring this theme in *The Amityville Horror*, let us consider the second entry in the film series, director Damiano Damiani's *Amityville II: The Possession* (1982). Less a sequel than a prequel to its 1979 predecessor, this film takes dramatic liberties in showing why DeFeo (here renamed Sonny Montelli [Jack Magner]) killed his father, mother, and younger siblings that fateful early morning. As denoted by its title, and in a manner that anticipates the aforementioned scene in *Amityville 3-D*, Damiani's film points toward supernatural causes for the killer's actions: an evil presence had taken up residence in 112 Ocean Avenue prior to the Montellis' arrival. Hearing a demonic voice in his Sony Walkman headphones (one of many historical anachronisms), Sonny gradually undergoes a physical as well as psychological change, becoming a hideously deformed monster who eventually guns down his bickering parents. His titular possession by a malevolent spirit occurs, notably, after he has descended into the basement. It is there, in that subterranean space, where a secret room had initially been discovered by a hired mover who is shown bringing in a large crate of rifles belonging to Mr. Montelli (Burt Young) during the film's opening sequence. Notably, when the worker pulls back the swinging panel and crawls into that dark, heavily cobwebbed compartment, slathered in a brown sludge of filth, he tells Sonny's mother, Dolores (Rutanya Alda), who is overseeing the move, that the copious leaking from the pipes probably means "a busted sewer line." "Lady, it stinks in here," he gripes against a soundtrack of dripping water and buzzing flies, before reemerging into the basement, covered in "shit," to advise her to "stay out of there." The man's shrewd warning can be extended to anyone who might enter the house, much less the basement, oblivious of the (false) fact that the earth below it was once the final resting place of the region's Native Americans—a bit of Amityville lore that Lisa, the seemingly well-informed (but, in actuality, ill-informed) possessor of "knowledge" in the previously mentioned 3-D production, likewise imparts to her credulous friend.

Based loosely on parapsychologist Hans Holzer's 1979 book *Murder in Amityville*, which was itself a sequel/prequel to Anson's earlier publication, and which erroneously claimed that the house had been erected on the sacred burial site of the Shinnecock Indians, *Amityville II: The Possession* further mythologizes the Lutzes' experience in the titular Long Island town by linking their troubles to the DeFeos' earlier misfortune. That connection would be paradoxically strengthened over the years with each additional entry in the franchise even as subsequent films suffer from weakening ties to the actual location where possession is said to have taken place. Indeed, with the made-for-TV and direct-to-video releases of *Amityville 4: The Evil Escapes* (1989), *The Amityville Curse* (1990), and *Amityville: It's About Time* (1992), the series moved farther and farther away from the original haunted residence, suggesting that such low-budget productions were sequels in name only. However, further indirect allusions to the DeFeos, coupled with an unabated focus on rank olfactory experiences and excremental terrors, render these—the fourth, fifth, and sixth entries in the film series—as thematically consistent extensions of the first motion picture's anal fixations.

Based on John G. Jones's book of the same title, *Amityville 4: The Evil Escapes* is set largely in the middle-class Californian home of the film's septuagenarian protagonist Alice Leacock (Jane Wyatt), whose basement, like that of the original house on Long Island, eventually becomes a site of putrid odors and fecal filth. When a plumber arrives on the scene to look into the cause of the black sewage issuing from Alice's pipes (mucky sludge that her oblivious granddaughter, Amanda [Zoe Trilling], unwittingly puts on her toothbrush in one comically grotesque scene), he sniffs the air, a tell-tale sign that something is amiss or afoot. Indeed, a hand—the amputated appendage once belonging to Amanda's boyfriend (who had a nasty run-in with the trash compactor upstairs)—is blocking the plumbing, and its sudden appearance inside one of the below-ground pipes is this film's most effective gross-out moment (figures 8.7 and 8.8). A brown torrent dislodges the hand and sends the handyman

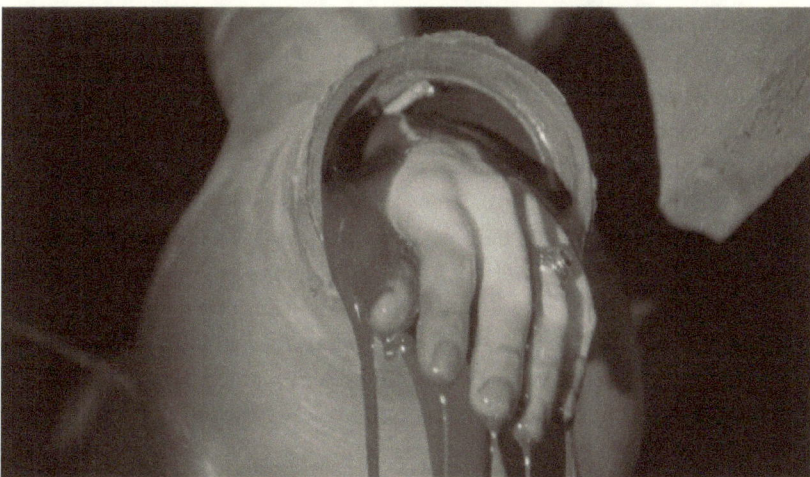

Figure 8.7. An amputated hand temporarily blocks the poo-filled plumbing of the California home where *Amityville 4: The Evil Escapes* (1989) has relocated.

Figure 8.8. One of the biggest gross-out moments in *Amityville 4: The Evil Escapes* occurs when Amanda (Zoe Trilling), the teenaged granddaughter of the main character, mistakenly brushes her teeth with the excremental stuff spilling out of the bathroom faucet.

to the ground, with drops of the slop falling into his mouth. This image, like the earlier bathroom scene in which Amanda unknowingly brushes her teeth with smelly, discolored water, links anality and orality; in other words, architectural and human orifices function as physical portals of disgusting eruption and ingestion. The simultaneously horrifying and humorous overlap of those antipodal trajectories creates a cross-hatching of movements *out of* and *into* bodies defined by their relative "cleanliness" or "dirtiness," with the former (according to Catholic theology) being next to godliness while the latter suggests "sinful" impurities of the soul. Such abject representations hint at the way in which physical and psychological terrors bleed into spiritual concerns about one's moral readiness for heavenly reward or hellish punishment—a thematic preoccupation of many horror films in which representatives of the Christian religion figure prominently.

How did the Amityville ghost come to take up residence in Alice's basement? As would be repeated with slight variation in *Amityville: It's About Time* and *Amityville: A New Generation* (1993), a cursed object from the former dwelling, imported into the new one, is all that is required for that transdimensional transferal to take place. In the case of *Amityville 4: The Evil Escapes*, the malevolent spirit of 112 Ocean Avenue comes to inhabit a hideously ugly, strangely anthropomorphic floor lamp after a young priest performs a ritual blessing and failed exorcism in the film's first extended sequence. Propelled by way of outlet and power cord into the body of that man-sized eyesore, the newly captured demon is eventually unleashed after the brass lamp is sold off in a yard sale and sent to the elderly protagonist as a gag gift by her sister on the East Coast. Once it comes into the matronly woman's possession, the haunted object begins to infect several of her other tools and household appliances besides the aforementioned kitchen sink disposal, including a tea kettle, a toaster oven, and (most distressingly) a chainsaw. Like the antique clock in *Amityville: It's About Time*, the ornate mirror in *Amityville: A New Generation*, and the titular miniature toy in *Amityville Dollhouse* (1996), the relocated relic in this film is presumed to have been a fixture from the now-unoccupied original house, as if the evil associated with that legendary street address has spread beyond the confines of its bowel-like basement into other subterranean spaces.

TIME FLIES AND SLIME OOZES

> The fly is an emblem of our mortal organic condition, our connection to the world of biological processes: digestion, dying, the soft and slimy. To be or become food for flies and worms—that is the most base level of human existence.
> —COLIN McGINN, "*The Fly* and the Human: Ironies of Disgust" (2012, 11)

In addition to providing expositional pretext for the scenes set in sunny Dancott, California, the comparatively dark, overcast opening sequence of *Amityville 4: The Evil Escapes* (the setting of which returns the viewer to Long Island) ushers forth one of the series' most persistent audiovisual motifs, as dependably present over the past forty years as the many spoken references to the DeFeo murders. Against the sonic backdrop of pattering raindrops and skittering violin strings, plucked with greater and greater intensity, the sound of buzzing houseflies increases in volume as the camera racks focus, showing a half-dozen priests arriving outside the storied house and then (in the same shot) a second-floor window inside it whose view to the world below is partially obscured by those winged insects. Other more recent entries in the franchise, from *Amityville: No Escape* (2016) to *Amityville: The Awakening* (2017), likewise fill the frame from time to time with houseflies. In the former production, a microbudget attempt to reproduce the scares of *The Blair Witch Project* (1999) and other "found-footage" films, dead flies are spotted by new homeowner Lina (Julia Gomez), a young woman who moves into the house in 1997 and records her experience via video camera. Visible on the windowsill as well as underfoot (Lina accidentally steps on several of the crunchy critters when entering a secret room upstairs), the tiny creatures are more than just a nuisance. With the benefit of hindsight, viewers can ascertain that the flies serve as a harbinger of the bad things to come, similar to what occurs in Ángel Gómez Hernández's *Don't Listen* (*Voces*, 2020), a Spanish horror film in which a fly-infested house, desperately in need of renovation, is abuzz not only with the constant noise of the bugs but also with ghostly voices coming through phone lines and walkie-talkies—all of which portend the tragic death of a young boy (early in the narrative), his grieving mother (a bit later), and his father (near the end, after he has found a hidden basement entrance through a hole in the wall where the flies had been buzzing). In these examples, flies—or, in the case of *Amityville Dollhouse*, wasps—point toward future events, whetting the spectator's appetite for unappetizing images. In a majority of films, however, flies gesture toward past events, serving as lingering indexical referents of a bad death or a smelly corpse, even when they too are dead.

For instance, around the midpoint of Pete Walker's proto-slasher film *The Comeback* (1978), Nick Cooper (Jack Jones), the main character, spots a smattering of dead flies outside the door of the London flat belonging to his ex-wife, Gail (Holly Palance). Sniffing the air and casting a suspicious look at the insects, he cautiously opens the door and says, "dead cats," fully expecting domesticated animals to be sprawled on the floor inside. Instead, he sees a large rat nibbling away at Gail's remains, her half-eaten head a pulpy mess of missing facial features and her decomposing body the cause of the foul odor wafting through the apartment. As one does in these kinds of situations, Nick retches at this grisly crime scene, leaning forward on a banister as if the contents of his last meal were about to "come back." The title of this British film is apt, and not simply because the protagonist is a once-successful recording artist on a six-year hiatus who plans to jumpstart his stalled-out career with a forthcoming pop album. *The Comeback* makes sense as a title given the way that it harkens back to several elements in that original proto-slasher film from 1960, *Psycho*, and also because one of the first events depicted in its narrative—Gail's murder at the hands of a man wearing a hag's mask—returns with the sudden force of a gruesome "reveal," unforeseen save for the anticipatory shot of the dead flies (which are soon echoed by the image of maggots crawling around on Gail's barely visible face).[3] The insects thus function in *both* of the aforementioned ways, marking the presence of a previous death but preparing audiences and characters for the literal and figurative stench of what is to come. They and the film in which they are found furthermore anticipate the imagery in the *Amityville* series, which would continue to "come back" to the same themes and settings as the franchise's initial film, as well as to Walker's *The Comeback*, which was made one year prior to *The Amityville Horror* and which is eerily similar to Rosenberg's film despite their different settings and narrative outcomes. Notably, both motion pictures show morally compromised male protagonists, beset by supernatural visions that force them to question their sanity, using axes to break through brick walls and entering cobwebbed secret rooms in search of the truth.

Like humans, "flies die easily." That, according to Colin McGinn, is one reason why this humblest, most degraded of creatures unsettles us; its vulnerability and mortality seems to mirror our own (2012, 11). Like that of a fly, our lives are "short and strenuous, with sudden death always a heartbeat away. We are easily squashed, quickly choked" (12). Not only do they "remind us of certain disagreeable facts about ourselves," McGinn states, but flies also invade our personal spaces, taking up residence where they are not wanted and feeding on "things we find most disgusting," including "human garbage, rotting flesh, and feces" (10). Given these characteristics, which are presented from an admittedly anthropocentric perspective (treating the "lowliest" of all animals as nuisances and objects of disgust rather than as short-lived subjects with their own reasons for hovering around spaces *invaded by humans*), it is easy to see why flies and their squirming, wingless progeny (maggots) might feature so prominently in horror films, especially those engaging the themes of contamination, defilement, pollution, and putrescence. What might be surprising, however, is the frequency with which these zigzagging insects become momentary agents of narrative disorder, inciting significant changes in a plot's course of events that can have serious consequences for human characters. This happens, for instance, in *Don't Listen*, when one of the many flies that can be heard buzzing around Daniel (Rodolfo Sancho) and Sara's (Belén Fabra) new fixer-upper house darts into the ear of the child psychologist who has come to visit their son, Eric (Lucas Blas). As if the fly has taken possession of the woman, she crashes her vehicle into a tree after she drives away from the house. It is a deadly head-on collision that the boy, attuned to the buzzing of the flies, has apparently seen in advance (having drawn a picture of if).

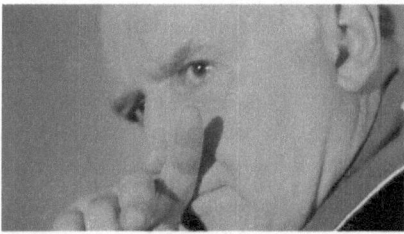

Figure 8.9. Preparing to bless the Lutzes' newly purchased house, Father Delaney (Rod Steiger) sniffs something awry and is covered with flies as soon as he steps into a second-floor room of the cursed structure in *The Amityville Horror* (1979).

As both an aural and visual metaphor for the otherwise unsniffable scents that permeate *The Amityville Horror* and other films, the swarm of buzzing flies is a synesthetic stand-in for something that cannot be directly represented in cinema (discounting, of course, "Smell-O-Vision," "Odorama," and other ballyhoo-style attempts to bring an olfactory experience to audiences). With the possible exception of crawling maggots, visible in several productions made around the time of *The Amityville Horror*'s theatrical release, such as Lucio Fulci's *City of the Living Dead* (*Paura nella città dei morti viventi*, 1980), Michael Wadleigh's *Wolfen* (1981), and Tobe Hooper's *Poltergeist*, nothing announces the arrival of malodorous forces quite so viscerally as houseflies. They, like the excremental visions and smells that flair up from time to time in *The Amityville Horror* and its many derivative offshoots, are "banal" in the sense of being commonly experienced outside of horrific fictions, in our everyday lives (unlike the sight and stench of dead, decomposing bodies, which relatively few people ever directly encounter). Beyond this particular franchise, countless other horror films, from Paul Solet's *Grace* (2009) to Anthony DiBlasi's *Dread* (2009) and Kiyoshi Kurosawa's *Creepy* (2016), link buzzing flies to disgusting aromas, as when a police investigator in the latter film covers his mouth and nose upon entering a cramped, wood-paneled shack where the blackened, rotting corpses of five cold-case victims have been hidden. Detective Nogami's (Masahiro Higashide) visceral response to the newly discovered bodies, which are wrapped inside sealed plastic bags, is registered in the sight and sound of those swarming insects, just as Father Delaney's swift departure from the Lutzes' house is prompted as much by the houseflies and their associated odors as by the otherworldly threat ("Get out!") spoken by some unseen spirit (a scene from the first film in the *Amityville* franchise, which I will return to momentarily) (figure 8.9).

In *Never Home Alone*, his tellingly titled study of the many tiny creatures with whom humans domestically cohabitate (from microbes to millipedes), Rob Dunn notes that houseflies are among our most ancient associates. And yet, for all their perennial familiarity, this species of arthropod has proven to be a "real problem" for people, "especially when sanitation is poor." As Dunn states, much more so than other insects (including cockroaches), houseflies (*Musca domestica*, of the suborder *Cyclorrhapha*) "vector pathogens, including many that cause diarrhea and are associated with more than five hundred thousand deaths a year" (2018, 171). Notably, it is from their own filthy feeding sites (including garbage cans and manure piles) that houseflies bring pathogenic organisms into structures designed for human activities (such as eating). Thus, the physical transmission of viral and bacterial diseases—including, as Gregory Dahlem notes, "typhoid fever, cholera, dysentery, and infantile diarrhea" (2009, 469)—hinges upon an unsavory association between consumption and defecation, something that would go largely unnoticed in popular culture were it not for "tasteless" horror films bringing these coprophagic insects to the forefront of our imagination. This is true not only of a handful of motion pictures, such as the critically panned made-for-TV movie *Island of the Dead* (2000), in which swarming flies are the actual "monsters" bringing death and disease to human characters, but also of those films like *The Amityville Horror* in which they are merely semiotic stand-ins or indexical referents of another, invisible/offscreen threat, as smoke is to fire.

The motion picture that most decisively moved the humble fly from the background to the foreground of horror fans' popular imagination is, not surprisingly, David Cronenberg's *The Fly* (1986), a film that Colin McGinn discusses at length in his aforementioned study of the world's filthiest flying insects. Notably, Cronenberg's sci-fi-horror hybrid, loosely based on a 1957 short story by George Langelaan (more than the 1958 Vincent Price movie of the same title), is among the slimiest, squishiest films of all time, an effect that makeup artist Chris Walas and his team achieved through practical means (e.g., animatronic puppets, facial prosthetics, foam latex suits) and which has not dampened the critical consensus around it as being one of the Canadian filmmaker's best, most edifying works. Featuring a physical metamorphosis that is at least as disturbing as that endured by the main character in *Septic Man* (only this time happening to a brilliant, introverted scientist [Jeff Goldblum's Seth Brundle] rather than a low-wage sewage worker), *The Fly* sits atop a gooey, gelatinous heap that includes other slimy films from the 1980s, such as *Scared to Death* (1981), *The Thing* (1982), *The Stuff* (1985), *TerrorVision* (1986), *Prince of Darkness* (1987), *The Blob* (1988), and *Society* (1989). That was an era when hideously grotesque bodies like that of Dr. Brundle, who slowly deteriorates into an insectoid monster after he steps into a teleportation pod inhabited by a common housefly and is taken over by the creature's DNA, rose to prominence alongside their more traditionally hypermasculine big-screen brethren (hardbody Hollywood stars like Arnold Schwarzenegger and Sylvester Stallone). It

Figure 8.10. Promotional material for the 1963 film *The Slime People*.

was a time, according to Susanne Wedlich, "when almost every film with a hint of spookiness was swimming in gunk . . . a tsunami of slime," including those such as Columbia Pictures' PG-rated *Ghostbusters* (1984) and *Ghostbusters II* (1989) that catered to adolescent audiences and family crowds (2021).

Drawing upon the work of Rebecca Bell-Metereau, one of the first media scholars to explore the relationship between slime, sexuality, and disease, Wedlich gestures toward the ubiquity of biological hydrogels in horror films from that socially volatile period, when "humanity's survival seemed under threat from radioactive contagions" (2004, 287–300). But, as she also acknowledges, ectoplasmic goo and other viscous fluids had been oozing into motion pictures long before the Reagan era (when twenty-four-hour cable news programs made political mud-slinging a spectator sport). One need only to consider Cold War–era sci-fi-horror hybrids like the original version of *The Blob* (1958) and actor-turned-director Robert Hutton's "laughably bad" *The Slime People* (1963), which were released as the top or bottom half of drive-in double bills.[4] Notably, the theatrical release of the latter film, which concerns a race of subterranean reptile men who are driven from their homes by underground atomic tests, was promoted through movie posters that not only encouraged audiences to put their ears up to the mouth of one of the titular monsters, but also announced that those monsters have come "up from the bowels of the earth" (figure 8.10). That, of course, is a phrase that would continue to make its way into subsequent horror films as surely as would the aforementioned gunk that Wedlich discusses (as highlighted in *The Amityville Horror*, which shows green slime seeping through keyholes and dripping down the walls of George and Kathy's newly purchased home).

As I have tried to show in this and previous chapters, horror films are as contradictory and slippery as the slime that oozes through so many of the most grotesque examples of the genre, making any attempt to get a handle on them more than a little difficult. That viscous substance, glistening under the fluorescent lights of a movie set and sickeningly slick yet paradoxically sticky to the touch for anyone who literally handles the props, costumes, makeup, and practical special effects during a horror film's production, thus functions metonymically, reminding us of the elusiveness of a text's meanings even as those meanings rise to the "surface" or require little-to-no "digging" on the spectator's part. According to bio-philosopher Ben Woodward, slime forms the material center of human existence, through which it both coheres and breaks apart. It is the sludgy, smudgy afterbirth of one of Earth's most advanced or evolved but excessively destructive species (2012). At once generative and degenerative, the organic, semi-solid stuff that lends Woodward's book *Slime Dynamics* its title is abject in the sense of being a marker of gross bodily decay or decomposition while simultaneously presenting us with the protoplasmic proof of our animal essence and primitive will to create (traceable to the earliest petroglyphs and cave paintings of the Paleolithic era, when animal fat, blood, and saliva were among the first gloopy ingredients in art). Just as *homo sapiens* is a slimy biological residue of this planet, so too do the things that we produce—including "lurid cultural artifacts" such as monster movies, slasher films, and trashy exploitation flicks—ooze with the "dark vitalism" of our own creative-destructive tendencies. Creating horror films is a slimy affair in more ways than one: a messy tangle of effects-work entailing the shedding of blood, sweat, and tears on the part of many artists and craftspeople, but also a fungal outgrowth of that seemingly self-annihilating urge to *make* things about the ruinous *unmaking* of things (Woodward 2012, 67–68).

Notably, *Amityville: It's About Time*, though a franchise outlier with little direct connection to the plot of *The Amityville Horror*, ushers forth the kind of abject, slimy, stench-summoning imagery that would not be out of place in that original film. Besides shots of black goo spilling out from a bathtub faucet and befouling its unsuspecting occupant (who rubs the stuff on his face), a scene set in the basement of yet another California home puts a peculiar twist on earlier depictions of excremental evil. When a sixteen-year-old girl (the daughter of the film's protagonist) lures her boyfriend to the house with the promise of sexual congress, the horny teenager succumbs not only to temptation (stripping off his clothes in anticipation) but also to the demonic force that has infiltrated this new yet uncannily familiar environment after the introduction of a possessed clock—another remnant from the original Amityville residence. A viscous swirl of bubbling poo encircles the young man, rising up from the drain in the floor and eating away at his skin until his

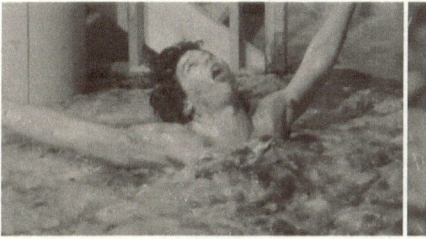 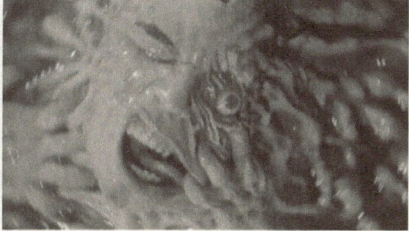

Figure 8.11. As highlighted in this scene, *Amityville: It's About Time* (1992) is the slimiest and grimiest of the many entries in the long-running "Amityville" franchise.

misshapen body disappears, as if he were "flushed" into the sewer from whence it came (figure 8.11).[5]

Audiences might snicker or groan, not from fright but in derision or disdain at the sight of such silliness, which puts a too-literal spin on the old adage—articulated most famously by Philip Brophy—that the "pleasure of the text" (in the context of horror film spectatorship) is "getting the shit scared out of you" (1986, 5). But one of the genre's appeals is its sometimes-tasteless, uninhibited embrace of those most banal, base activities in everyday life—i.e., pissing and defecating—that are typically performed outside of other genres' representational systems. In the words of I. Q. Hunter, such abjection exists beyond "the social and cultural order" (2014: 498), and the excessiveness of the horror film's compensatory drive is most offensive or odious to those who wish to keep bodily functions inside the bathroom, locked behind closed doors and away from prying eyes, ears, and nostrils. Like *The Amityville Horror* before it, *Amityville: It's About Time* flings open those doors—to bathroom and basement alike—and gives audiences a peek (and smell) inside. The film's willingness to wallow in nauseating displays of human degradation is a sign of the horror genre's capacity to do the kind of cultural work that is often passed over by filmmakers and critics who deride or dismiss such productions as "rubbish." The sight, sound, and (imagined) scent of the teenaged boy's revolting descent into a sewer drain are certainly execrable, reasons why some viewers might turn their noses up when faced with the prospect of watching (and smelling) such "trashy" productions. One could argue, though, that few images in the entire franchise are as unsettling as this literalization of the "powers of horror" that Julia Kristeva fleshes out in her groundbreaking book of the same title.

HOLY SHIT: THE PLEASURES OF THE TEXT AND THE (HEALING) POWERS OF *AMITYVILLE*'S HORRORS

> At last we reached the church.
> —CHARLES BOONE, the soon-to-be-possessed protagonist in Stephen King's "Jerusalem's Lot" (1978)

> Church smells funny.
> —ELLIE, describing the unusual odor of her recently resurrected cat, in Stephen King's *Pet Sematary* (1983)

As Kristeva notes in *Powers of Horror: An Essay on Abjection*, epistemological borders and presumably stable identities are threatened by the body's extrication of itself, its leaving behind of wastes that point toward our own eventual falling "beyond the limit" (i.e., from the living to the dead). "If dung," the abject everyday anticipator of one's own death, "signifies the other side of the border," the French philosopher writes, "the place where I am not and which permits me to be, the corpse, the most sickening of wastes, is a border that has encroached upon everything" (1982, 3–4). Corpses pile up in this multi-film Amitytext, but so too do the turd-like droppings of matter that cannot be so easily consigned to the grave. It might be flushed away, like the putrefying remains of the teenaged boy in *Amityville: It's About Time*, but the shit at the heart of this film series keeps coming back, floating to the signifying surface as a semantic element both within and beyond the symbolic order. This repeated visual element, this pollutive substitution for the Real that resides just below that surface, is an apt approximation of the way in which the DeFeo murders, at once unimaginable yet wholly within the realm of representation, resurface with each telling of the Amityville story.

Not surprisingly, the first time Ronald's homicidal act occurs in this franchise is during the first scene of the first film. Ricocheting off the similar sound of thunderclaps, rifle fire rings out on the tail end of the opening credits. Images of the now-iconic Dutch Colonial exterior, cloaked in early morning darkness but lit by the occasional burst of lightning, are intercut with close-up interior shots of the gun going off and lifeless bodies lying atop blood-spattered bedsheets. A slow dissolve indicating a passage of time shows law enforcement vehicles parked outside the house and stretchers carrying the recently deceased individuals into a waiting ambulance. Superimposed atop that establishing shot are the "facts" of what just took place, printed as onscreen text. The words inform the audience that on November 13, 1974, in Amityville, Long Island, "a mother, father, and four of their children [were] murdered," and that "no apparent motive" for the killer's actions can be discerned. Retrospectively viewed, the opening scene of *The Amityville Horror* thus offers an immediate "answer" or point of origin for what is about to occur as well as an endlessly replenished enigma for the series as a whole. That is, it supplies an abbreviated backstory for the unfolding narrative while forcing any spectator lacking context (and perhaps baffled by what has just transpired) to question why someone might have committed such a crime in the first place. Gradually, once the next occupants—the Lutz family—move in, the mystery surrounding those execution-style murders will be explained, but by way of a far-fetched, supernatural scenario that compounds the problem of finding a more reasonable "reason" for the DeFeos' deaths.

Following that introductory passage, the story of George and Kathy Lutz's terrifying brush with the unexplained begins. The cash-strapped newlyweds are given a tour of the house by a nervously smiling real estate agent, who accurately tells them that "there's nothing like it on the market." Priced at $80,000, but valued at $120,000, this "fixer-upper" is too good to pass up, even though Kathy literally bristles at the idea of living in a place once inhabited by a killer. "Houses don't have memories," George calmly says in an effort both to comfort his wife and to convince her that this is the perfect place to raise her three kids (all from a previous marriage). His comment, sure to be refuted in subsequent scenes involving paranormal encounters with the past, is further undermined by the fact that, throughout their inspection of the property, several flashbacks suddenly interrupt the diegesis, each one a violent shock-cut to the previous year's grisly murder scene. As the agent guides the prospective buyers into each room, discombobulating shots of the rifle-wielding Ronald DeFeo stop them in their tracks, halting the flow of narrative and suggesting a kind of regurgitative return to the Real. Glimpsed in quick fragments and accompanied by the now-familiar sound of gunfire, bursts of images flicker into the viewer's perception like a subconscious memory of something too traumatic to keep at bay, and anticipate the way in which the tragic history of the house will continue to rematerialize over the course of this film series' forty-two year run (as of 2021), even after the franchise has moved on to different characters and locales.

Not long after the Lutzes move into the house, a local priest, Father Delaney, arrives to offer his blessing. Finding the place empty, the priest proceeds to take his own tour of the structure, stopping at the window of the second-floor guest room to view the happy family outside. His benevolent smile shifts to a look of concern once he spots a cluster of flies on the window, which is stuck shut. Taking out his Bible, Delaney is startled by the sound of the door suddenly closing and the warm air blanketing the room. Perspiration beading on his forehead, he turns once more toward the window to see that a swarm of buzzing houseflies has now descended on the pane. Then, putting his finger to his nose, he hunches over in revulsion, clearly nauseated by the unidentified stench that has attracted the insects. Leaving no confusion as to

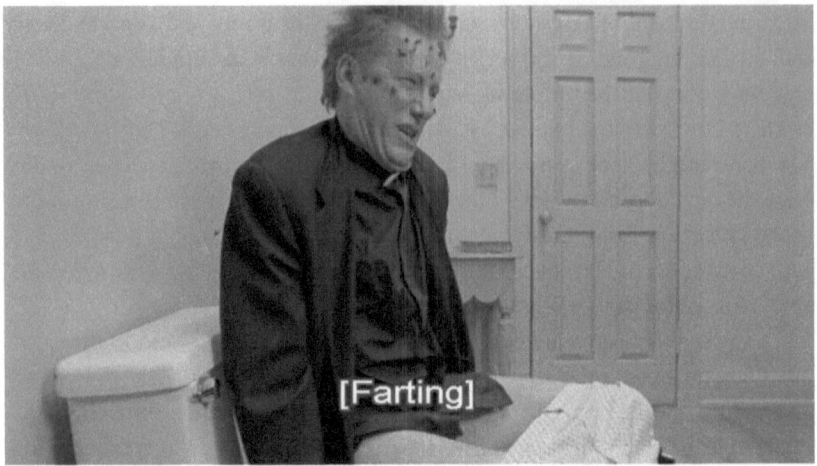

Figure 8.12. A parodic throwback to Rod Steiger's Father Delaney, James Woods's character in the spoof *Scary Movie 2* (2001), Father McFeely, produces a stench of his own while seated on a toilet bowl.

the deadly threat posed by the house, the door swings open and a demonic voice from somewhere inside the room orders the priest, who is covered in flies himself, to "get out."

Audiences who have accidentally stumbled onto (or willingly watched) Keenen Ivory Wayans's 2001 horror spoof *Scary Movie 2* might recognize this early scene in *The Amityville Horror* as a source of inspiration for the former film's most disgusting laugh-getter, a literal example of toilet humor that borrows not only from Stuart Rosenberg's 1979 production but also from William Friedkin's 1973 classic *The Exorcist*. Like that devil-possession film, *Scary Movie 2* hinges on a priest's attempt to rid a young girl, Megan Voorhees (Natasha Lyonne), of the evil inside her, first manifesting during a formal dinner party in which the teenager urinates on the floor for all of her mother's invited guests to see. Once Father McFeely (James Woods) arrives at the Voorhees residence, and before Megan's projectile vomiting assumes epic proportions, we see him turning his attention to the small legion of flies that have landed on a windowpane inside the bathroom. In a manner that recalls Father Delaney's response to the same insects in *The Amityville Horror*, McFeely coughs uncontrollably to the point of nearly choking. "Please, Lord, help me to release this demon," he beseeches, grimacing upwards as he unleashes a loud fart while seated on the toilet bowl (figure 8.12). The sickening release of his bowels, aurally accentuated for maximum comic effect, retroactively turns the buzzing of the bathroom flies into a harbinger of bad smells throughout the rest of the film. Although played for belly laughs, but just as likely to induce groans of revulsion (and perhaps recognition), this moment reveals much about horror and comedy as complementary body genres that test the limits of representation and cross thresholds that most forms of cinematic discourse shy away from.

If "grossly off-putting" to some audiences, this and other motion pictures noted for their aesthetic badness might also be understood "as a kind of security (or comfort) blanket," in the words of I. Q. Hunter, insofar as they are "transitional objects that enable rehearsal of emotional and physical responses to the abject" (2014, 498). Although he applies this logic to the study of properly "cult" phenomena ranging from classic low-budget exploitation fare like Herschell Gordon Lewis's *Blood Feast* (1963) to straight-to-DVD underground videos like *Slaughtered Vomit Dolls* (2006) and social media-driven sensations like *Birdemic: Shock and Terror* (2010), which converts horror into "accidental comedy," Hunter's words speak more broadly to the "phenomenology of bad film," which can include commercial productions aimed at large audiences and intentional (but potentially "failed") comedies like *Scary Movie 2*. Even though it does not require a "camp sensibility attuned to the alluring counter-merits of trash cinema," as do Harold P. Warren's technically incompetent, woefully inept *Manos: The Hands of Fate* (1966) and Joel M. Reed's "morally reprehensible" *Bloodsucking Freaks* (1976) do (484), *Scary Movie 2* arouses strong emotions in its viewers, including critics who have labeled it a "repulsive, vulgar, disgusting, over-the-top horror spoof," an "insufferable hodgepodge of phallic and fecal humor," and a "pocket of infection on the skin of the American body cultural." "The whole thing reeks of sequelitis, with an emphasis on the rude and crude," says Marjorie Baumgarten of the *Austin Chronicle*, throwing slightly less shade than her fellow critics at other online and print magazines, who called the film, variously, a "humanity-robbing experience" (Dave Kehr), "like Chinese water torture" (Stephanie Zacharek), and—in keeping with the slime theme of previous productions—a "hobgob blob" (Mark Ramsay).

With its 14 percent Tomatometer rating on Rotten Tomatoes reflecting critics' distaste for its "disgusting bathroom humor" and "gallons of bodily fluids," *Scary Movie 2* seems not unlike the kind of films Mikita Brottman had in mind when describing cinematic "offensiveness": those that arouse strong sensations "in the lower body—nausea, weakness, faintness, and a loosening of bowel and bladder control—normally by way of graphic scenes featuring the by-products of bodily detritus: vomit, excrement, viscera, brain tissue, and so on" (Brottman, 2005, 9; quoted in Hunter 2014). "Excremental" in more ways than one, *Scary Movie 2*, like the relatively "serious-minded" (but no less risible) first entry in the *Amityville* franchise, sits between "extreme" and "mainstream" poles, reveling in excessive moments of anal grotesquerie that might appeal to cult film fanatics while luring audiences of commercial cinema into a potentially nauseating world of corporeal abjection. These films' in-betweenness, in fact, contributes to their sliminess, if we perceive the latter as a liminal quality that is neither completely solid nor completely liquid.

Heightening their offensiveness is the presence of priests—Father Delaney in the more straight-faced supernatural film, and Father McFeely in the Wayans Brothers' comedy-horror film—whose physical predicaments hint at some of the more odious personal failings and public scandals that have rocked the foundations of the Catholic Church in recent years (including reports of widespread sexual abuse that top officials tried to hush). Certainly, far worse, more humiliating (and more humorous) things have happened to clergymen in horror films over the past few four decades than what is depicted in *Scary Movie 2*, and one need only to watch *Rawhead Rex* (1986) to catch a glimpse at a truly transgressive moment in the recent history of the genre. In this big-screen adaptation of a short story by Clive Barker, a verger at a small church in an Irish village becomes so besotted by an ancient, nine-foot-tall demon that, at the height of his insanity, he bends down at the feet of the creature and allows it to "baptize" him in the unholiest way possible: by having the monster pee on him in a cemetery next to the rectory. Considerably more "offensive" than any scene in *Holy Motors* (the ostensibly "bat-shit crazy" art film discussed at the beginning of this chapter), this fleeting moment in a poorly reviewed horror film reveals the extent to which the "lowliest" of genre productions, including those that are "aesthetically incompetent" or "morally suspect," can be, in I. Q. Hunter's words, both "genuinely disconcerting" and "culturally dislocating," so much so that they can leave audiences feeling "wonderfully alive" in their befuddlement (2014, 498). But the funniest parts of *Rawhead Rex* are those in which the verger in question, Declan O'Brien (Ronan Wilmot), exuberantly pulls faces and makes the underlying humor of this horror film explicit through broad smiles and crazed expressions that contagiously leap onto audiences' faces (at least, those who might delight in beholding such spectacles of performed eccentricity and bad taste).

Though he is not necessarily mugging for the camera or behaving like a clown, actor Wilmot, in the thankless role of a man of the cloth destined to be peed on by one of the cheesiest-looking demons in the history of the genre, brings to the surface the film's underlying gleefulness in breaking taboos and flouting the strictures of what a well-made motion picture is *supposed* to abide by. Similar to Dwight Frye's performance as the raving lunatic slave Renfield in Universal's *Dracula* (1931), the theatrically trained Shakespearean actor contributes much to *Rawhead Rex*'s flamboyancy, its exaggerated depictions of sacrilegious actions that are sure to elicit laughter among audiences not offended by such big-screen blasphemy. Indeed, his character O'Brien's own maniacal laughing and devilish grinning, prompted by comments that the church sits on "holy ground, *God's* ground," hints at the way badness bleeds

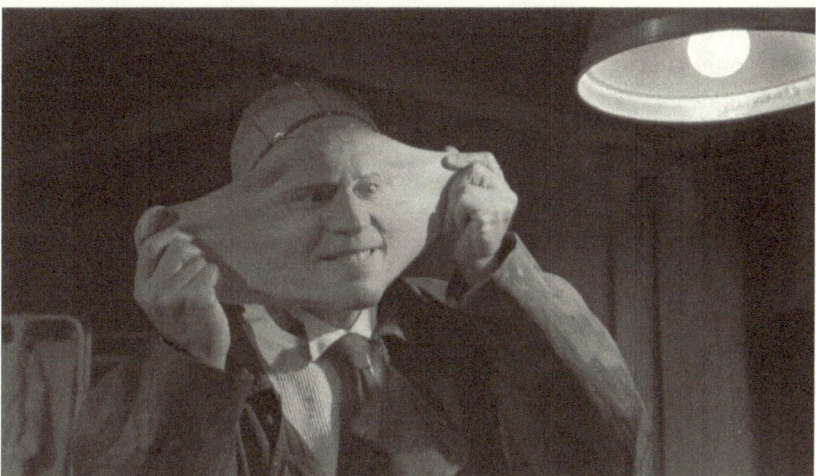

Figure 8.13. The killer's Silly Putty-like face in *Popcorn*, pulled into a broad toothy smile that is in keeping with this film's humorously terrifying action, hints at how the horror genre can "stretch" to accommodate textual incongruities.

into madness (and vice versa), with the latter term further suggesting the kind of circumvention of rules or rationality that J. Hoberman encourages in his own appreciation of bad (or "mad") films (1999, 150; Hunter 2014, 498). For Hoberman and other critics, an "anti-masterpiece" like this can "expand our definition of what a movie can be" (150), just as Wilmot's exaggerated facial reactions to the events transpiring around him help to push the boundaries of the horror film beyond the relatively limited sphere of negative emotions (e.g., dread, fright, revulsion, etc.) to encompass a broad range of feelings or (to modify the name of James Woods's flatulent, defecating cleric in *Scary Movie 2*) "feelies," including those that are associated with comedy (e.g., happiness, merriment, playfulness, etc.).

Significantly, during a key scene in the previously mentioned film *Popcorn*, the college-aged killer not only explains his modus operandi to his captive Maggie (whom he plans to kill in a literal showstopper inside the Dreamland movie theater), but also demonstrates his skills in the slimy, rubbery art of prosthetics by putting on one of his recently molded faces and stretching it like Silly Putty—pulling the left and right side of his head until it is three times wider than a "normal-looking" face (figure 8.13). At once disturbing and amusing, Toby's act of literally pulling a face—one that smiles toothily and with self-satisfaction in his own creation's ability to simultaneously horrify and fascinate his female victim (who is tied up and unable to escape, but who could close her eyes if she chose to)—neatly sums up this body genre's wide breadth of emotional valences and spectatorial solicitations. Like Toby's Silly Putty face, horror has been stretched well beyond what its first audiences imagined they would encounter onscreen over a century ago, though humor—which was an indelible part of the genre from its earliest stages—remains as central to horror's contradictory appeals as it has always been. The next chapter will bring this book to a close by ruminating on the seemingly contradictory "feels" of bodily fear, using an eclectic mix of comically infused horror films to illustrate just how funny and unpredictable this ostensibly scary and seemingly predictable genre is.

9

SPOOKY ENCOUNTERS OF THE HUMOROUSLY DISGUSTING KIND

Clutching Hands and Hopping Corpses, from Hollywood to Hong Kong

It felt like hands touching me!
—MADELEINE SHORT (Madge Bellamy) to her fiancé, Neil Parker (John Harron), after their horse-drawn carriage passes by evil voodoo master Murder Legendre (Bela Lugosi), in an early scene of *White Zombie* (1932)

As disgusting as it is to imagine smelling the horrible things referenced in the previous two chapters, including exposed organs, fungal growths, human wastes, and rotting corpses that attract flies (which "are themselves units of dirt, a measure of how mucky a place is," according to Colin McGinn) (2012, 10), *touching* that slick and squishy stuff—coming into direct physical contact with it—might be even more unappetizing to viewers. Thankfully for touch-averse audiences, no such literal entanglement is needed for it to be imagined by them, nor is it even possible, owing to the spectator's enfleshed separation from the text. No matter how immersed in a cinematic fiction one may be, including a film that intentionally or unintentionally foregrounds its own artifice as a work reliant on fake excrement, prop vomit, stage blood, and prosthetic makeup effects to depict moments of death, decay, disease, illness, and other pathological states, *actual immersion* in that liquid unpleasantness—that cold or warm bath of noxious secretions—is an impossibility to such a degree that it hardly requires further elaboration. Nevertheless, audiences can still be made to *feel* the surfaces of a diegetic world littered with touchable things that exist in the real world, including everyday objects such as axes, hammers, hooks, and knives, which take on a kind of vibrational life of their own in the hands of killers or victims displaying their own dismaying familiarity. Indeed, horror disturbs us partly because its textures are so terribly familiar, and no amount of integumentary protection can shield our skin from the memory of accidentally brushing up against something barbed, lumpy, mushy, scummy, viscid, or otherwise disgusting in real life.

As Jeffrey Lockwood notes in his discussion of the universal emotion that we call "disgust" (an English word etymologically tethered to the sense of taste, or gustation, and further related to smell as a means of chemical detection), humans are "keenly attuned to the tactile properties of substances that are likely to infect us—curdled, gooey, lukewarm, moist, mucky, oily, scabby, slimy, slithery, and squishy" (2013). Our bodies' biological defense systems are on constant guard against bacteria, fungi, viruses, parasites, and other pathogens that might bring illness or disease. It naturally follows, then, that horror fiction of the literary and cinematic varieties should be so thoroughly marinated in such organic matter, for the genre itself seems particularly well-suited to helping humans maintain their adaptive proficiencies vis-à-vis real and imagined threats to their survival. Taking aim at fears that are ancient and primal, horror thus prepares us for an existence that is fraught with peril and bound to end in physical rot and decay (in line with the lives and deaths of our ancestors), but which necessitates a continuous being-on-guard if we are to make it to that foregone conclusion at a ripe old age. Advocating for neuroscientific approaches to the genre, Mathias Clasen maintains that horror fiction is dependent on "deeply conserved defense mechanisms in the brain . . . that have their roots far back in vertebrate evolution" (2017, 4, 6), though I would add that those "danger-management circuits" extend beyond the amygdala and prefrontal cortex—indeed, beyond the central nervous system—into other areas of the body where evolved premonitions of the inevitable reside. When it comes to the diseases and illnesses that are spread via pathogens, skin is one of our first lines of biological defense. As the largest sensing organ (one that covers the whole of the human body, even the transparent cornea in the eye) (Hague 2014, 97), it acts as a waterproof barrier, shielding our internal organs from harmful outside agents. Ironically, so too do those slimy, sludgy, and watery external substances—bowel bacteria, mucus, saliva, stomach acid, tears, and urine flow—protect us from nastier stuff as part of that first line of defense, making our aversion to the previously mentioned textures somewhat ironic. Harkening back to an argument I made in the previous chapter, one substance in particular (slime) speaks to homo sapiens' many contradictions as a species attracted to yet repelled by dangerous materials and destructive acts.

As anyone who has children (or has ever been a child) knows, slimy, nontoxic toys and games have long been part of commercial kid culture in the United States and other countries around the world. Although there were rudimentary antecedents stretching back to the Depression era of the 1930s, rubbery silicone polymers like Silly Putty and Flubber (popularized in Walt Disney's live-action family comedy film *The Absent-Minded Professor* [1961]) were relatively cheap

Figure 9.1. Following a group of elderly friends as they confront a demonic figure named Mr. Big (Richard Brake), the recent Blumhouse production *Bingo Hell* (2021) is partly a tribute to the slime-filled Nickelodeon TV shows that writer-director Gigi Saul Guerrero grew up watching as a kid during the 1990s and early 2000s.

postwar playthings marketed to the middle-class and working-class parents of adolescents. Decades later, the US cable channel Nickelodeon partnered with Mattel and other companies to manufacture and release a line of products catering to kids' predilection for creating messes, including Green Slime Shampoo, Gak, Smell My Gak, Floam, Smud, Goooze, Smatter, Squeeez, Splish Splat!, and Zyrofoam. These and other relatively safe consumer items—most famously, Mattel's simply named Slime (a small plastic trashcan filled with Guar gum and PVA glue, and advertised to the public as "gooey, drippy, oozy, cold 'n clammy" fun for all ages, beginning in 1976)—attest to the American public's appetite for unappetizing things and suggest that people are groomed to consume one of the most iconographic features of cinematic horror from an early age. Interestingly, a major motivating force behind the making of Gigi Saul Guerrero's comedy-horror film *Bingo Hell* (2021) was the writer-director's desire to create something that her earlier adolescent self would have loved, one that would be "covered in green goo," as she says. As Guerrero stated in an interview following the film's online release on Amazon Prime (as part of the streaming platform's "Welcome to the Blumhouse" film series), "I was that weird child that wanted to be on the Nickelodeon show covered in slime"—a reference to the cable channel's longest-running game show *Double Dare*, which began airing in 1986 and which pitted teams of kids against one another in messy physical challenges and sent them shimmying across slimy obstacle courses (Ryan 2021). Hence Guerrero's decision to include in *Bingo Hell* a substance that her interviewer, Danielle Ryan, calls "disgusting," but which the director enjoyed working with (expressing delight in having to test out ten different slime consistencies provided by her film's prop master) (figure 9.1).

If the 1980s was a heyday of slick and slippery horror films in the United States (as argued in the previous chapter), on top of all the gooey kid-centric

Figure 9.2. Some of the gloopiest films ever made came from Hong Kong during the 1970s and 1980s, a "golden age" of goo, on top of the many "hopping corpses" that came to define locally produced horror films in the decades that followed.

television programs and consumer products aimed at parents' pocketbooks, that collective fascination in non-Newtonian fluids was not unique to the North American cultural context. A host of other national cinemas gave rise to similarly slimy works that are just as deserving of consideration, including a major film-producing region of the world that has heretofore gone unmentioned in this book but which played a vital role in revitalizing horror through the incorporation of cultural and generic hybridity. In fact, few film industries around the world were as soaked in slime at that time as that of Hong Kong, a former British colony where a slew of humorously infused horror movies were produced and/or distributed by the Shaw Brothers Studio, Golden Harvest, and other companies specializing in popular genres. Some of the slimiest films ever made, full of flesh-melting, maggot-squirming action, came from the likes of Kuei Chih-hung (director of *The Killer Snakes* [1974], *Hex* [1980], *Bewitched* [1981], *Corpse Mania* [1982], *Curse of Evil* [1982], and *The Boxer's Omen* [1983]), Ho Meng-hua (director of *Black Magic* [1975], *Black Magic 2* [1976], and *Oily Maniac* [1976]), and Ma Wu (director of *The Dead and the Deadly* [1982], *My Cousin, the Ghost* [1987], and *Exorcist Master* [1992]) (figure 9.2).

To paraphrase one film festival programmer, the lowbrow genre movies produced in Hong Kong from the late 1970s until the early 1990s offer a deliciously malicious and refreshingly seedy alternative to the current vogue for "snooty...highbrow, elevated horror" (e.g., David Robert Mitchell's *It Follows* [2015], Robert Eggers's *The Witch* [2015], Ari Aster's *Hereditary* [2018], John Krasinski's *A Quiet Place* [2018]). Made for a fraction of the cost of those recent Hollywood-backed releases, films such as Lo Wei's *The Bedevilled* (1975), Tsui Hark's *We're Going to Eat You* (1980), Hua Shan's *Bloody Parrot* (1981), and Chang Ren-chieh's *The Devil* (1981) "get down and dirty, squelching in the psychic muck of primal fear and revulsion" and—in keeping with the loosely translated English title of director Yeung Kuen's 1982 Shaw Brothers' production *Mo jie* (*Hell Has No Boundary*)—are virtually limitless or boundless in their ability to evoke a nightmarish "stew of sex and slime and all things sleazy and

Figure 9.3. One of the slimiest scenes in *The Devil* (1981) shows a witch cutting open a man's stomach and removing hundreds of nightcrawlers and snakes.

slippery" (figure 9.3).[1] Even the title-screen typefaces of some of these films, such as that of *The Bedevilled*, appear to drip down the screen, as if the characters of the Chinese alphabet and/or the letters of a title's English translation were soaked in the ichorous liquid and lavalike goop that courses through this gangly body of work.

Some of the genre productions from that period, such as Ho Meng-hua's *The Mighty Peking Man* (1977), Godfrey Ho's *Robo Vampire* (1988), and Lau Sze-yu's *Ghost Busting* (1989), are clearly indebted to US horror, science fiction, and fantasy films (in this case, *King Kong* [1976], *Robocop* [1987], and *Ghostbusters* [1984], respectively). Director Ronnie Yu's *The Trail* (1983), about a pair of opium smugglers masquerading as Taoist monks who lose a reanimated (and hopping) corpse in a sulfur swamp, begins by pilfering the Ennio Morricone–composed score from John Carpenter's *The Thing* (1982), which can be heard during its opening sequence (O'Brien 2003, 34). But even when they are directly or indirectly based on existing motion pictures (within the legal parameters of what an official remake of a copyrighted work is), the movies made by Kuei Chih-hung and his contemporaries are second-to-none and hardly derivative when it comes to expanding the boundaries of squishy screen content and transforming the eyes into an organ of touch.

Kuei's 1982 film *Curse of Evil*, for example, features a scene in which a small army of bloody, metal-toothed frogs slathered in black bile nibble at the entrails of their human victims (reminiscent of the way a woman is attacked by several tiny metameric creatures near the end of director Keith Li's slightly less slimy *Centipede Horror* [1982]). The fact that those frogs are obviously hand puppets does not detract from any negative feelings that might wash over a spectator's body (such as disgust, nausea, and revulsion). Instead, it contributes to the sense of tactility that settles upon the viewer, who applies his or her vision as he or she would fingers inside a glove, flexing and extending or contracting along the folds of the image as the fake monsters secrete themselves onto a woman's exposed flesh. Even less subtle is *Curse of Evil*'s depiction of rape, which occurs when a horned (and excessively horny), human-sized mutant-lizard covered in pink slime crawls out of a well and slithers atop a helpless woman, whose cries for help are answered too late, after she has expired under the weight of the phallic creature and its gelatinous demon semen, which, after so much applied pressure, appears like chunky Pepto Bismol (a viscous substance that the camera lingers on, as if challenging the audience to not turn away, to remain haptically stuck in the folds of those sticky fibers). Slightly less disturbing Hong Kong horror films will take center stage throughout much of this chapter, in part due to the frequency with which hands, fingers, and fists figure in humorously horrific narratives filled with martial arts and the spectacle of "hopping corpses." Before going any further, though, a few words about the perception of touch are in order.

HAPTICS AND THE HANDS OF HORROR

> No, don't touch it! It's dangerous. It *opens doors*.
> —the skinless sadomasochist FRANK COTTON (Oliver Smith) to his sister-in-law and lover Julia Cotton (Clare Higgins), when she reaches out to touch a mystical puzzle box, in *Hellraiser* (1987)

In his multisensory study of comic books and graphic novels, Ian Hague emphasizes how foundational somatosensation is to all of our senses, connecting us not only to a world that we perceive at a distance (through sight and hearing) but also to "the spaces we inhabit" more intimately, breathing in their odorants, tasting their flavors, and touching their surfaces so that we might have an understanding of our own physical limits relative to the those of other bodies and objects (2014, 97). That latter idea has a bearing on how we might conceive of genres since, as categories of things, they are partially defined by lines of separation. Genres mark the boundaries of distinct types of cultural production as surely as a person might conceive of her, his, or their own subjecthood by tracing the epidermal surface of the body. For all this separation, however, the materiality of media like comic books and graphic novels (and cinema, I hasten to add) can prompt a sense of "shared physical existence," according to Laura U. Marks (quoted in Hague 2014, 105). Besides Marks, several scholars, including Jennifer M. Barker, Giuliana Bruno, Miriam Ross, and Beth Carroll, have developed tactilo-kinesthetic and haptic-based approaches to the study of the motion-picture medium (and to particular case studies across genres). Nevertheless, work remains to be done in bringing such theorizations into the skin-crawling arena of cinematic horror. By stressing the importance of touch as an imaginary yet physically real interface between spectator and screen, and by foregrounding a few scenes in classic and contemporary films in which characters scream and laugh in quick succession (both in this chapter and the brief coda that will bring this book to a close), I hope to contribute to a better understanding of comedy-horror's complementary appeals and contradictory "feels."

As the aforementioned scholars have pointed out, touch is part of a larger somatosensory system or neural network that links body and brain and makes it possible for people to gain an inner sense—a cognitive understanding-of their external environment, relative to the pressure, surface, and temperature of the objects with which they come into physical contact. As a subset of the sensory nervous system, the somatosensory system is affected by auditory, gustatory, olfactory, and visual stimuli, though we tend to think of touch as a bodily phenomenon dependent primarily, if not entirely, on the *skin*; or, rather, on the skin's mechanosensitive and thermosensitive responsiveness to external stimuli. In other words, touch is a physically "felt" sensation that begins at the molecular level, starting with an electrical signal impulse and biological relay system reliant upon the skin's nerve cells. The endings of those nerve cells contain receptor molecules, or "ion channels," which respond to environmental information related to the force exerted by stimulants as well as their textures and their hotness or coldness relative to the temperature of the perceiver's body. However, as Jennifer Barker reminds us, *mentally grasping* (or wrapping our minds around) the tactility of screen signifiers entails first acknowledging the linked perceptions of kinesthesis (or the awareness of continuous movement) and proprioception (or the awareness of bodily position), both of which are mediated by mechanosensory neurons located in the joints, muscles, and tendons, though she adopts a surface-to-depth model of phenomenological analysis that takes her readers well below the epidermis to the "murky recesses of the body" (i.e., viscera) (2009, 2–4). The actual musculature involved in *physically grasping* an object—taking hold of it in one's hand, fingering its surface, and possibly gripping it tightly inside a clenched fist—is key to how we gain mental awareness of said object's *objecthood* and our own sensual subjecthood, its *thingness* as a touchable substance whose materiality is temporarily coterminous with our own. With that in mind, before returning to the sensory suggestiveness of horror films, or what Jack Halberstam has referred to as "skin shows" (owing to their tendency to render in purely epidermal terms—as surface monstrosities—the perennial themes of inside vs. outside and self vs. other) (1995), I want to dwell momentarily on the hand as an especially prominent anatomical feature of the genre.

Because touch involves several different sensory pathways, including those that relay information about temperature changes in the environment and painful or injurious encounters with rough, sharp, or slimy objects to different areas of the brain (to reference three of the most prevalent textures in horror), no one sensing organ or single part of the body can be expected to hold the secret as to what makes cinema so *affectively effective* in delivering tactile, kinesthetic, and visceral experiences to audiences. Nevertheless, the hand fulfills multiple functions in film, and fingers are one of the most sensitive parts of the body (second only to a person's lips). This makes it both mechanically and sensorially significant as an expressing and perceiving medium in its own right. Moreover, it deserves special consideration in this book given its prominence as a corporeal metaphor for the kind of unthinking or irrational violence that flares up so frequently in horror films, including comically suffused ones like *Evil Dead II* (1987) and *Idle Hands* (1999) that show characters locked in comically absurd battles *against their own hands* once those prehensile appendages become "possessed." Not unrelated to this is the fact that the hand plays a vital part in reversing subject-object relations, giving rise to a reciprocal interplay between subjective intimacies that makes empathy—the sharing of another person's feelings—conceivable if not always achievable through film. This is something that Barker alludes to in her discussion of the handshake as a gesture whereby two bodies "mimic one another's muscular behavior" and display "mutual recognition" of those similarities that might otherwise be lost to sight or other, non-physically intimate senses alone.

After exploring some of the ways that hands have figured in literary and cinematic texts, including those that benefit from a *textural* as opposed to strictly textual mode of analysis, I will direct the reader's attention to several important horror films produced in Hong Kong. My reason for focusing on that region of the world is due in part to the narrative and visual emphasis that is placed on hands, fingers, and fists, which appear conspicuously in humorously horrific narratives. Even prior to the theatrical releases of the case studies that I have selected to explore in the following pages, American audiences were being introduced to Hong Kong cinema as part of the "kung-fu craze" that was sweeping throughout the world in the 1970s. In an essay concerning that cultural phenomenon, film scholar David Desser pinpoints an unprecedented moment in motion-picture history when three foreign releases topped the US box-office charts (2000, 19–43). Those three films—*Fists of Fury* (aka, *The Big Boss*, 1971), *Deep Thrust: The Hand of Death* (aka, *Lady Whirlwind*, 1972), and *Five Fingers of Death* (aka, *King Boxer*, 1972)—ranked first, second, and third among all North American theatrical releases during the week of May 16, 1973. That initial success paved the way for what Desser refers to as the "high-point" of martial-arts cinema's commercial dominance the following month (23). Indeed, during the week of June 20, 1973, the above trio of releases was joined by several other Hong Kong productions, including *Duel of the Iron Fist* (1971), *Kung Fu: The Invisible Fist* (1972), and *Thunderbolt Fist* (1972), which not only contributed to stateside audiences' growing interest in Chinese martial arts but also similarly foregrounded—through their English-language titles—the centrality of hand-to-hand combat in the iconographic constitution of the genre. Subsequent productions such as the Shaw Brothers' *Shaolin Hand Lock* (1978) further solidified the cultural imaginary of kung-fu cinema, which has since been codified as a physically balletic and graceful, if also violently bloody and brutal, genre defined in part by the persistent presence of deadly thrusting hands.

Of course, hands are also central to another type of cultural production, one that, within China, has often incorporated kung-fu action and martial arts iconography. Although the genre can be traced back to the earliest years of Cantonese- and Mandarin-language sound film production (1930s), Hong Kong's horror cinema began to gain international prominence in the 1970s and 1980s, thanks to the circulation of works that were at least partially inspired by *jiangshi* fiction—literary texts featuring sundry forms of reanimated (or "hopping") corpses and (un)healthy doses of scatological humor. With examples ranging from Yiu Hua Hsi-men's *Demon Strike* (1979) and Sammo Hung's *Spooky Encounters* (1980) to Hwa I Hung's *Kung Fu Zombie* (1982) and Sun Chung's *Human Lanterns* (1982), horror films from that period played upon local and global audiences' familiarity with genre conventions, including the tendency to showcase human and nonhuman hands as both embodied and disembodied manifestations of physical danger or psychological dread. Although much has already been written about the prevalence of "clutching hands" in US and European motion pictures, particularly with regard to the converging strains of Gothic thrillers and monster movies that followed the release of Paul Leni's Universal Pictures production *The Cat and the Canary* (1927) (Koszarski 1994, 186), little has been made of the equally prominent place such imagery occupies in Hong Kong cinema. This chapter attempts to fill that gap by assessing a broad range of motion pictures that showcase hands in thematically complex and symptomatically relevant ways, be they the severed anatomical remnants of long-departed souls sprung back to life in *Witch from Nepal* (1986) or the skeletal appendages that comically grab the protagonist's crotch in the aforementioned *Spooky Encounters*.

That latter film, a spectacularly choreographed classic of the genre starring Sammo Hung as the tellingly named "Bold" Cheung, will serve as a key case study in the final third of this chapter—not only because it includes a humorous scene involving a possessed hand (anticipating a similar moment in Sam Raimi's low-budget American production *Evil Dead II*) but also for its demonstration of the mind-body division that structures *all* horror films (regardless of their national origins). "Bold" indeed boldly goes into an abandoned house where he encounters one frightful yet funny sight after another (including a terrorizing vampire), yet it is his own grasping hand (which he no longer controls thanks to black magic) that proves to be his worst nemesis. In attempting to get a handle on that hand (literally and figuratively), he and we strive to pin down the powerful forces that lay dormant within the genre, including its tendency to dredge up and display moments of excessive, otherworldly violence for which there is seemingly no rational explanation. The ethical dimensions of the genre are thus crystalized in that divide between the *hand* as a means of enacting such violence and the *mind* that might try to make sense of it. We should therefore consider the two distinct notions of the word "grasping" that underscore classic and contemporary horror films, such as *Spooky Encounters* and more recent productions like *Forest of Death* (2007) and *The Child's Eye* (2010), which demonstrate how physical and mental operations—the corporeal *clutching* as well as the cognitive *understanding* specific to the genre—can be bridged, if only momentarily, through hand imagery.

HANDS OFF:
A FAREWELL TO ARMS AND A FIGHT TO THE DEATH

> I didn't see anyone. Just a hand.
> —RAINIE, a traumatized young woman recounting the most terrifying part of her latest dream to her friends, in the 2002 Hong Kong horror film *The Child's Eye*

Prior to the advent of motion pictures as a medium of technological wonder, visual spectacle, and narrative storytelling at the turn of the twentieth century, Western literary texts in the Gothic tradition of the 1800s had foregrounded hand imagery as operative means of exploring the divide between sanity and madness, the conscious and unconscious minds. Such themes, according to Barry Langford, are also central to the horror film, which distinguishes itself from other genres partly by demonstrating how the "transgression of limits" is made experientially palpable or "graspable" (at the cognitive and corporeal levels) through images of bodily fragmentation and destruction (2005, 158). Cinema, it has been argued, has at least one advantage over literature: namely, the visual register that forms its ontological base and which, in the words of Barbara Antonucci, "gives thickness to words" (2007, 166). Covering a "wider range of direct sensory experience" than other types of cultural production, film literalizes or "fleshes out" what would otherwise be metaphorical ideas on the printed page, lending those concepts an "affective charge" (Langford 2005, 158; Costanzo 2004, 4–5). Still, a brief consideration of literary horror's fixation on hands will be useful as a preamble to the discussion of Hong Kong cinema that follows, for it situates the latter in a cross-cultural, cross-media lineage of international publications and productions that are similarly drawn to the body as a site of rational and irrational fears.

An exemplary English-language text in this light is Sheridan Le Fanu's "Narrative of the Ghost of a Hand," a much-anthologized short story that the Irish writer originally interpolated as an embedded tale within his 1863 mystery novel *The House by the Churchyard*. As denoted by its title, phalangeal fears are the root of this supernatural story, which anticipated the same author's more famous "sensation novel" *Wylder's Hand* (1864) by one year. "Narrative of the Ghost of a Hand" concerns a husband and wife, the wealthy Prosser family, who grow increasingly distressed by the sight and sound of a seemingly dismembered hand intruding upon their otherwise peaceful life in Dublin. The doors and windows of the couple's cottage do little to shield their insulated existence from this supernatural, unknowable threat, and as thresholds to the outside world these architectural features suggest a movie screen. Tellingly, the hand's first manifestation occurs one August evening when Mrs. Prosser, sitting alone in her parlor, catches sight of the weirdly moving object outside her window, which looks out onto the estate's beautiful orchard. Placed upon the stone windowsill, the "handsomely formed" hand, which is described as being "white and plump" with clenched knuckles, suddenly withdraws at the sound of the woman's loud scream (Le Fanu 1964, 402). Her "ejaculation of terror" in this scene hints at the correlation between sexual fulfilment and fear of the unknown—two recurring themes in horror film, which treats the screen as both a fleshy skin to be penetrated and as a "window onto the world" that grants temporary access to its many mysteries or "secrets." Like those perennial motifs, the severed hand does not depart for good in this Victorian-era story, but *keeps coming back* over several pages, inserting its ghostly yet physical presence into the lives of the cleaning and cooking staff in addition to the Prossers' bedridden son, a toddler whose "strange sickness" is attributed to it (406).

Lacking a properly conclusive conclusion, the tale culminates ambiguously with the narrator musing that "the person to whom that hand belonged never once appeared, nor was it a hand separated from a body, but only a hand so manifested and introduced that its owner was always, by some crafty accident, hidden from view" (407). Thus, the titular thing that cannot be caught or expelled from the house is paradoxically *corporeal* and *discarnate*, there but not there—the synecdochal stand-in for a larger threat that simply cannot be seen or "grasped" in its entirety. Metatextually, the hand, shorn from its ghostly owner's body, can be said to represent the story itself. That is, in being separately anthologized, this "dismembered" tale has been removed from its original container (the aforementioned novel *The House by the Churchyard*) and now exerts autonomy as a recontextualized narrative, as part of a larger whole that has been granted its *own* wholeness.

Le Fanu's "Narrative of the Ghost of a Hand" is certainly not the only example of Gothic literature to locate social anxieties and psychological traumas at the site of a body part that is unique—and uniquely contradictory—in its power to either create something of value or rob a person of life (through choking/strangulation or the wielding of a weapon), sometimes seemingly on its own accord. For example, several anonymously written detective stories published in its wake, including "The Mystery of the Bloody Hand" (1865), "The Maimed Hand" (1875), and "The Black Dogs and the Thumbless Hand" (1896), hinge on a shared narrative premise: that of a criminal or victim being identified by his or her wounded hand, which represents the violence committed by or inflicted upon a person who is "reduced" to that titular body part (Briefel 2015, 14). As explained by Aviva Briefel, the culprit in many of these and other stories is typically "recognized through a manual injury acquired while committing the crime." In other cases, "a dead victim's detached hand offers proof of the sort of violence done to its owner" (14). Moreover, Briefel argues that the otherworldly "racialized hands" of Egyptian mummies in several fin-de-siècle fantastical fictions (e.g., Edgar Allan Poe's "Some Words with a Mummy" [1845], Sir Arthur Conan Doyle's "Lot No. 249" [1892], etc.) occupy "a tenuous position between body parts and material artifacts." She states, "While they are remnants of the dead and evoke the productive hands of long-deceased artists, they also 'survive' as concrete remains from the past, material evidence of enduring manual productions" (24). As a detached part of the missing whole (i.e., the embalmed/mummified figure, which is both "a person and a thing"), the synecdochal hand in this context presents the reader with an "uncanny duality" (80). Much like M. C. Escher's iconic lithograph *Drawing Hands* (1948), which "breaks down the distinction between creator and created" by showing each feeding into the other, the mummy's hand brings together human labor and the inhuman products of that labor. Paradoxes mount as one recognizes that the Victorian-era mummy's hand is both a gruesome signifier of irreducible Otherness—something to be avoided at all costs—and a talismanic fetish object to be treasured by collector-consumers of the "mysterious" Orient.

Other works of nineteenth-century literature likewise tapped into the allegorical and sexual suggestiveness of hands, most notably Robert Louis Stevenson's 1886 novella *Strange Case of Dr. Jekyll and Mr. Hyde*. This classic tale of man's inherent dualities (civilization vs. barbarism, rational restraint vs. irrational desire) makes the hand a conspicuous part of its diegetic universe. As discussed by Elaine Showalter, the fractured protagonist's hands "seem almost to have a life of their own," with the right hand being indicative of "patriarchal respectability and constraint" (which Jekyll seems to have inherited from his father) and the left hand being suggestive of immorality and rebelliousness (soon to manifest in Hyde's sinister dealings with unsuspecting victims) (2000, 197). When Jekyll discovers that his metamorphosis is beyond his control, "he wakes up to find that his own hand, the hand of his father, the 'large, firm, white and comely' hand of the successful professional, has turned into the 'lean, corded, knuckly' and hairy hand of Hyde." In the words of Showalter, "the implied phallic image here also suggests the difference between the properly socialized sexual desires of the dominant society and the twisted, sadistic, and animal desires of the other side" (197). And yet, Slavoj Žižek reminds us, the hand, even when clenched into a fist, is "the organ par excellence not of spontaneous pleasure but of instrumental activity, of work and exploration" (1997, 16).

Tellingly, the first shot of Rouben Mamoulian's big-screen adaptation *Dr. Jekyll and Mr. Hyde*, produced by Paramount in 1931 and released the following year, is a POV from the title character's (Fredric March) position as he sits at a pipe organ inside his posh London residence, his arms outstretched before the instrument. His fingers explore the keys of the three-tiered organ in a way that anticipates his later interaction with bar singer Ivy Pearson (Miriam Hopkins), whose leg garter he impishly caresses before she halts the movement of his roving hand. As "organs" atop the organ, the English doctor's hands are initially presented to the audience as *producers* of (musical) pleasure, but they are eventually revealed to be *partakers* of (libidinal) pleasure. Later, once his smooth skin gives way to hirsute knuckles, the ape-like Hyde becomes, in the words of Monica Germanà, the "savage other"—a creature whose "protruding teeth, unkempt eyebrows, and [large] nose" lend credence to Barry Keith Grant's notion that "the experience of horror in the cinema is almost always grounded in the visual representation of bodily difference" (2015, 6). Indeed, the "dread of difference" (to borrow the title of Grant's 1996 book) that permeates the genre is exacerbated by the fact that, in many films, the monstrous Other is often only an arm's length away, literally "armed" with elongated hands that, Hyde-like, grasp at us (or, rather, our onscreen surrogates) just as *we* figuratively try to grasp at—to make sense of—it. What makes the opening scene of *Dr. Jekyll and Mr. Hyde* so disconcerting is the presence of arms and hands untethered to a body, which in its momentary absence has been replaced by the cinematic apparatus—the camera that adopts the title character's point of view (seated before the musical instrument). Even at this early stage of the narrative, Jekyll's internal struggle is externally divulged in the way that he keeps each hand on a different level of the tiered organ keys, as if these two "instruments" of creation and destruction can play the musical tune in unison only by being physically separated, one from the other.

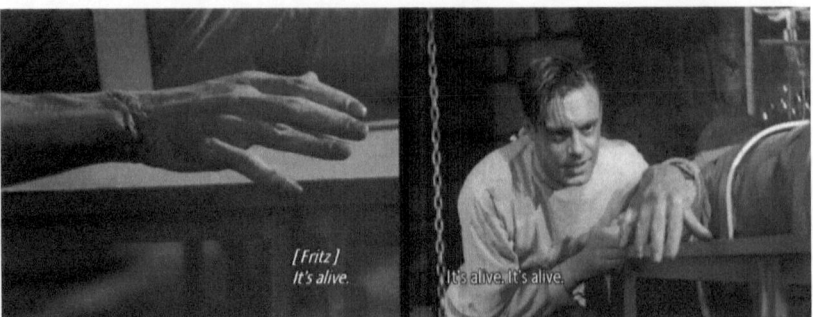

Figure 9.4. In this famous scene from James Whale's *Frankenstein* (1931), the title character witnesses the miracle of creation when the monster's hand (an anatomical part that will soon be linked to destruction) moves on its own.

Another studio-era horror film based on a nineteenth-century literary classic, director James Whale's Universal production *Frankenstein* (1931), foregrounds the monster's hands even earlier, during its opening credits. Following a brief curtain-parting prologue in which character actor Edward Van Sloan stands on a stage and warns the audience of the shocks and thrills that await them, the film's title card combines an image of savagely clawing hands with large staring eyes, two of the most frequently repeated visual motifs across the genre's history (Prawer 1980, 24). Although Henry Frankenstein's (Colin Clive) hideous progeny is a mishmash of cobbled-together body parts excavated from newly dug-up graves, its hands are given pride of place among that unholy assemblage. Indeed, the audience's first glimpse of the monster as a living creature is delivered as a close-up shot of its right hand moving—visible evidence that the mad scientist has succeeded in bringing his creation to life. Set in Henry's laboratory, this scene puts so much visual emphasis on the monster's hand that it seems detached from the larger body strapped onto the operating table (figure 9.4). This close-up is immediately followed by a medium shot of the scientist looking at the hand in awe, acknowledging its movement before delivering the film's most famous line: "It's alive! It's alive!"[2] Although the subject of Henry's exclamation is the entire creature to whom the hand belongs, his eyes are initially fixated on the latter, as if that individual body part's animation is what matters *most* to the man whose own hands worked to shape and create the thing. In that sense, the character's euphoria at seeing the monster move is a metatextual response to movement itself (a distinctive characteristic of the motion-picture medium) as well as an acknowledgment that his godlike power derives from being able *to produce the ability to produce*. With his own hands *he has made hands* that have the power to either create or destroy.

By the time that Whale's *Frankenstein* was theatrically released, several English-language horror films and mystery thrillers had already made the hand an entrenched part of the motion-picture medium's now-standardized "mise-en-scène of fear."[3] So entrenched was it that, for many critics, the image of "a hand gliding along a banister" had become as central and formulaic a scare-generating device as the presence of "Gothic manors lit by lightning" and "shadows glimpsed under doors" (White 1971, 1–18). As one critic states, "clutching hands" became a cornerstone of the genre following the 1927 release of *The Cat and the Canary*, a prototypical "old dark house" film that, besides fusing comedy and horror, also features such atmospheric elements as "sliding panels, thunderstorms, [and] billowing curtains in darkened hallways" (Hallenbeck 2003, 13). Beginning in the 1930s, numerous other films around the world would refine and expand the genre's repertoire of stock images, including US and UK studio productions such as director Karl Freund's *Mad Love* (1935), Robert Florey's *The Beast with Five Fingers* (1946), and Freddie Francis's *Dr. Terror's House of Horrors* (1964), three of the many motion pictures that deploy disembodied hands as metaphors of the "anxieties about bodily control and integrity" (Hutchings 2008, 99).[4] Regardless of whether these severed body parts are simply figments of characters' imaginations or the actual physical remainder of wronged individuals who seek revenge from beyond the grave, hands have been operationally encoded as signs of characters' "tortured consciousness" (be it that of the victim or the villain)—a fixture of the genre that Peter Hutchings alludes to in his discussion of Oliver Stone's psychological horror film *The Hand* (1981) (99). Not surprisingly, the promotional material (posters, lobby cards, etc.) surrounding this and other films (*The Hands of Orlac* [1960], *Hands of a Stranger* [1962], *The Crawling Hand* [1963], etc.) foreground the titular body part, free-floating in space as a weirdly static yet animated limb that appears to have a "mind of its own" (figures 9.5a and 9.5b).[5] And yet, as I will explain in my discussion of Hong Kong horror films, attributing cognition or even consciousness to the fleshy appendage conflates manual and mental operations, making it difficult to pull apart *action* and *intention* in stories that hinge on unimaginably gruesome acts (usually performed by, and sometimes *on*, hands).

The expression "at the hands of," which means "because of someone's actions" (rooted etymologically in the German word *hand-lung*, meaning "act" or "deed") (Rickels 2016, 85), is commonly used by cultural critics and genre specialists when describing the graphic, grisly violence that plays out both onscreen and offscreen—across the bodies of characters and spectators—in horror cinema. One example of this can be found in Angela Ndalianis's book *The Horror Sensorium: Media and the Senses*, in which she states that heroes and bystanders alike suffer such violence "at the hands of the monsters . . . hands that tear open an abdomen to reveal the slippery internal organs, the same hands that rip limbs from pulsating bodies" (2012, 5–6). But, in ascribing that abdomen-tearing and limb-ripping activity to *hands*, we ironically take the monster as a

Figures 9.5. Second only to eyes as the anatomical feature most frequently deployed in horror's promotional materials, hands seem to have a life of their own in these posters for 1940s and 1950s films.

whole out of the equation, reducing its uncanny (irreducible) presence in the text to individual instances of irrational action. All of the clawing, clutching, grasping, ripping, stabbing, strangling, and tearing that goes on in horror films is one sign that irrational impulses prevail in this genre, which, in the words of Isabel Cristina Pinedo, exposes in its transgressions "the limits of rationality" (1997, 23). Rhetorically framed in this way, it is as if the "head"—the monster's or villain's mental faculties—has nothing to do with such "mindless" actions, which are presented as automatic motor responses originating in the hand. However, media theorist Laurence Rickels offers a way forward (past mere transference) by reminding us that the hand, like an "externalized brain," translates thought into action. Quoting the German philosopher Ernst Kapp, Rickels emphasizes that this organ, which "grasps and concerns itself with bodily things," is also "the organ that essentially supports the release of ideas and their mental grasp" (2016, 85).

Not insignificantly, reviewers and general audiences who bemoan the privileging of graphic violence and visual spectacle over character development and dramatically compelling storytelling in both horror films and martial arts cinema sometimes resort to using the expression "mindless action" when describing scenes in which hands grasp at unsuspecting victims and fists fly with delirious abandon (Nguyen 2002). However, rather than being merely mind-numbing "gore-fests," the many expertly timed, show-stopping scenes in Hong Kong action films and monster movies have also been referred to by Stefan Hammond and Mike Wilkins (authors of *Sex and Zen & A Bullet in the Head: The Essential Guide to Hong Kong's Mind-bending Films*) as "poignant moments... packed full of rapid-fire mood swings" (1996, 38). Although Hammond and Wilkins are speaking specifically about action scenes in the "heroic bloodshed" crime thrillers directed by John Woo (such as *A Better Tomorrow* [1986] and *Hard Boiled* [1992]), which showcase ballistic gunplay rather than elaborate kung-fu acrobatics, their comments can be applied to Hong Kong horror films and martial arts cinema generally, given the many tonal shifts (e.g., between fright and laughter, dread and humor, etc.) that occur within those genres. Horror films in particular, with their fusion of broad physical comedy and terrifying bodily destruction, demonstrate Hong Kong cinema's aforementioned "mood swings" while illustrating how the hand is anything *but* "mindless" in its capacity to translate thought into action. Sure, silliness abounds in such productions as director Chu Yen-ping's *Fantasy Mission Force* (1983) and Ngai Choi Lam's *The Ghost Snatchers* (1986). But the hands that spring to life and terrorize the ill-fated characters in these seemingly mindless, horror-infused action films deserve serious consideration as instruments of patriarchal control, military authority, and religious doctrine that are made more disturbing by virtue of their apparent autonomy.

The above overview of Western literary and cinematic texts' adoption of hand imagery, though abbreviated, suggests the extent to which the iconography of horror was established early on and revised often over the course of its transmedia life as a type of cultural production that continues to cross national boundaries and corporeal thresholds. My reason for including this geographically uprooted prelude to the discussion of Hong Kong horror films that follows is twofold: first, it establishes some of the images and themes that will take on slightly different permutations in an East Asian context where issues of sexuality, transgression, and male power (or patriarchal authority) require additional or alternative interpretative frameworks than those adopted in North American and European contexts. Second, Hong Kong, a former British colony that is now officially recognized as a Special Administrative Region of the People's Republic of China (following the 1997 "handover" from the UK to China), has itself been mired in the rhetoric of national boundaries and corporeal thresholds for decades. An autonomous territory that is nevertheless part of the larger "body" of China proper, Hong Kong can be characterized as a culturally hybrid and spatially severed zone, and Great Britain's "handing over" of it does not erase the century-and-a-half history of colonial rule that continues to soak through its popular culture even after the transfer of sovereignty. Horror film expert Ken Gelder, describing Hong Kong as a "postmodern, global city that is also colonial," alludes to this paradoxical positionality, and for him and other scholars its "movement forwards" (towards China) is also "a kind of belated return" (2000, 351). In the words of Brian Chan Hok-shing, "[I]t is both Chinese and Western and yet neither (completely) Chinese nor (completely) Western." Although "geographically peripheral to the Chinese borders and politically separated from the motherland" (2007, 189), Hong Kong has been "imagined, fantasized, and claimed as 'authentically' Chinese" (Chu 2003, 63). This is thanks in part to the many Mandarin-language film productions shot at Shaw Brothers Studios and Cathay Studios beginning in the 1960s—*wuxia* films, period dramas, and horror films that, according to Mirana May Szeto and Yun-chung Chen, draw creative inspiration from the long tradition of "Chinese folk tales and literature on martial arts, romance, and ghost genres that have survived in Hong Kong film and print media while being censored in China and Taiwan during the Cold War" (2015, 91).

Thus, several films from that era, ranging from director Li Han Hsiang's costume fantasy *Enchanting Shadow* (1960) to *The Legend of the 7 Golden Vampires* (1974), a Shaw Brothers-Hammer Studios coproduction bringing together martial arts legends like David Chiang and Szu Shih and British star Peter Cushing, collectively attest to "the duality of Hong Kong's geopolitical identity" (Chu 2003, 63). As Kevin Heffernan points out, that duality is apparent in two horror films released within months of one another in 1974 and 1975, director Ho Meng-hua's *Black Magic* and Kuei Chih-hung's *The Killer Snakes*, which are "localized variations" on earlier Hollywood hits: *The Exorcist* (1973) and *Willard* (1971), respectively (2009, 60). Of these two Shaw Brothers productions, *Black Magic* is more representative as a text steeped in the themes and iconography of supernatural ghost stories involving sorcery, possession, resurrection, and reanimation. Flayed skin, rotting flesh, crawling worms, and copious amounts of spilled blood flood the screen over the course of this film's rollicking narrative, which revolves around two forest-dwelling witch-doctors—one good, the other evil—who lend their spell-casting services to men and women seeking romantic and sexual fulfilment. Although that latter element is a marked departure from the main storyline of director William Friedkin's *The Exorcist*, much of *Black Magic*'s thematic and visual material can be found in examples of cinematic (and literary) horror produced in other national and cultural contexts. And its various scare tactics, including the jolt-inducing intrusion of an old hag's dirty hand as it grabs the male protagonist's shoulder (sending him and the audience into a momentary state of shock), are not uncommon within Western texts.[6] However, other elements, including the presence of four female "hopping spirits" who haunt a young woman's dreams in the moments leading up to the film's final showdown between the dueling necromancers (set, incongruously, at a construction site in the modern metropolis), hint at

Black Magic's cultural ties to China, specifically, to the history of *jiangshi*-based storytelling that has been Hong Kong horror cinema's major source of inspiration for decades (going back to the 1930s, when such films as *Midnight Vampire* [1936], *Vampire of the Haunted Mansion* [1939], and *Three-Thousand-Year-Old Vampire* [1939] were theatrically released) (Bai 2013, 110).

Fittingly, the literary and folkloric genre of *jiangshi* fiction takes its name from the appropriately hybrid, frequently hopping creature that exists liminally between the world of the living and the world of the dead—a being that is neither wholly a zombie nor wholly a vampire, but a mixture of both. The *jiangshi*, typically adorned in Qing-era robes but also strangely redolent of the supernatural monsters that populate Western cinemas (particularly "ugly, strong, hairy creatures with long fingernails" who, like Mr. Hyde, delight in frightening young women with their "otherness"), is a sign of the duality that characterizes Hong Kong's cultural identity, situated between two worlds (Bai 2013, 109). The creature's name, rooted in the Chinese character for *jiang* (meaning "hard" or "stiff"), indicates its paradoxical status as an animated corpse in a frozen state of decay, with rigor mortis being the reason for its Frankensteinian flinging up of arms toward frightened victims. As one cultural historian explains, because of its inability to bend its limbs and body in a way that most humans can, the *jiangshi* moves around by jumping like a kangaroo "while keeping its arms outstretched for mobility" (Pettigrove 2005, 98). It feeds off the breath or "essence" (*qi*) of living humans, yet is unable to communicate verbally with them, having "lost the rational part of its mind with only the animal's desire remaining" (Bai 2013, 108). And, in general, the only person capable of dispatching or exorcising this unholy threat is a Taoist priest, hence the preponderance of traditional religious iconography (clothing, amulets, scriptures, paintings, architecture, etc.) not just in period pieces such as Ricky Lau's *Mr. Vampire* (1985) and Ching Siu-tung's *A Chinese Ghost Story* (1987), but also in urban horror films set in modern-day Hong Kong such as Stephen Tung's *Magic Cop* (1990) and Juno Mak's *Rigor Mortis* (2013). As viewers of *Magic Cop* and *Rigor Mortis* are aware, it is often through Taoist priests' elaborate hand signs (*shoujue*), which bear the influence of earlier Buddhist *mudras* or "hand seals" (Mitamura 2002, 235), that the *jiangshi* threat is eventually eliminated in these and other horror films, reminding us of the intrinsic way in which *Chinese* cultural references saturate tales that also bear passing similarities to Western horror films (figure 9.6).

Tellingly, the original title of *Rigor Mortis*—*Jiangshi* (in Mandarin) and *Goeng-si* (in Cantonese, the language in which the film was shot)—attests to the perennial status and centrality of this uncanny, liminal figure, which can additionally be situated between "masculine" and "feminine" identities, a gender binary that is both deconstructed and strengthened in many Hong Kong

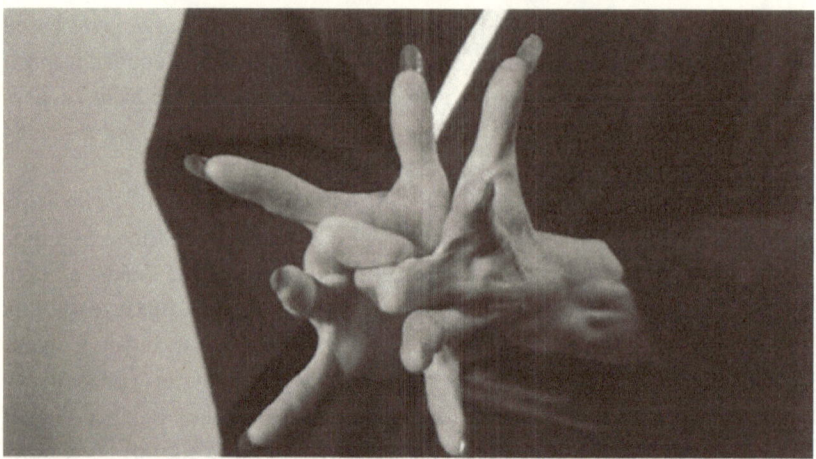

Figure 9.6. Elaborate Taoist hand signs frequently appear in Hong Kong horror films featuring hopping corpses and the reanimated dead.

horror films. Indeed, the creature is often distinguished by its long, claw-like fingernails, which can shoot out like phallic knives and pierce a person's flesh like butter, as witnessed in everything from *Spooky Encounters* to *A Chinese Ghost Story III* (1991). In the latter film, the evil spirit from "beyond" is given the name Butterfly and visually coded as female, with stereotypically feminine features like long flowing hair, jewelry, and makeup only partially masked by prosthetics. But in *Rigor Mortis*, the *jiangshi*—the reanimated corpse of a character named Uncle Tung (Richard Ng)—is coded as male, albeit one whose fingernails elongate and appear like those of a woman. The undead version of Uncle Tung can also be thought of as a "castrating" figure, who literally twists the arm off a retired demon hunter named Yau (Anthony Chan) in the film's penultimate scene.[7] The image of Yau's unattached member is one of several instances in *Rigor Mortis* when hands and arms are shown to be on the receiving end of both physical and psychic attempts at annihilation. One example is an earlier scene—the hallucination of a suicidal man, Chin (Chin Siu-ho) just before he tries to hang himself—depicting a middle-class family of three (Chin, his wife, and their young son) sitting down to eat at an all-white breakfast table that is suddenly stained by the red blood that pours from their hands and wrists. An even more disquieting moment occurs when a man rapes two women (a pair of twins), plunging a knife into one of their hands to keep her in place throughout the grueling ordeal (which ends when the other twin stabs the rapist with a pair of scissors). Significantly, director Juno Mak frequently cuts to close-ups of hands in order to show whether or not a character has died as a result of such violence (in the case of Chin, his suicide attempt fails, as denoted by a shot of his still-moving fingers). Moreover, at various points

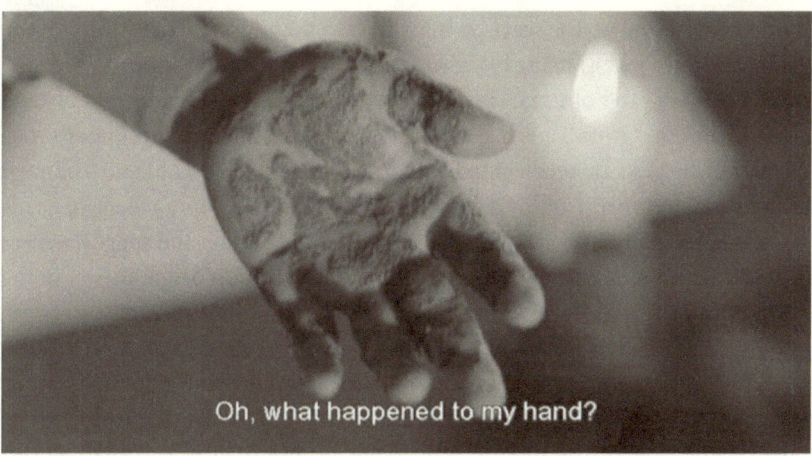

Figure 9.7. The male protagonist in *Black Magic* (1975), after seeking out a witch doctor to help him take revenge against the young men responsible for his wife's death, begins to notice crusty scabs developing on his hands (the price he must pay for using black magic for selfish, less-than-noble reasons).

in *Rigor Mortis*, sacred hand gestures "activate protective or exorcistic powers" on the part of those for whom "fingers have [a] cosmological significance" (Mitamura 2002, 246). As explained by Keiko Mitamura, besides being used "for exorcism of evil forces, control over spirits, [and the] healing of diseases," the hand helps to enhance a "transformation of the body into a locus of contact with, and merging into, the otherworldly realm of the Dao" (237).

While *Rigor Mortis* and several other Hong Kong films foreground the perennial hopping corpse more frequently than *Black Magic*, Ho Meng-hua's 1975 production puts tremendous emphasis on Taoist rituals and continues to be singled out by genre enthusiasts as a foundational text, setting the template for several of the "sleazy," "schlocky," and "exploitative" motion pictures that followed in its wake. These include the 1983 Shaw Brothers production *Seeding of a Ghost*, one of a series of so-called "fiendish fetus" films (e.g., *Ghost Nursing* [1982], *Devil Fetus* [1983]) that combines softcore titillation and gratuitous female nudity with Corman-meets-Cronenberg "body horror" and gross-out effects. Although the film's most notorious scene shows a slimy demonic placenta—or, rather, a "throbbing lump of pus and gristle"—exploding from an expectant mother's belly (recalling a similar moment in Ridley Scott's *Alien* [1979]) (Tombs 1998, 40), there are several instances when the hands of the male protagonist, a lowly cab driver whose wife has been raped and killed by a pair of horny hooligans, are singled out as small yet significant parts of a larger body that gradually succumbs to disease.

At the narrative's midpoint, the husband, assisted by an aging witch doctor (whose services he has enlisted as part of his vengeance plot), begins to notice crusty scabs on his hands (figure 9.7). When the young man asks about this sudden development, the sorcerer informs him that this new deformity "is the price [one pays when] using black magic." "It will get more serious in the next couple of days," the old man says, and indeed the brown epidermal blisters spread from the protagonist's hands to his arms, shoulders, and upper torso. Eventually, he pokes a needle into his arm, drawing the blood out and feeding it to the animated corpse of his dead wife, who is referred to as a *plazawa*. As his diseased limb palpitates, the audience is invited to consider the suggestiveness of this image: the idea that both corruption and salvation originate not in the brain but in the *hand*, which has the power to either destroy lives or restore hope—heady themes for so "mindless" and "sleazy" a motion picture.

For all of the weight given to gory images of blood-drinking, brain-eating, and worm-vomiting in *Seeding of a Ghost*, the film's most disturbing scene involves the rape of the main character's wife, an unfaithful woman who is forced to "pay the price" for her philandering in the most brutal way imaginable. This, lamentably, is a recurring feature of Hong Kong horror films produced in the 1970s and 1980s, but can also be found in martial arts films lacking the semantic and syntactical elements of the horror genre. For instance, director-star Sammo Hung's kung-fu classic *The Iron-Fisted Monk* (1977) features numerous shots of women being sexually violated by a high-ranking Manchu officer and voyeuristically framed by the camera as objects of a lascivious male gaze. No less problematic, the previously mentioned Shaw Brothers production *The Killer Snakes* begins with the offscreen sound of a woman being slapped by her sexual partner, grafted onto the black-and-white image of a young boy seated at a desk doing schoolwork and hearing the moans of his climaxing mother in the adjacent room. A brief insert shot—an extreme close-up of the woman's perspiration-dotted lips parting in preparation for a scream—suggests that all the slapping (dealt out by the hand of the unseen man) brings an equal measure of pleasure and pain to audiences of both martial arts films and horror films, which are littered with such scenes.

For instance, director Kuei Chih-hung's 1980 film *Hex*, a cross-cultural remake of Henri-Georges Clouzot's *Les Diaboliques* (1955), pivots on the impromptu decision of a deathly ill woman (who is wracked with consumption) and her conspiring nursemaid to murder her husband, a belligerent troll who doles out verbal and physical abuse whenever he is not busy drinking or gambling. Because of feudal China's marriage laws, divorce is not an option for Madam Chan (Tien Ni). Before she and her female servant Yi Wah (Chen Szu-chia) drown the man and dispose of his body in a nearby pond, he is shown beating and slapping the two women, to the point where the younger woman points her own finger at him and declares that he is "not a man." This is the first of several moments when hands emerge as accusatory or retaliatory instruments used by victims and villains alike, an image of finger-pointing that

Figure 9.8. In *Hex* (1980), a detached hand—one that belongs to a dead woman who seeks revenge from beyond the grave—crawls on its own toward the people responsible for her death.

anticipates similar shots in the Pang Brothers' more recent horror films *The Eye* (2002) and *Re-Cycle* (2006). Tellingly, as the seemingly lifeless body of this hideous man, this monstrous form of literally toxic masculinity, disappears into the swampy water, his right hand is the last thing to go under, submerging momentarily only to come back—albeit in spectral form—in a subsequent dream sequence. The widow, beset by guilt, wakes from a nightmare in which she is harassed by the dead man's grasping hands, which clamp down on the woman's throat and nearly kill her in her sleep. Eventually, Madam Chan does die, not from consumption but from fright. In the aftermath of her funeral we learn that her husband, who actually faked his death (holding his breath under the water), had been conspiring with Yi Wah, the double-crossing handmaiden, all along. But, in a manner that recalls the long-haired female spirits found in Japanese and South Korean horror films (e.g., *Ring* [1998], *Ju-on: The Grudge* [2002], *Acacia* [2003], *Bunsinsaba* [2004], *Arang* [2006], etc.), the wronged woman gets her revenge in the end, emerging from her coffin and using her own severed hand—a crawling appendage that looks suspiciously like a white plaster cast—to go after the priest who is performing the last rites (figure 9.8).[8]

The image of a crawling hand acting independently on its own, a throwback to earlier American, British, and French productions (ranging from Maurice Renard's 1920 horror novel *Les mains d'Orlac* to the US television series *The Addams Family* [1964–66] to a segment of the 1972 Amicus anthology film *Asylum*), can be found in other Hong Kong horror films theatrically released in 1980 (the same year that *Hex* created a stir among local audiences). Indeed, two films—director Tsui Hark's *We're Going to Eat You* and Sammo Hung's *Spooky Encounters*—employ severed and possessed hands as a means of demonstrating the relationship between victims and perpetrators of violence, but with more than a modicum of silliness to help offset (or distract from) the otherwise disturbing gender politics at the heart of these and other Hong Kong horror films.

For example, *We're Going to Eat You* incorporates a humorous gag in which the male hero, an agent of the Central Surveillance Agency who has tracked the movements of a notorious thief to an isolated village, mistakes a severed hand for his own (a shock moment, contained within the protagonist's dream, which wakes him from sleep). It also depicts a Taoist priest as the most "bumbling, ineffectual" village member, a portrayal that, with a few exceptions, runs counter to other *jiangshi*-laden horror films and which critic Daniel O'Brien sees as a sign of Tsui Hark's satirical approach to his subject (O'Brien 2003, 17). Not surprisingly (given its title), this film revolves around gruesome acts of consumption/cannibalism, but the repulsiveness of that subject is offset by dollops of slapstick action and comic pratfalls involving the emaciated, mask-wearing villagers, who are given "handouts" of human steak—the fleshy remains of unlucky passersby—as if living in a commune. Several critics have pointed out this film's blatant anti-communist message, not-so-subtly telegraphed in scenes showing the military uniformed village chief's "inequitable distribution of the 'meat' to his starving masses" (Morton 2001, 38). This, according to Lisa Morton, is one reason why the film has been interpreted as political satire, as an early warning of what might transpire once Hong Kong is handed over to China. But that allegorical reference perhaps gets lost amidst the copious, conspicuous nods to European mondo movies, spaghetti westerns, and other horror films of the 1960s and 1970s (everything from *The Texas Chain Saw Massacre* [1974] to the contemporaneous *Cannibal Holocaust* [1980]), which form the densely intertextual foundation for the appropriately titled *We're Going to Eat You*, a cannibal film about the literal and figurative ingestion of other "bodies" (38).

Few horror films of the 1980s have stood the test of time quite so well as *Spooky Encounters*, thanks mainly to Sammo Hung's inspired direction and fight choreography as well as his vigorous performance as the pedicab driver "Bold" Cheung, a commoner who is placed into extraordinary circumstances in a turn-of-the-century rural setting. Like other productions of that era, this film brings a number of traditional Chinese signifiers to bear on a scenario that is rooted in superstitions but also weirdly contemporary and even prescient in its hybridized mix of cultural elements and its satirical critique of corrupt, authoritarian public figures. Recalling the narrative premise of the aforementioned *Black Magic*, *Spooky Encounters* revolves around two dueling mystics—one good, the other evil—who each get entangled in the romantic troubles of local villagers. Chin Hoi (Jonny Chan), a Taoist mercenary priest, works for Cheung's tyrannical boss, Master Tam (Ha Huang), a town official who wishes to assassinate the dim-witted hero to prevent the discovery of his adulterous affair with Cheung's wife. Cheung, initially oblivious of his wife and the would-be-mayor's relationship, is counseled by another, more virtuous *sifu*, Tsui (Chung Fat). As the brother of Chin Hoi, Tsui lends support to the hero when the latter is forced to fend off a hopping corpse in a haunted temple over the course of two consecutive nights. Those midnight romps are some of *Spooky Encounters*' most memorable and hilarious scenes, a showcase for Sammo Hung's skills as a plus-sized performer as well as a demonstration of the way in which hands can be instrumentally employed as corporeal metaphors of an unthinking or irrational violence that will assume considerably less-funny, truly horrific connotations by the end of the film.

After being tricked into spending his first night in the dilapidated temple, Cheung climbs the rafters in fear, watching the coffins below with nervous anticipation. And, indeed, a reanimated corpse makes an appearance in this scene, thanks to the evil necromancer Chin Hoi, who controls the creature from afar through voodoo-like dark magic. When the top of the coffin slides open and the hideous looking corpse inside becomes visible, its hands appear first. Long, sharp fingernails point towards the ceiling, and the arms of the traditionally robed *jiangshi* stretch out to probe the room, like the dials of a compass or sensors in search of its prey. Each thud of the corpse's hop sends another spray of sweat from Cheung's brow. His fear begins to abate once the thing hops back into its coffin. The priest does not relent, however, and uses elaborate hand movements to whip the *jiangshi* back to its feet, leading to the first of many kung-fu fights in the film (not counting the opening title sequence, a confrontation with skeletons and flesh-eating monsters that is revealed to be a dream). Notably, the chopping movements of the *jiangshi*, performed in robotic-staccato fashion (in contrast to the fluid acrobatics of the chubbier Cheung), put additional emphasis on its hands, which appear to independently lead the creature toward its moving target, at least until the rising sun outside the temple sends it back to its coffin.

Against his will, Cheung's own hand takes the lead in a later scene, set in a village market, after he has escaped from prison (where he was held captive on suspicions of killing his wife, who is in fact alive). He and his famished protector, Tsui, sit down for bowls of rice. Meanwhile, Chin Hoi, who is in a nearby forest grove, unleashes yet another *fashu* (incantation)—a puppetmaster curse that takes control of the hero's right hand at the moment when he lifts his spoon to his mouth. Soon, a clearly mystified Cheung finds himself in a battle with himself and others, throwing punches at his fellow patrons and trying to control a part of his body that is no longer connected to his mind (figure 9.9).[9] That is, his hand seems to have a "mind of its own" and can only be brought back to the corporeal/mental fold once Tsui rushes to his aid, defeating Chin Hoi, who, before scampering away, promises that he will return. And return he does, in an epic battle that pits the two sorcerers against each other one final time outside Master Tam's residence. Tellingly, Chin Hoi is ultimately defeated by a long blast of fire shot by Tsui from his fingertips, although the latter also dies

Figure 9.9. Sammo Hung's character Cheung is locked in a battle against his own hand, which is being controlled by a sorcerer, in this scene from *Spooky Encounters* (1980).

from exhaustion. Having killed Master Tam by thrusting a sword through his chest, Cheung would appear to be the only person left alive in this final scene. However, his long-missing wife (Leung Suet-mei) emerges from the wings, crying crocodile tears and lying that his boss tried to rape her. No longer the rube he was at the beginning of the film, our hero suddenly pushes her away and lands seven punches to her stomach. "I knew you were having an affair," he screams at her, before viciously thrusting his hand into her abdomen one final time and launching the woman into the air with a degree of rage not yet seen in the film. Superimposed atop this last image of the film are the words "The End," rendered as a freeze frame that suspends time and leaves the audience with a bitter taste that is at odds with the generally sweet nature of the likeable main character. Culminating with this frankly shocking image of male violence directed at a woman, *Spooky Encounters*—despite its distinctiveness as an artfully choreographed and formally inventive horror-comedy—reveals itself to be just as misogynistic as the many other Hong Kong films from the 1970s and 1980s that treat the topics of rape and domestic abuse in an exploitative manner.

What makes this conclusion even more troubling, though, is the frequency with which hands had been foregrounded throughout the film as signs of an irrational, unthinking violence that gradually becomes understandable or "graspable" to an audience that yearns for the woman's comeuppance by the end. As early as its opening credits, *Spooky Encounters* has brought forth images of supernatural monsters clutching and grasping at the hapless hero, from the skeletal phalanges that comically pinch his bottom to a decomposing female ghost who, from the other side of a mirror, pokes her long red fingernails through the reflective surface in search of her male prey (figure 9.10). It is noteworthy that Cheung is able to fend off this spectral mirror-woman by cutting off her hand, which he then stabs with a knife—a precursor to the more ferocious, curiously spur-of-the-moment yet premeditated attack

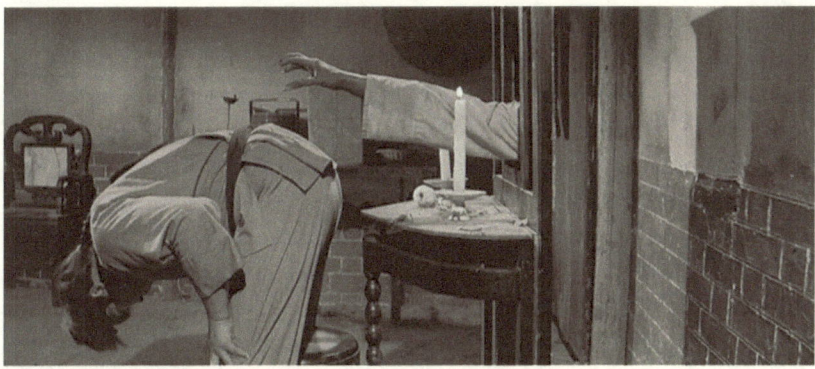

Figure 9.10. A localized spin on the old "clutching-hand" trope familiar to fans of 1920s and 1930s Hollywood horror films occurs near the beginning of *Spooky Encounters*.

that he launches against his wife in the film's final shot. Here, once again, we are invited to speculate on the ethical dimensions of a genre that is often reductively conceived of as grossly misogynistic, but which also highlights a gap between the hand as an instrument of violence and the mind that creates the conditions for violence to emerge in the first place. Those conditions are not always (or simply) a result of sexism, but are likely rooted in larger social divisions, including the separation of those wielding institutional power (for whom Master Tam is a representative) and those lacking that power (for whom Cheung is a representative).

CONCLUSION: HANDS UP AND HONG KONG PROTESTS

> Precisely because of its innocence it has become particularly dangerous.
> —ELIAS CANETTI, discussing the hand, in *Crowds and Power* (1960)

As stated above, Hong Kong cinema has long been described by cultural critics as having an "East-West identity," owing to the fact that, for years, filmmakers working in the mainstream industry have mixed "indigenous sources from legends, folklore and the supernatural . . . with different Western devices of narrativity" (Yue 2000, 365). This is especially true in the context of horror films, which "produce an ambivalent milieu where ghosts are modernized in a modernity that nevertheless longs for traditionalism" (365). But in the presence of so much discourse surrounding Hong Kong's liminal state, which is visually encoded in the *jiangshi*-based iconography of horror films featuring "Manchu-costumed vampires, Daoist priests, and the blood-sucking contagious qualities of the Western Dracula" (365), the relative absence of critical literature dealing with that most important yet understudied body part in the genre is made starker. As I have endeavored to illustrate through examples drawn from various corners of the world, the hand is an especially significant organ in the horror genre, presented as an independent agent of destruction, regardless of whether or not it is attached to a person's or monster's body. "Grasping" it, then, is of utmost importance if we are to make sense of the seemingly senseless violence and mindless action that has long characterized horror films.

More specifically, with the "reattachment" of Hong Kong to the larger body of China following the transfer of postcolonial sovereignty in 1997, the horror genre's corporeal tropes and predilection for what Barry Langford has called the "transgression of limits" become all the more noteworthy. Taking a cue from recent films like *Rigor Mortis*, which is "a horrifying statement about the older generation devouring the young and the specters of China crowding out the space of quotidian Hong Kong" (Szeto and Chen 2015, 96), we might speculate on the growing cultural "worth" or value of future horror films, which—even at their cheesiest or most slimy—confront viewers with their worst fears but also provide purgative social and libidinal release at times when free expression comes under attack. Of course, *not knowing* what will happen in the future of Hong Kong–China relations is what lends additional frisson to motion pictures in which the spread of dread *cannot* be stopped. Tellingly, the pro-democracy demonstrations that swept through the streets of this "Special Administrative Region" in September of 2014 were made up of young protesters who, inspired by the people of Ferguson, Missouri, raised their arms in unison and yelled, "Hands up, don't shoot." This peaceful, nonviolent reaction to the Chinese government's decision to renege on its promise to grant its citizens full democracy, while worlds away from the period setting and kooky antics of *Spooky Encounters*, presents a more chilling backdrop against which the hand has begun to assume allegorical significance as part of a larger effort to *unite*, rather than divide, thought and action. Here I am reminded of the words of Thomas M. Sipos, who, in his discussion of horror as an "emotive genre," states, "Horror audiences stick their hands into a black box, knowing something will bite, only uncertain as to how and when" (2010, 5). Just how deep that "black box" is, in terms of Hong Kong's cinema's capacity for generating both hope and fear in the midst of tremendous social and political change, is a question that horror films are perhaps best armed to explore.

Coda

PREPARING TO BE UNPREPARED

Horror Film's Predictable Unpredictability

> You cannot predict the workings of an insane mind!
> —INSPECTOR MATTHEW STRUDWICK (Philip Bourneuf), referring to the capricious nature of a wedding dress-obsessed killer on the loose, in *Chamber of Horrors* (1966)

In an early chapter of this book, I alluded to some of the paradoxical pleasures of cinematic horror, using Alfred Hitchcock's film *Psycho* (1960) as an example of a genre that has been referred to (by theorists such as Linda Williams) in terms reminiscent of amusement park "thrill rides," owing to the combined pleasure, delirium, and terror they inspire. As someone who has shown *Psycho* to large groups of undergraduate students (in courses devoted to horror cinema and to the films of Alfred Hitchcock), I can attest to its enduring power to frighten and entertain in equal measure. At different universities, on more than one occasion, I have witnessed audiences of varying ages (but mostly in the traditional college-age range of eighteen to twenty-two years old) reacting in an excessively showy way, by shouting, shrieking, and, yes, laughing whenever an unforeseen action—for instance, the cross-dressing killer Norman Bates (Anthony Perkins) rushing private investigator Arbogast (Martin Balsam) on a staircase landing, or the dead woman's sister Lila Crane (Vera Miles) letting out her own scream when she sees the skeletal remains of Norman's mother—occurs. Like Kendall R. Phillips, who alludes to the fact that "almost everyone" knows something about this "sordid, low-budget picture" (from its instantly recognizable score by composer Bernard Herrmann, to the identity of Marion's [Janet Leigh] attacker in the famous shower scene, to the initial reception of audiences who "howled, screamed, and threw popcorn into the air"), I am constantly surprised by *other people's surprise* (2005, 4, 62). Years of teaching the subject should have prepared me for such reactions, but I imagine that there are other media professors who have found themselves similarly disarmed by the ease with which horror filmmakers are able to generate audible bodily responses from those who should *know better*.

And why would they "know better"? The answer to that question can be found in dozens of studies of cinematic horror, including those written by scholars and cultural commentators whose professed interest in or abiding love for the genre is not dampened in the least by its "predictability" (Ford 2016, 170; 181–82). Variations of that latter word pepper academic and nonacademic texts as surely as does the recuperative language used to justify such studies and assert the importance of horror *because of*—not despite—its formulaic tendencies. For instance, in her discussion of surveillance in contemporary American cinema, Sandra Waters states that horror as "a Hollywood mainstay is more predictable and repetitive" than most other genres (2020, 41), offering a similar (if more generalized) take on the topic as that of Gail de Vos, who claims that "most horror films, with their predictable outcomes in a set, time-bounded narrative, have followed the same functional patterns as Ouija boards for adolescents and 'Bloody Mary' ritual games for pre-adolescents" (2012, 14). Notably, de Vos conceives of horror film viewing as a "rite of passage" for young people, allowing those viewers who are still learning the ropes of the genre—those who have not yet mastered its tropes—to dabble in darkness from a safe distance (thus quelling their curiosity in morbid subjects) while engaging in the parasocial pleasure of bonding with other neophytes around the same age (who are likewise discovering classics like *Psycho* for the first time).

On the other hand, the authors of the book *America in the Thirties* describe horror-viewing as a potentially cathartic experience, a way for Depression-era audiences to escape their day-to-day troubles and confront fears of the unknown through "the comfort of predictable plotlines, characters, and settings." In their words, "most horror films" produced in the United States during the 1930s "followed a similar pattern whereby someone—or something—upsets the natural, peaceful order," which is eventually restored "through the efforts of a heroic character who defeats the monster and wins the girl, who is often the monster's object of desire" (Olszowka et al., 2014, 230). Although there are nearly as many examples to the contrary as those that conform to the authors' sweeping generalization (so-called "outliers" such as *Freaks* [1932], *Night of Terror* [1933], *Maniac* [1934], *Condemned to Live* [1935], and *Mark of the Vampire* [1935], which progress in unexpected ways or feature final-reel plot twists), much of the genre's social value derives from the commonly held view that horror is as comforting in its narrative formulas as it is discomforting in its representational schemas, its tendency to test spectators' thresholds for pain and nail-biting suspense through either graphic displays of the body's undoing or more subtle suggestions of a malevolence that exists beyond our imagination.

The only thing more predictable than the conventions of cinematic horror is the critical tendency to use the word "predictable" when describing fictional scenarios that, apparently, need no introduction. Not only are the stock characters of today's horror films as flimsy as "cardboard" and the monsters who pursue them reminiscent of earlier manifestations of our worst fears, but so too can audiences' physical and emotional reactions to the genre's well-worn tropes be anticipated, as if they were scripted in advance. Variations of this all-too-familiar discourse, which *repetitively* insists upon the "repetitive" aspects of horror as well as the equally "predictable" way that viewers react to onscreen depictions of violence and dread, are found in countless essays and book chapters that stress the underlying *knowability* of a genre ironically believed to revolve around *unknowability*. However, T. S. Kord shows us a way out of this paradox by putting forth the idea that, contrary to popular belief, "horror films do *not* deal with the unknown" (2016, 181). Instead, by depicting "the same kind of character" getting into "the same kind of trouble, over and over again," they epitomize *knowability* and are thus our most reliable shields against fear:

> We *know* that Kirk will not stick with opening the door and calling down the hallway, but go into the house [in *The Texas Chain Saw Massacre* (1974)]. We *know* that Darry will lean so far down the pipe that he'll eventually fall in [in *Jeepers Creepers* (2001)]. We know that evil can be vanquished only provisionally, that our satisfaction in seeing the Creeper run over [in *Jeepers Creepers*], Michael Myers burned to a crisp [in *Halloween: Resurrection* (2002)], or Chucky melted into a puddle of plastic [in *Child's Play 2* (1990)] is temporary. We know they will all be back. We know these things whether we have seen the film or not. Horror reliably presents us with the worst-case scenario. Is it possible to fear it if we know it's coming, if we expect it, even rely on it? (181)

In fact, horror films, though sometimes colloquially referred to as "scary rides" (and theorized as such by Linda Williams), are less vehicles of fear than they are "guilt trips," according to Kord, who stresses the culpability of spectators in allowing themselves to be aligned "with a character with whom most people cannot possibly identify—the killer" (9). It would be easy to point toward the POV shot—the camera's framing of the culprit's ocular perspective as he or she hunts another victim (or, in the case of *Psycho*'s Norman Bates, looks through a peephole at a woman disrobing in the lead-up to her death)—as the chief means through which viewers are implicated in murderous or morally suspect actions (figure 10.1). Thankfully, Kord rejects the simplistic notion that spectatorial identification results from the act of seeing through the killer's eyes, though she insists that POV shots and other visual schemas work to make

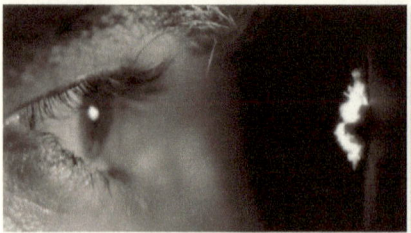

Figure 10.1. Norman Bates (Anthony Perkins) spies on Marion Crane (Janet Leigh) as she undresses and prepares for a shower, in Alfred Hitchcock's *Psycho* (1960).

"murder" in the abstract tangibly specific while inviting audiences to "revel in the spectacle of violence" without getting their own hands dirty. Therein lies the guilt that she believes supplants fear as horror's principal experiential mode: "guilt for enjoying the destruction of another human being" (9). Contrary to what Kristen Stewart's character, Maureen, believes in Olivier Assayas's supernatural psychological thriller *Personal Shopper* (2016), which shows her texting her reply to a mysterious caller's question of what most unsettles her about horror movies ("A woman runs from a killer and hides," she types on her cellphone), Kord contends that *fear* is only minimally operative or nominally present in a genre that instead forces us to confront our own worst tendencies both as spectators and as social actors at least partly responsible for far worse, real-world horrors.

Kord's contrarian view certainly expands our understanding of the subject and offers a refreshing break from traditional accounts of how and why other negative emotions besides guilt might be triggered by familiar scenarios and formulaic genre elements. However, her emphasis on the inherent "sameness" of cinematic texts—especially of the many sequels that comprise well-known franchises—paints with too broad a brush stroke. Reductively concluding that, "as anyone who has ever seen" any of the entries in the *Halloween, Friday the 13th, A Nightmare on Elm Street, Puppetmaster, Hellraiser*, and *Saw* series can attest, "sequels of horror films are not actually different films but the same film all over again, and appropriately so, since all horror films are fundamentally predictable" (182), she makes the mistake of letting the "big picture" obscure the "little details" of a genre that operates at the atomic or molecular level. Such top-down (as opposed to bottom-up) conceptualizing puts *knowing* (or thinking) ahead of *being* (or becoming), which runs counter to a phenomenological engagement with horror as something to be experienced first through the body and then through the brain. Of course, the latter body part, associated with higher-order executive functioning (or cognition) as well as the reception and processing of sensory information (conferring vision upon the eye, for instance) and the coordination of motor movements, is an embodied organ, making any such dualisms seem specious. Moreover, as William Brown points out, "visceral experiences" like those associated with horror (including, but not limited to, shock, revulsion, and nervous laughter), make "new modes of thought" possible, since "viscera are an inextricable part of higher-order processes" and thus cannot be so easily divested from the brain or the mind (2013, 141). Nevertheless, the point I wish to make is that the discourse of sameness that continues to swirl around horror films, predicated on their observable predictability as texts which rarely stray from narrative paths established by their forerunners, rhetorically smooths over the textual ruptures and literal bumps of individual works that are received differently by differently perceiving bodies.

Brown's comment about viscera as a higher-order process is echoed by Xavier Aldana Reyes, who notes the "inextricability" of the body from mind and thought in his 2016 book *Horror Film and Affect: Towards a Corporeal Model of Viewership*. This is one of a few recent publications to contest allegations of generic uniformity in favor of a more down-to-earth hermeneutics sensitive to the variables of individual motion pictures and of embodied viewing experiences. In it, Reyes makes the case that *affect*, or "the physical process whereby the body is affected by an external prompting," is a central feature of horror film spectatorship. He also goes on to note that the experience of watching, listening to, and feeling cinematic works as diverse as the Japanese "arthouse shocker" *Audition* (1999), the US "torture porn" movie *Hostel* (2005), the Spanish "found-footage" film *[•REC]* (2007), and the "New French Extremity" standout *Martyrs* (2008) "will naturally be different" for individual audience members based in part on their own bodily differences, and that it is "treacherous" to essentialize a genre that is perhaps less concerned with narrative than in a multitude of *effects*. Importantly, he cautions readers from putting too much emphasis on "thematic concerns or aesthetic tropes that push the genre into an all-too-formulaic box," suggesting that a pluralistic rather than reductive view of horror might result from moving affect theory more fully into the area of audience studies, thereby granting "its many and multiple incarnations their own specificity" (2016, 199). Following his and other scholars' lead, I have sought to bring an affectively charged "eye" to the study of horror. But I have also tried to go *beyond the eye* (and the brain which confers vision upon it) so that the body's "potential intensities" (to borrow Paul Elliott's Deleuzian wording) might be actualized and the "metaphysical distance that has become a major preoccupation of Western thought" might be replaced by a physical *closeness* to films which stimulate the proximate senses (smell, taste, and touch) (Elliott 2011, 14).

I have furthermore endeavored to show how the horizon of expectations that audiences bring to their viewing of motion pictures is frequently blown apart by horror's startling departures from the "straight and narrow path" of narrative causality, its gravitation toward figuratively and literally explosive or incendiary material that exists simply for its own sake and which—like the shower scene in Hitchcock's *Psycho*, or the shot of psychiatrist Steve Graham (Gabriel Byrne) suddenly erupting into flames in Ari Aster's *Hereditary*, or the lacerating flash of self-immolation that brings *Saint Maud* (2021) to a shocking end—can leave audiences shaken by the sheer audacity required to broach certain subjects or show certain things. As someone who has watched thousands of horror films in my lifetime and can reasonably say that I have a strong grasp of the genre's conventions (e.g., character archetypes, standard storylines of particular subgenres, etc.), I still find myself being "blindsided" by plot developments that I could not have fully anticipated, including those that occur near the conclusions of films as diverse as Robin Hardy's *The Wicker Man* (1973), Robert Hiltzik's *Sleepaway Camp* (1983), Fred Walton's *April Fool's Day* (1986), Alexandre Aja's *High Tension* (*Haute Tension*, 2003), James Mangold's *Identity* (2003), James Wan's *Dead Silence* (2007), Frank Darabont's *The Mist* (2007), J. A. Bayona's *The Orphanage* (*El orfanato*, 2007), Denis Villeneuve's *Enemy* (2013), and Jordan Peele's *Us* (2019). As surprising as those twist endings are, a more unsettling sense of being on shaky ground while traversing a horror film's detour-laden narrative is likely to affect audiences of Pascal Laugier's *The Tall Man* (2012), Justin Benson and Aaron Moorhead's *Spring* (2014), Veronika Franz and Severin Fiala's *The Lodge* (2019), and several other motion pictures that are just as powerful as *Psycho* is in terms of making audiences' footing unsure or by pulling the rug out from under them. Unable to predict where the narratives of these films are going, and giddy (if also nervous) at the prospect of encountering something for which my body and mind are unprepared, I find myself inhabiting a similar spectatorial space or experiential state as those moviegoers who encountered Hitchcock's film during its initial theatrical run in the summer and early autumn of 1960.

Ultimately, arguments like the ones advanced by Kord and other commentators fail to account for the many moment-to-moment surprises and small yet significant textual differences that occur within and across franchises (not to mention standalone movies that are not part of a larger series). Those textual differences include the actual *textures* of onscreen objects that might vary from film to film (for instance, the smooth dull surface of Jason Voorhees's hockey mask in *Friday the 13th Part III* [1982], the cracked, blood-caked version of that face covering worn by the same character in *Friday The 13th: The Final Chapter* [1984], and the grimy, scratch-marked version of it in *Freddy vs. Jason* [2003]). They are also to be found in the micro-performative elements of acting that make something like Gus Van Sant's ostensibly line-by-line, shot-for-shot remake of *Psycho*—a 1998 production starring Anne Heche as Marion Crane and Vince Vaughn as Norman Bates—considerably *different* from its source material ("in more ways than you can wave a butcher knife at," to quote Thomas M. Leitch, including those "that can be observed even by color-blind audiences") (2000, 269). Although audiences who are familiar with the story of *Psycho* (having already seen Hitchcock's black-and-white original) can accurately guess where Van Sant's version is heading, a smorgasbord of slight yet significant departures from the original is to be found in the way that he and his creative team pace the narrative, compose shots, stage scenes, and arrange objects within a mise-en-scène that simply *must* be seen and heard with the same eye and ear for detail that Leitch brings to his discussion of the film (pointing out, for instance, the new Norman's snorting sounds, the southwestern twang of his and other characters' vowel-stretched speech, and the squawking of birds that can now be heard emanating from the fruit cellar) (269). Indeed, to *see* how dissimilar the two films are, right down to the once-skeletal, now-mummified face of Mrs. Bates, entails being at once more eye-focused (in order to note things like blinks, winks, and Marion's dilating pupil at the time of her death) and more inclusively attuned to those textual and textural components of a given filmmaker's style or a particular actor's body that are in some ways the *substance* of cinematic horror.

If I may make my own contrarian claim, as a corporeal form and as a body genre (wherein no two bodies are the same), horror film is utterly *unpredictable*. Or rather, the physical stuff with which the present study is concerned—the limbs, organs, and viscera that spill out every which way and have their own granular, cellular specificity—cannot be so easily contained or abstracted away by critics who persist in thinking that horror films are all, or mostly, "the same." Even those elements that are frequently disparaged by genre enthusiasts as being rote and repetitive, such as the propensity of victims to behave stupidly and make bad, irrational decisions (e.g., going down into a basement to read from the Necronomicon, watching a cursed videotape despite dire warnings not to, discarding a weapon while a murderer is still on the loose, splitting up a group of characters so that they might be killed off one by one), remind us that *anything* can happen in a horror film. Indeed, such plot contrivances, lamented by more than a few critics, are the best insurance that unruliness will ensue and chaos will surely come. The inevitability of such disorder might seem to suggest a paradoxically predictable *order*, a logic behind all the illogical actions driving the plots forward. However, the process of getting from point A to point B (and so on) in a given narrative matters less than the time spent with people whose *bodies*—each distinct in its own way—shoulder much of the burden of that storytelling and make it possible for us to imagine how *we* would behave if faced with the same (or similar) moment-to-moment predicaments.

There has never been a time—certainly not during the modern industrial era—when the inescapable reality of death did not impress itself upon the cultural imagination of moviegoers, whose lives outside the multiplex, the drive-in theater, the arthouse theater, or the film festival setting are susceptible to literal and figurative infections as a result of environmental catastrophes and damages to the world's natural habitats (e.g., climate change, air pollution, ozone depletion), their governments' failed health and public service policies, and the proliferation of weapons of mass destruction in addition to the specter of endless war (including of the biological variety). But the moment of this writing, one-and-a-half years after the World Health Organization (WHO) declared COVID-19 a global pandemic (on the way to claiming nearly six million lives as 2021 comes to a close), is particularly fraught with the kind of fretfulness or foreboding that so often characterizes horror films. Without wishing to exploit a tragedy of truly epic proportions in the process of analyzing comparatively "small" cultural productions that are, in some respects, already exploitatively designed to capitalize on our susceptibility to real-world fears, I want to stress the increased relevance of horror—even that which is otherworldly and out-of-the-ordinary—to people's everyday lives. Never more so than now, in 2021, has the genre been so broadly applicable to real-world concerns, and the fact that the past year alone has witnessed the release of several coronavirus-themed horror films—from Rob Savage's *Host* (a 2020 feature shot on Zoom during the pandemic and based on the director's earlier short that went "viral") to Ben Wheatley's tellingly titled *In the Earth*—reminds us of its ability to replenish itself with each new set of generation-defining calamities.

NOTES

1. BOOKS, BODIES, BELIEFS:
INTRODUCING A GENRE THAT NEEDS NO INTRODUCTION

1. For an elaboration of the cultural values attached to the expression "elevated horror," a recent critical and marketing term that has come under increased scrutiny, see Church (2021).

2. In the forenote to the 2010 edition of his bestselling nonfiction book *Danse Macabre*, Stephen King writes, "Expensive CGI FX, elaborate makeup jobs, and exploding blood bags won't scare anybody over the age of fourteen (three years younger than you have to be to get into an R-rated movie). The kids have seen it all before. It's borrr-ing. If a horror movie is going to work, there has to be something in it beyond splatter" (2010, xiii).

3. For more on the longstanding claims of horror's social relevance, see Johnny Walker's recent work on the independently produced 2014 short *The Herd* (2022, 194–219). Directed by activist-artist Melanie Light after a successful crowdfunding initiative that foregrounded its creator's feminist credentials, the film revolves around the subjugation of women, allegorically linked to the exploitation and mistreatment of livestock in a factory farm setting that recalls the kind of gruesome iconography featured in videos produced by People for the Ethical Treatment of Animals (PETA). Unlike the majority of better-known horror films, such as *The Texas Chain Saw Massacre* (1974), which might gesture toward the plight of cattle and other caged or farmed animals in a rather superficial fashion, *The Herd* does not simply "reflect injustices" but was intentionally "designed to elicit change in a manner akin to street protest, activist video, and media campaigning," according to Walker. It thus "illustrates how horror has been, and can continue to be, used as activism" (198, 215).

4. As Donald C. Willis notes in his study of classic horror films of the 1930s, "human eyes and ears can't take in everything and process it all at once," and the dense combination of camera placement, mobile framing, editing, sound design, and the bodily and vocal aspects of acting (among other elements) ensure that no two people will see and hear the exact same things when watching and listening to a film (2019).

2. HEADS WILL ROLL, BODIES WILL SHAKE, SOULS WILL SHATTER:
HORROR FILM'S FORMATIVE STAGES AND PHYSICAL CHANGES

1. The expression "horror film" was used by production companies and promotional departments as early as late 1917. That was when director Emmett J. Flynn's silent drama *Alimony*,

perhaps best remembered today as an early acting gig on the resume of Rudolph Valentino (who has a supporting role in the film), was advertised in the pages of *Motion Picture News* (vol. 16, no. 21) as "NOT A HORROR FILM—NOT A PROBLEM PLAY" in advance of its December 3 release by First National Exhibitors. That ad copy presupposes that readers and audiences would know what a "horror film" is, so that no one would be confused about this motion picture's status as "A POWERFUL BLENDING OF GRIPPING DRAMATIC INTEREST, PATHOS AND SUPREME LOVE." Eleven years later, director Paul Leni's *The Last Warning* (1928) was referred to as a "Spook and Horror Film" in the pages of the same trade magazine, one of the first instances in which the generic designation "horror film" was used to positively identify a theatrical release (Anon. 1929, 126).

2. Some critics at the time of *Dr. Jekyll and Mr. Hyde*'s nationwide release did not respond favorably to the opening scenes and the use of POV shots. For instance, in his 1932 review of the film for *American Cinematographer*, William Stull begins by referring to Mamoulian's "excellent dramatic conception" of the introducing passages, but goes on to note that "it is executed, unfortunately, by means of a long sequence of trucking shots and free-head 'pans' which, though expertly photographed, begin the picture with a confused note that is totally at variance with the deft sureness of the rest of the production" (1932, 22).

3. CORPOREALITY, MATERIALITY, MORTALITY: THE HORROR FILM AS "BODY GENRE"

1. Other films in addition to *Psycho* have been described through metaphors befitting amusement parks and carnivals, either by critics, theorists, or the creators and performers involved in their production. For instance, during his commentary-track chat with Louis Morneau, the director of *Bats* (1999) (featured on the DVD release of a film clearly inspired by Hitchcock's *The Birds* [1963]), actor Lou Diamond Phillips states, "I think overall the whole film is designed to be a real thrill ride, a lot of fun. People like to be scared . . . to give them good scares but to give them some thrills . . . and a nice ride along the way."

2. In the words of Mark Kermode (who reviewed the 2008 DVD release of *Teeth* one year after it made its British debut at the London FrightFest Film Festival), this "delightfully outré slice of rubbery horror fun" would have given James Ferman, the New York-born former Secretary of the British Board of Film Censors (BBFC, later renamed the British Board of Film Classification), whose tenure lasted from 1975 to 1999, heart palpitations. Kermode's jesting comment, which alludes to the frequency with which the UK's chief censor and other regulators took "gardening shears" to violent, low-budget exploitation and horror films during the so-called "Video Nasties" era of the 1980s, draws attention to how much has changed over the past few two or three decades, and how relatively easy it now is for darkly satirical films (including those with "very strong sexualized gore" and "bleeding genitals," to quote the BBFC's content notes) to receive a wide release. This last point is perhaps true so long as distributors and exhibitors believe that there are audiences out there who will either be drawn to "a proto-feminist agenda" or be nostalgic for "the creaky body-horror of yore" (i.e., films that lean in to their "laughs-and-barfs bad taste") (Kermode 2018).

3. I am reminded of how the severing of sleazy pornographer Derrick Jones's (Jerry O'Connell) penis in director Alexandre Aja's *Piranha 3D* (2004) is "played for laughs," to quote one critic (Thurman 2020).

4. In one of the few analyses of *Teeth* to mention this title sequence, Casey Ryan Kelly points out the suggestive shape of the microbes, which echoes the "two phallic nuclear cooling towers" that can be seen befouling the air behind Dawn's mother's house in the pre-title scene (set several years earlier, when she first discovered her unusual "gift" while playing with Brad in a kiddie pool) (2016, 93–94). "Spewing toxic vapor into the air and disturbing the landscape's natural beauty," the power plant is part of a larger culture of "toxicity" that encompasses environmental as well as gendered signifiers of nature being harmed or spoiled in some way (93–94). These images during the opening credits are thus doubly significant: they point *forward*, establishing a horizon of expectations for first-time viewers who can perhaps intuit what the film's suggestive title and marketing campaign refer to but are likely unaware of how predatory behavior will be handled in the narrative; and they point *backward*, reminding us of the phallocentric parameters of a story in which practically *everything* looks like a penis (including young Brad's finger, which is bitten when he sticks it where he shouldn't during that pre-title kiddie-pool scene) while also hinting that environmental pollution might be the cause of the female protagonist's genetic mutation.

4. GOING DEEP, STICKING TO THE SURFACE: BAD DEATHS AND WET BODIES

1. For instance, director Terence Fisher's *Frankenstein Must Be Destroyed* (1969), the fifth in a series of Hammer Film productions centering on the scientific breakthroughs and exploits of Baron Victor Frankenstein (played in this and all of the preceding films by Peter Cushing), begins with a scene in which a medical doctor, Otto Heidecke (Jim Collier), is about to enter the building where his office and underground lab are located. He is stopped cold in his tracks when the blade of a scythe appears out of nowhere, slicing at the man in a sudden burst of mayhem. The only sign that audiences have of Dr. Heidecke's death comes from the spray of blood that spatters onto a literal sign that bears his name on that building. His badly damaged body, now a no-longer breathing corpse, remains below the frame as viewers are forced to quickly adjust to a storyworld that seems to be caught in-between the "telling" traditions of the past and the "showing" tendencies that will become a dominant mode of representation in future horror films.

2. Directing duties on Winchester Pictures Corporation's 1951 production of *The Thing* have sometimes been attributed to legendary Hollywood filmmaker Howard Hawks, who exerted a strong hand as coproducer and uncredited screenwriter.

3. Steve Jones, the author of *Torture Porn: Popular Horror after Saw*, likewise traces a movement from seeing (or showing) to touching (or feeling) in writer-director Eli Roth's *Hostel*, a 2005 film that reflects in microcosm the broader cultural shift alluded to by Laura Wilson and in my own chapter. Importantly, that cultural shift is enacted as a power shift in the film. As Jones states, the trio of young men who feel compelled to visit the titular lodging in Slovakia during their pleasure-seeking travels throughout Europe begin the narrative as distant observers—fairly innocuous sexual voyeurs drawn to the titillating sight of naked women. However, once they cross the threshold from harmless voyeurism to physical involvement with the hostel's resident temptresses, Natalya (Barbara Nedeljáková) and Svetlana (Jana Kaderabkova), the ill-fated protagonists are quickly abducted by sadistic individuals who have also made that transition from seeing (or surveilling) to touching (or torturing), effectively turning the three college-aged consumers into the "consumed." *Hostel*'s sole survivor at the end, Paxton (Jay

Hernandez), provides a further distillation of that trajectory toward tactility, having shared a personal recollection about his earlier "failure to rescue a drowning girl" (with whom he had notably made "eye contact") and eventually cutting off the dangling eye of another tortured victim to spare her from any more suffering. This "messy visceral engagement," according to Jones, underscores the film's thematic emphasis on inactive viewing giving way to active touching and proximal collapse. It furthermore suggests that the power to put one's hands on someone else against that person's will (which several of the characters in this film do) ultimately trumps the agency associated with distant witnessing and lends physical expression to the kind of "positional slippage" that is needed before a victim can gain power over his or her victimizers (Jones 2013, 103–4).

4. The spectatorial act of obscuring one's vision or closing one's eyes while viewing a horror film is metatextually suggested in a scene near the end of Kiyoshi Kurosawa's *Pulse* (*Kairo*, 2001), involving a college student named Ryosuke Kawashima (Haruhiko Kato) who comes face to face with a ghost. When the fuzzy black shape with a pale white face glides toward Ryosuke, the young man covers his eyes with his hands and shouts, "I refuse to acknowledge!" His defiant act is a will to ignorance in the presence of a life-draining spirit that simply cannot be wished away.

5. Here I am reminded of *Zombi 2* (1979) and producer Ugo Tucci's mind-bogglingly bad decision to send a second unit out to film Ramón Bravo in undead costume and makeup battling a real tiger shark in the ocean. It was a literally life-or-death scene that director Lucio Fulci did not want to shoot, and which was accomplished through the use of animal tranquilizers and careful editing.

6. On his director's commentary chat with moderator Chris Alexander (featured on the Vestron Video Blu-ray release of *Shivers* [1975]), David Cronenberg discusses the occasion during his film's production when actor Susan Petrie (whose character, Janine Tudor, needed to be in tears during a particular scene, but who was not able to cry on command) asked him to violently slap her across the face more than once. He complied, although, as he notes during the commentary, "Not being a sadist it wasn't something that was natural to me." Interestingly, Cronenberg was left with a permanent mark because of an on-set accident, when a cooking fork defensively brandished by Lynn Lowry (playing the character Nurse Forsythe) accidently struck his left bicep (which still bears the scar).

7. Similarly, the writer-director of the 2016 horror film *The Barn*, Justin M. Seaman, spends a portion of his Blu-ray commentary track discussing the moment when he "actually got electrocuted" during the shooting of one scene (when the power cords above his head got wet), only to later find himself on the receiving end of a plastic wrench to the face (which, according to him, "still hurts"). His were not the only injuries, though, and more than one unforeseen event—an exploding lightbulb, a Halloween pumpkin that caught fire, one young actor getting hit in the head with a wooden handle, and another actor being nearly run over by a speeding van that had lost control of its brakes—threatened not only to halt production but also to bring a premature end to a few of this film's performers.

5. SLICED EYEBALLS AND SEVERED EARS:
ON (NOT) SEEING AND (NOT) HEARING HORROR FILMS

1. Theatrically released during the week of Halloween in 1995, *Vampire in Brooklyn* was actually preceded by Rusty Cundieff's horror anthology *Tales from the Hood* (1995), which

premiered in US theaters on May 24. However, neither *Tales from the Hood* nor the earlier African American comedy-horror film *Def by Temptation* (1990), directed by James Bond III and starring Kadeem Hardison, were distributed as widely as Craven's studio-backed film (which, thanks to Paramount's publicity machine, managed to recoup its $14 million budget despite tepid reviews).

6. DEAD, BUT STILL BREATHING:
THE PROBLEM OF POSTMORTEM MOVEMENT IN HORROR FILMS

1. For instance, a white poof of air can be seen coming out of a mysterious woman's mouth when she loudly exhales near the beginning of Kiyoshi Kurosawa's *Séance* (2001). This appears to be real (the actor's actual breath), though in recent years filmmakers have used computer-generated imagery to create frosty exhalations of air (as Michael Dougherty, the director of the Christmas-themed horror film *Krampus* [2015], did when he solicited help from the visual effects team at Weta Digital to make the characters' breath visible during cold exterior scenes).

2. In the words of Peter Shelley, heavy breathing is "a corny horror movie convention for an antagonist" (2012, 152). Less parodic takes on the heavy-breathing killer (from roughly the same time period of *Student Bodies*' theatrical release) can be found in *Antropophagus* (1980), *The Boogey Man* (1980), *Tenebrae* (1982), and *Curtains* (1983). For a discussion of the marketing and reception of *Student Bodies*, see Nowell (2011, 244–45).

3. Greydon Clark's 1982 comedy-horror film *Wacko* spoofs the negative imperative of the genre during a scene in which a character named Mrs. Doctor Graves (Stella Stevens) reads a note from the Lawnmower Killer: "It says, 'It's Halloween, it's prom night, there's a psycho loose, so don't open the door, don't answer the phone, don't look in the attic, don't go to the bathroom, don't go into the ocean, and don't go into space 'cause no one can hear you scream.'"

4. Ironically, by loading up the frame with actors playing dead, a filmmaker can make it difficult for audiences to spot any one person's breathing (from the sheer number of bodies on screen). This happens, for instance, in director Greg McLean's *The Belko Experiment* (2016), when at least a dozen of the nearly ninety characters killed in the film—employees of Belko Industries, located in Bogotá, Colombia—are shown lying on the floor of the office building's main room.

7. SMELLING LIKE A SLAUGHTERHOUSE:
CINEMATIC OLFACTICS AND THE STENCH OF HORROR

1. The expression "Final Girl" was coined by Carol Clover in the early 1990s, in response to a narrative pattern that the film scholar had detected in the slasher subgenre going back two decades earlier. It refers to the lone female survivor who, having witnessed the grisly effects of murderous mayhem that have left her more sexually promiscuous friends dead (and often mutilated), "perceives the full extent of the preceding horror and of her own peril" (1992, 35). She is generally resourceful, strong (both mentally and physically), and morally unblemished by the kind of "bad behavior" that resulted in her companions' deaths. But because she embodies and enacts the frequently misogynistic peril directed toward women in this subgenre, by being "chased, cornered, [and] wounded" and unleashing scream after scream as she falls and rises repeatedly, she can be seen as "abject terror personified" (to borrow Clover's much-quoted phrase). For more information about the seemingly static but ever-evolving "Final Girl" trope,

which has been a mainstay of slasher films since the 1974 theatrical release of *Black Christmas*, see Christensen (2011, 23–47), Kawin (2012, 143–44), Muir (2007, 25–28), and West (2018, 28–29).

2. In *Film Theory: An Introduction through the Senses*, Elsaesser and Hagener mention smell only in passing, notably after discussing two pioneering works in the study of horror films: Linda Williams's exploration of excess-filled "body genres" that stimulate physical mimicry and close the distance between spectator and screen, and Barbara Creed's study of the taboo-breaking, boundary-transgressing potential of the abject (a core feature of horror, which displays "mutilated or dead bodies, bodily secretions, discharges and waste"). However, because the transmission of odors relies upon, in their words, "physical proximity," Elsaesser and Hagener maintain that the combined "disciplinary regime" of seeing and hearing (rather than smelling or touching) became central to cinema from its origins as a medium through which to engage urban environments (the favored subject of early filmmakers), which were kept at a safe "distance" from viewers (2010, 121–22).

3. Several critics have used the same expression in describing how audiences sometimes shift from a palpably felt to a practically smelt experience while watching horror films. For example, in his discussion of the 1972 British production *Death Line* (retitled *Raw Meat* for its North American distribution), Calum Waddell paints an evocative picture of a scene set inside the subterranean lair of the villain, a cannibalistic man who has kept the corpses of his many victims hidden within the tunnel systems adjoining the London Underground. As director Gary Sherman's camera slowly tracks into that quagmire of despair, showing a host of "decaying and mutilated bodies" while the unnamed monster slices a man's throat to the accompaniment of dripping water, the film attains a "putrid, 'you can almost smell it' feel" (2018). Similarly, Sean W. Fallon, a contributor to the website *Audiences Everywhere*, writes that "you can almost smell . . . [the] 'lo-fi, dirty' grittiness of Tobe Hooper's *The Texas Chain Saw Massacre* (1974) (2017); similarly, another Hooper-directed horror film, *Eaten Alive* (1976), which "offers a continuation of the vile rural backwater" depicted in that earlier masterpiece, inspires Shaun Anderson (a contributor to *The Celluloid Highway*) to muse, "You can almost smell the pungent stink of the surrounding swamp" (2012).

4. Marie Mulvey-Roberts, author of *Dangerous Bodies: Historicising the Gothic Corporeal*, notes the conspicuous manner in which the size and shape of Dracula's nose is dwelt upon by Stoker, who also lingers upon the "fetid body odour" (or *foetor judaicus*) of the vampire in a way that recalls anti-Semitic legends dating back to the Middle Ages, including the story of "a Jew falling into a privy" (which was used to racially associate his people with excrement) (2016, 48, 290).

8. SHITTY, SLIMY, SMELLY, SMILEY: DIRTY SPACES, FUNNY FACES, AND THE TEXTURAL PLEASURES OF "LAUGHABLY BAD" TEXTS

1. For instance, Horror.com's Staci Layne Wilson writes of *Zombie Nation* and its director: "The only way you'll get me to watch another Ulli Lommel film is to make me choose between that or having a loaded pistol taped to my temple which is rigged to an active landmine under my foot as you douse me with itching powder" (https://www.rottentomatoes.com/m/zombie-nation).

2. https://www.reddit.com/r/horror/comments/9e11h7/amityville_1992_is_one_of_the_best _movies_in_the/).

3. As Ian Fryer points out, the image of the dead ex-wife's body in *The Comeback* keeps returning over the course of the narrative, forcing the audience to see the corpse "in various stages of decomposition" and underlining once again why the title of the film is apt (2017).

4. Consider, too, the promotional gimmick concocted by drive-in film distributor Sam Sherman, who created buzz around the 1969 release of *The Mad Doctor of Blood Island* by inviting moviegoers to take the "Oath of Green Blood" by handing out small packets of liquid gel to be ingested during the screening (Corupe 2020, 24).

5. This scene from *Amityville: It's About Time* recalls a similarly disgusting moment from the independently produced horror movie *Spookies* (1986), when a brown muck monster—basically, a walking piece of poo that farts incessantly—dissolves into the basement floor of a mansion.

9. SPOOKY ENCOUNTERS OF THE HUMOROUSLY DISGUSTING KIND: CLUTCHING HANDS AND HOPPING CORPSES, FROM HOLLYWOOD TO HONG KONG

1. See https://nyc.metrograph.com/series/series/180/shaw-brothers-horror.

2. Tony Williams argues that close-up shots of hands in James Whale's *Frankenstein* are what most decisively connect Henry and his creature. Not only is the hand "the first object moving on the operating table," but an image of Henry's hand "stroking the coffin" during the film's earlier disinterment sequence further links the two, suggesting that production and destruction, life and death, are dialectically aligned. This corporealized theme is picked up again in the film's 1935 sequel, *Bride of Frankenstein*. As Williams points out, the film begins with a tête-à-tête between *Frankenstein* author Mary Shelley and poet Lord Byron, the latter admiring the former's creative process and remarking, "It was these fragile, white fingers that wrote the nightmare." When she accidentally pricks her finger with an embroidery needle, "the flow of blood causes Mary consternation." "This action," according to Williams, "anticipates the creatures attempt to stroke his bride's hands toward the end of the film, an action that leads to rejection" (Williams 2004, 39–40).

3. For example, director Roland West's horror-comedy *The Monster* (1925), one of many "old dark house" films made during the silent era, features a scene in which a hand reaches out from behind a curtain, about to grab the milquetoast hero, followed by a cutaway shot of the film's heroine, on a slab, being brought down by a pair of arms perched above her heaving chest.

4. In addition to the motion pictures mentioned in the body of this chapter, other US horror films showing severed hands include *The Beast Within* (1982), in which a dog carries a human hand in its mouth, and *Psycho III* (1986), which culminates with a shot of Norman Bates in the back of a squad car, caressing the disembodied hand of his "mother" as he is being driven to the mental institution.

5. In the case of Sam Raimi's *Evil Dead II*, the flapping hand, which pulls at Ash's (Bruce Campbell) hair and smashes dishes on his head, is given a mind of its own and is even endowed with both vocal and sight abilities (despite its lack of mouth and eyes).

6. Robert Baird points out that several popular US horror films, including *The Exorcist* (1973), *Jaws* (1975), *Halloween* (1978), and *Aliens* (1986) employ "the old tap-on-the-shoulder routine," a false startle effect that likewise occurs with frequency across the history of Hong Kong horror (2000, 12–24).

7. This arm-ripping scene in *Rigor Mortis* is reminiscent of the final showdown between the Chinese hero and his Japanese adversary in the Shaw Brothers' 1972 martial arts film *Thunderbolt*

Fist. As the culmination to a story about Japan's incursions into northeastern China, the film pits the protagonist Tie Wa (whose hand had been maimed by thugs when he refused to divulge the location of the resistance movement's hideout) against an opponent whose arm is torn off, resulting in an arterial spray and a final shot of the bloody body part lying next to the fallen man in the boxing ring.

8. Or, at least, that is what the audience is *led* to believe until the film's denouement reveals the truth behind Madam Chan's death and revenge, exacted on her behalf by her long-lost twin sister.

9. Another example of a character losing control of his arm and hand occurs in the Hong Kong-Malaysian coproduction *Hungry Ghost Ritual* (2014), when a man possessed by a demon stabs himself in the chest with a sharp talisman.

BIBLIOGRAPHY

Abbott, Stacey. 2007. *Celluloid Vampires: Life after Death in the Modern World*. Austin: University of Texas Press.

Abbott, Stacey. 2016. *Undead Apocalypse: Vampires and Zombies in the 21st Century*. Edinburgh: Edinburgh University Press.

Ackerman, Diane. 1990. *A Natural History of the Senses*. New York: Vintage Books.

Albright, Brian. 2012. *Regional Horror Films, 1958–1990: A State-by-State Guide with Interviews*. Jefferson, NC: McFarland & Company.

Anderson, Shaun. 2012. "Eaten Alive." *Celluloid Highway*, September 29. http://sonofcelluloid.blogspot.com/2012/09/eaten-alive-1977.html.

Andrews, Eleanor, Stella Hockenhull, and Fran Pheasant-Kelly. 2016. "Introduction." In *Spaces of the Cinematic Home: Behind the Screen Door*, eds. Eleanor Andrews, Stella Hockenhull, and Fran Pheasant-Kelly, 1–18. New York: Routledge.

Anon. 1929. "Theatre Screen Can Aid Local Authorities in Flu Situation." *Motion Picture News*, January 12, 126.

Anon. 1936. "Masters of Horror." *Movie Action Magazine*, February, 108–17.

Anon. 1936. "They're the Topics!" *Movie Classic*, February 8.

Anon. 2012. "Favorite Things About . . . *Creature from the Black Lagoon*." *The Motion Pictures*. https://themotionpictures.net/2012/10/24/favorite-things-about-creature-from-the-black-lagoon/.

Antonucci, Barbara. 2007. "Mediatic Metamorphosis and Postmodern Novels by Chuck Palahniuk, Bret Easton Ellis and Nick Hornby." In *Literary Intermediality: The Transit of Literature Through the Media Circuit*, ed. Maddalena Pennacchia Punzi, 163–82. Bern: Peter Lang.

Badley, Linda. 1995. *Film, Horror, and the Body Fantastic*. Westport, CT: Greenwood Press.

Badley, Linda. 1996. *Writing Horror and the Body: The Fiction of Stephen King, Clive Barker, and Anne Rice*. Westport, CT: Greenwood Press.

Bai, Meijadai. 2013. "Gothic Monster and Chinese Cultural Identity: Analysis of *The Note of Ghoul*." In *Thinking Dead: What the Zombie Apocalypse Means*, ed. Murali Balaji, 105–26. Lanham, MD: Lexington Books.

Bailey, Ian L., and Amanda Hall. 1989. *Visual Impairment: An Overview*. New York: American Foundation for the Blind.

Baird, Robert. 2000. "The Startle Effect: Implications for Spectator Cognition and Media Theory." *Film Quarterly* 53, no. 3 (Spring): 12–24.

Balázs, Béla. 1970. *Theory of Film: Character and Growth of a New Art*. New York: Dover.

Bampatzimopoulos, Sotirios. 2020. "*Jennifer's Body*." In *The Encyclopedia of Sexism in American Films*, eds. Salvador Jimenez Murguía, Erica Joan Dymond, and Kristina Fennelly, 181–84. Lanham, MD: Rowman & Littlefield.

Barton, Steve. 2012. "The Dead." *Dread Central*, January 25. https://www.dreadcentral.com/reviews/29878/dead-the-blu-ray-dvd/.

Beard, William. 2015. "Traces of Horror: The Later Films of David Cronenberg." In *The Canadian Horror Film: Terror of the Soul*, eds. Gina Freitag and André Loiselle, 209–30. Toronto: University of Toronto Press.

Belinkie, Matthew. 2010. "The Shocking Complexity of the *Saw* Movies." *Overthinking It*, October 26. https://www.overthinkingit.com/2010/10/26/saw-movies/.

Bell-Metereau, Rebecca. 2004. "Searching for Blobby Fissures: Slime, Sexuality, and the Grotesque." In *Bad: Infamy, Darkness, Evil, and Slime on Screen*, ed. Murray Pomerance, 287–300. Albany: State University of New York.

Bernard, Mark. 2013. "'LOOK AT ME': Serial Killing, Whiteness, and (In)visibility in the *Saw* Series." In *Murders and Acquisitions: Representations of the Serial Killer in Popular Culture*, ed. Alzena MacDonald, 85–104. New York: Bloomsbury Academic.

Blaisdell, George. 1913. "*Dr. Jekyll and Mr. Hyde*." *Moving Picture World*, March 1, 899.

Bonner, Hannah. 2016. "Top 12 Feminist Horror Films." *Den of Geek*, May 21. https://www.denofgeek.com/movies/top-12-feminist-horror-films/.

Bramesco, Charles. 2014. "Septic Man." *The Dissolve*, August 12. https://thedissolve.com/reviews/991-septic-man/.

Briefel, Aviva. 2015. *The Racial Hand in the Victorian Imagination*. Cambridge: Cambridge University Press.

Broderick, James F. 2012. *Now a Terrifying Motion Picture! Twenty-Five Classic Works of Horror Adapted from Book to Film*. Jefferson, NC: McFarland & Company.

Brogan, Jacqueline Vaught. 1986. *Stevens and Simile: A Theory of Language*. Princeton, NJ: Princeton University Press.

Brophy, Philip. 1986. "Horrality—The Textuality of Contemporary Horror Films." *Screen* 27, no. 1: 2–13.

Brown, Simon. 2018. *Screening Stephen King: Adaptation and the Horror Genre in Film and Television*. Austin, TX: University of Texas Press.

Brown, William. 2013. *Supercinema: Film-Philosophy for the Digital Age*. New York: Berghahn Books.

Canby, Vincent. 1976. "*Deep Red* Is a Bucket of Ax-Murder Clichés." *New York Times*, June 10, 58.

Carroll, Noël. 1999. "Film, Emotion, and Genre." In *Passionate Views: Film, Cognition, and Emotion*, eds. Carl Plantinga and Greg M. Smith, 21–47. Baltimore: Johns Hopkins University Press.

Chan Hok-shing, Brian. 2007. "Hybrid Language and Hybrid Identity? The Case of Cantonese-English Code-switching in Hong Kong." In *East-West Identities: Globalization, Localization, and Hybridization*, eds. Chan Kwok-bun, Jan W. Walls and David Hayward, 189–202. Leiden, The Netherlands: Koninklijke Brill.

Cherry, Brigid. 2002. "Refusing to Refuse to Look: Female Viewers of the Horror Film." In *Horror, the Film Reader*, ed. Mark Jancovich, 169–78. New York: Routledge.

Cherry, Brigid. 2009. *Horror*. London: Routledge.

Christensen, Kyle. 2011. "The Final Girl versus Wes Craven's *A New Nightmare on Elm Street*: Proposing a Stronger Model of Feminism in Slasher Horror Cinema." *Studies in Popular Culture* 34, no. 1: 23–47.

Chu, Yingchi. 2003. *Hong Kong Cinema: Coloniser, Motherland and Self*. New York: Routledge.

Church, David. 2021. *Post-Horror: Art, Genre and Cultural Elevation*. Edinburgh: Edinburgh University Press.

Clasen, Mathias. 2017. *Why Horror Seduces*. New York: Oxford University Press.

Classen, Constance, David Howes, and Anthony Synnott. 1994. *Aroma: The Cultural History of Smell*. New York: Routledge.

Clover, Carol. 1987. "Her Body, Himself: Gender in the Slasher Film." *Representations*, no. 20 (Autumn): 187–228.

Clover, Carol. 1992. *Men, Women, and Chain Saws: Gender in the Modern Horror Film*. Princeton, NJ: Princeton University Press.

Combs, C. Scott. 2014. *Deathwatch: American Film, Technology, and the End of Life*. New York: Columbia University Press.

Connolly, Ellen, and Mark Duell. 2012. "The Horror Movie So Terrifying It Made Audiences SICK." *Daily Mail*, January 31. https://www.dailymail.co.uk/news/article-2094187/V-H-S-horror-movie-Sundance-Film-Festivals-graphic-scenes-audiences-SICK.html.

Conterio, Martyn. 2015. *Black Sunday*. Leighton Buzzard, UK: Auteur.

Cooper, Ian. 2011. *Witchfinder General*. Leighton Buzzard, UK: Auteur.

Cooper, L. Andrew. 2012. *Dario Argento*, Urbana, IL: University of Illinois Press.

Cortez, Marisol. 2012. "From the Bedroom to the Bathroom, Stephen King's Scatology and the Emergence of an Urban Environmental Gothic." In *Fear and Nature: Ecohorror Studies in the Anthropocene*, eds. Christy Tidwell and Carter Soles, 153–73. University Park, PA: Pennsylvania State University Press.

Corupe, Paul. 2020. "Return of the Living Drive-In." *Rue Morgue*, no. 195 (July/August): 22–24.

Costanzo, William V. 2004. *Great Films and How to Teach Them*. Urbana: National Council of Teachers of English.

Costanzo, William V. 2014. *World Cinema through Global Genres*. West Sussex, UK: John Wiley & Sons.

Craig, Pamela, and Martin Fradley. 2010. "Teenage Traumata: Youth, Affective Politics, and the Contemporary American Horror Film." In *American Horror Film: The Genre at the Turn of the Millennium*, ed. Steffen Hantke, 77–102. Jackson: University Press of Mississippi.

Creed, Barbara. 1993. *The Monstrous-Feminine: Film, Feminism, Psychoanalysis*. New York: Routledge.

Creed, Barbara. 2015. "Horror and the Monstrous-Feminine: An Imaginary Abjection." In *The Dread of Difference: Gender and the Horror Film*, ed. Barry Keith Grant, 37–67. Austin: University of Texas Press.

Crowdus, Gary. 2017. "Cult Films, Commentary Tracks, and Censorious Critics: An Interview with John Bloom." In *Cineaste on Film Criticism, Programming, and Preservation in the New Millennium*, eds. Cynthia Lucia and Rahul Hamid, 234–46. Austin: University of Texas Press.

Dahlem, Greg. 2009. "House Fly: (Musca domestica)." In *Encyclopedia of Insects*, eds. Vincent H. Resh and Ring T. Cardé, 469–70. Burlington, MA: Academic Press.

Dancyger, Ken. 2010. *The Technique of Film and Video Editing: History, Theory, and Practice*. Burlington, MA: Focal Press.

Davies, Clive. 2015. *Spinegrinder: The Movies Most Critics Won't Write About*. London: Headpress.
Dee, John. 1931. "After Crooks—Spooks!" *The Bioscope*, May 6, 37.
Desser, David. 2000. "The Kung Fu Craze: Hong Kong Cinema's First American Reception." In *The Cinema of Hong Kong: History, Arts, Identity*, eds. Poshek Fu and David Desser, 19–43. Cambridge: Cambridge University Press.
Diffrient, David Scott. 2011. "TV Similes: Language, Community, and the Comparative Poetics of *Northern Exposure*." *Scope*, no. 21 (October): https://www.nottingham.ac.uk/scope/documents/2011/october-2011/diffrient.pdf.
Dixon, Wheeler W. 2010. *A History of Horror*. New Brunswick, NJ: Rutgers University Press.
Drain, Heather. 2016. "They are Just Like You: S. F. Brownrigg's *Scum of the Earth*." *Diabolique Magazine*. https://diaboliquemagazine.com/just-like-s-f-brownriggs-scum-earth/.
Dunn, Rob. 2018. *Never Home Alone: From Microbes to Millipedes, Camel Crickets, and Honeybees, the Natural History of Where We Live*. New York: Basic Books.
Ebert, Roger. 1989. *Roger Ebert's Movie Companion*, Kansas City, KS: Andrews and McMeel.
Elliott, Paul. 2011. *Hitchcock and the Cinema of Sensations: Embodied Film Theory and Cinematic Reception*. I. B. Tauris.
Elliott-Smith, Darren, and John Edgar Browning. 2020. "Introduction." In *New Queer Horror Film and Television*, eds. Darren Elliott-Smith and John Edgar Browning, 1–10. Wales: University of Wales Press.
Elsaesser, Thomas, and Malte Hagener. 2009. *Film Theory: An Introduction through the Senses*. New York: Routledge.
Everman, Welch D. 1993. *Cult Horror Films: From Attack of the 50 Foot Woman to Zombies of Mora Tau*. New York: Citadel Press.
Fahy, Thomas. 2019. *Dining with Madmen: Fat, Food, and the Environment in 1980s Horror*. Jackson: University Press of Mississippi.
Falvey, Eddie. 2021. "Revisiting the Female Monster: Sex and Monstrosity in Contemporary Body Horror." In *New Blood: Critical Approaches to Contemporary Horror*, eds. Eddie Falvey, Joe Hickinbottom, and Jonathan Wroot, 203–24. Wales: University of Wales Press.
Filipowicz, Chris. 2021. "Richard Styles' *Shallow Grave*." PopHorror.com, October 28. https://www.pophorror.com/richard-styles-shallow-grave-1987-2k-restoration-by-vinegar-syndrome-review/.
Fleming, Mike, Jr. 2012. "Moviegoer Faints in *V/H/S* Midnight Screening: Sundance." Deadline.com, January 25. http://deadline.com/2012/01/moviegoer-faints-in-vhs-midnight-screening-sundance-220225/.
Ford, Brian J. 2013. "Shining the Spotlight on Movie Microbes." *The Microscope*, 63–73.
Frey, Mattias. 2015a. "Introduction: Critical Questions." In *Film Criticism in the Digital Age*, eds. Mattias Frey and Cecilia Sayad. New Brunswick, NJ: Rutgers University Press, 1–20.
Frey, Mattias. 2015b. "The New Democracy? Rotten Tomatoes, Metacritic, Twitter, and IMDb." In *Film Criticism in the Digital Age*, eds. Mattias Frey and Cecilia Sayad, 81–98. New Brunswick, NJ: Rutgers University Press.
Fryer, Ian. 2017. *The British Horror Film: From the Silent to the Multiplex*. Millview, UK: Fonthill Media.
Gelder, Ken, ed. 2000. *The Horror Reader*. New York: Routledge.
Gilbert, Morris. 1930. "Parisian Cinema Chatter." *New York Times*, February 9, X6.
Givens, Bill. 1989. *Film Flubs: Memorable Movie Mistakes*. New York: Citadel.

Glasby, Matt. 2020. *The Book of Horror: The Anatomy of Fear in Film*. London: Frances Lincoln.

Glynn, Kevin. 2017. *Gasping for Air: How Breathing is Killing Us and What We Can Do About It*. Lanham, MD: Rowman & Littlefield.

Grady, Constance. 2018. "How *Jennifer's Body* Went from a Flop in 2009 to a Feminist Cult Classic Today." *Vox*, October 31. https://www.vox.com/culture/2018/10/31/18037996/jennifers-body-flop-cult-classic-feminist-horror.

Grant, Barry Keith. 2007. "Children of the Day: Sex, Gender, and the New Horror Film." In *Beauty and the Abject: Interdisciplinary Perspectives*, eds. Leslie Anne Boldt-Irons, Corrado Federici, and Ernesto Virgulti, 3–16. New York: Peter Lang Publishing.

Grant, Barry Keith. 2015. "Introduction." In *The Dread of Difference: Gender and the Horror Film*, ed. Barry Keith Grant, 1–16. Austin: University of Texas Press.

Grunzke, Andrew. 2015. *Educational Institutions in Horror Film: A History of Mad Professors, Student Bodies, and Final Exams*. New York: Palgrave Macmillan.

Guihot, Julie. 2012. "Cinema: A 'Thing' of Transformation." In *Rhizomes: Connecting Languages, Cultures and Literatures*, eds. Nathalie Ramière and Rachel Varshney. Newcastle: Cambridge Scholars Publishing.

Gunning, Tom. 1994. *D. W. Griffith and the Origins of American Narrative Film: The Early Years at Biograph*. Urbana: University of Illinois Press.

Gunning, Tom. 2007. "To Scan a Ghost: The Ontology of Mediated Vision." *Grey Room*, no. 26 (Winter): 94–127.

Hague, Ian. 2014. *Comics and the Senses: A Multisensory Approach to Comics and Graphic Novels*. New York: Routledge, 2014.

Halberstam, Jack. 1995. *Skin Shows: Gothic Horror and the Technology of Monsters*. Durham, NC: Duke University Press.

Hallenbeck, Bruce G. 2003. *Comedy-Horror Films: A Chronological History, 1914–2008*. Jefferson, NC: McFarland & Co.

Halliburton, David. 1973. *Edgar Allan Poe: A Phenomenological View*. Princeton, NJ: Princeton University Press.

Hammond, Stefan, and Mike Wilkins. 1996. *Sex and Zen & A Bullet in the Head: The Essential Guide to Hong Kong's Mind-bending Films*. New York: Fireside.

Hanich, Julian. 2010. *Cinematic Emotion in Horror Films and Thrillers: The Aesthetic Paradox of Pleasurable Fear*. New York: Routledge.

Hanich, Julian. 2018. *The Audience Effect: On the Collective Cinema Experience*. Edinburgh: Edinburgh University Press.

Harrington, Erin. 2018. *Women, Monstrosity and Horror Film: Gynaehorror*, New York: Routledge.

Haupt, Melanie. 2008. "This Kitty's Got Claws." *Austin Chronicle*, January 25. https://www.austinchronicle.com/screens/2008-01-25/584326/.

Hawkins, Joan. 2000. *Cutting Edge: Art-Horror and the Horrific Avant-Garde*. Minneapolis: University of Minnesota Press.

Heffernan, Kevin. 2009. "Inner Senses and the Changing Face of Hong Kong Horror Cinema." In *Horror to the Extreme: Changing Boundaries in Asian Cinema*, eds. Jinhee Choi and Mitsuyo Wada-Marciano, 57–68. Hong Kong: Hong Kong University Press.

Heller-Nicholas, Alexandra. 2021. *The Giallo Canvas: Art, Excess and Horror Cinema*. Jefferson, NC: McFarland & Company.

Henry, Claire. 2014. *Revisionist Rape-Revenge: Redefining a Film Genre*. New York: Palgrave Macmillan.

Higham, George. 2020. *Wax Museum Movies: A Comprehensive Filmography*. Jefferson, NC: McFarland & Company.

Hill, Derek. 2000. "The Face of Horror." In *The Horror Film Reader*, eds. Alain Silver and James Ursini, 51–62. Pompton Plains, NJ: Limelight.

Hillman, Gordon. 1933. "Keith's Has Rare Screen Thriller in *The Mummy*." *Boston Daily Record* (compiled in *Universal Weekly*), February 18, 14.

Hills, Matt. 2005. *The Pleasures of Horror*. London: Continuum.

Hobbs, Simon. 2018. *Cultivating Extreme Art Cinema: Text, Paratext and Home Video Culture*. Edinburgh: Edinburgh University Press.

Hoberman, J. 2010. "*Psycho* Is 50: Remembering Its Impact, and the Andrew Sarris Review." *Village Voice*, June 15. https://www.villagevoice.com/2010/06/15/psycho-is-50-remembering-its-impact-and-the-andrew-sarris-review/.

Horsley, Jasun. 2015. *Seen and Not Seen: Confessions of a Movie Autist*. Alresford, Hants: Zero Books.

Howarth, Troy. 2021. *Unholy Communion: Alice, Sweet Alice, From Script to Screen*. BearManor Media.

Hunter, I. Q. 2014. "Trash Horror and the Cult of the Bad Film." In *A Companion to the Horror Film*, ed. Harry M. Benshoff, 483–500. West Sussex, UK: John Wiley & Sons.

Hutchings, Peter. 2008. *The A to Z of Horror Cinema*. Lanham, MD: Scarecrow Press.

Hutchings, Peter. 2018. *Historical Dictionary of Horror Cinema*. Lanham, MD: Rowman & Littlefield.

Isaacs, Bruce. 2020. *The Art of Pure Cinema: Hitchcock and His Imitators*. Oxford: Oxford University Press.

Jancovich, Mark. 2014. "Horror in the 1940s." In *A Companion to the Horror Film*, ed. Harry M. Benshoff, 237–54. West Sussex, UK: John Wiley & Sons.

Jenner, Mark. 2000. "Civilization and Deodorization? Smell in Early Modern English Culture." In *Civil Histories: Essays Presented to Sir Keith Thomas*, eds. Peter Burke, Brian Howard Harrison, Paul Slack, and Keith Thomas, 127–44. Oxford, UK: Oxford University Press.

Jones, Steve. 2013. *Torture Porn: Popular Horror after Saw*. New York: Palgrave Macmillan.

Kane, Joe. 2010. *Night of the Living Dead: Behind the Scenes of the Most Terrifying Zombie Movie Ever*. New York: Citadel Press.

Kattelman, Beth A. 2010. "Carnographic Culture: America and the Rise of the Torture Porn Film." In *The Domination of Fear*, ed. Mikko Canini, 1–15. Amsterdam: Rodopi.

Kawin, Bruce. 2012. *Horror and the Horror Film*. New York: Anthem Press.

Keeley, Sean. 2018. "15 Years Later, Good-Bad Movie *Dreamcatcher* Remains Baffling in the Best Way." *The Comeback*, March 21. https://thecomeback.com/films/dreamcatcher-movie-stephen-king-15th-anniversary.html.

Kellner, Douglas. 1989. "David Cronenberg: Panic Horror and the Postmodern Body." *Canadian Journal of Political and Social Theory* 13, no. 3: 89–101.

Kelly, Casey Ryan. 2016. "Camp Horror and the Gendered Politics of Screen Violence: Subverting the Monstrous-Feminine in *Teeth* (2007)." *Women's Studies in Communication* 39, no. 1: 86–106.

Kermode, Mark. 2008. "DVD of the Week: *Teeth.*" *The Guardian*, October 19. https://www.theguardian.com/film/2008/oct/19/horror-dvdreviews.

Kern, Laura. 2010. "Best Worst Movie." *Film Comment* 46, no. 3 (May/June): 72.

Kinder, Marsha. 1993. *Blood Cinema: The Reconstruction of National Identity in Spain*. Los Angeles: University of California Press.

King, Charles. 1997. "*Dr. Jekyll and Mr. Hyde*: A Filmography." *Journal of Popular Film and Television* 25, no. 1: 9–20.

King, Stephen. 2001. *Dreamcatcher: A Novel*. New York: Pocket Books.

King, Stephen. 2010. *Danse Macabre*. New York: Gallery Books.

King, Stephen. 2012. *Night Shift*. New York: Anchor Books.

King, Stephen. 2018. *The Body*. New York: Scribner.

King, Stephen. 2018. *Needful Things*. New York: Gallery Books.

King, Stephen. 2018. *The Tommyknockers*. New York: Gallery Books.

Kord, T. S. 2016. *Little Horrors: How Cinema's Evil Children Play on Our Guilt*. Jefferson, NC: McFarland & Company.

Koszarski, Richard. 1994. *An Evening's Entertainment: The Age of the Silent Feature Picture, 1915–1928*. Berkeley, CA: University of California Press.

Kracauer, Siegfried. 2004. "Remarks on the Actor." In *Movie Acting: The Film Reader*, ed. Pamela Robertson Wojcik, 19–27. New York: Routledge.

Kristeva, Julia. 1982. *Powers of Horror: An Essay on Abjection*. New York: Columbia University Press.

Kuleshov, Lev. 1974. *Kuleshov on Film: Writings*, trans. Ronald Levaco. Berkeley, CA: University of California Press.

Kyrölä, Katariina. 2016. *The Weight of Images: Affect, Body Image and Fat in the Media*. New York: Routledge.

Landis, John. 2011. *Monsters in the Movies*. New York: DK.

Langford, Barry. 2005. *Film Genre: Hollywood and Beyond*. Edinburgh: Edinburgh University Press.

Lázaro-Reboll, Antonio. 2012. *Spanish Horror Film*. Edinburgh: Edinburgh University Press.

Leeder, Murray. 2016. "The Humor of William Castle's Gimmick Films." In *The Laughing Dead: The Horror-Comedy Film from Bride of Frankenstein to Zombieland*, eds. Cynthia J. Miller and A. Bowdoin Van Riper, 87–101. Lanham, MD: Rowman & Littlefield.

Leeder, Murray. 2018. *Horror Film: A Critical Introduction*. New York: Bloomsbury Academic.

Le Fanu, Joseph Sheridan. 1964. *Best Ghost Stories of J. S. LeFanu*. New York: Dover Publications.

Le Guérer, Annick. 1992. *Scent, the Mysterious and Essential Powers of Smell*. New York: Random House.

Le Guérer, Annick. 2002. "Olfaction and Cognition: A Philosophical and Psychoanalytic View." In *Olfaction, Taste, and Cognition*, eds. Catherine Rouby, Benoist Schaal, Danièle Dubois, Rémi Gervais, and A. Holley, 3–15. Cambridge, UK: Cambridge University Press.

Lehman, Peter. 1993. "'Don't Blame This on a Girl': Female Rape-Revenge Films." In *Screening the Male: Exploring Masculinities in the Hollywood Cinema*, eds. Steve Cohan and Ina Rae Hark, 103–17. New York: Routledge.

Leitch, Thomas M. 2000. "101 Ways to Tell Hitchcock's *Psycho* from Gus Van Sant's." *Literature/Film Quarterly* 28, no. 4: 269–73.

Lerner, Neil. 2010. "The Strange Case of Rouben Mamoulian's Sound Stew: The Uncanny Soundtrack in *Dr. Jekyll and Mr. Hyde* (1931)." In *Music in the Horror Film: Listening to Fear*, ed. Neil Lerner, 55–79. New York: Routledge, 2010.

Lindner, Katharina. 2017. *Film Bodies: Queer Feminist Encounters with Gender and Sexuality in Cinema*. London: I. B. Tauris.

Lockwood, Jeffrey. 2013. "How to Cultivate Disgust." *The Atlantic*, October 29. https://www.theatlantic.com/health/archive/2013/10/how-to-cultivate-disgust/280858/.

Loiselle, André. 2003. *Stage-Bound: Feature Film Adaptations of Canadian and Québécois Drama*. Montreal: McGill-Queen's Press.

Lowenstein, Adam. 2014. *Dreaming of Cinema: Spectatorship, Surrealism, and the Age of Digital Media*. New York: Columbia University Press.

Mank, Gregory William. 2010. *Hollywood Cauldron: Thirteen Horror Films from the Genre's Golden Age*. Jefferson, NC: McFarland & Company.

Marcucci, Dario. 2020. "Strangers at the Door: Space and Characters in Home Invasion Movies." In *The Spaces and Places of Horror*, eds. Francesco Pascuzzi and Sandra Waters, 251–64. Wilmington, DE: Vernon Press.

Marks, Laura U. 2002. *Touch: Sensuous Theory and Multisensory Media*. Minneapolis: University of Minnesota Press.

Marks, Laura U. 2013. "Thinking Multisensory Culture." In *Carnal Aesthetics: Transgressive Imagery and Feminist Politics*, eds. Bettina Papenburg and Marta Zarzycka, 144–57. London: I. B. Tauris & Co.

Marriott, James, and Kim Newman. 2018. *The Definitive Guide to Horror Movies*. London: Carlton Books.

Martin, Scott. 2016. "'King for a Day': Performance and Expression in the Cinematic Space of the Basement." In *Spaces of the Cinematic Home: Behind the Screen Door*, eds. Eleanor Andrews, Stella Hockenhull, and Fran Pheasant-Kelly, 45–59. New York: Routledge.

Mathijs, Ernest. 2013. *John Fawcett's Ginger Snaps*. Toronto: University of Toronto Press.

McCloud, Sean. 2010. "New and Homegrown Religions." In *The Blackwell Companion to Religion in America*, ed. Philip Goff, 636–48. Blackwell Publishing.

McCormack, Olivia. 2021. "*Jennifer's Body* Has Become a Hallmark of Queer Horror." *The Lilly*, October 30. https://www.thelily.com/jennifers-body-has-become-a-hallmark-of-queer-horror-these-fans-explain-why/.

McDonagh, Maitland. 1994. *Broken Mirrors/Broken Minds: The Dark Dreams of Dario Argento*. New York, Citadel Press.

McGinn, Colin. 2012. "*The Fly* and the Human: Ironies of Disgust." In *The Philosophy of David Cronenberg*, ed. Simon Riches. Lexington: University Press of Kentucky.

Means Coleman, Robin R. 2011. *Horror Noire: Blacks in American Horror Films from the 1890s to Present*. New York: Routledge.

Mitamura, Keiko. 2002. "Daoist Hand Signs and Buddhist Mudras." In *Daoist Identity: History, Lineage, and Ritual*, eds. Livia Kohn and Harold D. Roth, 235–55. Honolulu: University of Hawai'i Press.

Morgart, James. 2013. "Gothic Horror Film from *The Haunted Castle* (1896) to *Psycho* (1960)." In *The Gothic World*, eds. Glennis Byron and Dale Townshend, 276–87. New York: Routledge.

Morton, Lisa. 2001. *The Cinema of Tsui Hark*. Jefferson, NC: McFarland & Company.

Muir, John Kenneth. 2002. *Horror Films of the 1970s*. Jefferson, NC: McFarland & Company.

Muir, John Kenneth. 2004. *The Unseen Force: The Films of Sam Raimi*. New York: Applause Theatre & Cinema Books.

Muir, John Kenneth. 2019. *Horror Films of the 1990s*. Jefferson, NC: McFarland & Company.

Mulvey-Roberts, Marie. 2016. *Dangerous Bodies: Historicising the Gothic Corporeal*. Manchester, UK: Manchester University Press.

Murphy, Bernice M. 2013. *The Rural Gothic in American Popular Culture: Backwoods Horror and Terror in the Wilderness*. New York: Palgrave Macmillan.

Murray, Noel. 2011. "Santa Sangre." *AV Club*, February 9. https://www.avclub.com/santa-sangre-1798167188.

Nair, Kartik. 2021. "Unfinished Bodies: The Sticky Materiality of Prosthetic Effects," *JCMS: Journal of Cinema and Media Studies* 60, no. 3: 104–28.

Nayman, Adam. 2021. "The Best Horror Movies of 2021 (So Far)." *The Ringer*, April 28. https://www.theringer.com/movies/2021/4/28/22406653/best-horror-movies-2021.

Ndalianis, Angela. 2012. *The Horror Sensorium: Media and the Senses*. Jefferson, NC: McFarland & Co.

Neale, Steve. 1990. "'You've Got to Be Fucking Kidding!': Knowledge, Belief and Judgement in Science Fiction." In *Alien Zone: Cultural Theory and Contemporary Science Fiction Cinema*, ed. Annette Kuhn, 160–68. London: Verso.

Newman, Kim. 2011. *Nightmare Movies: Horror on Screen Since the 1960s*. New York: Bloomsbury Publishing.

Nguyen, Ed. 2002. "Review: Iron Monkey," *DVD Movie Central*, March 26. http://www.dvdmoviecentral.com/ReviewsText/iron_monkey.htm.

Nowell, Richard. 2011. *Blood Money: A History of the First Teen Slasher Film Cycle*. New York: Continuum International Publishing Group.

Nuland, Sherwin B. 1993. *How We Die: Reflections on Life's Final Chapter*. New York: Knopf.

O'Brien, Daniel. 2003. *Spooky Encounters: A Gwailo's Guide to Hong Kong Horror*. Manchester: Headpress.

Och, Dana, and Kirsten Strayer. 2014. "Introduction." In *Transnational Horror Across Visual Media: Fragmented Bodies*, eds. Dana Och and Kirsten Strayer, 1–16. New York: Routledge.

Olszowka, John, Marnie M. Sullivan, Brian R. Sheridan, and Dennis Hickey. 2014. *America in the Thirties*. Syracuse: Syracuse University Press.

O'Pray, Michael. 2003. *Avant-garde Film: Forms, Themes and Passions*. London: Wallflower Press.

Ornsdorf, Brian. 2009. "The Collector," *DVD Talk*, July 31. https://www.dvdtalk.com/reviews/38051/collector-the/.

Palmer, James, and Michael Riley. 1995. "Seeing, Believing, and 'Knowing' in Narrative Film: Don't Look Now Revisited." *Literature Film Quarterly* 23, no. 1: 14–25.

Paszkiewicz, Katarzyna. 2018. *Genre, Authorship and Contemporary Women Filmmakers*. Edinburgh: Edinburgh University Press.

Perkins, Claire, and Constantine Verevis. 2014. "Introduction." In *B is for Bad Cinema: Aesthetics, Politics, and Cultural Value*, eds. Claire Perkins and Constantine Verevis, 1–18. Albany: State University of New York Press.

Perry, Dennis R. 2017. "The Recombinant Mystery of Frankenstein: Experiments in Film Adaptation." In *The Oxford Handbook of Adaptation Studies*, ed. Thomas Leitch, 137–53. New York: Oxford University Press.

Petley, Julian. 2017. "Horror and the Censors." In *A Companion to the Horror Film*, ed. Harry Benshoff, 130–48. West Sussex, UK: John Wiley & Sons.

Pettigrove, Cedrick. 2005. *The Esoteric Codex: Supernatural Legends*. Creative Commons Attribution 2.0.

Peucker, Brigitte. 2007. *The Material Image: Art and the Real in Film*. Stanford, CA: Stanford University Press.

Pheasant-Kelly, Frances. 2013. *Abject Spaces in American Cinema: Institutional Settings, Identity and Psychoanalysis in Film*. London: I. B. Tauris.

Phillips, Kendall R. 2005. *Projected Fears: Horror Films and American Culture*. Westport, CT: Praeger Publishers.

Phillips, Kendall R. 2018. *A Place of Darkness: The Rhetoric of Horror in Early American Cinema*. Austin: University of Texas Press.

Piatti-Farnell, Lorna. 2017. *Consuming Gothic: Food and Horror in Film*. London: Palgrave Macmillan.

Pinedo, Isabel Cristina. 1996. "Recreational Terror: Postmodern Elements of the Contemporary Horror Film." *Journal of Film and Video* 48, nos. 1–2 (Spring/Summer): 17–31.

Pinedo, Isabel Cristina. 1997. *Recreational Terror: Women and the Pleasures of Horror Film Viewing*. Albany: State University of New York Press.

Plantinga, Carl. 1999. "The Scene of Empathy and the Human Face on Film." In *Passionate Views: Film, Cognition, and Emotion*, eds. Carl Plantinga and Greg M. Smith, 239–56. Baltimore: Johns Hopkins University Press.

Plantinga, Carl. 2009. *Moving Viewers: American Film and the Spectator's Experience*. Los Angeles: University of California Press.

Poe, Edgar Allan. 2015. *The Annotated Poe*, ed. Kevin J. Hayes. Cambridge, MA: Harvard University Press.

Pollard, Tom. 2016. *Loving Vampires: Our Undead Obsession*. Jefferson, NC: McFarland & Company.

Purse, Lisa. 2016. "The New Hollywood, 1981–1999: Special/Visual Effects." In *Editing and Special/Visual Effects*, eds. Charlie Keil and Kristen Whissel, 142–55. New Brunswick, NJ: Rutgers University Press.

Quinlivan, Davina. 2012. *The Place of Breath in Cinema*. Edinburgh: Edinburgh University Press.

Reinarz, Jonathan. 2014. *Past Scents: Historical Perspectives on Smell*. Urbana: University of Illinois.

Reyes, Xavier Aldana. 2016. *Horror Film and Affect: Towards a Corporeal Model of Viewership*. New York: Routledge.

Rhodes, Gary D. 2001. *White Zombie: Anatomy of a Horror Film*. Jefferson, NC: McFarland & Company.

Rhodes, Gary D. 2018. *The Birth of the American Horror Film*. Edinburgh: Edinburgh University Press.

Rickels, Laurence. 2016. *The Psycho Records*. New York: Columbia University Press.

Robertson, Kate. 2018. "13 Feminist Horror Movies That Will Make You Appreciate the Genre in a Whole New Way." *Marie Claire*, July 19. https://www.marieclaire.com/culture/news/a28961/best-horror-movies/.

Rosenberg, Scott. 1995. "Murphy Sinks His Teeth into Vampire Comedy." *San Francisco Examiner*, October 27. https://www.sfgate.com/news/article/Murphy-sinks-his-teeth-into-Vampire-comedy-3124874.php.

Ryan, Danielle. 2021. "*Bingo Hell* Director Gigi Saul Guerrero Dishes on Slime and Senior Citizens." *SlashFilm.com*, October 1. https://www.slashfilm.com/621338/bingo-hell-director-gigi-saul-guerrero-dishes-on-slime-and-senior-citizens-interview/.

Schaefer, Dennis, and Larry Salvato. 2013. *Masters of Light: Conversations with Contemporary Cinematographers*. Berkeley: University of California Press.

Sconce, Jeffrey. 1995. "'Trashing' the Academy: Taste, Excess, and an Emerging Politics of Cinematic Style." *Screen* 36, no. 4: 371–93.

Sconce, Jeffrey. 2003. "Esper, the Renunciator: Teaching 'Bad' Movies to Good Students." In *Defining Cult Movies: The Cultural Politics of Oppositional Tastes*, eds. Mark Jancovich, Antonio Lazaro Reboll, Julian Stringer, and Andy Willis, 14–34. Manchester: Manchester University Press.

Sconce, Jeffrey. 2014. "Explosive Apathy," in *B is for Bad Cinema: Aesthetics, Politics, and Cultural Value*, Claire Perkins and Constantine Verevis (eds.), Albany, NY: State University of New York, 21–42.

Sevastakis, Michael. 1985. "The Stylistic Coding of Characters in Mamoulian's *Dr. Jekyll and Mr. Hyde*." *Journal of Film and Video*, vol. 37, no 4 (Fall): 12–26.

Shelley, Peter. 2012. *Australian Horror Films, 1973–2010*. Jefferson, NC: McFarland & Company.

Shipka, Danny. 2011. *Perverse Titillation: The Exploitation Cinema of Italy, Spain and France, 1960–1980*. Jefferson, NC: McFarland & Company.

Showalter, Elaine. 2000. "Dr. Jekyll's Closet." In *The Horror Reader*, ed. Ken Gelder, 190–97. New York: Routledge.

Sikov, Ed. 2010. *Film Studies: An Introduction*. New York: Columbia University Press.

Sipos, Thomas M. 2010. *Horror Film Aesthetics: Creating the Visual Language of Fear*, Jefferson, NC: McFarland & Company.

Smith, Barry C. 2015. "The Chemical Senses." In *The Oxford Handbook of Philosophy of Perception*, ed. Mohan Matthen, 314–52. New York: Oxford University Press.

Smith, Don G. 2006. *H.P. Lovecraft in Popular Culture: The Works and Their Adaptations in Film, Television, Comics, Music and Games*. Jefferson, NC: McFarland & Company.

Smuts, Aaron. 2002. "The Principles of Association: Dario Argento's *Profondo rosso*." *Kinoeye* 2, no. 11 (June 10). http://www.kinoeye.org/02/11/smuts11.php.

Smuts, Aaron. 2003. "Haunting the House from Within: Disbelief Mitigation and Spatial Experience." In *Dark Thoughts: Philosophic Reflections on Cinematic Horror*, eds. Steven Jay Schneider and Daniel Shaw, 158–73. Lanham, MD: Scarecrow Press.

Smuts, Aaron. 2014. "Cognitive and Philosophical Approaches to Horror." In *A Companion to the Horror Film*, ed. Harry M. Benshoff, 3–20. West Sussex, UK: John Wiley & Sons.

Sobchack, Vivian. 1992. *The Address of the Eye: A Phenomenology of Film Experience*. Princeton, NJ: Princeton University Press.

Sobchack, Vivian. 2004. *Carnal Thoughts: Embodiment and Moving Image Culture*. Los Angeles: University of California Press.

Sobchack, Vivian. 2013. "The Dream Olfactory: On Making Scents of Cinema." In *Carnal Aesthetics: Transgressive Imagery and Feminist Politics*, eds. Bettina Papenburg and Marta Zarzycka, 121–43. London: I. B. Tauris & Co.

Stanfield, Peter. 2011. *Maximum Movies: Pulp Fictions: Film Culture and the Worlds of Samuel Fuller, Mickey Spillane, and Jim Thompson*. New Brunswick, NJ: Rutgers University Press.

Stull, William. 1932. "Concerning Cinematography." *American Cinematographer* 12, no. 11 (March): 22–24.

Szeto, Mirana May, and Yun-chung Chen. 2015. "Hong Kong Cinema in the Age of Neoliberalization and Mainlandization." In *A Companion to Hong Kong Cinema*, eds. Esther M. K. Cheung, Gina Marchetti, and Esther C. M. Yau, 89–115. West Sussex, UK: John Wiley & Sons.

Thomas, Eric Austin. 2015. "Camera Grammar: First-Person Point of View and the Divided 'I' in Rouben Mamoulian's 1931 *Dr. Jekyll and Mr. Hyde*." *Quarterly Review of Film and Video* 32, no. 7: 660–66.

Thrower, Stephen. 2014. "*Don't Look in the Basement*." *Horrorpedia*. https://horrorpedia.com/2014/01/13/dont-look-in-the-basement-1972-horror-film-s-f-brownrigg-cast-plot-review-trailer/.

Thurman, Trace. 2020. "The Public's Perception of the Penis in Horror." *Certified Forgotten*, November 3. https://certifiedforgotten.com/penis-horror/.

Tombs, Pete. 1998. *Mondo Macabro: Weird and Wonderful Cinema Around the World*. New York: Macmillan.

Totaro, Donato. 2003. "The Italian Zombie Film: From Derivation to Reinvention." In *Fear Without Frontiers: Horror Cinema Across the Globe*, ed. Steven Schneider. Godalming, Britain: FAB Press.

Turner, George E. 2020. "Two-Faced Treachery: *Dr. Jekyll and Mr. Hyde*." *American Cinematographer*, October 30. https://ascmag.com/articles/two-faced-treachery-dr-jekyll-and-mr-hyde.

Vander Kaay, Chris, and Kathleen Fernandez-Vander Kaay. 2016. *Horror Films by Subgenre: A Viewer's Guide*, Jefferson, NC: McFarland & Company.

de Ville, Donna. 2010. "Menopausal Monsters and Sexual Transgression in Argento's Art Horror." In *Cinema Inferno: Celluloid Explosions from the Cultural Margins*, eds. Robert G. Weiner and John Cline, 53–75. Lanham, MD: Scarecrow Press.

de Vos, Gail. 2012. *What Happens Next? Contemporary Urban Legends and Popular Culture*. Santa Barbara, CA: ABC-CLIO.

Vrabel, Ani. 2009. "Jennifer's Body." *Paste*, September 21. https://www.pastemagazine.com/movies/diablo-cody/jennifers-body/.

Waddell, Calum. 2018. *Minds of Fear: 30 Cult Classics of the Modern Horror Film*. Albany, GA: BearManor Media.

Walker, Johnny. 2022. "Activist Horror Film: The Genre as Tool for Change." *New Review of Film and Television Studies* 20, no. 2: 194–219.

Waters, Sandra. 2020. "Surveillance, Narrative, and Spectatorship in Recent American Horror Films." In *The Spaces and Places of Horror*, eds. Francesco Pascuzzi and Sandra Waters, 41–54. Wilmington, DE: Vernon Press.

Weaver, Tom. 2003. *Eye on Science Fiction: 20 Interviews with Classic SF and Horror Filmmakers*, Jefferson, NC: McFarland & Company.

Weaver, Tom, David Schecter, Robert J. Kiss, and Steven Kronenberg. 2017. *Universal Terrors, 1951–1955: Eight Classic Horror and Science Fiction Films*. Jefferson, NC: McFarland & Company.

Weaver, William R. 1953. "*Abbott & Costello Meet Dr. Jekyll and Mr. Hyde*." *Motion Picture Daily*, July 24, 2.

Weismann, Brad. 2021. *Lost in the Dark: A World History of Horror Film*. Jackson: University Press of Mississippi.

Wenson, Rebecca. 2020. "The Demonization of Fat Bodies in Horror." *Medium.Com*, August 11. https://medium.com.
West, Alexandra. 2018. *The 1990s Teen Horror Cycle: Final Girls and a New Hollywood Formula*. Jefferson, NC: McFarland & Company.
White, Dennis L. 1971. "The Poetics of Horror: More than Meets the Eye." *Cinema Journal* 10, no. 2 (Spring): 1–18.
Williams, Linda. 1976. "The Prologue to *Un Chien Andalou*: A Surrealist Film Metaphor." *Screen*, vol. 17, no. 4 (Winter): 23–33.
Williams, Linda. 1991. "Film Bodies: Gender, Genre, and Excess." *Film Quarterly* 44, no. 4: 2–13.
Williams, Linda. 2000. "Discipline and Fun: *Psycho* and Postmodern Cinema." In *Reinventing Film Studies*, eds. Christine Gledhill and Linda Williams, 351–78. London: Arnold.
Williams, Tony. 2014. *Hearths of Darkness: The Family in the American Horror Film*. Jackson: University Press of Mississippi.
Willis, Andrew. 2005. "The Spanish Horror Film as Subversive Text: Eloy de la Igelsia's *La Semana del Asesino*." In *Horror International*, eds. Steven Jay Schneider and Tony Williams, 163–79. Detroit, MI: Wayne State University Press.
Willis, Donald C. 2019. *Chronology of Classic Horror Films: The 1930s*. Parkville, MD: Midnight Marquee Press.
Wilson, Laura. 2015. *Spectatorship, Embodiment and Physicality in the Contemporary Mutilation Film*. New York: Palgrave Macmillan.
Wilson, Lena. 2020. "Jennifer's Body & Me." *New York Times*, August 8, C1.
Wilson, Scott. 2011. *The Politics of Insects: David Cronenberg's Cinema of Confrontation*. New York: Continuum.
Winkler, Martin M. 2020. *Ovid on Screen: A Montage of Attractions*. Cambridge: Cambridge University Press.
Woodward, Ben. 2012. *Slime Dynamics*. Alresford Hants, UK: Zero Books.
Worland, Rick. 2007. *The Horror Film: An Introduction*. Malden, MA: Blackwell Publishing.
Yeshurun, Yaara, and Noam Sobel. 2010. "An Odor is Not Worth a Thousand Words: From Multidimensional Odors to Unidimensional Odor Objects." *Annual Review of Psychology* 61, no. 1: 219–41.
Young, Harvey. 2005. "The Black Body as Souvenir in American Lynching." *Theatre Journal* 57, no. 4 (December): 639–57.
Yuan, Jada. 2012. "An A to Z Guide to Cannes' Weirdest Film, *Holy Motors*." *Vulture*, May 29. https://www.vulture.com/2012/05/holy-motors-cannes-weirdest-film.html.
Yue, Audrey. 2000. "Preposterous Hong Kong Horror: *Rouge*'s (Be)Hindsight and a (Sodomitical) *Chinese Ghost Story*." In *The Horror Reader*, ed. Ken Gelder, 364–73. New York: Routledge.
Yue, Genevieve. 2021. *Girl Head: Feminism and Film Materiality*. New York: Fordham University Press.
Žižek, Slavoj. 1997. *The Plague of Fantasies*. New York: Verso.

INDEX

abattoir, 169, 171, 190, 192. *See also* slaughterhouse
Abbott, Bruce, 3
Abbott, Stacey, 72, 74, 156
Abbott & Costello Meet Dr. Jekyll and Mr. Hyde (film), 34
ABCs of Death, The (film), 68
abdomens, 59, 88, 146, 249, 260
abjection, 54, 55, 76, 84, 86, 116, 145, 161, 179, 181, 196, 204, 208, 214, 220, 226–28, 231, 276n2
ableism, 6, 14, 93, 132
abnormality, 23. *See also* normality
Absent-Minded Professor, The (film), 236
abstinence, 68
Acacia (film), 257
Achilles tendons, 46
Ackerman, Diane, 171, 173, 182, 186
Adamson, Al, 75
adaptations, 32, 44, 88, 93, 155, 180, 187, 206, 207, 213, 232, 247
Addams Family, The (TV series), 257
aesthetics, 7, 10, 12, 122, 141, 192, 199, 203, 231, 232; counter-, 194
affects, 5, 8, 9, 17, 56, 78, 101, 126, 143, 163, 166, 176, 204, 242, 245, 267
African Americans, 109–10, 112, 148, 155, 275n1
Aftermath (film), 46
Aguirre, Javier, 153
AIDS, 74
air fresheners, 189–91, 192, 193, 195
Aja, Alexandre, 268, 272n3
Alamo Drafthouse, 68, 71

Albright, Brian, 4, 7
Alda, Rutanya, 218
Alexander, Chris, 274n6
Alice, Sweet, Alice (film), 179–80, 195
Alien (film), 204, 255
Aliens (film), 277
Alimony (film), 271n1
Almendros, Néstor, 36
Álvarez, Fede, 132, 143, 168
American Humane, 15, 113, 119
American Mary (film), 67
American Werewolf in London, An (film), 35, 107
Amirpour, Ana Lily, 93
Amityville: A New Generation (film), 220
Amityville: It's About Time (film), 10, 218, 220, 226–27, 228, 277n5
Amityville: No Escape (film), 189, 221
Amityville: The Awakening (film), 221
Amityville Asylum, The (film), 186
Amityville Curse, The (film), 218
Amityville Dollhouse (film), 220, 221
Amityville 4: The Evil Escapes (film), 10, 218, 219, 220–21
Amityville Horror, The (film), 9, 172, 196, 213–15, 217, 222–23, 224, 225, 226, 228–29, 230, 231
Amityville Horror, The (novel), 212–13
Amityville II: The Possession (film), 217–18
Amityville 3-D (film), 215–16, 217
amputees, 52, 87, 103
amusement parks, 28, 50, 86, 263, 272n1; roller coasters, 58, 59, 60
anality, 212, 214, 219

And Now the Screaming Starts (film), 124
Anderson, Shaun, 276n3
Andrews, Eleanor, 144
Angel for Satan, An (film), 163
Angel Heart (film), 41
animals, 15–16, 42, 48, 71, 88, 102, 104, 106, 107, 112, 113–14, 117–20, 121, 122, 133, 143, 155, 169–70, 187, 190, 204, 222, 253, 271n3; alligators, 82; armadillos, 118, 120; bats, 15; crocodiles, 82; cruelty towards, 28, 113, 121, 152, 190; fat, 226; frogs, 239; and horror, 19; rats, 15, 118; tranquilizers for, 274n5. *See also individual names*
animation, 42, 248, 249, 253; stop-motion, 29, 35; suspended, 156
Ankle Biters (film), 64
Anson, Jay, 212, 213, 218
anthology films, 68, 257, 274n1
anthropocentrism, 15, 121, 222
Antonucci, Barbara, 244
Antropophagus (film), 275n2
ants, 30, 83, 84, 108, 117
anuses, 6, 202, 205, 213, 214
Appleman, Hale, 69
April Fool's Day (film), 268
Aranda, Vicente, 192
Arang (film), 257
Arbors, The (film), 189
Archibald, Chad, 62
Argento, Dario, 85, 94–96, 97, 100, 101, 104, 123, 124, 125, 142, 158, 159
Armstrong, David A., 139
Arnold, Jack, 157
"AromaRama," 203
Aronofsky, Darren, 167
Arora, Vardaan, 47
Arrow Video (distributor), 17–18
arterial spray, 100, 278n7
artifice, 12, 48, 54, 88, 89, 93, 138, 162, 167, 235
asphyxiation, 138, 157
Assayas, Olivier, 266
Aster, Ari, 29, 68, 181, 238, 268
Asylum (film), 257
auteurism, 7, 12, 22, 85, 87, 95, 101, 109, 122, 145, 194
autopsies, 83, 87, 140, 153, 155–56

Avati, Pupi, 94
Averback, Hy, 50, 54
axes, 14, 28, 53, 106, 146, 147, 222, 235

Babadook, The (film), 178
Babysitter: Killer Queen, The (film), 82
Bach, Johann Sebastian, 38
Backus, Richard, 155
bacteria, 72, 74, 98, 224, 236
Bad Ronald (film), 85
Badley, Linda, 39, 175
badness, 10, 48, 90, 198–99, 201–2, 207, 231, 232
Badon, Joe, 64
Baggot, King, 32, 33
Bailey, John, 36
Bailey-Bond, Prano, 20
Baird, Robert, 277n6
Baker, Rick, 35
Balázs, Béla, 49
Balsam, Martin, 263
Baltake, Joe, 106
Banner, Jill, 110
Bannister, Reggie, 90
Bark, Peter, 186
Barker, Clive, 181, 183, 232
Barker, Jennifer M., 240, 241, 242
Barn, The (film), 274n7
Barrymore, John, 42
basements, 96, 98, 132, 144–48, 150–51, 167, 184, 214, 216, 217, 218, 220, 221, 226, 227, 269, 277n5
Basil, Harry, 64
Basket Case (film), 144, 208
Bataille, Georges, 209
bathrooms, 138–39, 214, 219, 227, 275n3; showers, 45, 58–59, 86, 96, 121, 125, 202, 207, 263, 266, 268; toilets, 139, 182, 201, 203, 204–5, 206, 207–9, 211, 212, 213, 230, 231; tubs, 45, 96–97, 101, 190, 226
Bats (film), 272n1
Baumgarten, Marjorie, 231
Bava, Lamberto, 132
Bava, Mario, 162, 164
Bay of Blood (film), 64
Bayona, J. A., 268
Bazin, André, 203

Beard, William, 87, 88
Beast with Five Fingers, The (film), 249, 250
Beast Within (film), 277n4
Beck, Scott, 97, 100
Bedevilled, The (film), 238, 239
Bedlam (film), 87
Beheading the Chinese Prisoner (film), 28
Behind the Great Wall (film), 203
belief, 21, 23, 32, 33, 38, 47, 150
Belko Experiment, The (film), 275n4
Bell, Tobin, 138
Bellamy, Madge, 235
Bell-Metereau, Rebecca, 225
Benson, Justin, 268
Berman, Shari Springer, 46
Bernard, Mark, 139
Bertino, Bryan, 20, 46
Bessenger, Mark, 177
Best Worst Movie (film), 11
Better Tomorrow, A (film), 251
Bewitched (film), 238
Beyond, The (film), 82, 133, 144
Beyond the Darkness (film), 189, 191, 194, 195
Bianchi, Andrea, 186, 187
bile, 76, 239
Bingo Hell (film), 237
Birdemic: Shock and Terror (film), 231
birds, 121, 122, 124–25, 269
Birds, The (film), 124, 272n1
bisexuality, 191
Bite (film), 62
Bite Marks (film), 177
Black Christmas (1974 film), 85, 141, 142, 276n1
Black Christmas (2006 film), 123
Black Magic (film), 238, 252, 253, 255, 258
Black Magic 2 (film), 82, 238
Black Sunday (film), 162, 163–64
Blacula (film), 112
Blade (film), 107, 180–81
Blair, Linda, 121, 177
Blair Witch Project, The (film), 221
Blaisdell, George, 32–33, 35
Blas, Lucas, 222
blaxploitation films, 109, 212. *See also* exploitation films

blindness, 48, 108, 123, 131–33, 143, 144, 145; to color, 269
Blob, The (1958 film), 225
Blob, The (1988 film), 224
Bloch, Robert, 183
blood, 5, 13, 17, 30, 44, 45, 46, 53, 55, 56, 59, 63–64, 71, 76, 86, 89, 96, 106, 109, 117, 122, 139, 145, 153, 158, 159, 163, 170, 174, 178, 182, 184, 188, 190, 196, 204, 205, 209, 226, 228, 235, 252, 254, 256, 268, 271n1, 273n1, 277n2; cells, 74, 75; fake, 7, 36, 95; suckers, 107, 156, 181, 261; vessels, 129, 165
Blood and Black Lace (film), 64
Blood Bath (film), 64
Blood Ceremony (film), 15
Blood Diner (film), 64, 199
Blood Drinkers (film), 64
Blood Feast (film), 15–16, 18, 62, 231
Blood for Dracula (film), 13, 64
Blood Glacier (film), 64
Blood Harvest (film), 89
Blood Junkie (film), 64
Blood Moon (film), 64
Blood Orgy (film), 64
Bloodeaters (film), 7
Blood-Spattered Bride, The (film), 64, 192–93
Bloodsucking Freaks (film), 7, 231
Bloodthirsty (film), 20
Bloody Birthday (film), 82
Bloody Parrot (film), 238
Bloom, John Irving (Joe Bob Briggs), 89–93
Blue Eyes of the Broken Doll (film), 15
Blue My Mind (film), 75
Blue Velvet (film), 108, 117
Blumhouse Productions, 237
bodies, 9, 12, 29, 37, 38, 41–43, 45–48, 55, 56, 69, 70, 75, 79, 82, 83–84, 86–88, 93, 97, 101, 125–26, 137, 138, 139, 146–47, 148, 150, 154, 155–61, 163, 173, 174, 176, 180–84, 187, 188, 190, 202, 204, 205, 207, 220, 227, 228, 236, 239, 240, 241–42, 244, 245, 253, 256, 257, 259, 264, 266, 267, 273n1; -as-text, 80; cast, 153–54; counts, 89; decomposing, 108, 112, 153, 156, 175, 189, 192, 194, 221, 223; doubles, 58–59; excretory, 206; genre, 5, 6, 8, 13, 14, 24, 44, 57, 62–63, 65, 73, 77, 80,

81, 90, 94, 104–5, 107, 162, 169, 179, 197, 231, 233, 269, 276n2; hard, 224; horror, 3, 11, 27, 88, 89, 122, 177, 196, 212, 255, 272n2; language, 6; parts, 3, 6, 7, 16, 24, 64, 68, 108, 111–13, 128, 129, 214, 246–49, 262, 278n7; politic, 6, 262; spray, 189

Body, The (novella), 175

Boggy Creek II: And the Legend Continues (film), 207

Bogliano, Adrián García, 132

Boland, Brian, 121

Bond, James, III, 275n1

Bong, Joon-ho, 99, 199

Bonner, Hannah, 71

Boogens, The (film), 144

Boogey Man, The (film), 275n2

Booth, Walter R., 31

Bordello of Blood (film), 64

Borzage, Frank, 34

Bottin, Rob, 88–89, 99, 100

Botting, Fred, 74

Bouchet, Barbara, 160

Bourneuf, Philip, 263

Bousman, Darren Lynn, 62

Bouwer, Jaco, 20

bowels, 4, 145, 186, 220, 230, 231, 236

"bowels of the earth," 212–13, 216, 225

Boxer's Omen, The (film), 238

Bradburn, John, 64

Bradshaw, Peter, 198

Brain Damage (film), 207, 208

brains, 6, 8, 12, 15, 36, 48, 93, 125, 158, 166, 167, 176, 178, 182–83, 203, 236, 241, 242, 250, 256, 266, 267; nasal, 173, 202; stems, 92, 176; tissue, 231

Brake, Richard, 237

Bram Stoker's Dracula (film), 74, 75, 188

Bramesco, Charles, 209

Bravo, Charly, 192

Bravo, Ramón, 274n5

breasts, 13, 65, 67, 78, 79, 80, 89, 90, 91, 158, 162, 164–65

breaths, 4, 18, 97, 137, 138, 140, 141, 142, 145, 149, 151, 152, 154, 156, 157, 159, 161, 163, 166, 167, 253, 257, 275n1

breathing, 6, 7, 9, 19, 29, 35, 100, 171, 183, 214, 240, 273n1, 275n2, 275n4; communal, 137; heavy/labored, 141–42, 275n2; rate, 143

Brenon, Herbert, 32

Brice, Patrick, 46

Bride, The (film), 42–43

Bride of Chucky (film), 82

Bride of Frankenstein (film), 277n2

Bride of Re-Animator (film), 3

Briefel, Aviva, 246

British Board of Film Censors, 195, 272n2

Brogan, Jacqueline Vaught, 173

Brolin, James, 213

Brood, The (film), 87

Brophy, Philip, 49, 88, 227

Brottman, Mikita, 231

Brown, Jason David, 209

Brown, William, 267

Browning, Tod, 31, 41, 44

Brownrigg, S. F., 10, 145, 146, 149, 150, 152

Bruckner, David, 20, 46

Bruno, Giuliana, 240

Bucket of Blood, A (film), 64

Bunsinsaba (film), 257

Buñuel, Luis, 114, 115, 116, 117, 119, 121, 122, 124, 125

'Burbs, The (film), 185

Burd, Tim, 209

Burial Ground (film), 186, 187

Burning, The (film), 141, 154–55

Burns, Anthony Scott, 20

Burns, Marilyn, 35, 169

Burstyn, Ellen, 98

Byrne, Gabriel, 268

Cabin by the Lake (film), 82

Cabin Fever (film), 198

Cabin in the Woods (film), 21–22

Cabinet of Dr. Caligari, The (film), 33, 44, 116

Cage, Nicolas, 118, 119

Caiano, Mario, 163

Calandra, Giuliana, 96–97, 101

cameras, 7, 13, 29, 38, 39, 45, 51, 54, 58, 73, 90, 97, 98, 103, 117, 137, 139, 145, 148, 151, 155–56, 157, 158, 159, 166, 184, 221, 232, 240, 247, 256, 265, 271n4; angles, 22, 95; handheld,

153; lenses, 36, 42, 52, 64, 96, 124, 127, 130, 138, 162; movement, 16, 36, 160–61, 276n3
Campbell, Bruce, 277n5
Campbell, John W., Jr., 88
Canby, Vincent, 94
Candyman (film), 98, 129, 208
Canetti, Elias, 261
Cannibal Campout (film), 4
Cannibal Ferox (film), 194
Cannibal Holocaust (film), 3, 15, 93, 118, 196, 258
Cannibal Man, The (film), 172, 190, 192–96
cannibalism, 20, 93, 165, 178, 190, 191, 196, 258, 276n3
Canter, Kieran, 190
Car: Road to Revenge, The (film), 123
Carax, Leos, 198, 199, 206
Cardiff, Jack, 203
carnality, 70, 116, 145
"carnographic culture," 85, 89
Carone, Joe, 87
Carpenter, Horace B., 150–51
Carpenter, John, 85, 86, 87, 88, 94, 100, 137, 141, 239
Carr, Camilla, 146
Carrie (film), 76–77
Carroll, Beth, 240
Carroll, Larry, 169
Carroll, Noël, 49
Case of Charles Dexter Ward, The (novella), 187
Castle, Nick, 141
Castle, William, 5, 48, 50, 51, 52, 62, 194, 210, 211
Castle of Otranto, The (novel), 185
castration, 14, 59, 64, 68, 69–70, 71, 132, 254
Cat and the Canary, The (film), 243, 249
Cat O' Nine Tails (film), 159
Cat People (film), 87
Cathay Studios, 252
Catholicism, 158, 192, 219, 232
cats, 15, 150, 180, 221
causality, 119–20, 267
Cell, The (film), 138
cemeteries, 170, 188, 232
Censor (film), 20

censorship, 13, 81, 83, 152, 162, 164, 193, 194, 252, 272n2
Centipede Horror (film), 239
Chamber of Horrors (film), 50–55, 62, 263
Chan, Anthony, 254
Chan, Jonny, 258
Chan Hok-shing, Brian, 252
Chandler, Betty, 146
Chaney, Lon, Jr., 109
Chang, Ren-chieh, 238
Changeling, The (film), 91
Changeling, The (novel), 173
Chapman, Ben, 157
Chapman, Michael, 36
Checchi, Andrea, 163
Chen, Szu-chia, 256
Chen, Yun-chung, 252
Cherry, Brigid, 53, 196
Chiang, David, 252
Chiba, Sonny, 93
chickens, 15, 18, 118
Chien Andalou, Un (film), 114–17, 119, 122, 124, 125, 126
Children Shouldn't Play with Dead Things (film), 85
Child's Eye, The (film), 129, 244
Child's Play 2 (film), 265
Chin, Siu-ho, 254
Chinese Ghost Story, A (film), 253
Chinese Ghost Story III, A (film), 254
Ching, Siu-tung, 253
choking, 97, 157, 180, 230, 246
Chu, Yen-ping, 251
Chung, Fat, 258
Church, David, 271n1
Cinefantastique (magazine), 88
"cinema of attractions," 57, 93
City of the Living Dead (film), 125, 223
clairvoyancy, 133
Clark, Alfred, 27, 29
Clark, Bob, 85, 141, 155–56
Clark, Greydon, 122, 139, 275n3
Clasen, Mathias, 60, 236
Classen, Constance, 171
Cliffe, Louise, 165
Climax (film), 20

Clive, Colin, 248
Clouzot, Henri-Georges, 256
Clover, Carol, 8, 38, 57, 60, 65, 67, 137, 275n1
cockroaches, 103, 107, 113, 224
Cody, Diablo, 65, 67, 71, 77, 79, 81, 178
Coffy (film), 109
cognition, 8, 9, 23, 37, 173, 176, 182, 202, 241, 244, 249, 266
Cohen, Emma, 192
Cohen, Larry, 85, 93
Cold War, 19, 83, 225, 252
Coleman, Robin R. Means, 110
Collection, The (film), 82
Collector, The (film), 83
Collette, Toni, 182
Collier, Jim, 273n1
colors, 94–95, 111, 179; blindness to, 269; cinematography, 162
Combs, C. Scott, 153
Combs, Jeffrey, 3
Come True (film), 20
Comeback, The (film), 221–22, 277n3
comedy, 8, 9, 10, 17, 19, 24, 34, 50, 51, 53, 65, 68, 69, 81, 89, 91, 93, 107, 111, 118, 122, 141, 185, 190, 202, 204, 206, 207, 219, 231–34, 236, 237, 238, 242, 243, 249, 258, 260, 275n3; accidental, 231; and laughter, 7, 12, 16, 18, 22, 48, 49, 54, 60, 64, 71, 86, 106, 113, 126, 127, 145, 196, 212, 230, 232, 241, 251, 263, 267, 272n3; slapstick, 110, 258
comic books, 41, 178, 180, 240
coming-of-age, 69, 71, 175, 178
computer-generated imagery (CGI), 9, 42, 74, 113, 114, 130, 271n2
Condemned to Live (film), 264
Congia, Vittorio, 159
Conjuring, The (film), 60, 144
Connors, Kevin, 90
Conrad, William, 51
Conrich, Ian, 6, 202, 205, 214
Constantine (film), 41, 114, 133
contagion, 74, 225, 261; emotional, 49, 232
Conterio, Martyn, 163
continuity, 54, 119, 120; error, 7
controversy, 12, 14, 55, 65, 193, 213
Cook, Jesse Thomas, 5, 208

Cooper, L. Andrew, 94, 95, 124
Copperhead (film), 118
Coppola, Francis Ford, 74
Corman, Roger, 93, 255
corpse, 42, 80, 96, 107, 122, 139, 140, 145, 150, 153, 156, 160–61, 166, 172, 175, 182, 184, 187, 194, 202, 221, 223, 228, 235, 273n1, 276n3, 277n3; animal, 102; hopping, 238, 239, 240, 243, 254, 255, 259; mummified, 158; reanimated, 124, 186, 253, 256
Corpse Mania (film), 238
Cortez, Marisol, 204, 206, 207
Coscarelli, Don, 85, 90
Cosmatos, Panos, 68
Costanzo, William V., 116, 117, 245
Court, Hazel, 165
Crampton, Howard, 33
Craven, Wes, 85, 86, 93, 94, 99, 107, 112, 177, 208, 275n1
Crawl (film), 82
Crawling Hand, The (film), 249, 250
"creature feature," 19, 83
Creature from the Black Lagoon (film), 157
Creed, Barbara, 8, 14, 52, 54, 68, 70, 276n2
Creeping Terror, The (film), 199
Creepshow (film), 35, 82
Creepy (film), 223
Cronenberg, Brandon, 68
Cronenberg, David, 12, 13, 85, 87–88, 94, 224, 255, 274n6
crucifix, 31, 123
Cujo (film), 155
cult cinema, 3, 16, 57, 65, 89, 110, 151, 194, 231
Cundieff, Rusty, 274n1
Curse of Evil (film), 238, 239–40
Curtains (film), 275n2
Curti, Roberto, 163, 165
Cushing, Peter, 41, 252, 273n1

Dahlem, Gregory, 224
Dalí, Salvador, 108, 114, 115, 116, 124, 125
D'Amato, Joe, 133, 189, 190
Damiani, Damiano, 217
Damici, Nick, 132
damnation, 41, 42, 43, 46
Danielewski, Mark Z., 173

Dante, Joe, 19, 21, 22, 23
Danton, Ray, 139, 140
Danziger, Allen, 169
Darabont, Frank, 268
Dark Age (film), 82
Dark and the Wicked, The (film), 20, 46
Dark Circles (film), 129
David, Lou, 154
Davis, Essie, 178
Davis, Sonja, 99
Dawn of the Dead (1978 film), 82, 86
Dawn of the Dead (2004 film), 123
Day of the Beast, The (film), 41, 89
de la Iglesia, Eloy, 190
De Palma, Brian, 77, 85, 94
de Vos, Gail, 264
Dead, The (film), 101–4
Dead & Buried (film), 123
Dead and the Deadly, The (film), 238
Dead Rising 3 (video game), 180
Dead Silence (film), 268
Dead Snow (film), 48
deafness, 78, 108, 126
Death Bed: The Bed That Eats (film), 181
Death Line (film), 276n3
Death Screams (film), 29
Deathdream (film), 85, 155–56
Deathgasm (film), 91, 92
deaths, 4, 16, 21, 23, 27, 28, 29, 30, 36, 39, 40–42, 45–49, 53, 54, 62, 67, 73, 74, 86, 87, 90–92, 94–97, 101, 106, 110, 111, 113, 116, 122, 123, 138–41, 144, 146, 149, 150, 152, 156, 157, 158, 159, 161–62, 165, 166, 167, 169, 175, 179, 180–83, 185–88, 192, 195, 222, 224, 228, 229, 235, 236, 255, 257, 265, 269, 273n1, 275n1; and animals, 15, 118, 119, 120; bad, 45, 46–47, 82–83, 84, 91, 96, 97, 114, 138, 183, 205, 208, 221; faked, 29, 153, 257; wet, 82, 86
decapitation, 15, 27–30, 48, 106, 159
Dee, John, 116
Deep Red (film), 93–97, 100, 101, 104, 158, 159
Deep Thrust: The Hand of Death (film), 242
Def by Temptation (film), 275n1
defecation, 102, 177, 224, 227, 233; open, 206
DeFeo, Ronald, 215–16, 217, 220, 228, 229

Dekker, Fred, 207
del Toro, Guillermo, 116
Demme, Jonathan, 196
Demon: Hell's Hitman, The (comic book), 178
Demon Strike (film), 243
demonologist, 133, 213
Demons (film), 132
Denis, Claire, 75
DeNoble, Alphonso, 179
Dentist, The (film), 82
Deodato, Ruggero, 93, 94, 196
Descent, The (film), 82
Desser, David, 242
Devil, The (film), 238–39
Devil Fetus (film), 255
Devil's Advocate, The (film), 41
Devil's Backbone, The (film), 20
Devil's Castle, The (film), 31
diarrhea, 103, 181, 224
DiBlasi, Anthony, 183, 223
disabilities, 10, 14, 78, 103, 104, 108, 112, 122, 131, 132, 133, 143
disbelief, 23, 38, 42; mitigation of, 9, 33, 139; suspension of, 9, 39, 138, 149, 157
diseases, 23, 74, 101, 102, 103, 224, 225, 235, 236, 255, 256
disembowelment, 14, 78, 82, 138, 190
disfigurement, 5, 154
disgust, 3, 14, 15, 47, 59, 83, 126, 173, 179, 181, 193, 195–96, 214, 219, 222, 223, 230, 231, 235–36, 237, 239, 277n5
Disney, Walt, 55, 236
dogs, 69, 71, 118, 122, 143, 144, 155, 187, 204, 207, 211, 277n4; guide, 112, 133
donkeys, 117, 118, 121
Don't Answer the Phone (film), 145
Don't Be Afraid of the Dark (film), 85, 145
Don't Breathe (film), 132, 141, 143–45, 146, 167–68
Don't Go in the House (film), 145
Don't Go in the Woods (film), 145
Don't Listen (film), 221, 222
Don't Look in the Basement (film), 10, 145–50, 151
Don't Open the Door (film), 145
Don't Open the Window (film), 145

Don't Torture a Duckling (film), 145
doppelgangers, 44, 211
Double Dare (TV series), 237
Dougherty, Michael, 275n1
Doyle, Arthur Conan, 246
Dr. Blood's Coffin (film), 64
Dr. Jekyll and Mr. Hyde (1913 film), 32–33, 35
Dr. Jekyll and Mr. Hyde (1920 film), 42
Dr. Jekyll and Mr. Hyde (1931 film), 19, 24, 36–39, 41, 44, 48, 97, 247, 272n2
Dr. Terror's House of Horrors (film), 249
Dracula (film), 31, 41, 232
Dracula (novel), 73, 74, 188, 276n4
Dracula III: Legacy (film), 107
dread, 7, 23, 38, 49, 50, 83, 147, 167, 170, 176, 186, 213, 217, 233, 243, 247, 251, 262, 265
Dread (film), 144, 172, 183–85, 223
Dreamcatcher (film), 5, 172, 200–202, 204–6, 207
Dreamcatcher (novel), 201, 204, 207
drive-in theater, 17, 18, 75, 225, 269, 277n4
drowning, 48, 82, 124, 153, 256, 274n3
D-Tox (film), 123
Ducournau, Julia, 62, 178, 179
Duel of the Iron Fist (film), 243
Dunn, John, 152, 153, 154
Dunn, Rob, 223–24
Dunne, Griffin, 107
DVD/Blu-ray, 13, 16, 18, 36, 65, 78, 81, 94, 95, 97, 98, 100–101, 104, 111, 114, 128, 129, 142, 152, 154, 189, 191, 194, 195, 231, 272n1, 272n2, 274n6, 274n7
Dysart, Richard, 87

ears, 5, 7, 33, 40, 44, 55, 57, 60, 104, 106, 107, 109–12, 126, 173, 202, 225, 227, 271n4; severed, 108, 110
Eaten Alive (film), 82, 276n3
Ebert, Roger, 12, 67
Edge of the Axe (film), 9
Edison Manufacturing Company, 27, 28
editing, 29, 39, 88, 115, 146, 157, 271n4, 274n5; continuity, 54, 120; lap dissolve, 32, 35, 39, 45, 228; shock cuts, 19, 229
Edwards, Eric, 180–81
Eggers, Robert, 238

8th Night, The (film), 46
Eisenstein, Sergei, 36
Electrocuting an Elephant (film), 28
electrocution, 48, 82, 83, 280n7
"elevated" horror, 3, 4, 29, 30, 238, 271
Ellinger, Robert, 17
Elliot, Paul, 171, 182, 202, 203, 267
Elliott-Smith, Darren, 129, 130, 131
Elsaesser, Thomas, 171, 276n2
Elwes, Cary, 138, 182
embodied subjectivity, 24, 37, 38, 171
empowerment, 67, 70, 76
Empty Man, The (film), 20
Enchanting Shadow (film), 252
Enemy (film), 268
Englund, Robert, 153
Enlow, Darla, 64
Ennis, Garth, 178
Enter, Night (novel), 173
Ephraim, Molly, 121
Epps, Omar, 33
Escher, M. C., 246
Esper, Dwain, 10, 150, 151, 152
Etheredge-Ouzts, Paul, 129, 131
ethnicity, 104, 111
Evans, Shaun, 184
Even Lambs Have Teeth (film), 64
Everson, William, 167
evil, 32, 33, 40, 133, 188, 202, 214, 216, 217, 220, 226, 230, 252, 254, 255, 258, 259, 265
Evil Dead, The (film), 35, 144
Evil Dead II (film), 242, 243, 277n5
Evil Dead Trap (film), 123
excess, 10, 44, 46, 48, 57, 61–63, 72, 77, 86, 93, 104, 107, 109, 110, 148, 151, 154, 165, 168, 180, 204, 227, 231, 244, 263, 276n2
excrement, 86, 88, 177, 181, 196, 197, 198, 204, 205, 206, 207, 208, 209, 212–15, 218, 219, 222, 223, 226, 231, 235, 276n4
Execution of a Murderess (film), 28
Execution of Mary, Queen of Scots (film), 27–29, 30, 31, 55
Exorcist, The (film), 27, 35, 98, 121, 177, 217, 230, 252, 277n6
Exorcist II: The Heretic (film), 126
Exorcist Master (film), 238

exploitation films, 3, 7, 10, 85, 89, 93, 109, 141, 145–46, 150, 152, 167, 172, 189, 194, 196, 209, 212, 226, 231, 272n2
Exte: Hair Extensions (film), 182
Exterminating Angel, The (film), 122
Eye, The (2002 film), 64, 257
Eye, The (2008 film), 129
eyes, 4, 5, 6, 7, 14, 17, 19, 21, 23, 27, 31, 33, 34–36, 37, 38, 39, 40, 41, 44, 45, 48, 52, 55, 57, 58, 60, 83, 91, 104, 107, 108, 114–18, 120–21, 122, 123–26, 128–33, 137, 138, 150, 152, 154, 170, 173, 177, 181, 202, 210, 227, 236, 239, 248, 250, 265, 266, 267, 269, 271n4, 274n3, 274n4
Eyes Without a Face (film), 116, 198

Fabra, Belén, 222
face, 5, 8, 17, 37, 45, 47, 48–50, 55, 60, 61, 79, 84, 87, 90, 92, 96, 113, 115, 128, 131, 153, 156, 158, 159, 163, 166, 170, 181, 210, 222, 226, 232–34, 269, 274n7
facial feedback, 49
factory farm, 271n3
Faculty, The (film), 123
Fahy, Thomas, 180
Fail-Safe (film), 155
failure, 12, 67, 100, 131, 141, 145, 168, 202
fairy tale, 115, 116, 173
fakeness, 7, 8, 12, 17, 29, 36, 95, 97, 112, 113, 118, 153, 154, 212, 235, 240
Fallon, Sean W., 276n3
Falls, Matt, 210
Falvey, Eddie, 70, 71
fandom, 10, 13, 22, 29, 41, 46, 50, 58, 61, 62, 63, 80, 93, 97, 99, 106, 123, 124, 126, 167, 224; anti-, 207, 215
Fangoria (magazine), 88
Fantasy Mission Force (film), 251
fatness, 179, 181
Favela, Adrian, 47
Fawcett, John, 7, 77, 118
Feagin, Hugh, 146
Fear, Inc. (film), 123
"fear-jerking," 62
Feher, Friedrich, 34
Feldman, Corey, 185

feminism, 12, 58, 65, 69, 70, 81, 164, 271n3, 272n2; post-, 67, 76
Fergus, Dylan, 129
Ferman, James, 272
Fernandez-Vander Kaay, Kathleen, 145, 167
fetishism, 14, 24, 36, 52, 58, 94, 145, 246
fetuses, 87, 177, 255
Fiala, Severin, 268
fight choreography, 143, 258, 260
film festival, 20, 68, 71, 103, 129, 179, 194, 199, 210, 238, 270, 272n2
film flub, 138, 145
filth, 180, 182, 184, 192, 196, 208, 218, 224
Final Destination (film), 21
Final Destination 2 (film), 189
"final girl," 77, 132, 170, 275n1
Fincher, David, 181
Findlay, Michael, 194
fingers, 33, 69, 83, 103, 112, 178–79, 240, 241, 242, 247, 254–55, 256, 259, 273n4, 277n2; nails, 83, 253, 254, 259, 260
Fingerprints (film), 64
Fisher, Terence, 41, 273n1
Fists of Fury (film), 242
Five Fingers of Death (film), 242
flavors, 176, 177, 178, 179, 188, 240
Fleischer, Richard, 215
Flesh Feast (film), 7
Flesh for Frankenstein (film), 13
flies, 36, 184, 215, 218, 220–24, 229–30, 235; maggots, 184, 222, 223, 238
Florey, Robert, 249
Fly, The (1958 film), 224
Fly, The (1986 film), 6, 87, 224
Flynn, Emmett J., 271n1
focalization, 56
foley, 36, 77
food, 9, 176–79, 187, 214; poisoning, 103, 177; rotting, 175, 189
Ford, Howard J. and Jon, 101–4
foreignness, 32, 34, 107
Forest, The (film), 138
Forest of Death (film), 244
Forte, Joseph, 83
Foster, Jodie, 132
Foster, Meg, 176

found-footage films, 121, 142, 221
Four Flies on Grey Velvet (film), 142
Fox, Megan, 65, 67, 79, 178
Foxy Brown (film), 109
Fragasso, Claudio, 11
Frailty (film), 144
franchise, 10, 21, 57, 75, 88, 90, 92, 138, 183, 204, 212, 215, 218, 221, 222, 223, 226, 227, 228, 229, 231, 266, 268
Francis, Freddie, 249
Francis, Matthew Sean, 64
Franco, Francisco, 192, 193, 194
Franju, Georges, 116, 198
Frankenstein (film), 31, 116, 248, 277n2
Frankenstein Created Woman (film), 41–42
Frankenstein Must Be Destroyed (film), 138, 273n1
Frankenstein Unbound (film), 129
Franz, Veronika, 268
Freaks (film), 264
Freaky (film), 82
Freddy vs. Jason (film), 268
Fredriksson, Horacio, 164
Freeman, Morgan, 201, 206
Freeman, Rob, 102
freeze-frame, 52, 155–56, 159, 260
French, Edward, 153–54
Fresnadillo, Juan Carlos, 75
Freud, Sigmund, 148
Freund, Karl, 31, 249
Frey, Mattias, 199, 200
Friday the 13th (film), 57, 266
Friday the 13th: The Final Chapter (film), 268
Friday the 13th Part III (film), 123, 268
Friday the 13th Part V: A New Beginning (film), 124, 208
Friedkin, William, 98, 121, 177, 230, 252
Friedman, Brent V., 187
Friedman, David F., 16, 18
Friedman, Richard, 17–18
Fright Night (film), 35
Fright Night 2: New Blood (film), 123
From Within (film), 189
Frontière(s) (film), 20
Frye, Dwight, 232
Fryer, Ian, 277n3

Fulci, Lucio, 94, 124, 125, 126, 133, 165, 223, 274n5
Funhouse, The (film), 18, 86, 142
Funhouse Massacre, The (film), 123
furnace, 167
Furst, Stephen, 98

gagging, 208, 209, 212
Gaia (film), 20
Gallows, The (film), 60
Gance, Abel, 36
Ganja & Hess (film), 109
Garateguy, Tamae, 68
Gavin, John, 59
Gawlikowski, David, 155
gaze, 7, 24, 35, 54, 59, 94, 95, 131, 159, 160, 161, 192; disciplinary, 61; forensic, 5; hypnotic, 163; male, 67, 256; medical-scientific, 74, 75
Gebbe, Katrin, 68
Gelder, Ken, 251
gender, 13, 56, 59, 60, 65, 77, 79, 96, 131, 191, 253, 257, 273n4
genitalia, 14, 68, 77, 81, 162
German Expressionism, 33, 73, 118
Germanà, Monica, 247
Get Out (film), 137, 148
Ghost Busting (film), 239
Ghost Nursing (film), 255
Ghost Rider (film), 41
Ghost Snatchers, The (film), 251
Ghostbusters (film), 225, 239
Ghostbusters II (film), 225
ghosts, 31, 96, 187, 213, 220, 221, 245–46, 252, 260, 261, 274n4
Ghoulies (film), 138
giallo, 93, 95, 100, 106, 125, 159, 160, 165, 179
Gilbert, Morris, 116, 117
Ginger Snaps (film), 75, 76, 77, 118
Girl Walks Home Alone at Night, A (film), 93
Glass, Rose, 20, 46
Glover, Kate, 208
Glynn, Kevin, 166, 167
God Inside My Ear, The (film), 64
God Told Me To (film), 85
Goddard, Drew, 21
Goldblum, Jeff, 6, 224

Golden Harvest (studio), 238
Goldman, William, 200
Golem, The (film), 44
Gomez, Julia, 221
Gondry, Michel, 199
Gonjiam: Haunted Asylum (film), 20
gore, 4, 19, 35, 71, 85, 88, 122, 128, 164, 251, 272
Gothicism, 44, 108, 145, 163, 204, 243, 244, 249; literature, 31, 32, 74, 188, 246; romance, 185; rural, 22
Gottowt, John, 73
Goya, Francisco, 193
Gozier, Bernie, 157
Grace (film), 223
Graduation Day (film), 65, 138
Grand Guignol, 50, 159, 190
Grant, Barry Keith, 115, 116, 120, 121, 122, 247
Grapes of Death, The (film), 165
gratuitousness, 57, 92, 93, 255
Grau, Jorge, 15
"Gray Matter" (short story), 175
Greasy Strangler, The (film), 82
Green, Adam, 128
Green Inferno, The (film), 3, 62
Gremlins (film), 13, 138
Grier, Pam, 109
Griffith, D. W., 36
grindhouse, 13, 89
gross-out moments, 5, 62, 123, 204, 209, 218–19, 255
Grudge, The (film), 129
Gruesome Twosome (film), 122, 144
Guadagnino, Luca, 68
Guerrero, Gigi Saul, 237
Guihot, Julie, 88
guilt, 257, 265, 266
Guinea Pig 2: Flower of Flesh and Blood (film), 54
Gulf War, 132, 143
Gunn, Bill, 109
Gunning, Tom, 57, 59, 73–74
gustation, 126, 171, 176, 177, 179, 185, 190, 236, 241
guts, 4, 77, 80, 81, 83, 104, 175, 190
"gynaehorror," 70

Ha, Huang, 258
Hagener, Malte, 171, 276n2
Hague, Ian, 236, 240
hair, 7, 40, 53, 78, 124, 180, 182, 254, 277n5
Halberstam, Jack, 241
Hall, Conrad, 36
Hallahan, Charles, 87
Halliburton, David, 185
Halloween (film), 86, 100, 137, 141, 142, 266, 277n6
Halloween: Resurrection (film), 265
Halloween Horror Nights, 27, 35
Halloween II (1981 film), 96
Halloween II (2009 film), 100
Hammer Films, 41, 138, 164, 252, 273n1
Hammond, Stefan, 251
Hand, The (film), 64, 248
hands, 6, 15, 33, 35, 37, 38, 52, 54, 55, 78, 83, 91, 92, 100, 101, 106, 107, 115, 128, 129, 147, 163, 208, 237, 240, 241–42, 243, 244, 245, 246–51, 254–56, 259–62, 274n3, 277n2, 277n3, 277n5; clutching, 243, 244, 249, 257, 261; crawling, 249–50, 257; disembodied, 53; gloved, 96, 97, 158; racialized, 246; severed, 53, 57, 122, 218–19, 245, 257, 258, 277n4; signs, 253–54
Hands of a Stranger (film), 249
Hands of Orlac, The (film), 249
Hands of the Ripper (film), 123
Hanich, Julian, 7, 8, 56, 127, 128
Happy Hell Night (film), 123
haptics, 86, 88, 96, 153, 171, 177, 202, 203, 240
Hard Boiled (film), 251
Hard Candy (film), 71
Hardison, Kadeem, 107, 108, 109, 275n1
Hardy, Robin, 268
Harper, Tess, 216
Harrington, Erin, 69–70
Harron, John, 235
Hart, James V., 74
Hartman, Valerie, 208
Harvey, Michael, 146–47
Haunt (film), 97, 100
Haunted Curiosity Shop, The (film), 31
haunted houses, 27, 35, 46, 50, 142, 216, 218
Haunting of Hill House, The (novel), 188–89

Haupt, Melanie, 71
Hawkins, Joan, 89, 122
Hawks, Howard, 273n2
Häxan (film), 116
Hayes, Jeff, 152
Hazing, The (film), 123
Hazmat (film), 123
heads, 6, 27–30, 31, 47, 48, 52, 75, 78, 79, 82, 88, 90, 91–92, 95, 96, 97, 101, 109, 117, 118, 122, 124, 138, 139, 153, 159, 174, 212, 221, 233, 250, 274n7
hearing, 5, 6, 7, 78, 80, 112, 126, 137, 139, 144, 169, 171, 173, 174, 183, 188, 189, 202, 240, 276n2
hearts, 15, 18, 40, 62, 78, 79, 80, 112, 137, 138, 152, 166; palpitations, 272n2; rate, 139, 141, 143; staking, 107–8
Heart-Shaped Box (novel), 187
Heche, Anne, 268
Heffernan, Kevin, 252
Heise, William, 29
Hell Has No Boundary (film), 238
Hell House LLC (film), 142
Hell Night (film), 57
Hellbent (film), 129–32
Heller-Nicholas, Alexandra, 12, 95
Hellraiser (film), 240, 266
Hemmings, David, 95, 159
Henenlotter, Frank, 208
Henry, Claire, 69
Henry, Gloria Lynne, 90
Hensley, John, 69
Herbert, Holmes, 19, 38
Herd, The (film), 271n3
Hereditary (film), 3, 29–30, 181, 182, 238, 268
hermeneutics, 7, 40, 64, 80, 95, 100, 118, 172, 267
Hernández, Ángel Gómez, 221
Hernandez, Jay, 274n3
Herrera, Lola, 192
Herrier, Mark, 209
Herrmann, Bernard, 59, 263
Hex (film), 238, 256–57
Hide and Go Shriek (film), 29
Higashide, Masahiro, 223
Higgins, Clare, 240

High Tension (film), 20, 189, 268
Hill, Derek, 49
Hill, Jack, 5, 109, 111
Hill, Joe, 187
Hills, Matt, 13, 194
Hills Have Eyes, The (1977 film), 93, 122
Hills Have Eyes, The (2006 film), 123
Hills Have Eyes Part II, The (film), 133
Hiltzik, Robert, 152, 153, 154, 208, 268
Hitchcock, Alfred, 44, 45, 50, 57, 59, 60, 61, 62, 65, 84, 86, 94, 101, 104, 116, 144, 162, 207, 263, 266, 268, 269, 272n1
Ho, Godfrey, 239
Ho, Meng-hua, 238, 239, 255
Hobart, Rose, 43
Hobbs, Simon, 100
Hoberman, J., 60, 233
Hobgoblins (film), 138
Hockenhull, Stella, 144
Hodder, Kane, 128
Holotik, Rosie, 146
Holy Motors (film), 198–99, 205, 206, 232
Holzer, Hans, 218
homosexuality, 68, 129–32, 191, 193
Honeymoon (film), 67
Hong Kong, 15, 24, 118, 173, 238–40, 242–43, 245, 249, 251–62, 277n6
Hooper, Tobe, 18, 85, 86, 94, 100, 118, 169, 170, 189, 223, 276n3
Hornaday, Ann, 67
"horrality," 49
Horror of the Blood Monsters (film), 75
Horsley, Jasun, 22–23
Host (film), 270
Host, The (film), 99
Hostel (film), 88, 267, 273n3
Hough, John, 208
Houlihan, Carolyn, 154
House at the End of the Street, The (film), 144
House by the Churchyard, The (novel), 245, 246
House of Dracula (film), 74
House of Leaves (novel), 173
House of 9 (film), 129
House of the Dead (film), 186
House of Wax (1953 film), 50, 162

House of Wax (2005 film), 9
House on Haunted Hill (film), 48
House on Sorority Row, The (film), 101
House that Dripped Blood (film), 64
Howard, Trevor, 133
Howarth, Troy, 180
Howden, Jason Lei, 92
Howes, David, 171
Howling, The (film), 19
Hua, Shan, 238
Human Centipede, The (film), 88
Human Centipede 2 (Full Sequence), The (film), 55, 180, 189
Human Lanterns (film), 243
Humanoids from the Deep (film), 93
Hunchback of the Morgue (film), 118, 153
Hung, Sammo, 5, 243, 256, 257, 258, 259–60
Hunger, The (film), 74
Hunger and Thirst (novel), 172
Hungry Ghost Ritual (film), 278n9
Hunter, I. Q., 227, 231, 232, 233
Hurst, Elliott, 211
Hutchings, Peter, 124, 249
Hutton, Jim, 140
Hutton, Robert, 225
hypnosis, 98, 163

I Drink Your Blood (film), 64
I Eat Your Skin (film), 7
I Saw the Devil (film), 29
I Spit on Your Grave (film), 12–14, 65
I Stand Alone (film), 50, 55
I Walked with a Zombie (film), 87
id, 144–45, 148
identification, 24, 54, 56, 57, 59, 265
Identity (film), 268
Idle Hands (film), 242
immolation, 48, 138; self-, 268
immortality, 40, 43
impalement, 48, 82, 83, 92
In a Glass Cage (film), 54
In the Earth (film), 20, 123, 270
inbreeding, 109
Incident in a Ghostland (film), 16
incineration, 82
Incubus, The (film), 208

infections, 74–75, 201, 208, 231, 270
Inferno (film), 96
Ingram, Rex, 167
injuries, 83, 84, 95, 122, 242, 246; on-set, 16, 98–100, 102, 118, 128–29, 274n7
insects, 19, 36, 83–84, 113, 117, 118–19, 221–22, 223, 224, 229, 230. *See also individual names*
Inside (film), 20, 80
intertextuality, 21, 30, 115, 143, 185, 258
intertitles, 28, 33, 34, 35, 115, 116, 151
Interview with a Vampire (film), 107
intestines, 85, 86, 178, 204, 213, 214
Intruders (film), 144
invisibility, 14, 17, 41, 54, 73, 104, 127, 137, 139, 142, 146, 152, 160, 174, 213, 224
Invisible Ray, The (film), 34
Irigaray, Luce, 137
Iron-Fisted Monk, The (film), 256
ironic detachment, 10, 23, 107
Isabelle, Katharine, 75
Island of the Dead (film), 224
Isle of the Dead (film), 87
It Follows (film), 238
Italian Americans, 107, 112
It's Alive (film), 85

Jack Frost (film), 92
Jackson, Shirley, 188
Jancovich, Mark, 87
Jane, Thomas, 205
Janiak, Leigh, 67
Jeepers Creepers (film), 124, 169, 189, 265
Jeffory-Nelson, Dawn, 166
Jenner, Mark, 171
Jennifer's Body (film), 14, 65, 67, 76, 77–81, 178
"Jerusalem's Lot" (short story), 185–86, 188, 228
jiangshi, 243, 253–54, 258–59, 261
Jodorowsky, Alejandro, 108, 138
Jones, Duane, 155
Jones, Jack, 221
Jones, John G., 218
Jones, Steve, 273n3
Jug Face (film), 122
Julia's Eyes (film), 20, 129, 131

jump scare, 19, 86–87, 277n6
Juno (film), 71
Ju-On: The Grudge (film), 20, 257

Kaluuya, Daniel, 148
Kamp, Louise, 18
Kandel, Stephen, 50, 54
Kapp, Ernst, 250
Karlatos, Olga, 124, 126
Karloff, Boris, 31, 34, 113
Kasdan, Lawrence, 5, 201, 204
Kattelman, Beth A., 85
Kaufman, Lloyd, 93
Kawin, Bruce, 35, 36, 138
Keaton, Camille, 13
Keeley, Sean, 205–6
Keene, Brian, 173
Keenleyside, Eric, 205
Kehr, Dave, 231
Kelly, Casey Ryan, 273n4
Kent, Jennifer, 178
Kentis, Chris, 98
Kermani, Natasha, 20
Kermode, Mark, 272n2
Kidder, Margot, 213
Killer Klowns from Outer Space (film), 82
Killer Snakes, The (film), 238, 252, 256
killers, 52, 53, 55, 59, 80, 94, 95, 97, 109, 123, 131, 132, 139, 153, 156, 159, 165, 210, 215, 217, 228, 229, 233, 235, 263, 265–66, 275n2; gloved, 123, 158; masked, 33, 47, 86, 96, 130, 137, 141, 155, 166; serial, 20, 33, 50, 52, 142, 193
Kim, Tae-hyoung, 46
kinesthesis, 240, 241, 242
Kinetograph, 27
Kinetoscope, 28
King, Charles, 32
King, Stephen, 15, 45, 115, 155, 174–75, 183, 185, 186, 188, 200, 201, 204, 205, 206, 207, 228, 271n2
King Kong (film), 239
King of the Zombies (film), 110
Kirk, Phyllis, 162
Kirkwood, Bryan, 130
knives, 18, 45, 47, 58, 76, 79, 86, 99, 111, 184, 254, 260, 268; prop, 59

knowability, 265
Kölsch, Kevin, 68
Kord, T. S., 265–66, 268
Kovács, László, 36
Kracauer, Siegfried, 31, 166
Krampus (film), 275n1
Krasinski, John, 238
Krauss, Werner, 34
Kristeva, Julia, 161, 227, 228
Ku Klux Klan, 111
Kuei, Chih-hung, 238, 239, 252, 256
Kuleshov, Lev, 154
kung fu, 5, 90, 242–43, 251, 256, 259
Kung Fu: The Invisible Fist (film), 243
Kung Fu Zombie (film), 243
Kurosawa, Kiyoshi, 223, 274n4, 275n1
Kurtzman, Robert, 113
Kusama, Karyn, 14, 65, 67, 77, 79, 81, 178
Kyrölä, Katariina, 181

Lady Frankenstein (film), 8
Laemmle, Carl, 32
Lagos, Vicky, 195
Lake Mungo (film), 82
Lake Placid (film), 82
Landis, John, 19, 22, 23, 35
Lang, Fritz, 36
Lang, Stephen, 132, 143
Langelaan, George, 224
Langford, Barry, 244–45, 262
Last Drive-in with Joe Bob Briggs, The (TV series), 89–93
Last House on the Left, The (film), 65
Late Phases (film), 132
Latham, Matt, 128
Lau, Ricky, 253
Lau, Sze-yu, 239
Laugier, Pascal, 268
LaValle, Victor, 173
Lázaro-Reboll, Antonio, 193, 194
Le Fanu, Sheridan, 245–46
Lee, Jason, 205
Legend of the 7 Golden Vampires, The (film), 252
Lehman, Peter, 13, 14
Leier, Nicole G., 208

INDEX

Leigh, Janet, 45, 58–59, 65, 101, 144, 263, 266
Leitch, Thomas M., 269
Leni, Paul, 243, 272n1
Lenzi, Umberto, 194
Leopard Man, The (film), 87
Lerner, Neil, 38, 40, 48
Let the Right One In (film), 9
Leung, Suet-mei, 260
Levant, Denis, 198–99
Levine, Ted, 132
Levy, Jane, 143
Lewis, Damian, 205
Lewis, Herschell Gordon, 15, 16, 18, 62, 122, 231
Lewis, Matthew, 185
Lewton, Val, 87
Li, Han Hsiang, 252
Li, Keith, 239
Lichtenstein, Mitchell, 14, 68, 70–71, 72, 75, 77
Light, Melanie, 271n3
Light at the End, The (novel), 173
Lights Out (film), 144
liminality, 43, 133, 140, 232, 253, 261
Lindner, Katharina, 79
Lips of Blood (film), 64
Little Shop of Horrors (film), 93
Living Skeleton, The (film), 157–58, 159, 162
Lo, Wei, 238
Lockwood, Jeffrey, 236
Lodge, The (film), 268
Loiselle, André, 160–61
Lommel, Ulli, 200, 276n1
Long Hair of Death, The (film), 64, 163
Lords of Salem, The (film), 176
Losada, Jan-Michael, 128
Lost Boys, The (film), 181, 186
Loughlin, Lori, 215
Lovecraft, H. P., 3, 174, 177, 185, 187
Lowe, Alice, 67
Lowry, Lynn, 274n6
Lucky (film), 20
Lucky Ghost (film), 111
Lugosi, Bela, 235
Lumet, Sidney, 155
Lumière brothers, 28
lungs, 15, 137, 165, 214

Luque, Pedro, 168
Lust for a Vampire (film), 164
Lustig, William, 93
Lutz, George, 213, 214, 215, 217, 218, 223, 229
Lutz, Kathleen, 213, 214, 215, 218, 223, 229
Lynch, David, 85, 108, 117
lynching, 110, 112
Lyonne, Natasha, 230

Ma (film), 68, 189
Ma, Wu, 238
Macabre (film), 62
MacAdams, Rhea, 146
MacColl, Catriona, 133
MacLachlan, Kyle, 108
Mad Doctor of Blood Island, The (film), 277n4
Mad Love (film), 249
mad scientists, 6, 150, 158, 248
made-for-TV movies, 85, 125, 224
Madman (film), 186
Madsen, Virginia, 98
Magee, Patrick, 61
Magic Cop (film), 253
Magician, The (film), 167
Magner, Jack, 217
Mains d'Orlac, Les (novel), 257
Mak, Juno, 253, 254
makeup, 10, 17, 35, 54, 88, 92, 99, 113, 128, 138, 153, 154, 156, 200, 224, 226, 235, 271n2
Malfatti, Marina, 160
Mamoulian, Rouben, 32, 36, 37, 39, 40, 41, 42, 44, 48, 97, 247, 272n2
Mancinelli, Dusty, 20
Mancuso, Nick, 141
Mandy (film), 68
Mane, Tyler, 100
Mangold, James, 268
Manhunter (film), 132
Maniac (film), 10, 150–52, 264
Maniac Cop (film), 93
Manitou, The (novel), 177–78
Mank, Gregory William, 42, 43
Manos: The Hands of Fate (film), 231
March, Fredric, 19, 37, 38, 40, 247
Marcucci, Dario, 80
Margheriti, Antonio, 64, 163

marginalization, 14, 192, 197
Marillier, Garance, 178, 179
Mark of the Devil (film), 62
Mark of the Vampire (film), 264
Marks, Laura U., 171, 176, 179, 240
Marriott, James, 124
Marsillach, Cristina, 123
Martin, Scott, 144, 145
Martino, Sergio, 64, 106
Martyrs (film), 20, 267
Martyrs of the Inquisition (film), 28
masculinity, 60, 77, 131, 224, 253; toxic, 70, 257
masks, 6, 27, 33, 47, 86, 87, 96, 130, 137, 141, 153, 155, 163, 166, 198, 210, 211, 222, 258, 268
masochism, 9, 12, 64, 65, 124; sado-, 55, 57, 64, 240
Masque of the Red Death, The (film), 61
Masterton, Graham, 177
Mastrocinque, Camillo, 163
materiality, 9, 12, 18, 29, 30, 33, 39, 41, 43, 44, 48, 56, 59, 63, 74, 86, 88, 89, 93, 112, 126, 141, 166, 170, 177, 226, 240, 241, 246
Matheson, Richard, 172
Matsuno, Hiroshi, 157–58, 159
Matsuoka, Kikko, 157–58
Matthews, Brian, 154
May the Devil Take You (film), 144
Maylam, Tony, 155
Mazzantini, Margaret, 133
McCambridge, Mercedes, 98
McCue, Mathew, 83
McGhee, Bill, 146
McGinn, Colin, 220, 222, 224, 235
McLean, Greg, 275n4
McMinn, Teri, 169
McTee, Dylan, 47
meat, 15, 76, 116, 118, 121, 155, 169, 184, 195–96, 258; rancid, 16, 172
Medium, The (film), 46
Méliès, Georges, 28, 31
melodrama, 31, 49, 57, 61, 62, 63, 64, 127, 131, 166, 203
melting, 82, 207, 238, 265
memorabilia, 195
memory, 96, 126, 127, 155, 169, 170, 171, 173, 174, 178, 182–83, 184, 195, 203, 204, 229, 235

Men Behind the Sun (film), 15, 35, 36
Mendes, Eva, 198
mercy killing, 48
meta-emotion, 58, 60
metafilms, 21, 80, 86, 139, 143, 165, 167, 210, 212, 245, 248, 274
Mickle, Jim, 68
microbe, 72, 223, 273n4
microscopy, 71–76, 80, 182
Midnight Movie (film), 123
Midnight Vampire (film), 253
Midsommar (film), 68
Mighty Peking Man, The (film), 239
Miles, Terry, 64
Miles, Vera, 144, 263
Miller, Jason, 98
Miller, Robert, 71
Milling, Bill, 149
Minarovich, Adam, 64
Minnette, Dylan, 143
Miraglia, Emilio P., 160–61
mirrors, 37, 39, 48, 78, 126, 220, 260; rearview, 189–90
misogyny, 12, 53, 58, 65, 67, 69, 76, 162, 164, 165, 260–61, 275n1
Mist, The (film), 268
Mitamura, Keiko, 253, 255
Mitchell, David Robert, 238
molecules, 72, 75, 156, 189, 241, 266; odor, 182
Monk, The (novel), 185
Monreale, Cinzia, 133
Monster, The (film), 277n3
monsters, 5, 20, 21, 34, 38, 41, 43, 44, 48, 56, 63, 73, 75, 80, 93, 98, 99, 106, 117, 128, 131, 132, 139, 143, 154, 156, 157, 177, 201, 208, 210, 217, 224, 225, 226, 232, 240, 243, 248–50, 251, 253, 259, 260, 262, 264, 265, 276n3, 277n5
"monstrous-feminine," 14, 68, 70
Moorhead, Aaron, 268
Morales, Guillem, 129, 131
Moreland, Mantan, 110–11
Morneau, Louis, 272n1
Morrissey, Paul, 13
Morton, Lisa, 258
Mortuary (film), 142
Moses, Amelia, 20

INDEX

Mother! (film), 167
Mother's Day (film), 13, 92
Motion Picture Association of America, 107
mouths, 4, 15, 17, 52, 60, 83, 92, 126, 129, 132, 137, 143, 152, 153, 172, 176–77, 208, 210, 211, 214, 219, 223, 225, 259, 275n1, 277n4, 277n5; -feel, 176
Mr. Vampire (film), 118, 253
Ms .45 (film), 13
mucus, 6, 86, 236
Muir, John Kenneth, 138, 149, 150, 155, 164, 179, 276n1
Mulvey-Roberts, Marie, 188, 276n4
Mummy, The (film), 31–32
Murder-Set-Pieces (film), 55
Murnau, F. W., 36, 39, 44, 72, 73, 74
Muro, J. Michael, 93, 207
Murphy, Bernice M., 21–22
Murphy, Charlie, 112
Murphy, Eddie, 107, 112
muscles, 78, 131, 159, 167, 170, 241; relaxers, 152
mutations, 11, 20, 24, 35, 69, 72, 74, 88, 273n4
Mutilator, The (film), 29, 82
My Bloody Valentine (film), 123
My Cousin, the Ghost (film), 238
Mysteries of Udolpho, The (novel), 185

Nair, Kartik, 88–89
Naschy, Paul, 15, 153
Native Americans, 177, 213, 218
Naughton, David, 35
nausea, 21, 54, 59, 177, 185, 188, 190, 208, 214, 215, 227, 229, 231, 239
Nayman, Adam, 20–21, 22
Ndalianis, Angela, 9, 125–26, 249
Neal, Edwin, 170
Neale, Steve, 89
Neck (film), 64
necks, 27, 80, 83, 96, 146, 155, 157, 159, 188; biting, 107, 108
necrophilia, 50, 53, 55
Needful Things (film), 41
Needful Things (novel), 183
Nekromantik (film), 55
Nelson, Mike P., 20
New French Extremity, 55, 267

New York Ripper, The (film), 125, 165
Newman, Kim, 124
Next of Kin (film), 93, 123
Ng, Richard, 254
Nicotero, Gregory, 113
Night Feeder (film), 138
Night House, The (film), 20, 46
Night of Bloody Horror (film), 4
Night of Terror (film), 264
Night of the Creeps (film), 207
Night of the Living Dead (film), 84, 109, 144, 155, 196
Nightbreed (film), 181
Nightmare Beach (film), 167
Nightmare Castle (film), 163
Nightmare on Elm Street, A (film), 35, 86, 153, 167, 266
nightmares, 99, 104, 155, 163, 213, 257, 277n2
976-Evil (film), 208
Nishimura, Kō, 158
Noé, Gaspar, 50, 55
Nonguet, Lucien, 28
normality, 14, 23, 45, 118, 132
Noroi: The Curse (film), 20
noses, 5, 6, 7, 9, 11, 126, 137, 143, 170–72, 173, 174, 177, 179, 181, 182, 183, 185, 186–87, 188, 193, 195, 208, 210–11, 214, 223, 227, 229, 247, 276n4
Nosferatu: A Symphony of Horror (film), 44, 72–73, 74, 107
Nothing Bad Can Happen (film), 68
Nuland, Sherwin B., 166
Nyby, Christian, 88
Nyong'o, Lupita, 56

O'Brien, Daniel, 258
O'Brien, Declan, 108
Och, Dana, 24
O'Connell, Jerry, 272n3
ocularcentrism, 24, 35, 129
"Odorama," 203, 223
odors, 9, 16, 89, 169–73, 175–77, 179–90, 192–95, 202–3, 206, 208–9, 211, 212, 213–15, 219, 221–23, 226, 228, 229, 230, 240, 276n2
Oily Maniac (film), 238
Okada, Masumi, 158

olfaction, 126, 170–77, 179, 182, 183, 185, 186–89, 194, 195, 202, 203, 208, 211, 215, 218, 223, 241
Olson, Astrid, 15
Olyphant, Timothy, 205
Omen, The (film), 82
One Cut of the Dead (film), 20
One Missed Call (film), 20
O'Neal, Patrick, 52
Open Water (film), 98
opening credits, 72, 115, 156, 169, 170, 188, 228, 248, 260, 273n4
Opera (film), 96, 123–25
organs, 5, 7, 9, 15, 23, 24, 33, 36, 37, 40, 42, 43, 73, 75, 80, 81, 107, 108, 109, 111, 114, 115, 121, 122, 123, 124, 126, 160, 170, 176, 182, 188, 190, 210, 235, 236, 239, 242, 247, 249, 250, 262, 266, 269
orifices, 45, 129, 178, 211, 214, 219
Orphanage, The (film), 20, 268
ozone, 174, 270

pain, 9, 15, 22, 36, 47, 50, 54, 56, 59, 61, 92, 95, 97, 102, 111, 112–13, 123–24, 129, 169, 205, 212, 242, 256, 264
Pais, John, 69
Palance, Holly, 221
Palmer, James, 31
Pang Brothers, 64, 257
Pan's Labyrinth (film), 116
paracinema, 10, 12, 89, 145, 150, 151, 152, 168
Paranormal Activity (film), 60
Paranormal Activity 2 (film), 121
paratextuality, 16, 18, 34, 55, 64, 90, 99, 100, 129, 130, 195
Parra, Vicente, 190, 193
Partain, Paul A., 169
Paszkiewicz, Katarzyna, 65, 76, 77
patriarchy, 70, 76, 216, 247, 251
Peele, Jordan, 56, 148, 268
Pendergraft, Robert, 128
penises, 14, 68–69, 71, 77–78, 80, 88, 272n3, 273n4
People Under the Stairs, The (film), 144
perception, 9, 80, 94, 96, 104, 115, 137, 174, 176, 202, 213, 240, 241

Perkins, Anthony, 59, 122, 144, 207, 263, 266
Perkins, Claire, 198, 199
Perkins, Emily, 75
Personal Shopper (film), 266
perspiration, 46, 102, 125, 180, 226, 229, 256
Pet Sematary (novel), 228
Pet Sematary Two (film), 82
Petridis, Sotiris, 5
Petrie, Susan, 274n6
Peucker, Brigitte, 132
Phantasm (film), 85
Phantasm III: Lord of the Dead (film), 90, 91
Phantom of the Opera (film), 123
Pheasant-Kelly, Fran, 144, 145
Phenomena (film), 96
phenomenology, 9, 17, 33, 48, 56, 79, 112, 125, 126, 127, 137, 174, 231, 241, 266
Phillips, Kendall R., 31–32, 263
Phillips, Lou Diamond, 272n1
Piatti-Farnell, Lorna, 86, 171, 176
Picerni, Paul, 162
Pieces (film), 106, 142
Pierce, Charles B., 207
Pierce, Jack, 113
Pig Hunt (film), 123
pigs, 15, 118, 121, 213
Pinedo, Isabel Cristina, 22, 23, 82, 86, 90–91, 250
Pink Flamingos (film), 204
Piranha (film), 19
Piranha 3D (film), 272n3
Pisanthanakun, Banjong, 46
"Pit and the Pendulum, The" (short story), 185
Pitt, Ingrid, 165
Plantinga, Carl, 49, 60
"playing dead," 139, 146, 147, 149, 153, 275n4
pleasure, 9, 12, 13, 20, 22, 49, 50, 51, 53, 54, 57–59, 61, 70, 90, 91, 92, 93, 102, 106, 109, 113, 126, 127, 141, 171, 186, 189, 195, 210, 214, 227, 247, 256, 263–64; negative, 56
Podgayevsky, Svyatoslav, 42
Poe, Edgar Allan, 44, 150, 185, 213, 246
point-of-view (POV), 37, 38, 44, 48, 54, 56, 97, 124, 125, 131, 142, 143, 247, 265–66, 272n2
Polak, Fernando Sanchez, 192

Pollard, Tom, 165
Poltergeist (film), 189, 217, 223
Polyester (film), 203
polyps, 73, 74
Poncela, Eusebio, 193
Popcorn (film), 204, 209–12, 233
pornography, 57, 61, 62, 63, 64, 65, 166
Porter, Edwin S., 31
possession, 56, 65, 76, 217, 218, 220, 222, 230, 252
Possessor (film), 68
postfeminism, 67, 76
postmodernism, 21, 57, 58, 82, 86, 251
postmortem movement, 137, 138, 152, 158, 159, 168
practical effects, 9, 35, 39, 54, 97, 177
predictability, 20, 22, 67, 68, 234, 263, 264, 265–69
Prevenge (film), 67
Price, Vincent, 50, 224
Primeval (film), 82
Prince, Diana, 90
Prince of Darkness (film), 224
Prior, David, 20
Prom Night (film), 142
prosthetics, 7, 8, 17, 35, 54, 85, 88, 89, 93, 99, 108, 111, 112, 114, 129, 130, 153, 156, 210, 211, 224, 233, 235, 254
provocation, 24, 64, 75, 163, 172, 183, 197
Prowler, The (film), 92
Psychic Killer (film), 139–40
Psycho (1960 film), 44–45, 50, 57–60, 61, 65, 70, 84, 86, 96, 101, 116, 122, 142, 144, 145, 162, 179, 201, 207, 221–22, 263–64, 265–66, 268, 272n1
Psycho (1998 film), 268–69
Psycho (novel), 183
Psycho Cop 2 (film), 123
Psycho III (film), 207, 277n4
Public Cemetery Under the Moon, A (film), 99
Pulcini, Robert, 46
Pulse (film), 20, 274n4
punishment, 44, 54, 59, 70, 165, 180, 220
Puppetmaster (film), 266
Purge, The (film), 82
Purse, Lisa, 35

Queen of the Damned (film), 107
queer, 14, 67, 79
Quiet Place, A (film), 3, 144, 238
Quinlivan, Davina, 137, 140, 142–43, 166

Rabid (film), 13, 87
race, 20, 104, 111–12, 246, 276n4
Radcliffe, Ann, 185
Raffill, Stewart, 93
Raimi, Sam, 243, 277n5
Ramsay, Mark, 231
rape, 55, 69, 80, 240, 254, 255, 256, 260; as revenge, 12–13, 14, 65, 70
Rathbone, Jackson, 184
ratings, 107–8, 113, 119, 231
Raven, The (film), 8
Raw (film), 9, 20, 62, 172, 178–79
Rawhead Rex (film), 232
razor blades, 115, 129, 170
[REC] (film), 20, 267
"recreational terror," 22, 82, 90, 91
rectums, 204, 214
Re-Cycle (film), 257
Red Queen Kills Seven Times, The (film), 160–61
Red Shoes, The (film), 123
Reddit, 215
Reed, Joel M., 231
Reeker (film), 172, 190, 208
Reeves, Keanu, 114
Reeves, Michael, 84
Regnoli, Piero, 186
Reitman, Jason, 71
remakes, 100, 215, 239, 256, 268
Renard, Maurice, 257
Renfro, Marli, 59
respiration, 4, 15, 137, 141–42, 143, 145, 148, 152, 160, 162, 165, 167
Resurrected, The (film), 187–88
Return, The (film), 129
Revenge of the Zombies (film), 110
revulsion, 12, 23, 38, 89, 116, 172, 176, 202, 208, 213, 229, 230, 233, 238, 239, 267
Reyes, Xavier Aldana, 8, 9, 22, 56, 60, 75, 267
Reynolds, G. W. M., 44
Rhodes, Gary D., 5, 28, 29, 31

Richardson, John, 163
Richardson, Sallye, 169
Rickels, Laurence, 249, 250
Rigor Mortis (film), 253, 254, 255, 262, 277n7
Riley, Michael, 31
Ring (film), 116, 257
Rising, The (novel), 173
RKO Pictures, 87
Roberts, Tony, 215
Robo Vampire (film), 239
Robocop (film), 239
Robson, Mark, 87
Rogue (film), 82
Rollin, Jean, 64, 165
Romasanta: The Werewolf Hunt (film), 123
Romero, George A., 84, 85, 86, 94, 109, 155, 196
Room, The (film), 10
Rose, Bernard, 98, 208
Rose, Felissa, 153
Rosemary's Baby (film), 9
Rosenberg, Stuart, 230
Rosman, Mark, 101
Ross, Gene, 146
Ross, Miriam, 240
Rostock, Thomas, 97
Roth, Eli, 62, 88, 198, 273n3
Rotten Tomatoes, 11, 198, 199–200, 201, 206, 207, 209, 210, 231
Rowe, Michael, 173
Russell, Kurt, 100
Ryan, Blanchard, 98
Ryan, Danielle, 237
Ryan, Meg, 215

safety protocols, 15, 98, 100, 104, 113
Sage, Bill, 47
Saint Maud (film), 20, 46, 268
saliva, 226, 236
Sancho, Rodolfo, 222
Santa Sangre (film), 108, 138
Sarandon, Chris, 187
Satan, 41, 76, 163, 176, 178
Satan's Little Helper (film), 82
Satan's Slave (film), 123
Savage, Rob, 270
Savini, Tom, 35, 156

Saw (film), 21, 88, 92, 138–39, 182, 184, 266
Saw III (film), 62
Scanners (film), 87
Scared Stiff (film), 17–18
Scared to Death (film), 224
Scary Movie 2 (film), 230–32, 233
Scent of Mystery (film), 203
schlock, 7, 12, 17, 139, 167, 213, 255
Schmidt, Rob, 20
Schoelen, Jill, 210
Schoenbrun, Jane, 20
Schumacher, Joel, 181
Schundlur, Rudolf, 60
Schwarzenegger, Arnold, 224
science fiction, 32, 74, 83, 85, 88, 180, 239
Scissorpenis (film), 64
Scob, Edith, 198
Sconce, Jeffrey, 10, 145, 150, 152
Scott, Ridley, 255
screams, 5, 7, 12, 22, 27, 39, 46, 52, 54, 57, 58, 60, 62, 69, 71, 87, 96, 124, 126, 127, 129, 147, 163, 170, 172, 212, 241, 245, 256, 263, 275n3
Scream 2 (film), 208
Scrimm, Angus, 90
scythes, 123, 129, 130, 273n1
Seaman, Justin M., 274n7
Séance (film), 275n1
Sedgwick, Laura, 6, 202, 205, 214
See No Evil (film), 132
Seeding of a Ghost (film), 255, 256
seeing, 5, 6, 7, 17, 18, 21, 22, 23, 41, 47, 86, 112, 113, 121, 133, 137, 139, 162, 171, 173, 202, 248, 265, 273n3, 276n2
semen, 86, 240
sense-making, 6, 173, 203
senses, 9, 23, 27, 126, 144, 167, 171, 172, 173, 176, 179, 188, 192, 202, 240, 242, 249, 267
sensorium, 6, 9, 14, 169, 249
Sentinel, The (film), 123
Septic Man (film), 5, 208–9, 224
sequels, 11, 19, 85, 100, 139, 204, 207, 208, 215, 216, 217, 218, 231, 266, 277n2
Serbian Film, A (film), 55
Sevastaki, Michael, 38
Se7en (film), 181
Seventh Victim, The (film), 87

Severance (film), 9
sewers, 107, 108, 189, 198, 202, 203, 206, 207, 209, 218, 227
sex, 57, 63, 74, 108, 116, 122, 152, 164, 226, 238, 275n1; and abuse, 20, 67, 232, 260
sexism, 13, 85, 261
sexuality, 43, 54, 65, 67, 68, 70, 74, 75, 77, 107, 146, 163, 186, 191, 225, 247, 251
Seyfried, Amanda, 67, 178
Shallow Grave (film), 13
Shaolin Hand Lock (film), 243
Shapiro, Milly, 29
sharks, 98, 274n5
sharpness, 5, 59, 78, 95, 96, 124, 125, 126, 129, 174, 242
Shaw Brothers (studio), 238, 243, 252, 255, 256, 277n7
She Wolf (film), 68
sheep, 15, 16, 121
Shelley, Mary, 277n2
Shelley, Peter, 275n2
Sheppard, Paula, 179
Sherman, Gary, 276n3
Sherman, Sam, 277n4
Shipka, Danny, 192
Shiraishi, Kōji, 64
Shirakawa, Takeshi, 64
Shivers (film), 13, 87, 274n6
Shocker (film), 82
Sholder, Jack, 155
shot-on-video (SOV), 4, 118, 138
Showalter, Elaine, 246, 247
shudders, 44, 45, 63, 64
Sikov, Ed, 160
silence, 28, 34, 39, 114, 126, 143, 144
Silence of the Lambs, The (film), 132, 144, 196
silent films, 4, 21, 31, 33, 34, 36, 39, 44, 73, 114, 122, 126, 167, 271n1, 277n3
Silent Hill (film), 48
Silent Night (film), 123
Silent Night, Deadly Night Part 2 (film), 92
Silly Putty, 233, 236
Simón, Juan Piquer, 106
Sims-Fewer, Madeleine, 20
Sipos, Thomas M., 138, 262
Six, Tom, 88, 180

Sjöström, Victor, 36
skeletons, 31, 42, 259
Skeleton Key, The (film), 129
skepticism, 21, 33, 38, 48
skin, 5, 7, 48, 54, 78, 81, 117, 125, 126, 128, 143, 148, 171, 181, 226, 231, 235, 236, 241, 245, 247, 252; chicken, 18; crawling, 20, 241; grafting, 87
Skinned Alive (film), 7
Skipp, John, 173
skulls, 48, 83, 90, 190
slasher films, 3, 13, 18, 20, 22, 29, 47, 57, 65, 67, 77, 86, 97, 100, 106, 122, 128, 129, 132, 137, 138, 142, 145, 152, 153, 154, 155, 171, 179, 207, 208, 221, 226, 275n1
Slaughter High (film), 65
Slaughtered (film), 214
Slaughtered Vomit Dolls (film), 231
slaughterhouses, 169–70, 185, 187, 189, 190, 191, 192, 193, 195 196
slavery, 110, 232
sleep, 34, 144, 150, 156–57, 158, 167, 174, 216, 257, 258
Sleep Tight (film), 20
Sleepaway Camp (film), 29, 152–54, 208, 268
Sleepaway Camp II: Unhappy Campers (film), 207
Sleepaway Camp III: Teenage Wasteland (film), 82
Sleepwalkers (film), 15
slime, 6, 81, 86, 88, 115, 126, 175, 180, 185, 207, 212, 220, 224–26, 231, 233, 236–38, 240, 242, 255, 262
Slime People, The (film), 225
Slit-Mouthed Woman, A (film), 64
Slugs (film), 48
smell, 5, 6, 9, 16, 27, 57, 102, 114, 126, 133, 144, 169–71, 172–96, 198, 202–5, 210–12, 213, 217, 221, 223, 227, 228, 230, 235–36, 267, 276n2, 276n3; of death, 186–88; as memory, 204; scape, 171
"Smell-O-Vision," 203, 223
Smith, Barry C., 176, 183
Smith, Dick, 35
Smith, Oliver, 240
Smith, Paul Julian, 194

Smuts, Aaron, 9, 95–96, 169
snakes, 118, 152, 153, 239
Snuff (film), 194
Sobchack, Vivian, 9, 79, 171, 174, 203–4, 217
Sobel, Noam, 186
Society (film), 92, 224
Sole, Alfred, 180
Soler, Ivette, 211
Solet, Paul, 223
somatosensation, 171, 240–41
Sono, Sion, 182
Sorority Row (film), 82
Sorum (film), 20
Soska, Jen and Sylvia, 67
souls, 19, 24, 37, 38, 39, 41–44, 46, 48, 87, 186, 189, 220, 243
sound effects, 36, 77
soundtracks, 38, 40, 77, 80, 95, 121, 218
Spacek, Sissy, 77
Spanish Inquisition, The (film), 28
Spawn (film), 41
special effects, 3, 7, 10, 29, 31, 35, 44, 99, 106, 113, 118, 122, 226
Spector, Craig, 173
Spider Baby (film), 5, 109–12
Spiliotopoulos, Evan, 46
Spookies (film), 89, 277n5
Spooky Encounters (film), 5, 243, 244, 254, 257, 258–61, 262
Spring (film), 268
Springsteen, Pamela, 208
Squid Game (TV series), 22
stabbing, 48, 58, 92, 94, 122, 250, 254, 260, 278n9
Stadie, Hildegarde, 152
Stafford, Tamara, 133
Stallone, Sylvester, 224
Stand By Me (film), 175
Stanwyck, Barbara, 49
Starry Eyes (film), 68
startle effect, 19, 86, 277n6
Steele, Barbara, 163–64, 165
Steen, Hanne, 183
Steiger, Rod, 213, 223, 230
Steinmann, Danny, 98
Steinþórsson, Steinþór Hróar, 68

Stella Dallas (film), 49
Stevens, Andrew, 17
Stevens, Katie, 97, 100
Stevens, Stella, 275n3
Stevenson, Robert Louis, 32, 44, 246
Stewart, Kristen, 266
still frame, 52, 154, 155–56, 159, 260
Stipe, Michael, 106
Stitches (film), 48
Stoker, Bram, 73, 74, 75, 188, 276n4
Stomach (film), 64
stomachs, 78, 125, 138, 139, 140, 177, 214, 236, 239, 260; aches in, 205; churning of, 3, 22, 62, 83, 178, 190
Stone, Oliver, 64, 249
stop-motion, 29, 35. *See also* animation
Story of the Eye (novella), 209
Strange Case of Dr. Jekyll and Mr. Hyde, The (novel), 32, 44, 246
strangulation, 28, 53, 82, 157, 158, 159, 246
Strayer, Kirsten, 24
Street Angel (film), 34–35
Street Trash (film), 82, 93, 207
Stringer, Julian, 99, 104
Struss, Karl, 39, 42
Student Bodies (film), 65, 66, 142, 275n2
Stuff, The (film), 85, 93, 224
Stung (film), 129
stunt work, 17, 98–101, 128
Styles, Richard, 13
Subtitles for the Deaf and Hard-of-Hearing (SDH), 7, 78, 80, 126, 142
Suicide Club (film), 20
suicides, 20, 42, 46, 138, 254
Sullivan, Tim, 18
Sunrise (film), 39
superhero films, 41, 180, 181, 209
superimposition, 39, 73, 228, 260
Superstition (film), 29
surrealism, 44, 108, 114, 116, 122, 199
Suspiria (1977 film), 96
Suspiria (2018 film), 68
Sutton, Travis, 14
sutures, 54, 119, 120, 207
Sweet House of Horrors, The (film), 125
synchronized sound, 34–35, 36, 40

synesthesia, 78, 172, 173, 204, 223; and intersensoriality, 127, 176, 185
Synnott, Anthony, 171
Szaloky, Melinda, 126
Szeto, Mirana May, 252, 262

taboos, 32, 53, 87, 196–97, 201, 206, 214, 232, 276n2
tactility, 86, 88, 96, 126, 236, 239, 240, 241, 242, 274n3
Tale of Two Sisters, A (film), 20
Tales That Witness Madness (film), 8
Tall Man, The (film), 268
Tammy and the T-Rex (film), 93
taste, 10, 12, 57, 126, 150, 171, 172, 174, 176, 178–79, 188, 202, 210, 211, 236, 260, 267
taxidermy, 15, 121, 190
Taylor, Tate, 68
Taylor-Compton, Scout, 100
teenagers, 3, 20, 46, 65, 69, 71, 76, 77, 78, 80, 86, 122, 142, 143, 153, 155, 156, 178, 185, 208, 215, 216, 219, 226, 227, 228, 230
teeth, 56, 77, 79, 83, 95, 112, 180, 184, 187, 188, 219, 247
Teeth (film), 14, 68, 69–73, 74, 75, 76, 77–78, 81, 272n2, 273n4
telekinesis, 77, 140
Tenebrae (film), 96, 100, 275n2
TerrorVision (film), 224
Terry, John, 187
Tetsuo: The Iron Man (film), 89
Texas Chain Saw Massacre, The (film), 9, 35, 36, 100, 118, 120, 169–70, 185, 190, 194, 258, 265, 271n3, 276n3
textual analysis, 99, 126, 242, 268, 269
textural analysis, 86, 88, 242, 269
textures, 59, 81, 203, 235, 236, 241, 242, 268
Theatre Bizarre, The (film), 129
Them! (film), 83–84, 210
There's Someone Inside Your House (film), 46–47
Thigh Meat (film), 64
Thing, The (film), 86, 87, 88–89, 99, 100, 224, 239
Thing from Another World, The (film), 88, 273n2

Thing with Two Heads, The (film), 212
Things (film), 89
Things Heard & Seen (film), 46
Thirst (2009 film), 20
Thirst (2019 film), 68
30 Days of Night (film), 82
Thomae, Robert, 29
Thomas, Eric Austin, 43
Three on a Meat Hook (film), 194
Three-Thousand-Year-Old Vampire (film), 253
thrillers, 71, 80, 93, 98, 101, 107, 108, 132, 155, 243, 248, 251, 266
throats, 108, 133, 156, 158, 159, 176, 256; slitting of, 48, 91, 92, 154, 276n3
Thunderbolt Fist (film), 243, 277n7
Tien, Ni, 256
Tingler, The (film), 5, 62, 210
titillation, 13, 57, 60, 65, 77, 116, 162, 165, 255, 273n3
Toe Tags (film), 64
tombs, 150, 163, 186
Tommyknockers, The (novel), 174–75
Tomomatsu, Naoyuki, 64
tongues, 5, 15–16, 79, 83, 132, 146, 172
Torso (film), 64, 106
torsos, 58, 110, 112, 159, 165, 256
torture, 15, 46, 55, 71, 85, 138, 144, 152, 192; porn, 13, 83, 88, 122, 267, 274n3
Totaro, Donato, 155
touch, 5, 10, 33, 57, 59, 171, 174, 188, 196, 202, 203, 226, 235, 239, 240–42, 267, 273n3, 276n2
Tourist Trap (film), 92, 166
Tourneur, Jacques, 87
Toxic Avenger, The (film), 209
Trail, The (film), 239
Train to Busan (film), 20, 89
Transfiguration, The (film), 153
Trauma (film), 82
traumas, 29, 30, 47, 55, 64, 68–69, 70, 71, 93, 106, 112, 115, 124, 125, 138, 149, 156, 170, 175, 178, 182, 184, 186, 229, 246
Travers, Peter, 67
Travis, Daniel, 98
Trick (film), 33
trick photography, 31, 35, 39, 157, 166

Trilling, Zoe, 218, 219
Trilogy of Terror (film), 85
Troll (film), 11
Troll 2 (film), 10–12
Troma's War (film), 93
Trouble Every Day (film), 75
Tsui, Hark, 238, 257, 258
Tucci, Ugo, 274n5
Tucker and Dale vs. Evil (film), 82
Tung, Stephen, 253
turtles, 15, 188
28 Weeks Later (film), 75
Twilight (film), 19
Twins of Evil (film), 138

Úlfarsson, Gaukur, 68
Ulmann, Helga, 158
Ulmer, Edgar, 44
Unborn, The (film), 123
Uncle Josh's Nightmare (film), 31
Unger, Anthony B., 98
Unholy, The (film), 46, 133
Universal Studios, 31, 32, 34, 41, 44, 74, 100, 113, 116, 232, 243, 248
Unseen, The (film), 98–99, 118
urine, 86, 179, 180, 195, 212, 236
Us (film), 56, 268

vaginas, 88; dentata, 68–69, 70, 76, 78
Vail, William, 169
Vampire in Brooklyn (film), 16, 99, 107, 108, 109, 112–13, 274n1
Vampire of the Haunted Mansion (film), 253
vampires, 43, 68, 74, 99, 107–8, 109, 112–13, 155, 156, 173, 180, 181, 188, 244, 253, 261, 276n4
Vampire's Kiss (film), 118–19
Van Riper, A. Bowdoin, 15
Van Sant, Gus, 268–69
Van Sloan, Edward, 248
Vander Kaay, Chris, 145, 167
Vaughn, Vince, 268
Veidt, Conrad, 34
Vengeance of the Zombies (film), 15
Verevis, Constantine, 198, 199
verisimilitude, 15, 103, 178

Verónica (film), 20
V/H/S (film), 62
V/H/S: Viral (film), 68
V/H/S/2 (film), 123
V/H/S 94 (film), 181
victimization, 13, 62, 69, 76, 125, 143, 144, 274n3
Victor Crowley (film), 128–29
"Video Nasties," 194–95, 196, 272n2
Video Recordings Act of 1984, 194
Videodrome (film), 35, 87
Vidor, King, 49
Vietnam War, 85, 132, 146, 155
Villard, Tom, 204, 210
Villeneuve, Denis, 268
Violation (film), 20
viruses, 72, 236, 270
Visani, Alex, 64
viscera, 46, 231, 241, 267, 269
Visions of Light (film), 36, 39
visual effects, 21, 39, 44, 54, 114, 130, 275n1
voiceovers, 42, 51, 78, 188
vomit, 9, 76, 77, 86, 104, 176, 177–78, 179, 180, 184, 204, 208, 211–12, 231, 256; bags, 62; projectile, 230; as prop, 177, 235
voyeurism, 13, 54, 67, 256, 273n3

Wacko (film), 275n3
Waddell, Calum, 276n3
Wadleigh, Michael, 223
Wagner the Wehr-Wolf (novel), 44
Wahlberg, Donnie, 205
Wailing, The (film), 20
Wait Until Dark (film), 132
Walas, Chris, 224
Walker, Johnny, 271n3
Walker, Pete, 221, 222
Walpole, Horace, 185
Walters, Thorley, 42
Walton, Fred, 268
Walton, Karen, 75
Wan, James, 88, 138, 182, 268
Warren, Harold P., 231
Waters, John, 203, 204
Waters, Sandra, 264
Wayans, Keenen Ivory, 230, 232

We Are Still Here (film), 144
We Are What We Are (film), 68
Weber, Lois, 36
Wedlich, Susanne, 225
Weenick, Annabelle, 146
Weiner, Rob, 15
Weixler, Jess, 68
Wenson, Rebecca, 180
We're All Going to the World's Fair (film), 20
We're Going to Eat You (film), 238, 257, 258
werewolves, 19, 75, 77
Wes Craven's New Nightmare (film), 177
West, Roland, 277n3
Whale, James, 31, 44, 248, 277n2
Whannell, Leigh, 138, 182
Wheatley, Ben, 20, 270
When Animals Dream (film), 75
White Zombie (film), 5, 235
Whitford, Bradley, 137, 148
Wicker Man, The (film), 268
Widmyer, Dennis, 68
Wiene, Robert, 33, 44
Wilkins, Mike, 251
Willard (film), 252
Williams, Linda, 8, 44, 57–58, 59, 60–63, 64, 65, 77, 86, 107, 116, 127, 166, 263, 265
Williams, Tony, 93
Williamson, Chase, 128–29
Willis, Andy, 191, 193, 194
Willis, Donald C., 271n4
Wilmot, Ronan, 232, 233
Wilson, Laura, 88, 273n3
Wilson, Staci Layne, 276n1
Winkler, Martin M., 42
Winston, Stan, 35
Winther, Peter, 46
Witch, The (film), 3, 238
Witch from Nepal (film), 243
witches, 31, 193, 239; craft, 163, 186; doctors, 252, 255; hunts, 188
Witchfinder General (film), 84–85
Without Warning (film), 122

Wolf Guy (film), 93
Wolfen (film), 223
Wolff, Alex, 29
Woo, John, 251
Woods, Bill, 150
Woods, Bryan, 97
Woods, James, 230, 233
Woodward, Ben, 226
Worland, Rick, 43–44, 45–46
Would You Rather (film), 129
Wright, N'Bushe, 180
Wrists (film), 64
Wrong Turn (2003 film), 123
Wrong Turn (2021 film), 20–21, 47, 48
Wrong Turn 3: Left for Dead (film), 165
Wrong Turn 5: Bloodlines (film), 109
Wyatt, Jane, 218
Wylder's Hand (novel), 245
Wyss, Amanda, 153

Yamaguchi, Kazuhiko, 93
Yeshurun, Yaara, 186
Yeung, Kuen, 238
Yiu Hua, Hsi-men, 243
Young, Burt, 217
Young, Harvey, 112
You're Next (film), 138
Yu, Ronnie, 239
Yue, Audrey, 261
Yue, Genevieve, 27, 29

Zacharek, Stephanie, 231
Zarchi, Meir, 13
Žižek, Slavoj, 144, 148, 247
Zombi 2 (film), 124–26, 129, 274n5
Zombie, Rob, 100, 176
Zombie Nation (film), 199, 200, 276n1
zombies, 4, 43, 48, 85, 86, 89, 90, 91, 92, 101–4, 124–25, 142, 152, 155, 158, 173, 180, 186, 200, 209, 253
zoom shots, 24, 110, 160, 209
Zovatto, Daniel, 143

ABOUT THE AUTHOR

David Scott Diffrient is professor of film and media studies in the Department of Communication Studies at Colorado State University. His articles have been published in *Black Camera, Cinema Journal, Historical Journal of Film, Radio, and Television, Journal of Fandom Studies, Journal of Film and Video, Journal of Popular Television, Journal of Popular Film and Television, New Review of Film and Television Studies, Quarterly Review of Film and Video, Post Script,* and *Velvet Light Trap,* as well as in several edited collections about film and television topics. He is the coeditor of *Screwball Television: Critical Perspectives on Gilmore Girls* (Syracuse University Press, 2010) and *East Asian Film Remakes* (Edinburgh University Press, 2023), and the author of *M*A*S*H* (Wayne State University Press, 2008), *Omnibus Films: Theorizing Transauthorial Cinema* (Edinburgh University Press, 2014), *Comic Drunks, Crazy Cults, and Lovable Monsters: Bad Behavior on American Television* (Syracuse University Press, 2022), and (with coauthor Hye Seung Chung) *Movie Migrations: Transnational Genre Flows and South Korean Cinema* (Rutgers University Press, 2015) and *Movie Minorities: Transnational Rights Advocacy and South Korean Cinema* (Rutgers University Press, 2021).

www.ingramcontent.com/pod-product-compliance
Lightning Source LLC
Chambersburg PA
CBHW030334240426
43661CB00052B/1633